Dear Dad,
Merry C

Salt beneath the skin

By the same author:

Night Race to Kawau
Jellybean
Alex
Alex in Winter
Alessandra – Alex in Rome
Songs for Alex
Waitemata – Auckland's Habour of Sails
Crossing (with Agnes Nieuwenhuizen, anthology)
Nearly Seventeen (anthology)
Falling in Love (anthology)
Personal Best (anthology)
Mercury Beach
The Tiggie Tompson Show

Salt beneath the skin

Seafaring Kiwis tell their stories

Edited by
Tessa Duder

HarperCollins*Publishers New Zealand*

First published 1999
Reprinted 2000
HarperCollins*Publishers (New Zealand) Limited*
P.O. Box 1, Auckland
Selection and linking text copyright © Tessa Duder, 1999
Extracts copyright © individual authors (see acknowledgements)

Tessa Duder asserts the moral right to be identified as the author of this work.

All rights reserved. No part of this publication may be reproduced, stored in a retrieval system or transmitted in any form or by any means, electronic, mechanical, photocopying, recording or otherwise, without the prior written permission of the publishers.

ISBN 1 86950 332 5

Designed by Craig Humberstone
Typeset by M & F Whild
Printed on 80 gsm Ensobelle by Griffin Press

CONTENTS

Acknowledgements   7
Foreword   11

Part 1: On Board
Greg Whakataka-Brightwell in Jeff Evans, *The Discovery of Aotearoa*   17
Captain Jim Cottier, *Søren Larsen – Homeward Round the Horn*   24
Ronald Carter, *A Yachtsman's Memories of Long Ago*   29
Peter Smith, *Rebecca – the restoration of an old yacht*   34
Michael Brown and Sue Neale-Brown, *The Taming of the Crew*   41
Jim Lott, 'The Cruise of the Victoria'   50
Steve Dickinson, 'God is a woman'   56
Rebecca Hayter, 'New boat blues'   62
J.C. Rutherford, *The Founding of New Zealand: The Journals of Felton Mathew, First Surveyor-General of New Zealand, and his wife, 1840–1847*   69
John Logan Campbell, *Poenamo*   76
Captain Augustus Samson, Personal log of the *Countess of Kintore*   82

Part 2: Working on Water
Ted Ashby, *Phantom Fleet – the scows and scowmen of Auckland*   91
Percy Eaddy, *Neath Swaying Spars*   98
William Sanders, Personal logbook of the New Zealand Government steamer *Hinemoa*, 1906   104
Con Thode, 'Submariner in the Med'   109
Heather Heberley, *Flood Tide*   113
Sally Fodie, *Waitemata Tales*   121
Liz Light, 'The Floating World of the Rich and Famous'   124

Part 3: Drama at Sea
Jack Churchouse, *The Pamir Under the New Zealand Ensign*   135
Thayer Fairburn, *The Orpheus Disaster*   140
Royal New Zealand Navy, *Tales from Sea – the Royal New Zealand Navy in the Second World War*   143
Earling Tambs, *Cruise of the Teddy*   145
Ronald Carter, *Caught in a 60 m.p.h. Gale*   150
Colin Quincey, *Tasman Trespasser*   155
Captain Barry Thompson, *'Man Overboard!'*   163
George Brasell, *Boats and Blokes*   170
Commander Larry Robbins, *'The 1994 Pacific Rescue'*   178
Tom Neale, *An Island to Oneself*   193
Wade Doak, *Dolphin, Dolphin*   199
James Siers, *Taratai II – a continuing Pacific adventure*   206
Bill Belcher and Aileen Belcher, *Shipwrecked on Middleton Reef*   212
Robert McIntyre, *Satan's Eye*   220
Naomi James, *At One With the Sea*   230
David Lewis, *Ice Bird*   239
John Glennie, *The Spirit of Rose-Noëlle*   251
James Nalepka, *Capsized*   258
Adrian Hayter, *Sheila in the Wind*   266

Part 4: Racing Ahead
Leah Newbold, *The Emerald Highway*   279
Glen Sowry and Mike Quilter, *Big Red – the Round the World race on board Steinlager 2*   290
Grant Dalton and Glen Sowry, *Endeavour – Winning the Whitbread*   297
Russell Coutts in Paul Larsen, *Russell Coutts: Course to Victory*   307

ACKNOWLEDGEMENTS

Thanks are due to a number of people who helped in the selection and writing of the contributions to this book.

For those who provided suggestions and books to consider, I am grateful to the staff of the National Maritime Museum of New Zealand, especially former curator Pete McCurdy and librarian Pamela Collins; Diane Lamont of the New Zealand Navy Library Service and Rear-Admiral (Rtd) Jack Welch, RNZN; Captain Tim Ridge of Boat Books, Auckland; Lieutenant-Commander Peter Dennerly of the Royal New Zealand Navy Museum; and ever-helpful librarians at the Auckland Public and various North Shore libraries.

For access to the Williams Sanders archives I am indebted to his family, especially Tricia McRae, also to Pete McCurdy who alerted me to existence of archival material on New Zealand's only naval V.C.

Most of the contributions are from published material. However, a number of people responded enthusiastically to a request to view unpublished material or to write pieces especially for this anthology, and here I would especially like to thank Commander Larry Robbins, RNZN, Jim Lott, Pete McCurdy, Captain Barry Thompson, Con Thode, Liz Light, Steve Dickinson and Rebecca Hayter.

Measurements (of distances, boat length etc) have been given in either metres or the more traditional miles, yards and feet, as appropriate to the extract.

CONTRIBUTORS

The publishers are grateful to the following authors, publishers and copyright holders for their permission to reproduce copyright material:

Part 1:

Greg Whakataka-Brightwell in Jeff Evans, *The Discovery of Aotearoa* (Reed, 1998); Captain Jim Cottier, *Søren Larsen – Homeward Round the Horn* (Bush Press of New Zealand, 1997); Ronald Carter, *A Yachtsman's Memories of Long Ago* (Mallinson Rendel, 1980); Peter Smith, *Rebecca – the restoration of an old yacht* (Heinemann, 1978); Michael Brown and Sue Neale-Brown, *The Taming of the Crew* (Random House, 1994); Jim Lott, 'The Cruise of the Victoria' (unpublished); Steve Dickinson, 'God is a Woman' (*New Zealand Fisherman*); Rebecca Hayter, 'New boat blues' (*Boating New Zealand*); Pete McCurdy for Captain Augustus Samson, Personal Log of the *Countess of Kintore* (1875).

Part 2:

Ted Ashby, *Phantom Fleet – the scows and scowmen of Auckland* (Reed, 1975); PA Eaddy, *Neath Swaying Spars* (Whitcombe & Tombs, 1939); Mrs Olwyn Welsh for William Sanders, Personal logbook of the New Zealand government steamer *Hinemoa* (unpublished); Con Thode, *Submariner in the Med* (unpublished); Heather Heberley, *Flood Tide* (Cape Catley, 1997); Sally Fodie, *Waitemata Tales* (Collins 1991); Liz Light, *The Floating World of the Rich and Famous* (unpublished).

Part 3:

Jack Churchouse, *The* Pamir *Under the New Zealand Ensign* (Millwood Press, 1978); Royal New Zealand Navy, Able Seaman Bill Black, *Tales from the Sea – the Royal New Zealand Navy in the Second World War* (RNZN, 1995); Earling Tambs, *Cruise of the Teddy* (Collins, 1989); Paul Titchener for Ronald Carter, *Caught in a 60 m.p.h. Gale* (Mallinson Rendel, 1980); Colin Quincey, *Tasman Trespasser* (Hodder & Stoughton, 1977); Captain Barry Thompson, 'Man Overboard!' (unpublished); George Brasell, *Boats and Blokes* (Daphne Brasell Associates,1991); Commander Larry Robbins, 'The 1994 Pacific Rescue' (unpublished); Tom Neale, *An Island to Oneself* (Collins, 1966); Wade Doak, *Dolphin Dolphin* (Hodder & Stoughton, 1981); James Siers, *Taratai II – A Continuing Pacific Adventure* (Millwood Press, 1978); Bill Belcher and Aileen Belcher, *Shipwrecked on Middleton Reef* (Collins, 1979); Robert McIntyre, *Satan's Eye* (Hodder & Stoughton, 1977); Naomi James, *At One with the Sea* (Hutchinson, 1979); David Lewis, *Ice Bird* (Collins, 1975); John Glennie with Jane Phare, *The Spirit of the Rose-Noëlle 119 Days Adrift: a survival story* (Viking, 1990); James Nalepka, *Capsized* (HarperCollins, 1992); Rebecca Hayter for Adrian Hayter, *Sheila in the Wind* (Collins, 1959).

Part 4:

Leah Newbold, 'The Emerald Highway' (Reed, 1999); Glen Sowry and Mike Quilter, *Big Red – the Round the World race on board Steinlager 2* (Hodder & Stoughton, 1990); Grant Dalton and Glen Sowry, *Endeavour – Winning the Whitbread* (Hodder & Stoughton, 1994); Russell Coutts in Paul Larsen, *Russell Coutts: Course to Victory* (Hodder Moa Beckett, 1996).

While every attempt has been made to contact copyright holders and secure permission to reproduce copyright material, it has not always been possible to do so. Copyright holders are invited to contact the publisher.

FOREWORD

New Zealanders, according to writer Monte Holcroft, all share the collective memory of a sea voyage. In 1951 he wrote, 'Wide seas were crossed by the parents or near ancestors of most people now living in New Zealand. Exciting psychological possibilities are to be found in the influences, latent or active, of the long journey that remains a part of the collective mind.'

Even forty years ago, most of those long journeys were still undertaken by sea, as they had been for over a thousand years. Today people come and go in great numbers by wide-bodied jumbo jet. But even at 35,000ft, even by young people who would regard a long sea voyage as impossibly tedious, to get from New Zealand to anywhere else an ocean has to be crossed – nearly three hours minimum flying time in any direction.

This is a book of sea experiences, the first to bring together some true, first-person accounts of New Zealanders grappling with the Element which surrounds their country like no other of its size on the planet, and which is deep in their psyche.

It is not meant to be a comprehensive, quasi-historical collection covering significant canoe passages, landfalls, naval battles, disasters or race triumphs, but rather a personal selection, from a surprisingly rich and extensive literature, of lively, well-written pieces chosen to reflect New Zealanders' love of the sea and their deep understanding of it, in all its many and various moods.

Some are set in New Zealand waters, others in distant seas. With a few exceptions, carefully considered (Frederick Butler, Earling Tambs and James Nalepka), the writers are all New Zealanders, not always by birth but certainly by choice.

The range of experience is as varied and vivid as the sea itself. Greg Whakataka-Brightwell takes us aboard the *Hawaiki-Nui* canoe on its historic passage from Tahiti to Aotearoa. With pioneer settlers John Logan Campbell and Sarah Mathew, we sail into the Waitemata harbour even before New Zealand was declared a British colony and Auckland its first capital.

In wartime, Able Seaman Bill Black gets torpedoed in the Atlantic, Con Thode fires off torpedoes in the Mediterranean. In peacetime, a young Captain Barry Thompson falls overboard into the Pacific, and Leah Newbold willingly jumps off her Whitbread yacht into the icy southern ocean. The great names of New Zealand yachting, Russell Coutts, Grant Dalton and two from Sir Peter Blake's world-beating crews, Mike Quilter and Glen Sowry, share their race triumphs.

Then there are the courageous single-handers, Dr David Lewis, Dame Naomi James, Colin Quincey and Adrian Hayter, battling on to triumph against all the odds; and those who survived hurricanes, capsizes or groundings and the loss of their ships: Frederick Butler, John Glennie and Jim Nelapka, James Siers, Bill Belcher, Tom Neale and Robert McIntyre.

Professional seamen Commander Larry Robbins and George Brasell memorably describe their role in famous sea rescues; Frances Renner sees the great square-rigger *Pamir* through a fearsome Pacific storm; Captain Jim Cottier takes us, also under squares, around Cape Horn. Ted Ashby and Percy Eaddy share something of the scowman's rugged working life, and Captain Augustus Samson describes a record 82-day passage only once sighting land between Gravesend and Napier aboard an emigrant ship in the 1880s.

There are also quieter, more reflective moments: Heather Heberley drives a family runabout around the Marlborough Sounds; Jim Lott takes his family yacht through the French canals. Peter Smith lovingly restores and sails the classic yacht *Rebecca*. Steve Dickinson goes match racing for the first time, and Rebecca Hayter and Ronald Carter discover the realities of boat owning and maintenance. Sally Fodie tells some Waitemata ferry tales, and Liz Light what it's like to work on yachts of the rich and famous in the Med. Wade Doak and his wife Jan go dancing with dolphins.

All the writers draw on the maritime tradition which began with the arrival of the first Polynesians maybe a thousand years ago after some of the greatest ocean passages of discovery in recorded history; continued with the 17th and 18th century European discoveries by Dutch and British (and, some argue, Portuguese) ships; and continued into the 20th century with the emigrant ships, the ships regularly carrying cargoes of meat and dairy products to the northern hemisphere, the fishing fleets. Currently, it is most recognisable in the country's extraordinary pre-eminence in yacht racing, design and building.

New Zealanders, as Air New Zealand's television advertisement told us, are the world's greatest travellers. To that, I'd add some of its greatest sailors. It is no accident or good luck that this isolated country, similar in size to two other great maritime nations Britain and Italy but with only 3 million-odd people, has within the last twenty-five years won a number of Olympic sailing golds and many of the yachting world's major trophies, notably the One Ton Cup, the Admiral's Cup, two Whitbread round-the-world trophies and in 1995, unforgettably in San Diego, the ultimate prize of the America's Cup.

Auckland, with its fabled cruising (and training) grounds known on the charts as the Hauraki Gulf, is currently hosting the America'a Cup regattas, scheduled to climax in March 2000. From Auckland came the two earlier Whitbread-winning campaigns of Sir Peter Blake and Grant Dalton, also the vision that created the country's two youth sail training ships *Spirit of Adventure* and *Spirit of New Zealand*. The city has been home to the Royal New Zealand Navy since 1840, a long time in New Zealand terms, and the country's major port for over a hundred years. With an estimated one craft to every eight people, the Waitemata harbour and inner Hauraki Gulf has long been the undisputed centre of recreational boating.

In acknowledging Auckland, however, this is not to diminish maritime traditions developed in harbours and river mouths all around the coast. The rugged nature of the interior meant that it was easier to transfer cargo and passengers by sea; thus, until quite recently, the many hundreds of scows and similar small trading and fishing vessels, many of them owned by Maori. The ports of the West Coast and Dunedin, the Kaipara and Hokianga, Wellington, Napier, New Plymouth and Tauranga among others also once bustled with ships under sail, and later steam; today all our major cities, excepting only Rotorua, Hamilton and Palmerston North, are also major ports. Changing weather, which with little warning can bring a gale up from the icy southern wastes or from the vast north-east fetch of the Pacific, has wrecked ships on most stretches of the long, treacherous coastline or on rocky offshore islands; at the last count, more than 2,000 shipping casualties. And as for yachting, some of the toughest sailors in New Zealand are those who regard the Cook Strait/Marlborough Sounds region as their cruising grounds, or the area from Coromandel to East Cape, or the coast between Christchurch and Stewart Island.

> '... the sea was no place for free thought,
> break the code and you're dead.'
>
> Auckland poet-novelist **Kevin Ireland**.

I hope you enjoy these stories as much as I enjoyed, during the summer of 1998–99, reading the books and manuscripts from which they were taken. To the writers who knowingly broke the code and survived to tell us their stories, and to those who have respectfully, if less dramatically, honoured the code of the sea – my thanks and salutations.

Tessa Duder

Auckland, September 1999

PART ONE

On Board

THE DISCOVERY OF AOTEAROA

IN 1979 Greg Whakataka-Brightwell, a young apprentice carver, felled two mature totara in the Whirinaki State Forest. It was the first step to realising his dream of building a traditional double-hulled canoe and sailing across the Pacific in the wake of Kupe. The voyage would be from from Tahiti via Rarotonga to Aotearoa.

Four years later the 22m Hawaiki-nui, *hand-built from the hollowed totara trunks, sennit ropes, manila and wooden dowels, was launched in Tahiti. A year of sea trials followed. In late 1985, she set sail on her epic voyage. On board were Greg, named Matahi by the Tahitians, Francis Cowan, his Tahitian father-in-law, a renowned Polynesian navigator and the expedition's leader, and a crew of three.*

The first legs of the voyage, from Tahiti to Ra'iatea and Rarotonga, were accomplished safely, despite gear problems and having to set up a jury rig when the main mast broke in a storm three days out from Ra'iatea. In Rarotonga a new mast was fitted and the waka provisioned for the voyage to Aotearoa. Across some of the world's most dangerous oceans, they would continue to be without any support vessel or radio contact, navigating entirely by the ancient and traditional Polynesian methods.

A little over two weeks after we sailed into Rarotonga we were ready for the last and longest leg of our voyage. The canoe was ready, and we had more than enough provisions. The people of Rarotonga had come forward and showered us with fresh produce in the days leading up to our departure. The deck was covered with cases and cases of tomatoes, pawpaw, bananas and coconuts. And wild honey. We probably had 20–30 kg of sweet, sweet honey. The honey, along with the fresh lime, was probably our favourite food until it ran out.

As with Tahiti and Ra'iatea, we had a fantastic send-off from the local population. Before we left, the Rarotongans insisted that we erect a stone on their sacred marae site at Ngatangiia. It was to stand alongside the stones for Te Arawa, Takitimu and the five other migration canoes that, according to their traditions, left Tangiia Harbour over a thousand years before us for Aotearoa. It was a huge honour for *Hawaiki-nui*, and truly an emotional ceremony for us all.

After the ceremony at the marae, we returned to the canoe for the final speeches and the send-off. We left Tangiia Harbour on 29 November feeling confident, but ran into trouble immediately. I have to take full responsibility. It turned out that the foot of the new mast hadn't been secured to the mast shoe. I don't know how I missed lashing it, but fortunately Francis noticed the mast pitch backwards slightly as soon as we started sailing. So there we were, sitting out in the channel off Rarotonga being jostled around in very bumpy seas while Ace tried to re-lash the foot of the mast with heavy rope. However much we tried, we couldn't correct it, and we certainly weren't in the mood to return to the wharf and own up to it. In the end, Ace managed to do a decent job despite us not being able to risk taking the sail down because we were so close to land, and he secured the mast well enough for us to sail on.

On the 22-day crossing from Rarotonga we had three days of fine weather at the most, so we were virtually constantly walking around in wet clothes. Any time it looked like it was going to clear up, out came all the clothes and bedding for airing. The dry spells usually only lasted for an hour or two before it would start to spit again. Then it was a rush to get everything back inside and wrapped up before it got wet. The rain wasn't always a bad thing, especially when we were running short of fresh drinking water. Every time it rained we had a water brigade and caught as much of the water that ran down the sails as possible.

Personal hygiene was something that Francis was particularly hot on. Even so, we could only wash in salt water with a little Lux Liquid thrown in for the suds. We certainly didn't have any flash soap, and, unbelievably, none of us took a mirror along, so our shaving was sort of half-pie as well. Francis had a big toilet bag with all the goodies inside it that he used to keep in the cabin. Because our lips were cracking and sore, and our skin was peeling off, Ace and I used to get into it while he was asleep during his break from navigating, and put a bit of this mousse stuff on our faces to ease the discomfort. I think Francis knew, but he didn't say anything.

As I said earlier, Ace was the cook for the voyage, as well as being in charge of the rationing. In the mornings we had a light snack to keep us going until the evening, when we had our one main meal of the day, at about six o'clock, which we always ate together. I remember one particular meal early on in the voyage, when we were still well stocked with pawpaw, kumara, coconut, wild honey and dried banana. The menu started off with freshly caught raw fish sprinkled with lime along with a couple of crackers. Then it was the main course of kumara, tropical fruits and honey. Absolutely fantastic! I'd never eaten so well.

It became a daily ritual to ask Ace what was on the menu, and Ace always replied, 'One coconut shared between five of us, dried fruit, and raw fish.' It doesn't sound too appetising, and we only had limited rations, but believe me, Ace put together some memorable meals. The only reason any of us lost weight during the voyage was due to the fear of dying at sea – it certainly wasn't through Ace's cooking.

Each evening after the meal we had to take a look at the food distribution on board. Both the food and water were stored in the two hulls, and if we took too much food or water from one hull it would upset the balance and cause the canoe to pull to the heavy side. We had to redistribute provisions between the hulls on a regular basis to keep a good balance. In the end we only just had enough food for the voyage, because we had been counting on some fresh fish being caught along the way. And, from memory, we were allocated only about 1.5 litres of water each, per day.

As well as being in charge of food stocks, Ace was the second fisherman behind Rodo. Because we were having such a hard time catching fish to supplement our food stores, Ace decided to try to catch a shark. There were a few that were following us, so it didn't take him too long to entice one to take a hook. The only problem was that once we lassoed its tail and got it alongside the canoe, it was too heavy to pull on board. Ace's solution was probably the most astonishing thing I have ever seen. He actually jumped onto the back of the shark – it was still alive – and gutted it right there and then in the water. God knows how many other sharks were nearby! He split its stomach right down the middle and emptied it of all of its guts to make it light enough to manhandle onto the canoe. I really couldn't believe it when he jumped onto that shark. It was incredible.

During the voyage from Rarotonga to Aotearoa, Venus was one of our primary navigation aids. In December Venus was setting on the starboard bow, and could only be seen for three hours each night.

While we were taking our initial direction from Venus, we also had the Southern Cross to our port side. If we went off course it didn't take too long to realise it. Suddenly Venus disappeared from the rigging and the Southern Cross was no longer in place to our left. It was really like we had a narrow corridor to sail down.

We also knew that we were likely to encounter little cloud cover to obstruct our view of the heavens at night during November and December. As it turned out, there were very few nights when we didn't get at least a glimpse of the stars every couple of hours or so, although it was usually clear for most of the night. On the odd occasion when the stars weren't visible for long periods at a time, we were able to use our streamers and the consistency of the wind's direction during the hours of darkness to keep our course. We also had the rope trailer out behind us as an additional aid.

On the last leg to New Zealand, our physical strength was being quickly sapped. Our skin, being constantly wet for so long, started to peel off our faces, fingers and feet. I myself couldn't wear shoes, and was constantly soaked all the way through. During the long, cold, lonely hours through the night I thought a lot about my wife. Before we left she said, 'When you're cold and lonely and afraid, just think of me – my warmth and my support and my love.' Her words helped me a lot.

Along with the physical hardship, we also had to deal with inner fears as well. It's hard to describe, and I don't think you could really capture the feeling unless you experience it for yourself, but the sheer size and power of the sea when you're out there on a small canoe with your life in the hands of the gods can be a terrifying thing. One day I was leaning on the cabin and it was like we were riding on the roof-tops of the waves. I was looking down and could see right to the bottom of these huge troughs. It seemed such a long way down, and it was like we were balancing on the edge. I'll never forget that feeling. We tried to put the ocean's power out of our minds, but it was always there, reminding us, haunting us.

Another psychological problem for us came in the shape of the sharks that followed us for well over a week. They were following in our wake, happy to wait for any food scraps that might fall off the canoe or be thrown out after meals. They were big black-tipped sharks, about four metres long. Francis had encountered them before and described them as the butchers of the sea. They had no fear of anything. After a while they really started to get to us. It got to the point where we had to stop the canoe and let them circle us for a day without feeding them before they would leave us alone.

Going to the toilet was certainly an experience with those sharks hanging around! We ran out of toilet paper halfway through the final leg and had to start sitting off the back of the canoe. Each time a wave came up we'd wash ourselves with one hand, all the while looking out for those black-tipped sharks to come and bite our arses! Our toilet sessions were very fast.

We have previously had an indication of their intent when we caught the shark that Ace jumped on earlier in the voyage. Ace and Rodo cut the head off, took the jaw out, and threw what was left of the head back into the ocean. To our disbelief, its partner actually sat there with its head out of the water, and chewed its mate's head in front of us, all the while seemingly watching us on deck. That sent shivers up our spines. It had absolutely no fear of us whatsoever. It was like he was giving us the message: 'Put your arm, put your hand, put your leg in the water and I'll bite it off. Just try.'

About a week into the Rarotonga–Aotearoa leg, Francis decided that we were being pushed too far to the west, and he ordered the sails to be brought down. We sat there for about four days drifting with the currents. I've got no idea how far we drifted during the four days, but it was hard just sitting there. It transpired that Francis was waiting for a change in the wind direction. The wind was pushing us too far to the west, and Francis had calculated that if we continued on the course we were sailing, we would make landfall up near the Bay of Islands rather than further south as intended. The predominant wind direction was from the south-west, and we just needed it to move a little. Finally after four days it obliged us and we were off again. Not before time either.

It was another three or four days before we came across the Kermadec Chain. From memory, Francis had a booklet that had all the silhouettes of the Kermadec Islands, and he identified the island as L'Esperance Rock. We think it was that, but we can't be sure. Anyway, as we passed the island, Rodo asked Francis to anchor in its shelter so we could swim to the shore with the hope of gathering some birds' eggs. Francis thought about it for a while because he knew we could have done with some fresh eggs, but in the end decided instead to keep going and clear the Kermadecs' notorious waters while the winds were favourable. It was night as we crossed the Kermadec Chain, and Francis took point guard and walked the perimeter of the canoe keeping an eye out for rocks with his big, heavy torch until the crash of the breakers was well and truly out of earshot. I remember it was raining and very cold, and the sea was black and rough. Despite missing out on the eggs, we were very happy to clear the danger.

Another problem we had to worry about by this stage was that both of our steering paddles had been severely weakened. Both paddles had fractures and were flexing quite badly. It was just due to inexperience and the technique some of our crew were using, but it caused a real problem. Rather than letting the canoe run on, they tried to fight the natural run of the canoe and held the steering paddle too rigid. It was a fight the ocean wasn't going to lose.

Despite the hard times, we have a few highlights to look back on as well. Just after the episode with the sharks, Alex showed his experience and played the fool for the good of the crew. One morning when we were all up and about, he jumped out from the cabin, stark naked and wearing an old wig, just playing the clown. His fooling around really came at just the right time for us. It lightened the mood on board and it put the shark fears right to the back of our minds.

A bit later, up by the Kermadecs, we encountered a pod of whales that was probably on its annual migration to feed in Antarctic waters. They never moved any closer than about 200 metres from us, but all the same we had no doubts that they were the lords of the ocean. They were completely at home in their environment. It was an unforgettable experience to be so close to them – just them and us. It was as if we were the only two groups of living things on the planet – an awesome experience.

Another highlight was watching an albatross that latched onto us for the final ten days of the voyage. It was a beautiful bird. I remember it swooping down into the troughs catching fish without even landing, before gracefully flying back up. It was beautiful to watch.

Landfall in Aotearoa

Our official landfall in Aotearoa was Motiti Island in the Bay of Plenty. It took us 22 days to reach there from Rarotonga, and another ten days to actually land at Hicks Bay on the East Coast. The first clues that we were close to land came about 300 km out from Aotearoa. We were in the open sea and exposed to the elements. Heavy dew in the morning, the insects landing on the canoe and a distinct drop in the temperature were all unmistakable signs that we weren't far from home. Then a couple of nights later we actually saw the long cloud that often sits over New Zealand. We were still about three days out.

After all of our deep-water voyaging, it was coastal sailing that caused the most problems. We got caught in another storm just off Tauranga and decided the safest option was to shoot out a hundred miles or so and wait offshore for the storm to pass before we made our final approach. It was a hard decision to accept because we were so tired, but we had no real choice. At the same time Francis decided that we should try to contact the emergency channel monitored from Auckland to let them know where we were as a precaution. The radio operator was able to tell us our exact position after we sighted an emergency beacon out at sea and counted how many flashes of the light there were per minute. As it happened we had been pushed further south by the storms and were now off Whangaparaoa Harbour, one of the traditional landing places on the East Coast, just out of Whanau-a-Apanui land. We had to sail offshore again to avoid being wrecked on the coast. It was 28 December, two days before we finally landed.

About this time we were buzzed by an aeroplane just off East Cape. We were running about a week behind schedule due to the storms, and Gerard had flown to Aotearoa and organised a private search. Of course we couldn't have known who was on board the plane, but as it swept down towards us, Francis called out, 'That's my brother. Just like him to do that. To make sure we are safe right to the end.' And sure enough, it was Gerard.

Within a day of being sighted by Gerard's plane, the emergency channel operator contacted the Watties' fishing trawler *Kaiti* and asked her to tow us in. They were concerned because of our ongoing difficulties fighting the storms. That decision left a bit of a sour taste in my mouth, because I believe we could have made landfall under sail with the help of the strong north-easterly that had sprung up. In any case, the *Kaiti* towed us to Hicks Bay, where we landed.

There was a good number of people waiting for us, including my mother and father and brothers. Most of our supporters were still in Auckland, waiting at Orakei marae. Those on land told us later that *Hawaiki-nui* looked like a ghost canoe as it approached the wharf, with the light shining on the heavy dew. It was New Year's Eve, 1985.

In the morning the locals took everything out to dry in the sun and then cleaned the canoe out. They bailed the water out from the hulls, washed the canoe down and fed us. The last part of the voyage had really taken it out of all of us, but Francis in particular. It was decided that Francis should leave for Auckland as soon as possible because he was very sick.

Even in the comparative safety of Hicks Bay, the tail end of the storm was still strong enough to have one last go at us. With the canoe tied at the wharf, the big swell coming into the bay was lifting her up and banging her into the wharf. I had to make the decision to have the canoe towed around to Whakatane where we would wait for Francis. We would have loved to have sailed there but we were just too tired. We got another great reception at Whakatane, and were happy to rest up for a week before the final tow up to Okahu Bay in Auckland.

When we did get to Okahu Bay we ran the canoe up onto the beach. Although we had been towed to Auckland, and had first made landfall down-country a bit, we got a fantastic reception at Okahu Bay. There were absolutely thousands of people there to see us. Maori and Tahitian representatives performed the welcoming ceremony. It was a special day for all of us who had been involved in the voyage. Francis had recovered enough to rejoin us and led our side of the ceremony.

Greg Whakataka-Brightwell in **Jeff Evans'**, The Discovery of Aotearoa, *1998*

SØREN LARSEN – HOMEWARD ROUND THE HORN

CAPTAIN *Jim Cottier has clocked up something over 700,000 miles at sea in a career of more than fifty years. His commands have included, among others, yachts on delivery runs, square-riggers on sail training ocean passages, and the Greenpeace protest vessel to Antarctica in 1987–88.*

In 1991 he was asked by owner-skipper Tony Davies to sail as Mate on a ten-month voyage from Sydney to Liverpool on the Søren Larsen, *a sturdy oak Colchester packet built in Denmark in 1949 and now working out of Auckland. With a motley crew of twelve paying passengers, she left Sydney on October 5, 1991. Ahead lay a call into Auckland, and then the longest leg, that legendary 6390-mile run through the wild southern ocean to the Falkland Islands. She would be the first British square-rigger to round Cape Horn for over fifty years.*

The afternoon of December 8 is grey and threatening. There's heavy overcast cloud with a biting wind and the barometer is falling. But excitement is rising with our midday position a scant 35 miles from the islets. After 42 days and 6000 miles of sailing this 35 miles seems incredibly little. On the track chart in the saloon the noon position seems right there at the tip of the land.

All afternoon there is activity with binoculars, mental calculations, speculation and frequent checking of the speed, but it is 1600 hours before the welcome cry from the fore crosstrees – 'Land ho.'

'Where away?' the Old Man yells.

'Fine on the port bow.'

Within minutes there are 35 souls on deck; some scrambling aloft, others impatiently scanning the dull horizon where the outstretched arms are pointing. Yes, eventually even the weakest eyes can see the two faint dark bumps curtsying on the unsteady horizon – Diego Ramirez – outposts of the Horn.

Tony wears a quiet smile. It has been a long passage, much longer than anticipated, but his ship has stood the strain well and been thoroughly tested. Spars, sails, hull and fittings have all come through unscathed and, with only one or two minor injuries his crew have been safely delivered this far too. Fresh water, although rationed, has been adequate, food has lasted well and now the navigation has been proved accurate. The passage is not finished yet, but this is a major milestone for him especially. The 40-day run, land to land, is the longest either the ship, or Tony, has ever made.

He has been keeping watch as well as having the captain's responsibility. All our lives are in his hands in a very real way. He could carry too much sail and damage the rig, he could carry on running too long in bad weather rather than heaving-to, thus endangering us all. His decision (taken after consultation with Tiger) to run on ahead of *Eye of the Wind* means that if they got into difficulties we would not be able to assist them readily because we would have to beat back against the westerlies. There are dozens more non life-threatening decisions too; water rationing, for example, affects morale, which is extremely important on a long passage. Tony doesn't make his decisions lightly, so his mind is heavily engaged even off watch.

It's a lonely job being captain. Not that Tony hides himself away, or is an introvert, but the final responsibilities he cannot share. He must stand just a little removed, be just slightly autocratic, for the effective maintenance of alertness and seamanlike discipline onboard.

This necessary attitude augments the loneliness. Traditionally a ship's master was the very personification of autocracy but those days are past fortunately. Tony manages his ship well. Firmly in control, no nonsense, but he's able to join in the fun too; the singing, the social flux. Recently he's been reading Villiers' *The War With Cape Horn* to his watch each evening and then dispelling the horror of the harrowing episodes by leading some shanty singing.

Slowly, we haul the islands up over the horizon and since the weather continues to moderate we alter course to pass within a mile or so. Rugged is the only way to describe the Diego Ramirez islets standing brazenly in the full sweep of the wild west winds and suffering the onslaught of the world's greatest seas. Chile lays claim to them; even maintains a tiny military garrison there, huddled in a few huts in an eastward facing bay. We hope they are suitably impressed to see a square rigger swinging past under full sail, but if they are they don't say so when they call us by radio. They just want our name, nationality and port to which we are bound. Very formal although Mabel thoroughly enjoys the lovely flow and roll of Spanish when she talks with them.

If they are not excited, we certainly are and there's much singing and jollification on deck. The famous homeward bound shanty 'Rolling Home' gets an airing and one verse is very topical:

Bullies, sweat yer weather braces,
For the wind is freshnin' now,
And we're roundin' Digger Ramrees,
To the north our ship will plough.

We'll be up with the mighty Cape tomorrow morning with any luck, but we are ready to celebrate now. So Gabrielle's new flag goes aloft for its first airing and looks good. She has worked on it for days, after she and James settled on the design. The name of Tony's company is 'Square Sail Pacific' and he wanted the flag to reflect the name. Finally it is a square blue flag with a large white square-sail in the centre; simple, clear, smart. House flags, as they are technically called, go at the mainmast head, ensigns right aft or at the end of the gaff (at sea), and courtesy flags – the ensigns of the country the ship is visiting – go on the foremast.

Gabrielle has made a Falkland Islands ensign too, during this passage, so she can almost claim to have served a flag maker's apprenticeship. We also toast Tony for getting us here, we sing of the Spanish Ladies of South America and of *Eye* who reports on the evening radio schedule that they have found a favourable breeze, although they are nearly 200 miles astern. I devise a new verse for 'Colchester Packet' which is bellowed across the Drake Passage.

The Eye of the Wind's comin' up from astern
She's doin' eight knots but no cause for concern,
'Cause we're doin' ten with the t'gallant stowed,
She's a Colchester Packet, O Lord let her go.

We don't stop at one verse, of course, or one shanty. I hope the ghosts of the Cape Horn seamen lingering here appreciate their modern counterparts giving voice to their old favourites. Those old timers would have been happy with our weather, that's for sure.

Reluctantly people take to their bunks. The mood is gay but everyone expects to be called in the early hours and there are still watches to be kept. Daybreak is before 0300 in this high latitude – it's almost midsummer.

The night watch continue with songs and many a story. No one can relax. Questions fly and I tell of my other voyages this way, none of which have been in really stormy conditions. I explain that even here, in summer, statistics have it that on only about nine days a month will there be winds of gale force or more, so there's nothing abnormal about conditions today. I'm in the middle of a yarn about the worst seas I've ever encountered (in the Great Australian Bight) when, in the first faint flush of dawn I see, under the main boom, the unmistakable dark cone of the world's greatest cape.

'There it is!'

My story is never finished!

Quite quickly other land appears fanning out on the port bow, and from the chart we can confirm Hoste Island with False Cape Horn at its southern tip, the Hermite Islands all overlapping themselves and, as the light grows, the mountains of Navarin Island show too; mountains which frown to the north on Ushuaia across the Beagle Channel.

Land. Suddenly lots of it. But there's no mistaking the Cape Stiff of the British sailors who coined this familiar title with a nice flair for double entendre.

'Call all hands! Get the kettles on and tell Andy we'll need the rum before breakfast! Yes – everybody. We're the first people to see Cape Stiff from the deck of a British square rigger for 55 years. Can't have anyone sleeping through that! I'll call the Old Man.' I think some of my watch would prefer to contemplate the scene quietly and by themselves!

The deck sprouts crew. Some, clutching blankets, take a quick look and dive back to their bunks for another hour, others clutching hot mugs of coffee and cameras stand in knots peering forward with sleepy eyes and the oncoming watchkeepers (for it's almost 0400) struggle into jumpers and mittens, seaboots and balaclavas against the chill.

By 0500 everyone is on deck, and it's 0520, December 9, when the Cape is due north of us. We send up a mighty cheer and Andy pops the first champagne (not very traditional but there are no objections). Tony produces a specially minted Cape Horn lapel badge for everyone and Tish and Squizzy unveil the biggest, most beautifully decorated fruit cake I've ever seen. It has the same striking design as the badges: royal blue ground, light blue compass, white albatross and circular inscription – '*Søren Larsen* – Cape Horn – 91'. What a beauty! It was made in Auckland and must have been brought onboard in the dead of night. I had no inkling of its presence and I can smell a fruit cake at 20 paces. It goes down really well with the traditional tot of rum that Tony dispenses. He has a wide smile this morning. He's waited many years for this moment. Now he asks for a minute's silence in remembrance of all the sailors who passed this way and especially for those who did not return. It's a nice gesture and there are some wet eyes. Since Schouten named Cape Horn thousands of seamen have perished in these waters, hundreds of ships met their ends. Our festive mood is somewhat chastened by these thoughts and the colourless day. Grey, heavy clouds; but high enough to clear the Horn at 1400 feet. A dull sea running steadily from the southwest driven by a cold and rising wind.

There are enough white caps to liven the scene a little, but the land is forbidding, crouched on the horizon; the Horn itself a dark wedge of bare cliff, a dismal sentinel. There is some disappointment that we are not rounding in storm force conditions, or that there is no fanfare of trumpets, but Sandy has it right:

'I reckon we've sneaked past the dragon while he's snoozing, and who would want to wake a dragon?'

Chris parades in a special Cape Horn tee shirt and shivers for an hour or more to claim empathy with the ill-clad sailors of old. He also presents similar shirts to Tony, Joel and myself; a thoughtful memento. Soon afterwards I find a new personal card on the galley noticeboard designating Chris as a 'Cape Horner'. He came fully prepared. He's certainly cheerful today.

Joel has the wheel as we enter the Atlantic. I'm not at all sure that he fully realises the uniqueness of the occasion, as he has no background of seafaring, but I hope he will remember it always. As a lad, I would have been beside myself with pleasure and pride to be aboard a square rigger around the Horn (I still am!) never mind at the wheel. Perhaps Joel is too but if so, he's playing it very 'cool'.

Tony is outwardly calm too, but his emotions must be in tumult. He's had a vision of doubling Cape Horn for so long and here he is in his own square rigger! It's a sublime moment for Margaret thinking of her grandfather passing this way and how amazed he would be to see her here peering at the dark cape. Gabrielle's great grandfather of the *Cromdale* will be twitching in his grave no doubt. Let's hope we don't meet with the vast fleets of icebergs that great ship experienced.

I've been this way twice before but this time, under sail, it is different and very special. This time it feels like the culminating point of 40 years at sea. There's a powerful sense of fulfillment.

Captain Jim Cottier, *Søren Larsen* - Homeward Round the Horn, **1997**

A YACHTSMAN'S MEMORIES OF LONG AGO

IT'S sometimes said that the two happiest days of a man's life are the days he buys a boat – and the day he sells it. Ronald Carter, author of the classics Little Ships *and* The Glory of Sail, *writes wistfully of his two happiest days with his first boat, the clinker-built* Seabird, *sixteen feet overall, going for one pound sterling . . .*

> *And all I ask is a windy day*
> *with the white clouds flying.*
> *And the flung spray and the blown*
> *spume and the sea-gulls crying.*

John Masefield

This story is not for the yachtsmen of wealth, nor yet again for the men of moderate means; they would not understand it fully. No, this story is not for those to whom things have come easily during their lives – it is for the poor man. And I, who am still not rich, and I suppose never shall be, was once a poor man.

I say poor, because though I had a good job, I was not earning much money, and I wanted two things – desperately. I wanted to get married, and I wished to own a boat, and I put my marriage first; that is, I saved every penny I could for this happy event, and, as you will see, I got my boat, too.

In August 1925, I returned from Suva, having just been discharged from the War Memorial Hospital, where I lay for over three months, critically ill with typhoid fever. My strength was slowly returning, but I now found that I was in the grip of another fever – Sea Fever. Yes, it had gripped me just as firmly as the other disease, but time would not cure this ailment as it did the former. There was, I knew, only one cure – a yacht – and the open sea. And I yearned for this just as thousands of other men have done, and still do.

Well, here is the story.

It was on a lovely evening in February 1926, that we drifted into Hobson Bay on the last of the flood tide. I was on board my old friend's yacht *Kahawai* in the last year of her ancient life. She became a total wreck on the newly-formed railway embankment, two months later, in April. A dying summer nor'easter fanned us gently across the Bay. Suddenly I saw the tip of a small vessel's bow sticking out of the water. 'Hallo,' I said to my friend, 'That looks like an old yacht under the tide.'

'Yes,' he said. 'We call her "the wreck of the Hesperus"; she's no good; she's done for.'

I was not so sure.

The next morning at low water I walked across the mud-flats to find out for myself. She proved to be a ballasted centre-boarder, sixteen feet overall, seven feet in beam, about eighteen inches draught, and clinker built.

She was in a pretty bad state; no doubt about it. Her port side was in good order, but her starboard bilge was stove in, and her cockpit, coamings, cabin-top and deck had been badly chopped about by some vandal.

She was half-full of mud, sea-shells, rusty tins, broken bottles, and old bits of wire and rope. But she was a boat of sorts, so I bought her. Yes, for the sum of one pound sterling, I again became a boat-owner, and my spirits began to soar.

I floated her up on the beach at the top of the tide, and for six glorious winter months I patched her up. I put new planking in her starboard bilge, seven new birch timbers inside, new cockpit coamings, house-top, and patches in the deck made her look good to my eyes; yes, very good. And when I had finished the painting of her old hull, my heart swelled with pride.

One day I had a great compliment paid to me, during the old ship's rebirth. I was working in the bilge in the cockpit when I heard a voice just above me say: 'Well, I always thought that the British race was deteriorating; I made a mistake.'

I glanced up, somewhat startled as I had not heard the approach of this man, and looked for the first time upon the weather-beaten countenance of George Honor, who later became my friend. A great yachtsman was George. He did much for the poor man in the field of yachting. He left his monument in all the waters of New Zealand; the square bilge yacht, the answer to a poor yachtsman's prayer.

Yes, George always a man of few words, paid me a great compliment when he made that remark. He understood. A poor man, gripped with Sea Fever, working on an old wreck, in order to cure this strange malady.

For some time now my thoughts had been troubling me. I had my ship — for the modest sum of about five pounds. She was ready for the open sea. But I had no sails, no mast, spars, rigging, or blocks. I knew this would all cost money, and I did not have the money, at least not to spend on these items. And then a bit of luck came my way, in the shape of a newspaper advertisement: 'For Sale: Mast, spars, and sails, suit sixteen footer.'

Like a hound on the scent, I followed the ad to St Helier's Bay on a borrowed bicycle, and met for the first time my friend Walter Ure, who sold me the lot for 30 shillings. That's all I paid, and the mast and spars were freshly scraped and varnished into the bargain, but I must admit that the sails were pretty 'ripe'.

I lashed all this heavy gear to my bicycle and walked the lot home over Coates' hill, where the State settlement of Orakei now stands, to my home in Remuera. It was mid-winter, the roads were bad, and I frequently got bogged. But I was extremely happy with my bargain. The rest of the re-fit was easy. In my brother-in-law's workshop I made my own blocks, cleats, rudder, tiller and cabin table. In my mother's kitchen in the evening, on the floor, I spliced my standing and running rigging. It was great fun.

Sometimes my mother would poke her head through the door and say: 'Whatever are you doing with all those bits of rope and wire?' I would just look up at her and smile. I knew that she would not understand. No woman would ever understand the secret I was hugging to my breast. My thoughts were so far away – a little ship on sun-kissed water, or fighting to windward in a breeze. I knew that even if I told her, she would not understand.

Early in October we launched her at the top of high water. On a cold Sunday morning six of us stood round her and pushed her into the tide. Just before she was water-borne my other brother-in-law pulled a bottle of beer from his hip pocket, and we solemnly passed it round for the christening of *Seabird* as I had re-named my little ship. I had been told that her original name was *Duke*, but I did not like the sound of this word much. *Seabird* seemed much more pleasant to my ears.

Followed a glorious summer's sailing, and at the end of it a minor tragedy. Out sailing one fine afternoon late in March, and by myself, I was caught by a white squall just as I was rounding up to fetch my mooring in Hobson Bay. I missed.

My old mainsail ripped from leach to luff; the hastily-lowered anchor dragged, and ten minutes later the little *Seabird* struck the rocks on the railway embankment. She slowly filled and slid to the bottom, with her after starboard bilge stove in. I was heartbroken.

The following day Arthur Clare came down with his punt, jib and winch. Placing a line beneath the crosstrees, which were just above water, we slowly winched my ship to the surface. As she rose from the water I nearly burst into tears when I saw the damage which had been done.

I was so upset, I said to Arthur, 'Drop her back, she's done for this time'.

'Don't get your tail down, son,' said kindly Arthur Clare. 'I've seen boats in a lot worse condition than this. Quick! Make up your mind.'

'All right,' I said. 'I'll give it a go. Swing her in.'

I 'gave it a go' and *Seabird* sailed through another glorious summer the following year, although it cost me another six months of hard toil patching up the damage, and an ill-spared sum of two pounds ten shillings for a salvage bill.

I had two staunch pals who sailed with me, but I noticed they seemed to be getting restless – they wanted something bigger. Before I fully realised what I was doing, I had sold my ship. Yes, the realisation came very suddenly, as I walked out of a yachtbroker's office with seventeen pounds ten shillings in my hand. I had sold my dream.

I felt stunned as I looked at the little bundle of notes in my hand. I wanted to rush back and tell that broker that I did not really want to sell; that I had made a mistake; been talked into it. Too late. I knew in my heart that I was too late.

However, busy and eventful days were to follow, and I soon got over the parting, though I never lost my affection for the little *Seabird*. I love her memory still.

We now had a much larger yacht – 24 feet – straight-stemmer *Mahoe*. But she is another story.

The two young chaps who bought my boat had the misfortune to wreck her in their first season, on an out-lying reef off Rangitoto Island. They had her dragged off, and up into Hobson Bay, and there, right up in the corner, just in from No. 1 railway bridge, they left her bottom up and abandoned.

I used to pass her each time we went out in our new ship, and although I was quite happy in my partnership with *Mahoe*, I sometimes had a wistful longing to be a sole owner in my own little *Seabird* again …

'What are you going to do with her?' I asked, addressing the young man standing before me.

'I'm going to chop her up,' he said, looking me straight in the eye.

'You're what?' I said, in astonishment and dismay.

'Yes,' he repeated, 'I'm going to chop her up. She'll make good firewood.'

I was talking to my old ship's owner. It was Sunday morning, and I had come for a wander round the beach in Hobson Bay, as *Mahoe* was away for the weekend, and I had been unable to join her.

'Do you mean to tell me that you are going to chop her up? She's not so bad. I think you could fix her up.'

I knew in my heart that he could not. But I was pleading for my old ship. I wanted to save her; to let her lie where she was. But it was too late. She was afloat, and the owner was on the point of stepping into his dinghy to tow her up to Ponsonby, where she was to be chopped up.

'She's finished,' he said. 'Done for. No good wasting any more time on her.'

I knew he meant what he said.

'Do you mind if I come a little way with you?' I asked.

'No, that's all right; hop in.'

I hopped in; into the cockpit of my ancient, broken-down wreck of a boat. It was our last ride together, on the salt seas that had borne her on its bosom for nigh on sixty years.

It was a perfect day; brilliant sun, and a faint southerly breeze. The tide was running in. Yes, I thought, as we glided under the No. 1 railway bridge, he has picked the right day for it. Everything is in his favour, to take her home, and chop her up.

We halted at the Royal Akarana Yacht Club, and he put me ashore. Reluctantly, I stepped from her cockpit for the last time. I hardly trusted myself to say goodbye to the owner. I felt a great lump sticking in my throat as I hastily walked away. I never turned again to look at her. I knew that I dared not; my tears were pretty close; and I am not ashamed of it, even today – over twenty years later.

I have owned five sailing vessels in my time. One boat, a little 12 foot flattie, I never liked, for she tried to drown me on several occasions and almost succeeded on the last. That was the time I lost her. For the other four I will always retain the greatest affection.

But one stands out above them all – the little *Seabird*. How I scrimped and scraped to put her into sailing trim. How poor I was when I knitted her ancient frame together. It was a labour of love and she returned it four-fold in the happy hours we spent together. Youth and old age. We got on famously together.

Is there still some thin thread of connection between that ancient shell, no longer in existence, and the young man now growing old himself, who ministered to her with loving hands? I wonder.

I cannot ever remember having dreamed of any of the other yachts I have owned, but I frequently dream of the *Seabird*, and the dream is always the same. She stands upon the beach, and I climb aboard her, and immediately start scheming and planning how I can patch her up.

Is it possible that there is such a thing as 'the soul of a boat'? Some sort of bond between a ship and her lover, that even time and distance cannot break apart. I wonder . . .

This story is not for the yachtsman of wealth. He will not understand it, fully. It is not for the man of the fields and streets. He will most probably sneer at its sentimentality.

No, this story is for the men without wealth. The men who are starving for the sea, and cannot get there, even as I, so long ago, starved, but did get there, in a worn-out husk of a little ship, the ownership of which was akin to the touch of a soothing and gentle hand on the brow of one who suffered so much with Sea Fever.

Ronald Carter, A Yachtsman's Memories of Long Ago, *1980*

REBECCA – THE RESTORATION OF AN OLD YACHT

ONE *of the most handsome nautical books produced in New Zealand in recent decades was Peter Smith's story of the restoration during 1973 of the 1902 Whangarei yacht* Dolphin. *Every stage of the re-construction, from Bermudan ketch back to gaff cutter, was as lovingly detailed with plans and sketches assembled into coffee-table book format as was the restoration itself.*

After nearly a year of painstaking, concentrated work, Auckland teacher, painter and yachtsman Peter Smith was ready to return the 24ft hull back to its natural element, prior to that first, sublimely satisfying moment of hoisting the sails . . .

During the eight months of reconstruction the grass had been mown in an untidy halo around the work place and cradle. On the morning of the launching we stacked, raked and burned the accumulation of shavings, dead grass, paint flakes and timber scraps that obscured the blocks under the cradle. The lawn sloped down to the rear of the yacht so that the starboard bow corner of the cradle was at ground level with the opposite corner blocked up eighteen inches. The cradle had to be lifted bodily twelve inches to slide the low loader platform beneath it. To avoid lifting the stern dangerously high we took the weight on jacks and pulled away the blocks. *Rebecca* tilted so that her bowsprit pointed to the sky, but she was steady enough. There was little to do but wait for the transporter, other than label and lash the rigging along the mast.

At last we heard the rumble of the big diesel of the transporter grinding down the hill in low gear. The loader platform was backed across the neighbour's lawn and angled towards the cradle. Placing it under the cradle was comparatively easy, as each of its wheels swivelled, allowing it to be steered precisely into position, and the slope gave it its own momentum. Pulling it around the sharp corner formed by the wall of our courtyard was much more difficult. The winch cable from the truck angled it too sharply so that, despite the direction

34   SALT BENEATH THE SKIN

given, the wheels, the whole platform and *Rebecca* slid sideways too close to the wall for comfort. In spite of persistent jacking, blocking and winching, the whole lot inexorably inched closer to the wall. Finally the truck was taken around the corner and backed across the footpath so that the winch cable could be led directly to the platform. *Rebecca* gave a small creak and groan as she was eased from her resting place, then was quickly pulled clear. The truck returned to the entry point, the cable was shackled on again and in no time the platform was winched onto the road transporter. Straps fore and aft held her down firmly, and the mast and other gear was lashed along the deck. I rode with the transporter, admiring the easy and smooth handling of the big rig through intersections and awkward corners.

At Okahu Bay a small but well-known crowd waited. We were two hours late and there was little time for social niceties, but I noticed quite a few strangers present. Mostly they were onlookers who had seen the vintage yacht on her journey and, curious, had followed her to the launching ramp. There were a few old hands, asking the question that was to confront us so often from now on.

'Who was she?'

'*Dolphin* – E 15.'

'Ah, *Dolphin*! I remember her, and *Mahoe*, and *Why Not* . . .'

As they ran their hands appreciatively over the hull it was suddenly a new kind of reward to have brought back a little of the past to old yachtsmen.

The tide was dropping quickly. Many hands were ready to take the spars and gear from the deck. The transporter lined up on the ramp, winched the low loader off the road trailer. Jill clambered onto the deck and took the line which had been rowed out to the pile offshore. I stood on the cradle bracings and *Rebecca* rolled gently down the concrete slab and touched water again. The water rose steadily, until it was eighteen inches off the water line. It stopped. The platform wouldn't roll further. We looked at the tide. There should be plenty of depth, but I certainly didn't want her pitching off the cradle in shallow water. She was winched up the ramp again. It was just as well we had thought a champagne christening out of order! This time the winch was put out of gear, the brake released to let the cable drum freewheel, and the platform rumbled down the slope. As the water swirled around me and the cradle arms I could feel *Rebecca* lift at the stern, then she slid easily backwards, dipping her bow momentarily, to be checked by the bow line. I don't know if anyone cheered but Jill and I looked at each other as I scrambled aboard.

'She's back,' and I dived below to pull up the inspection panels and check for water. All was well. There was no spurt of water through dry planking, no leaky seacock connections, and the bung was in. When I launched *Moana* I had to sleep aboard for she needed pumping every three hours for the first two days. The very slight ooze reassured me that *Rebecca* was much tighter.

My brother Ru joined us. He was curious as to how the engine would perform. It started easily, popping away and pushing a satisfying gush of cooling water through the exhaust port. When the clutch was eased in, however, the motor slowed and died. We restarted it. Perhaps we didn't have enough revs? We opened the throttle a little more and engaged the clutch. Again the engine stalled.

'I don't know,' said Ru, 'I'm sure it should turn that prop. How tight is the stuffing box?'

'It's firm but I didn't think it was tight.'

'Well, try slackening it off a little. Surprising how much friction it applies. Better to have a weep of water than put drag on the shaft!'

It was getting dark, friends were waiting and there was tidying up to be done. We decided to leave the engine to later, rowed *Rebecca* to a temporary mooring nearby and went ashore. It was not until then that we had been able to stop and take a look at her. She rode gently and prettily but to our astonishment she was a good ten inches above her marks! Although her inside ballast, spars and gear would put her down a bit, ten inches was a lot of displacement. 'Oh well, better than the reverse,' we thought. 'And that engine isn't holding the stern down.'

We gathered on the ramp, passed around the wine, and were quietly happy. There is always something good about putting a boat back into its proper element. *Rebecca* sat on the evening tide, nodding to an occasional wake, her bowsprit making small arcs against the evening sky. It was too late to step the mast, and our friends were coming to dinner.

From the kitchen window of the flat there was an unnatural hole in the backyard, and a dried patch of earth and a scatter of dunnage was the only reminder of our long-time company.

After dinner brother John and I rowed out to check the water. She had made very little, perhaps a gallon. Nothing to worry about. We looked at the engine and gave in to temptation. Not a drop oozed through the stern gland so the stuffing box nut was released one and a half turns until the shaft turned easily by hand. This time the engine merely slowed a little to a driving beat, and there was a flurry of water under the counter. John dropped the mooring and *Rebecca* picked up way, slipping without fuss through the lines of sleeping boats. She spun quite readily with the helm down, considering the length of her keel. Reluctantly we took a last turn through the anchorage and picked up the mooring.

Summer sun early in the morning was a reminder of Christmas five days away. We were down at the jetty early to ensure a position under the mast derrick. *Rebecca* was carefully secured so that the derrick hook hovered exactly over the mast hole. There was no breeze and the water was satisfactorily still. A strop was passed around the mast under the crosstrees and a heave on the tackle swung the spar high enough to lift the heel over the jetty rail and guide it down towards the step. I went below to steer it in, Jill eased the tackle and the mast dropped with a pleasing little bump into its position.

Without her ballast and with the mast as a pendulum *Rebecca* rolled easily so we moved carefully on deck to avoid the mast colliding unnecessarily with the derrick arm. The upper shrouds were lashed temporarily to chainplates and bowsprit to hold the mast sufficiently firmly to allow me to climb the derrick and swing the arm and the tackle out of the way. It was then a matter of systematically setting up the rigging, checking the mast angles from time to time as the turnbuckles were tightened. The backstay tackles were rove and cleated down and the boom dropped into the gooseneck, set in the crutch, and the topping lift shackled on. It was now possible to climb out on the bowsprit to check the tensions there. It did not seem so long now, and the bobstay and whisker shrouds supplied plenty of hand and footholds.

Curious onlookers handed down the gaff and the rest of the gear on the jetty. They were keen to see her sail, but there was a lot to do before that happened. Most urgent was the business of ballasting her to her marks. I had already brought what I estimated to be the equivalent in lead of the iron and rock she had carried. Since she was a few inches higher at the bow, this lead was now stowed under the floorboards in the mast area, but even with the mast in her, she sank only a few inches. Obviously we would have to spend more than we had bargained for on extra lead, and the bilges were going to be full, which was a pity, as there would in consequence be little room for water to accumulate before flowing up the side when she heeled. The extra lead certainly put the car down on its springs and when finally pushed into place in awkward corners and crevices, and carefully wedged to prevent movement, it took the yacht to within three inches of the waterline. It seemed the best we could do in the meantime; she looked well enough and the centre of gravity must now be reasonably well down for the weight we had placed in the bilge was previously contained in timber work above the deck line. The chief concern was that the propeller, installed at a minimum distance below water was now close to the surface, and indeed without crew on board the tips broke the surface in the swells. With two in the cockpit, however she trimmed to the mark; although the propeller thrashed up some white water when someone was on the bow, it was driving her satisfactorily.

The day had slipped by. *Rebecca* was shipshape, with the gear stowed. The sailbags at in the forepeak, waiting. The jib fairleads were yet to be set. It was three days to Christmas.

The inevitable tasks of Christmas shopping, provisioning and packing had been sadly neglected; we rushed into the city, frustrated by the crowds, anxious only to do the final jobs, hoist sail and disappear to quieter places. By late afternoon I was able to slip down to the bay again where a light North East breeze barely lifted the yacht club pennants. By now I was getting once more accustomed to *Rebecca*'s movement and clambered less clumsily about the deck as I laced on the mainsail to gaff and boom. A line, stopped at the throat, was rove loosely around the mast and through the luff eyelets. Although mast hoops may appear more romantically traditional, on a small yacht a lacing works best, I think. Once the sail had been hoisted and the line tightened down to hold the luff firmly against the mast, the sail can be lowered and rehoisted without further adjustment. The line drops naturally into its own coils as the sail is lowered and takes up the proper tension again when the sail is set.

Apart from a brief affair with a Norwegian gaff rigged yacht in the Mediterranean I had not hoisted a gaff rig since I had owned the eighteen footer *Arline* in the 1940s, but the routine came back quickly as I topped up the boom and laid hands on peak and throat halyards. It's hoist and tighten the throat first, then top up the peak. It's the same on the way down; don't let the peak drop faster than the throat or the gaff jaws may jam.

There is a natural rhythm to hoisting. You take a heave on each halyard and check that the peak of the gaff has cleared the topping lift. Then you give a double haul on the triple-purchased peak halyard to each single haul on the throat and the gaff will ascend horizontally. After sweating up and belaying the throat halyard you top up the peak until the sail drops in folds at the throat. The amount of fold depends on the setting you want for the weather, but if you do not put in some bag at the luff the sail will be too flat at the head, and may even have a hard line running diagonally from the throat to the leech. The halyards are coiled down. A hand is passed through the coil to pick up a bight of the line running from the belaying pin, drawn back through the coil and given a half turn so that the resultant loop can be dropped over the pin where it holds the coil firmly in place. The halyard is freed to run merely by lifting the coil which trips the twisted bight off the pin automatically. The coil is then dropped on its face so that the line flakes off without fouling.

The main when hoisted and with the topping lift slackened hung quietly into the light breeze, the leech fluttering gently. The setting looked good with a reasonably full belly close to the mast and a clean flat run off the leech. I left it up to let the creases blow out and hooked on the jib by its snap shackles, which I hoped would not only allow easy release, but with their swivels avoid nasty twists in hoisting a sail not hanked to a stay. The clew was hauled out to the bowsprit end; it was another version of a traveller, although it did not permit an adjustment to any position along the sprit. I tried hoisting the sail with the tackle loose, but immediately it careered behind the crosstrees and dropped itself over the side. With the clew hauled to within a foot of the bowsprit, it was easy to hoist the sail so that the halyard eye came to a stop against the masthead block, then tighten down the foot with the double purchase outhaul which provided all the tension required.

This jib had a double purchase on its sheets. Double pendants, each with its block were shackled to the tack. The sheets were fastened to a shackle in a spare eye on the backstay chainplates, led through the pendant block and back to the deck where I had to find the correct position for the fairlead. It was important to place them carefully to ensure the best setting for there was no adjustable track to provide a variety of positions. The mitre angle of the sail provides a starting point; the sheet should lead in line with the mitre, but it is more important to check the relationship of the curve of the leech and foot. If the foot is flattened too much the leech will sag off and flutter and if the leech is too tight it may hook back badly or direct the airflow too sharply against the mainsail. The fairleads ended up about a foot ahead of the chainplates, as far outboard as possible. A narrow beamed yacht like *Rebecca* gives little choice here, for it is important to keep a reasonable gap between main and jib, and in this instance the gap would be split by the insertion of the staysail.

The staysail was by contrast a toy to set. Only sixty square feet in area and hanked to the stemhead stay, it was a docile little sail that could be whisked up and down in a moment. Its fairleads were set to provide an even gap between mainsail and jib. With all sail set and the sheeting organised it was tempting to test her out then and there, but it was growing late and I wanted Jill to be aboard for our first sail. It was two days to Christmas and cruising!

It was nearly Christmas Eve by the time we had finished our chores, cleaning up the yard, mowing lawns and loading supplies. At four o'clock the wind was still holding North East, about ten knots and easing with the evening. This was about the only opportunity to test the yacht before we departed on Christmas Day. The buoy was dropped with mainsail and staysail set, for the big jib tended to make her charge about on the mooring. She fell off very slowly, even with the staysail backed. The main quietened, there was positive pressure from the tiller and a gurgle from the towed dinghy. She obviously needed to be sailed free without the jib to balance the big mainsail area, but once it was up she came alive. We reached across towards Devonport, checking the sheet leads, trimming the main and watching the mast as the staying took the new pressures. The forestay sagged off a bit as was to be expected. With the running backstays secured with rope tackles it was very hard to get a consistent, firm tension. The ten knot breeze held her down to the rail, with an occasional swell lipping over and along the deck.

She moved easily and fast, with no pressure on the helm, and was noticeably responsive to small changes in wind strength, a lively lad indeed in contrast to the stolid old girl we had sailed out of Tauranga. F-buoy loomed up.

Time to go about. John and Jill shared the backstay tackles and would soon sort out a routine. Tightened down and heading for Bean Rock *Rebecca* settled into her stride over the small swells through the channel. There was a crunch and scatter of spray at the forefoot, now, each time she dipped, and the myriad exploding bubbles of foam streaming along the lee deck talked to the hull. The long evening light gilded Motuihe, Waiheke and Coromandel beyond, glinted on varnish and paint and threw soft shadows on the three arcs of sail. It was a golden evening.

Peter Smith, Rebecca – the restoration of an old yacht, **1978**

THE TAMING OF THE CREW

TELEVISION reporter Michael Brown, his wife Sue, their two sons Andrew, aged ten, and Sam, six, and three adult crew left Lyttelton harbour on April 25, 1992 in their 14.3 m steel sloop Alderman *bound for the Tonga and Fiji. They were not to know that off the Kaikoura cost and again off Wairarapa they and their little ship were to be severely tested by two of the worst autumn gales for decades.*

It was a rugged introduction to ocean cruising for the family. Behind the voyage lay four years of planning, and not a little criticism of parents taking innocent children on dangerous ocean passages. Having weathered their first two gales, they put in to Gulf Harbour in Auckland. There they met other yachts taking part in a 'fun' family regatta to Tonga. Surely this time – but the start took place in a 40 knot southerly and some yachts turned back or retired within the first three days. But not the hardy folk aboard Alderman. *Their luck was about to change.*

On 14 May, three weeks after leaving Lyttelton, five days out of Gulf Harbour, we caught up with the dream we had nourished for so long. And it allowed us a generous embrace.

Calm seas.

Wind five knots, warm on the cheeks.

A half moon wafting west over a silver evening gown laid out for the night.

We were forty miles west of Raoul Island, above the thirtieth parallel, with more than half the voyage behind us. We'd been beam reaching in perfect conditions half the day and making good speed. Now we were slow, down to three knots, and loving every drifting moment.

All of us were well again. We showered away the last of the blues. We ate our first real meal: chicken nuggets and mashed potato – ordinary at home, but exquisite there – and topped it off with plunger coffee. Then we didn't speak much, but absorbed the sights and sounds that were at last gentle on the senses, taking in the subtle connections between vessel and sea and air. Except for Sam.

'Sam, hush a minute. Listen to the water. Look at the stars. Isn't that something?'

Sam looked up, surprised. He took it in for all of three seconds.

'Yeah. It's great. Can I have a biscuit?'

'OK. Then sit down and don't say a word for a while.'

At eight o'clock we inaugurated the *Alderman* branch of the Dead Poets Society, inspired by the movie. *Carpe Diem*, the movie's theme says: Live for the day. We were also inspired by a growing dislike of recorded entertainment. The rules are simple. First, unplug the stereo. Second, perform (yourself) any song, act, riddle, prose or poetry that appeals to you, especially if it's your own. It doesn't have to appeal to anyone but you.

Out came a guitar and a school recorder, several books, pens and papers. We put a Chinese lantern in the radar stand. Johnny Windvane took care of steering and with tiller out of the way we slipped on into the evening, creating our own silver wake to join the moon's. Cruising is not cruisy, but there are moments of pure magic and this was the first.

Sue and I sang 'Johnny Sands', about a man with a foolproof way of sending his spouse to a watery grave without laying a finger on her. Aileen read out a poem, *Names*, written by Dave's uncle Donald McDonald, who was killed at the age of thirty-two, in World War II:

> *As I walked the streets of Damascus*
> *A boy said unto me,*
> *'Where is the land from whence you came?'*
> *'It's far away over the sea!'*
>
> *'What is the name of the land?' he said.*
> *'New Zealand's the name,' quoth I.*
> *'And where is your home in that land?' he said.*
> *'Ngaroma,' I said with a sigh.*
>
> *'Ngaroma, Ngaroma,' he softly said.*
> *And in his eyes was a look*
> *That my eyes held when once I read*
> *Of Damascus in a book.*

Ngaroma: it referred to the family farm and the name means many streams, or ocean currents. Dave and Aileen had often thought of Donald McDonald and what he might have become had the war not taken him so early. The steel sloop they were building back in Christchurch would be called *Ngaroma*.

I started to read from *The Prophet*, Kahlil Gibran, not realising what effect it was having on Andrew until he interrupted.

> *And a woman who held a babe against her bosom said,*
> *Speak to us of Children.*
> *And he said:*
> *Your children are not your children.*
> *They are the sons and daughters of Life's longing for itself.*
> *They come through you but not from you,*
> *And though they are with you they belong not to you.*
>
> *You may give —*

'Oh no?' Andrew cried out. We all looked at him. His face was screwed up with distress. 'I don't want to listen.'

'What's the matter?'

'That's a horrible thing to say!'

'What?'

'To say that we're not your children!' His eyes were threatening tears.

'But —' I couldn't think of a quick explanation, so I settled for urging him to listen to the rest of the famous poem, then he would understand. He stayed reluctantly, ready to depart.

> *You may give them your love but not your thoughts,*
> *For they have their own thoughts.*
> *You may house their bodies but not their souls,*
> *For their souls dwell in the house of tomorrow, which you*
> *cannot visit even in your dreams.*
> *You may strive to be like them. But seek not to make them*
> *like you.*
> *For life goes not backward nor tarries with yesterday.*
> *You are the bows from which your children as living arrows*
> *are sent forth.*
> *The archer sees the mark upon the path of the infinite,*
> *and He bends you with His might that His arrows may go swift and far.*
> *Let your bending in the Archer's hand be for gladness; for even as He loves the*
> *arrow that flies, so He loves also the bow that is stable.*

I looked up from the page at Andrew.

'OK?'

He nodded, biting his lower lip. 'Yes. I understand.'

Sam was suddenly inspired and put pen to paper while we continued. When he came back he was so eager to read the result that he bounced from bottom cheek to cheek.

> *I went to somebody's place and I saw a green pillow.*
> *I felt it and I felt it and I felt it until I felt where you lay*
> *all the time.*
> *I felt it a wee bit more and I felt it a wee bit more until I could*
> *feel where you lay the very second you were born.*

That was followed by a few sighs of appreciation, most of them from Sam.

'Did you just make that up?' I asked.

'Yes, Dad!' he said scornfully.

I kept my peace. Interrogations were not in keeping with the spirit of the Dead Poets Society. Sam vented hurt feelings by venting his bladder. Into the wind.

'Other side,' Dave suggested, protecting his wine glass.

'Oh,' Sam up-troued, bounded over and re-aimed towards the last glow of day, the fastest little squirt in the west.

On the sked, we heard that a yacht anchored at Raoul has lost a diver. A fifty-four-year old woman had suffered a heart attack on the way to the surface and never made it.

The same night, at three in the morning, we heard the most puzzling of the strange sounds following us round the Pacific. I had just woken Andrew to steer for me so that I could go forward to take down the main. The wind had dropped to zero. I just completed that when a boy's voice called out.

'Dad!'

The tone was urgent, so I went swiftly back to the cockpit and found Andrew looking astern. 'What's the matter?' I asked.

'Did you hear that?'

'No? What?'

'Someone called out "Dad".'

I stared at him. 'What are you talking about? *You* did. You called me. I'm here.'

'No I didn't.' He was indignant and mystified at the same time, and flapped his hand at the starlit night out the back. 'I didn't say anything. It was out there.' I checked below, then came back slowly. Sam was fast asleep and it hadn't been his voice anyway.

Andrew and I both stared astern for a while. The roll was still deep, but the water surface was so smooth that it reflected the starlight.

There was definitely nothing out there.

'That's weird, Dad,' Andrew said, then went to bed.

I had a theory, of sorts: maybe a background of wind and water is like 'white' noise, acting on the ear the way an over-busy painting acts on the eye. The beholder hears or sees according to the promptings of the subconscious. And yet tonight, the background was non-existent if you didn't count the engine and we had both heard the same thing. Precisely the same thing. Or does the best answer lie in Sam's book *The Big Friendly Giant*? Perhaps the sea, the source of all life, holds all possible sounds like dreams in a bottle, uncorked by the imagination.

The next day was gloriously windless. The only remainder of the days of torment was the long molten-glass roll from the south. The sky was utterly clear and lightest of blues. Clear even of birds. Perhaps we had seen our last albatross.

Overnight, it seemed, the ether had changed colour. Gone was the cold-grey. In its place an exquisite deep radiant-blue, like the contents of the old school ink-wells exposed to the sun. We dubbed the colour 'Tonga blue'. Its darkness must have been something to do with depth, because when we threw in an empty can we could see the shape flickering for up to minute after it sank.

Sam liberated his poem in a bottle. Some day the world will open it and know that it was written by Sam Brown aged six.

We thought again about the boys' correspondence lessons and let the thought go by. The day was too good to waste. We abandoned any urge to keep the race pace going and tried out the 'MO' button on the GPS. In theory it goes like this. Whoever sees the victim take an unscheduled bath screams, "Man overboard!". The crew nearest the GPS immediately stabs the 'man-overboard' button. The machine makes an electronic note of the co-ordinates and then tells which direction to steer to get back there. If it happens in the dead of night and no once notices until morning, pushing the button is optional.

That was the theory of the MO button. But it didn't work. We cast floating objects forth, then crisscrossed the water, tracing every geometric shape known to man on the surface. The objects are still out there.

Sobering.

We got more serious. We shortened the update time on the GPS. We lowered the dinghy and Sam and I climbed in. Dave pushed the MO button, then motored *Alderman* away from us. He would attempt to relocate us on electronics alone while the women kept an eye on us. I noticed that Sue and Aileen were looking more than apprehensive.

Quarter of a mile away *Alderman* looked peculiar. When in the valleys between the swells, we could see only her mast growing out of the water. Then she started moving about in every direction but the right one. The MO location system still wasn't working.

From the distance, we could hear nothing at all. In fact, apart from our own breathing, we were in total silence. No birds flew, no bug hummed, no breeze or fish disturbed the rolling glass. I persuaded Sam that it might be worth his while to sit totally still and listen very very carefully. And there it was: as near as possible to absolute silence short of taking a space walk without a suit. The funny thing is that absolute silence isn't silent. It has its own sound that seems like a vibration as long and slow as the roll that moved us up and down. Maybe the human ear and brain are incapable of hearing no sound and create their own.

Not that I discussed it with Sam. He wanted to talk about the possibility of meeting a shark in the very near future. Still, I can testify for the record the unlikely fact that Sam has experienced total silence.

I stood up and waved arms, pulling *Alderman* round towards us within seconds. When we clambered back up the ladder, the women all looked relieved. All three had been spooked by the experience, also imagining a Jaws attack. While we could always see the mast, the roll had often hidden us. In that shining expanse it was as if we had vanished altogether.

That failure didn't spoil a second perfect evening. We put Frankie to sleep again to make the most of it. We held a knot-tying competition–the possessor of the fastest bowline to be awarded immunity from dinner dishes. Andrew had it down to three seconds. We dined on gin and tonics, spaghetti bolognaise and contentment. We sang songs together and in that vast space it seemed important to sing softly, so softly that our voices blended perfectly and 'Greensleeves' seemed part of the pale pastel light.

Dave and Aileen took their three-and-a-half-dollar boat off the market. Andrew noticed how much detail I was writing in the log and asked if I was going to write a book about the trip.

'I don't know,' I said. 'I think so.'

'You can look in my diary, if you like.'

'I can?' I looked at him sideways. What had happened to his inalienable right to privacy?

'Sure, but I want a cut.'

'Oh. How much?'

'Fifty per cent.'

'Outrageous. Ten per cent is my last offer.'

He nodded. 'You got yourself a deal.'

As we became sleepy, a breeze of five to seven knots pranced in from the west. We raised sail to catch it, setting Johnny to direct a broad reach. Just before dark, dolphins joined us to play. They rolled and swayed alongside, eyeing us as we called to them. But our low speed made us poor company and they left us to the night.

Andrew moved his mattress back into the doghouse. And for the first time on passage, Sue and I moved into the forward cabin. In a sea, it's the place of most violent vertical movement, but in good weather it's the most comfortable sleeping pit. We lay listening to the sounds. The forward cabin is a sound box. It transmits not only the creakings and rustlings of the vessel, but also the endless sigh of the bow parting the water and the voices of the sea's inhabitants. Squeaks and squeals and chatterings, and a moan so deep I couldn't imagine what produced it.

We read. Gen had purloined my book again, so I reopened the book that had influenced our anticipated path amongst the islands – *Friendly Isles*, by Patricia Ledyard, an American woman who went to Tonga to teach, loved what she saw, and stayed. She became one of the island's best-known Europeans. I would try to find her when we reached the Vava'u island group in the far north.

We slept, the best on any passage so far, waking only once when Gen dipped too deeply into my *Prince of Tides* and allowed *Alderman* to turn ninety degrees into a short chop. Waking from a flying dream in a forward cabin that has become a trampoline is a good way to develop a heart condition.

On the morning of 18 May, just after midnight, I turned off the satellite navigation system.

In the previous twenty-four hours we had done 150 nautical miles, charging through the waves with a humming rig and a thrumming hull. If a vessel ever enjoys itself, it would be a time like this. And we had done it effortlessly. Johnny Windvane steered, we slept and read books and yarned. Sam begged to climb the mast and was allowed to go up only on to the spinnaker boom close to the mast. Andrew said that he was an individual and therefore had the right to read *Penthouse*, should there be one on board. Which there wasn't. Instead he hooked a magnificent yellowfin tuna. But it was going to dwarf our freezer, so we swiftly photographed the proud hunter with his catch to make sure that he need never tell another lie, and reluctantly gave the tuna back to the deep.

Now, after eight days at sea, we would be sighting land sometime in the afternoon. Ata Island, the most southern in Tonga.

I didn't just turn off the GPS system, I disconnected its supply in the electrics cupboard so no one could do a quiet, faithless shifty behind my back. Then I pulled the sextant out of its case and fondled it.

Even back in the planning stages, long before we knew of *Alderman*'s existence, I had visualised this day. I had dreamed, in vivid colour, of using a sextant to plot a running fix on the chart and to predict exactly when the first spike of the first land would come up on the horizon.

The sextant is arguably the most powerful, simple and beautiful tool ever invented. Take a beam of starlight and bounce it off two mirrors in succession, rotating one of them until the star appears to lie on the horizon. Attach a scale to measure the angle of rotation – and therefore the angle of the star above the horizon – and you have a sextant. Now record the time you measured it, run time and angle through tables to work out where you are, and you have navigation.

That's the kind of simplicity that takes a genius to bring into existence. When John Hadley did so in 1730, its accuracy consolidated the power of the British Empire at sea. My up-to-date chart for approaching Ata Island, for example, still used coordinates recorded by Captain Pelham Aldrich on H.M. Surveying Ship *Egeria* in 1888–90. One sextant reading puts you somewhere on a line of possible positions. Two readings give you two lines, and where they cross is where you are.

It's a science that's also an art, and exponents have drawn the shape of earth and sea in much the same way for two centuries.

But the art of navigation is dying. The science is decaying into technology. Soon, cheap GPS (Global Position Systems) will be stacked in redundant threesomes in instrument panels that will look like the bridge of the Starship Enterprise and do all our thinking, seeing, hearing and smelling for us. If we're lucky we may be able to fetch our own mugs of hot soup.

Don't get me wrong. When you're off a stormy coast in the middle of the night, it's handy to punch a button and know exactly where the rocks are and how long you've got before you pile up on them. But this was my very first landfall. This day of all day, I wanted to follow in the wake of the likes of James Cook: adjusting the sextant, bracing against the movement of the ship, aiming, luring heavenly body down to earthly horizon, waiting for the kiss, marking the moment, debriefing the sextant, poring over the charts.

I took the first reading from the full moon, just before dawn when the globe was golden and the horizon a razor edge. That became the first line on the chart. There was nothing else to shoot then, so I trod impatiently between navigation desk and cockpit, making bad jokes about the lack of heavenly bodies. The dawn flared with colour and the moon paled away.

Two hours after dawn I shot the sun, turning it into the second line on the chart and adjusting for the travel between readings. The intersection gave the position, I fiddled with a few more figures, then went up on deck.

'This is it,' I announced. 'The heading is 347 degrees. Ata Island will appear on the bow at quarter to one. If we keep our present speed,' I added.

My obsession caused some amusement with the crew. Someone suggested that if I got it wrong, I would be honour bound as a gentleman and an officer to dangle myself from the yard-arm. But then they were a scurvy bunch of landlubbers, their ancestors were probably barnacles, and we didn't have a yard-arm.

For one hour, I cultivated an image of relaxed, authoritative assurance. I would have tried a deeper voice, but the crew lying about helpless with laughter tended to erode authority. At half past eleven, I couldn't handle the suspense and my cool blew away on the breeze. I climbed the mast.

And there it loomed, a dark, bleak and beautiful triangle of rock, right on the bow. I didn't need to announce anything – a smile that wide is like another sunrise.

Such kudos is difficult to lose in a short time, but I found a way. Twenty miles out we spotted three yachts close to Ata. No surprise because we knew some of the fleet were intending to fish there before heading in to Nuku'alofa. I called them.

'Vessels at Ata Island, this is *Alderman*, you copy?'

No answer.

Ten miles out. They were barely moving even though their mains were up.

'Looks like we're going to have a quiet night,' I said knowledgeably.

'Dark sails,' Dave observed, looking through his binoculars.

I called up again, loudly and repetitively, coming away puzzled that not one of the three had their VHF on.

'They don't want to know us,' I complained.

'Could be because they're triangle-shaped rocks.' Dave said helpfully. The interesting thing about Dave is his ability to keep a straight face when his insides are suffering from internal combustion.

Ata is part of Tonga, but unlike Tonga.

There were people there once, on the bush-covered eastern saddle. But last century, the 'blackbirders' came, travel agents with pressing arguments about free accommodation and alternative lifestyles in places like the silver mines of Peru. The Peruvians were getting a bit low on Inca Indians and somebody had to do the work. The Tongans were renowned for their fierceness as warriors, but their own empire was dying and on Ata they were vulnerable. Too few, too far from help. In 1860, when the raids had reduced the population to 200, the King of Tonga ordered everyone out to Eua Island, closer to Tongatapu and protection.

The Ata islanders never returned.

On the east side, what looks bleak from a distance is downright unfriendly at close quarters. No harbour, no coral. The sheer faces of the extinct volcano plummet nearly 300 metres into the water and keep right on going as if the sea were only a casual visitor.

We came in close anyway, fascinated by the forbidding atmosphere. Black frigate birds fell on us out of the heights, swirling elbowed wings, screeching round the rigging like lost-valley pterodactyls. When darkness crept over the bastions, we coiled the empty trolling lines and pointed the bow thankfully toward Nuku'alofa, ninety miles away.

Michael Brown and *Sue Neale-Brown*, The Taming of the Crew, *1994*

'THE CRUISE OF THE VICTORIA'

JIM Lott *is an Auckland maritime teacher, examiner, safety officer for Yachting New Zealand, director for Coastguard Education and volunteer master of the STS* Spirit of New Zealand. *After many years spent building his handsome 16m cutter* Victoria *in his back garden, he put to sea in 1993 with wife Karin and son Andrew, then fourteen. Over a two-year-old period they raced first to Japan, sailed on to Alaska, Panama, Cuba, New York, Ireland, Scotland, England, France, Gibraltar, the West Indies and home.*

The long trip southward through the French canal system between the Bay of Biscay and the Mediterranean was to prove a highlight. With 159 locks to negotiate, however, these picturesque but busy waterways were not without their hazards, especially for a yacht that drew 17cm more than the authorised maximum draught.

From Paris we had two choices of route. We could go east along the Marne through Champagne country before turning south to the Rhône; or we could go south through the canals alongside the Loire River then across to the Rhône through the southern Burgundy district. We chose the latter route which is a little less busy and supposedly more picturesque. Partly our decision was based on the planned canal closures for maintenance. But we did have the problem of our draught which varied between 1.93 and 1.99 metres. A book I had bought before we built the boat assured 1.97 metres was the maximum draught for these canals, but we were to find that the author was the only one in step. All other references, and all official sources quoted 1.80 metres. We asked everyone we met and made many phone calls to try and find out whether it was possible for us to get through. Finally in Paris we were referred to the Captain of the English 'Little Ship Club' in France, and phoned her where she lived on a canal barge in the town of St Mammès. With the official authorised limit of 1.80 metres 'without exception' always emphasised, she quietly did some research and was advised by barge operators and lock-keepers that we would probably make it but with many difficulties.

It took all day to escape the suburbs of Paris, but by dusk we had moored in the gentle countryside to await the arrival of Sue and Tom, family accompanying us in a little grey Peugeot. Eventually it appeared, and with only a hitch or two, did so each evening for the next six weeks. The only real drawback to the system was that we had to plan our stop for the night in advance by looking at the charts. Mostly we chose well, but more by good luck than good management. We missed being able to pause at will and spend the night at some of the really beautiful places that passed by. Perhaps it would have been a good idea to have hired a couple of portable telephones, but that is hindsight.

The next day we pushed on to arrive at St Mammès, and met up with our advisor Ronnie Townson and her lively wire-haired terrier on their delightful barge moored to the canal bank. She gave us the most wonderful information about the canals, the wine, the history and much else besides. After a few days investigating the narrow ancient lanes and roaming the countryside where Sisley did many of his tranquil impressionist paintings, we entered the Canal du Loing garbed in tyres and fenders and we were on our way.

With our deep draught we bumped and banged, got stuck here and there, and had to use our ladder most nights to get ashore, but had no real problems till the bottom lock at Rogny, where we stuck inside the lock. The lock-keeper kindly trotted up to the next lock and let go a load of water which lifted us nicely over the sill.

Apart from bangs and scrapes with the odd rock, and we suspect, a supermarket trolley or two, there were no further incidents until one fine Saturday with heaps of traffic and us stuck in the lock at Maimbray. We hit hard on the sill while exiting, and water sent down from the next lock was just enough to lift us on top of the sill before the tide went out again.

Lines run to bollards and winched tight, to trees and wound bar-taut with the windlass did nothing to extricate us from our perch, and all the while the row of boats in the river grew longer. Most were very kindly and sympathetic, but one German in a charter cruiser had plenty to say about the delay. No one took much notice since he seemed to think the lock-keepers were there to do his line handling and everything else, while his crew sat drinking wine and trying to look decorative. The lock-keeper used his phone to contact the next four locks to send some water our way, with each lock building the 'wave' up as it passed. This held up the whole system for over an hour, and many boats were aware of the New Zealand yacht which was stuck in a lock.

In the meantime we had managed to winch ourselves back off the sill and into the lock, dropping down and out to let the queue through and get on their way. After an hour or so the water was pouring over the top of the gates, and we had sufficient depth to get over the sill. However, because we had thought we would not get through, Karin had hitched a lift on a launch ahead of us to tell Sue and Tom in the car where we were held up, but there was no way Andrew and I were going to waste the opportunity to make as much progress as we could.

After a couple more locks, we spied Karin and her new friends still in a lock up ahead and managed to entice her back aboard the yacht in spite of all the embarrassments that could now be assured. Our arrival in St Satur was well after dark, and Sue and Tom were aboard 'Karin's launch' drinking wine and well aware of our entertaining day. It took a day staying at St Satur and a visit to the superb country around the wine making district of Sancerre to bring the nerves back to something near normality.

We also took the opportunity to blow up our large inflatable dinghy which we loaded with our 30 kg anchor and 80 metres of 12 mm chain. This raised our waterline a couple of much needed centimetres and posed no problem towing since we could attach a stern line from the dinghy to our long overhanging mast. Some had warned that such long overhangs would pose problems, but we did not find that to be the case.

Our journey continued through beautiful countryside, forests which brushed the rails as we passed, and blue-grey herons that squawked and flew off in protest at the disturbance we caused in the quiet waterways. But the disturbance we caused was minor in comparison with the clamour that seemed to come from the forest itself one morning. The loud thumping and booming increased for many minutes and finally manifested itself from an approaching motor cruiser. The foredeck mounted speakers were blaring what is referred to by some of today's generation as 'music', all being powered by a portable generator which could not be heard above the all-pervading cacophony. As the cruiser passed and peace was restored we stared at each other in wild surmise; her name was *Mozart*.

By now we had used most of our fuel and hit no more lock-sills, but we nevertheless entered each very gently while holding our breath. With a total of 159 locks to negotiate we had plenty of time to be anxious. The maximum speed we could achieve was four knots without setting up a large stern wave, but this was fast enough with the sides of the canals about 30 metres apart. The locks themselves were much narrower at 4.5 metres wide and 25 metres long. This left just a handspan clear each side of our fenders and it took a while to get used to entering locks where it was impossible to see the sides which were below gunwale level and hidden from my view. Most of the lock gates at each end butt together in a simple mitre join, a system designed by that famous engineer Leonardo da Vinci.

In spite of these ever present problems we had a wonderful time of it all. The pure serenity as oak and plane trees stretched to hold hands above our heads while ferns and willows bowed to stroke the water; the long fields of sunflowers awaiting harvest for seeds and oil; the clearly efficient larger farms between the 10 acre holdings so heavily subsidized; the distant villages always adorned by a tall steeple; the warmth of the Loire valley in stark contrast to the Seine; the anglers who would quickly reel in and give a cheery wave as we puttered by; the textured patterns the vines made as they climbed the slopes for mile after mile in the wine districts; the people who paused from daily routines to wave or chat as we made our way through the centre of the many villages and towns: all left a lasting impression that we tried to capture on film and video.

Another lasting impression was made when our bow rose high and we shuddered to a sudden stop. Tom, who was steering, looked up from the cockpit floor where he had fallen amidst his morning coffee and said, 'I thought I was in the centre of the canal where you said.' He certainly was, but we managed to back off and crept past the obstacle close to the canal bank. At the next stop the lock-keeper asked if we had hit anything. Our answer was strongly affirmative, and he said that they thought there was a car in the canal! We greeted his comment with mirth, after all it was too ridiculous to think we could have collided with a car. Some months later when swimming in warmer water I had a good look only to find a large scrape and some timber torn from the bottom along the keel line up forward. The car had been just beneath the murky surface.

Low bridges also presented a challenge. We had to take down our radar post and GPS aerial to achieve the stated clearance. Even so at times our davits would scrape the bottoms of the hundreds of steel or concrete bridges under which we passed.

Gradually we rose higher and higher towards the centre of France to perhaps 300 metres above sea level. On the way, this amazing highway providing a transport route throughout Europe, built long before trains or cars were invented, led us over an aqueduct high above the river Loire. This bridge full of water is several hundred metres long and fifty metres above the river as it bubbles over the stones below. Looking down as we chugged slowly over in *Victoria* was indeed a weird sensation. We later returned by car to inspect the structure. It is beautifully built of rivetted iron and designed by Eiffel, an engineering masterpiece equal to his more famous erection. In its hundred years it was only closed once for any time, and that was due to bomb damage in the second world war.

Our adventures continued as we bumped and ploughed our way across France, but with no major incidents until our last aqueduct at Digoin. This 'pont-canal' is about 300 metres long, and while not as large or spectacular as the one we crossed at Briare, is made of concrete, I think. We bumped heavily at each frame as the boat jumped several centimetres. With full power we managed to make the end, and were heartily relieved not to be stuck, unable to go ahead or astern in the middle of a town aqueduct with less than half a metre clearance each side of the boat. Of course I had dreams of the worst-case scenario where we punched a hole in the bottom of the aqueduct! At times of minor stress one's imagination can be a little theatrical, providing a good laugh later when all is under some semblance of control. Much to our amusement was a plaque on the side of the aqueduct 'T.E. 2.4m'.

It was a happier skipper who reached the 'top' of the Canal Centre, and had begun the descent to the Saône. We now felt confident of achieving our goal without having to turn back and face the prospect of autumn gales in the Atlantic and Bay of Biscay.

The Burgundy region, so famous for its wines and particularly those wonderful reds made from the pinot-noir vines, was good reason for us to dally a while. From Santenay in the south, to the village of Nûits-St Georges in the north we explored, tasted, and spent a grand few days. The châteaux with their variegated tiled roofs are now often wineries, and many cellars encourage tasting. The quality is excellent and prices are moderate. Together with crisp French bread, the many cheeses, grapes and all manner of other foods, the wines made us over indulge until our belts needed that extra hole. Before we left Santenay, a completely unnecessary incident left us with a cracked railcap. We had moored in a section of canal where there were bollards, and with a good view of the canal in either direction. Several boats and peniches had passed without incident, but one, registered in Ghent, approached at more than twice the speed of any other traffic. The surge caused our mooring lines to carry away and as our bow was sucked out, the aft quarter of the barge struck our gunwale with a mighty thump. The bargee's wife abused us roundly using a wide vocabulary of English epithets, and they continued on without slowing. We had jumped onto the canal bank to try and hold onto the yacht, but she was dragged along in the peniche's wake for over 50 metres before we were able to catch up and regain some control. As the barge disappeared my only consolation was being able to add a few choice nouns and adjectives to the woman's range of oaths.

Finally, a lock with a drop of twelve metres and out into the Saône perhaps a hundred metres wide. We had become so used to about thirty metres that it seemed like going to sea. We stopped for the night in Tournus, but with only just a tiny clearance between our keel and the hard bottom. Next morning we were less than delighted to find the Saône had dropped 0.3 of a metre. But I felt that it was likely to come back up soon. During the morning it dropped even further, and so we laid out a heavy anchor with its chain and started winching towards deeper water. Getting a bite in the anchor was difficult, but we did manage to move things a bit, and then we waited for a deep-laden fast barge to give the wash that would do the rest. Of course, the river was amazingly quiet, but towards evening a kindly Dutchman in a large yacht came to our aid. Using his weight, a couple of firm pulls had us afloat again, and enjoying some burgundy with yet more new friends. He was heading north via the route we came with a draught just a tiny bit greater than ours. I hope we were able to give him some helpful advice.

Jim Lott, The Cruise of the Victoria, in Spirit, magazine of the Spirit of Adventure Trust, *1995*

'GOD IS A WOMAN'

Steve Dickinson, editor of New Zealand's oldest boating magazine Sea Spray, *grew up surfing on Northland's east coast and has been a teacher and author of children's books. As a freelance photographer and journalist, he has travelled the South Pacific, diving, fishing, windsurfing and surfing, but he came to serious sailing relatively late. This story of his own first experience in Waitemata harbour match racing, is, he says, really a dig at how some sailors take themselves way too seriously.*

There are times in every fisherman's life when he has to make sacrifices. You may have to miss the mother-in-law's birthday because the tides are just right, or late shopping with the kids because it's the only time the fish are biting according to Bill's fishing calendar. However, sacrifices have to be made. It is what sport is all about.

It seems a simple quirk of fate that the guys who own boats are always the guys who you would least want to ask. These individuals give credence to the fate that God is in fact a woman. If your general bloke had a boat, and his mate rang up and wanted to go fishing, there would be a simple discussion on who would bring the bait and who would buy the beer. The fishing would follow as a matter of course. But no. God has allowed a small number of individuals to hold sway over the fishing fraternity, blokes with names like Russell, Rupert or Randolph.

One of these Russells asked if I'd like to go fishing one afternoon. No discussion about cut lunches, fuel costs or even picking up the bait. Russell, I marvelled, had rejoined the realms of being a real bloke. But one final squeak down the line cast a dark shadow.

'Er, Steve, if we go for a fish in the afternoon, do you think you could help me crew the yacht in the morning for the wife's big race?'

What could you say, fingers crossed that this was just a hairline crack in the new veneer of testosterone.

'Sure, Russ, I'll be there, mate . . . no problems.'

'Er, the name's Russell, Steve. The little lady thinks 'Russ' sounds a bit common!'

I had known Russ ... Russell since school and had followed the chipping away of his manhood as he became more and more involved with yacht racing. Now in his late twenties, the metamorphosis from 'mate' to emasculate' had taken place.

Anticipation of something getting worse does not stop the natural drama and decline of events happening. As I walked down the marina, towards the yacht, I had that terrible sinking feeling, something akin to the captain of the *Titanic*. Russ – Russell – stepped off the transom in bright blue rubber leggings pulled up to his chin and luminous white boots, holding a coffee cup emblazoned 'Captain'. Had the cup said 'Poofter' or 'Skipper Jerk', the ownership of the cup would never have been in doubt, but 'Captain' seemed a grandiose title for someone looking like a Smurf into rubber bondage. The visual association was bad enough, but the deafening greeting that resounded across the harbour – 'Ahhah there, ship mate!' – made me flush the same colour as my tackle box, and preempted the need of a neck brace as I swung in every direction to make sure there was no one I knew within a five km radius.

'Hi Russ ... er, Russell,' I muttered. 'Where shall I put the tackle?'

Standing on one leg and partially closing one eye, Russ – 'Captain Russell' – chanted, 'Stow 'er below, me hearty!' Feigning seasickness might be the only way I was going to back out of this Errol Flynn movie. Any moment now Rita Hayworth was going to appear. Under full sail we would to sail off into the wild blue yonder, with me pressganged into this real bloke's nightmare!

The payment for an afternoon's fishing seemed to be way too high.

Then, as if by some unseen divine intervention, that which seemed so unfair, so unjust, got worse. Not only did rubber-coated Russ hold the key to an afternoon's fishing, the boat and a bloke's ability to hold his head up on the marina, but he was also married to the boating version of Marilyn Monroe. She moved away from the hatch cover and, as radiantly as the dawning sun, slowly made her way into the cockpit, so aptly named.

'Hi! I'm Janine,' she sang, standing with her frame against the light. 'Do you like what you see?' she purred.

'Excuse me?'

'Do you like her?' Russell boasted. I gaped at him. 'Do you like the boat?'

'Oh, yes, it has wonderful bows ... I mean bow,' I bumbled.

'You're going to help me do my thing, Russell tells me,' she whispered, bending over to adjust the straps that apparently maintained her voluptuous form.

'Excuse me?'

'Win the race.'

'Oh yeah, that's me. I'm here to give you all the hand you need.'

Russell's rubber pants seemed to come right up to his chin. His wife's gear neatly tucked the waistband under her assets, helping to lift and separate. In her hand she had a coffee cup that read in bright red lettering 'First Mate'. Was Russell not only blessed with this goddess of a wife, but also a second, a third and a fourth?

'Coffee?' she mused.

I stared at the array of coffee mugs and settled for a Daffy Duck with a quizzical look on its face. I sat in the cockpit, one of the crew, as Janine thrust her copious chest and silk-white finger at each of us in turn and labelled us with our positions for the race. 'You're the bowman,' she said to me. I knew the bow as the sharp bit at the front, and that big flappy things were somehow attached up that end, but not wishing to sound like Daffy Duck, I replied in confident, nautical fashion.

'No problems.'

There probably is a law of reasonable karma. Big Kev was assigned to assist with the bowman's job and he by the grace of God knew what to do. Unfortunately, he also had a hangover caused by copious amounts of red wine the night before. Although he looked the part in his rubber gear, and although he knew the words for all the ropes and sheets and cleats and sails and coloured bits, asking questions of him was a problem. Giving answers, his breath was enough to make a monkey's rear end a pleasant confrontation in comparison. Slapping his lips together, sticking out his yellow-coated tongue, he asked more than once, 'Cactus growing on it, mate?'

At a reasonable distance, with a sail between the two of us, Kev explained the workings of the sharp end: the different sails, poles and ropes. As long as it wasn't too rough, and he could keep his breakfast down, we'd be just fine.

'I'm gonna cast off,' cried Janine. Hoping that this was prelude to 'First Mating', I leapt to my feet expecting rubber pants and garters scattered in all directions, but it was only ropes that fell into the water.

Kev and I mellowed up the sharp end, him giving me quiet nautical advice and me trying to keep downwind of his breath. I was thrown my own set of rubber diapers, a pair of freezing worker's white rubber boots and a pair of biking gloves. I noticed that everybody had these biking gloves on. The team started to unwrap things, tie things and lash things down as the gentle waters of the marina took on a slightly wobblier stance. Thinking that this would be a good time to show off my own pirate-like skills I stood up the front bit, legs akimbo and stared out to sea.

What I saw was a fearful sight: fifty other yachts, each with a full complement of rubber-coated, white-booted gnomes all rushing about. The sea had come up and the moment we moved outside the harbour wall my composure went down the gurgler. I grabbed the first rope I saw and hung on. This rope unfortunately was not attached to anything. As I hit the deck, my rubber pants up over my eyes, I heard Janine authoritatively yell, 'We're gonna tack!'

I felt that this was no time to be laying carpet as sheets of white water came tumbling over the bow. Also, the rest of the boats on the Auckland harbour were bearing down on us.

'No, we're not going to tack,' parried Russell.

'Oh yes we are!'

'Oh no we are not!'

The next ten minutes were like a scene from a movie, Russell cast as Mr Fletcher on the *Bounty* and Janine screeching like Long John Silver's parrot. Up the sharp end, Kev seemed pretty relaxed, legs over the high side and hanging on the wire thing. I joined him up wind and took the same perch.

'Should put those pants over ya boots, bud,' Kev advised. No sooner had the words come out of his mouth than a large wave raised and broke, filling both gumboots to the brim.

'Told ya,' he said laconically. 'And, mate, when we tack, keep your head down and watch out for the boom.'

Not all together sure what the boom was, I guessed it could however do serious damage.

The big flappy things were now looking very tight and the yacht started to lean to one side. Everybody seemed fairly content. I on the other had was most concerned that someone had shut the round windows down below, as by now they would be well under water.

Janine, at the wheel, yelled, 'Prepare to come about!'

'No, not *yet*,' said Russell, his voice caustic.

'Yes, right now!'

'No, not yet!' he screamed.

'Yes, *now*!'

The argument got louder and louder. The thought of Janine flattening Russell was more than I could hope for. Disregarding Big Kev's advice, I sat up straight and looked towards the cockpit in the hopes of seeing Janine deal the deathblow. At the same moment, 'coming about' was no longer an issue for discussion but an actual event. All those who had done it before made like rubber-bellied snakes, and went slithering across the deck. I, still enthralled by the prospect of seeing Russell minus his dentures, was still on the high side looking back. The big flappy things went whoosh! . . . the rope things went whang! . . . and the boat started to capsize. The impact of the change in horizon threw me headlong across the deck, and a slight change in my hair parting caused by the movement of the boom was met with loud exclamations from Kev and the rest of the crew.

Not only did I almost lose my head but as I tumbled and rolled across the pitching deck, ending up with my head through the wire railing, the full icy contents of my gumboots ran up the inside of my rubber leggings. When asked by those around me if I was all right, I failed to answer, not due to any major injury but because of the ice cold water now gurgling round my good bits. With my male genitalia turned to those of a small boy on a cold night, I gathered myself with as much decorum as possible and tried to get the surprised look off my face. No sooner had I seated myself than the terror words of 'tacking' came again and the whole debacle repeated. This time I too made like a slithery snake, but due to my terror of the boom and the arctic environment of my jocks I stayed down there for at least fifteen minutes after we had finished the tack.

Throughout the next half an hour we tacked several times each with its own brand of horror. Each tack was precluded with furious debate about whether to tack or not. This furore may have well been an indication why they had never had children, with neither being able to make any sort of decision about when, where or even how.

'See the buoy! You little *beauty*!' screamed Russell, possibly giving some real clue to his sexual preference. Looking where he was pointing, I could not see any buoy, not even a pimply faced teenager. I did however see other yachts going around an orange balloon-shaped obstacle in the water, and busily changing the size and shape of their sails.

Before we got anywhere near the buoy, there was all sorts of consternation on board. Big Kev stood up and said, 'We'll be up soon, mate, let's get a few things organised.'

Kev and I crawled around the sharp end getting bits of rope clipped on and organising the sails. As we approached the orange balloon, Janine and Russell renewed their debate.

'I'm gonna heave!' yelled Big Kev, looking over the side. Wanting to be helpful, I was just in time to see last night's cab sav hit the briny.

'Get ready to gybe!' screamed Russell. Could Janine be my partner? With all the stress of getting around the orange balloon, it seemed an inappropriate time to boogie. No one else moved and no music filled the air, so I took it that gybing would be put on hold till later. No sooner had we gone around the balloon it was time to put up the sphincter.

'I want to put up the sphincter,' yelled Russell. Once again I wondered as to his sexual preference. It seemed an awful affront to Janine and unworthy criticism over a mere argument over whether to tack or not. The sphincter filled out in front of the boat and everybody seemed happy that the pole thing was in the right place.

The rest of the race continued in a struggle of tipping boats, slashing booms, big flappy things going whoosh and cold wet feet. After three hours of waves, wind and incomprehensible nautical terms, there was the sound of a gun. We threaded our way between two stationary boats, an indication of how seriously the race was taken. The yacht settled down, the wind mercifully dropped and we chugged back into the harbour under power.

Laying prone on the deck, I took stock. My back was displaced in several places due to the constant snake slithering across the deck. My backside had been ripped and bruised by the hard bits of metal that seem strategically placed to rip a hole in a young boy's butt. Hot and sweaty in my portable sauna, listening to Russell and Janine fight over where to park the boat, it had been an interesting introduction to yacht racing.

Eventually we tied up at the mooring. I heard the sound of footsteps and looked up to see silhouetted against the sun, the nautical version of Marilyn Monroe.

'Did you have a fun day, Steve?'

'Oh yes, sure, it was . . . fun!' Slowly I tried to sit up, but not having the full use of my spine, I gave an impression of a jellied eel.

'So, you boys going fishing now?'

'Eh?'

'You were going fishing, remember?'

Looking heavenward, I quite clearly saw the clouds part and heard angels singing. God in all her finery smiled down at my discomfort, my back out, soaked to the skin, no skin left on my fingers, hair parted by the boom, feet looking like two frozen prunes, stomach heaving from the pounding seas and my privates shrivelled to unrecognisable wrinkles. She in her heavens was laughing at me, knowing that her work was done and I was in no fit state to make a cup of tea, let alone go fishing.

'I've had so much fun I'm stuffed,' I muttered. 'I might give it a go next week.'

'Hey, Steve, that's great. You could crew for me next Saturday again, before you head out!'

Steve Dickinson, God is a woman, New Zealand Fisherman, *1997*

'NEW BOAT BLUES'

AT 31, Rebecca Hayter decided she'd had enough, took a deep breath and bought her first keelboat, a Raven 26.

She had grown up around boats with her father, Adrian Hayter, first while he was an instructor at Outward Bound at Anakiwa, later when he was a commercial fisherman. She'd pottered around in dinghies, owned a Laser, had her Boatmaster and Coastal Yachtmaster tickets and was beginning a career as a respected yachting journalist (currently, editor of Boating New Zealand). In theory and in practice, she was often better qualified than the guys who took her sailing. But when she took delivery of the Raven, she found there were plenty of unseen – and not entirely agreeable – challenges lying in wait for a female boat owner.

The yacht broker played along with my game – at first. Then, as I peered under floorboards and scrambled over the decks in my office clothes, his expression changed.

'What do you want to buy a yacht for?' He said it gently, so he wouldn't hurt my feelings.

Later, a friend told me I should have given him the answer he probably expected: 'I want to drink champagne on it and sunbathe in my bikini.'

Instead, some would say typically, I leapt to the defensive. I rattled off my boating CV: Boatmaster, Yachtmaster, Laser owner for three years, the winter series – over the next few weeks and brokers I would get tired of making that speech.

I found her on my thirty-first birthday: a Raven 26. That night at my party I was ecstatic, happy, thrilled. Two weeks later when it came to take her out I was nervous, worried, terrified. Twenty-five knots, gusting 35, didn't help.

Coming home from Islington Bay the wind was on the nose, we were sliding fifteen degrees off other boats' headways and the mainsail was a bag of wrinkles. At North Head, we finally, shamefully, eased the topping lift-but at least we weren't high and dry on Bean Rock.

'Maybe she's a hire yacht,' Graham suggested.

'Well, she's certainly higher than ours.'

Monday morning's *Herald* had the story: that yacht, too, had been on her first outing with new owners. The forgotten topping lift didn't seem so bad after all.

I was looking forward to bringing my new baby out of the water. Then I would work like a Trojan, do the tasks on my list, make her mine. Making that list was easy.

Haul-out day was calm and I almost enjoyed the trip from Northcote to Okahu Bay. The boat in line before us had the painter around the prop – another mistake we hadn't made – but while we awaited our turn, the wind increased to around eighteen knots.

'Put a stern line on the weather pile and row a bowline ashore,' the man had told me but if I ever do it again, I'll put a bowline on the weather pile. There we were, hanging straight downwind, while my flatmate Roger tried vainly to row three tonnes of boat against the wind.

The man on the next boat was obviously thinking about how he would do it. So I asked him.

'A longer line would help,' he drawled. Obvious. A one-month-old baby who had never read a sailing book could have figured that out. Eventually the boat was safely on the hard.

'Who's going to use the water blaster?' asked the man in charge.

'I am.' I fronted up to be shown how. General laughter all round.

'The little lady's going to do it!'

While the 'little lady' blasted her hull, her flatmate fielded comments ranging from 'nice boat you've got there,' to 'you've got her well trained'.

Afterwards we were towed to our spot. Ian and Maryon went to retrieve my car from Northcote, and Roger had other things to do. I stood alone on my boat and not a clue where to start. What had I done?

'Osmosis,' the man on the next boat said. 'Every person in this boatyard is going to tell you what to do about it.' He was the first.

Sanding the tiller seemed an easy place to start. The broken tiller extension clip came off easily but the actual extension had me stumped. It was the first job in a series that would involve replacing the exhaust pipe, removing the rudder, packing the stern gland (or something like that) and riding the bosun chair, and I was beaten by a two centimetre split pin.

Chauvinists, men who reckon women are 'totally impractical' – you're gonna love what follows. Feminists, independent women fighting for equal opportunities, you will think I have deserted you. I haven't; I just wish I had been given plastic drills to play with in the sandpit rather than dolls, that my home economics class had included woodwork and metalwork, and that every skipper I have ever sailed with had shared out the jobs evenly between the sexes. But that was enough of that. I just had more to learn, that was all.

I eyed the split pin; it eyed me. It didn't flinch, not even when I whacked it from beneath. Not even when I applied pliers and pulled hard. I sanded around it. Split pin: one; Beckie: nil.

Graham arrived and showed me how to lever out the split pin, but the screw beneath it merely turned with the nuts. I proudly produced all my tools which showed every sign of having been on a boat for a few years.

'You're never going to do with those,' he told me.

Ian arrived the next day and showed me how to break the lock nut. At the rate of one easy lesson a day, I'd be out of the water until Christmas.

Enter Graham WKE – Graham Who Knows Everything. As bluewater sailor, boatbuilder/painter and aircraft engineer, he has all the information a girl with her first keeler could need.

Graham inspected the hull and recommended scraping it back to the gel-coat and starting again. It seemed like a lot of work but the man on the next boat had done it and his boat was heaps bigger than mine. Graham gave me a lesson and left me to it.

Two days later I rang him. 'I can't do it, I'm wrecking the hull. It's too hard.'

Another lesson, a pat on the head. Ian helped and covered the same area in an hour that had taken me four days. My hands had blisters. My eyes were full of grit despite the goggles. My shoulders ached and every time I took a drink I forgot I was wearing a mask. I gave up.

'You're not a quitter!' Graham WKE said.

'Yes, I am. I'll paint over it and sandblast it next year.'

Meanwhile the boat had blisters too. A lesson on the angle grinder from Graham and I began cutting away pieces of my precious hull. Surprisingly, it wasn't that difficult. In fact, it was fun. In fact, I was going to have a boat that looked like Swiss cheese. I stopped.

'He gives you all the hard jobs, doesn't he?' a voice called from above as I went to retrieve the extension cord. A guy poked his head over a bow. He introduced himself as Warren.

'It's my boat,' I said proudly.

'You know, I don't want to be offensive, but I've never seen a girl doing that kind of work before.'

'Neither have I,' I said, standing up to my full five foot, four inches.

'I came down here and I thought: that's a girl. Then I thought: it can't be. But, yep, you're a girl. Like a beer?'

Sometimes I didn't feel so clever. Like when I mixed my first batch of epoxy, forgot to put it in a shallow container and it cooked into a hard mass of hokey pokey before I'd used a quarter of it. Like when I mixed the next batch and, terrified of using too much hardener, had to wait four days for it to go off. My learning curve was vertical and every time I made some upwards progress, I would lose my grip and fall in a heap back at the bottom.

The cockpit seats were a problem. The teak panelling had been done professionally but badly. The survey said leakage underneath could have left permanent damage. It had. I removed the teak panels – by now quite hard-hearted about wrecking things – and when I jumped on the worst one, it squeaked and squirted up foul smelling brown water.

'You'll have to clean those holes out and fill them with epoxy,' Graham said. 'Dry them out with your hair dryer first.' At last – I had the right tool for the job!

It was time to tackle the split pin in the spreader. Graham WKE was the only person I trusted to winch me up. I don't have a problem with heights, I just want to know that I'm safe.

'Can't I have two halyards holding me up on two winches?' I asked.

'You don't need two, one's enough. People do this every day on boats,' Graham told me.

'I still want two halyards, just in case.'

'Look. One halyard is designed to take strains of 30,000 pounds. Are you going to tell me you weigh more than that?'

Hell, no.

What a fuss about nothing. The split pin went in easily. I didn't even drop the pliers on the deck.

Grant, automotive engineer by trade, told me to clean the engine, change the oil, and change the filters. He also gave me pointers on removing the exhaust pipe: remove the hose clip there and pull it out, cut it there with the hacksaw blade and rejoin the new piece. Simple. He left me to it.

Straightaway, I could see quite plainly Grant didn't know what he was talking about. There was no point cutting the pipe when there were three bolts obviously holding it on. By dismantling part of the casing around the quarter berth, squeezing in through the small hole and sweating away five to six kilos, it would be a simple matter to remove those bolts.

Three hours later, I was still wedged into the Houdini practice position, when I heard a knock on the hull. I was getting used to visitors: friends, people wishing to compare Ravens, others curious to meet 'the bird with the boat'. Visitors were nice but I had had enough.

'If it's not an engineer, an electrician or a boat builder they can bugger off,' I muttered.

It was John, whom I had met the day before. He had advised me to drill out the holes in the cockpit seats to clean them. I'd hired a drill, got bits far too small – the exact size of the screws I had removed, how silly of me – and got nowhere.

However, John is a professional sailing tutor. He was also holding a drill. From between my blackened hands and greasy hair, I found my most beaming welcome. We drilled out the holes and filled them with epoxy. It took.

After he had gone, I tackled the oil change. This was supposed to be easy. Let it out, plug it in, fill it up. Considering it's the most commonly undone nut on the engine, it seemed strange it was also one of the most inaccessible – or at least it would have been a week before. I was learning.

More constipated-sounding grunts, more nothing. The nut was placed so that if any spanner, socket or crescent was fitted onto it, the handle came slap up against another part of the engine. Mark, ex-fitter and turner, arrived and we spent a further three or four hours struggling with the exhaust manifold. Beaten.

'The first part of learning a man's work is to swear like a man,' he told me. A few minutes later when I dropped the spanner in the bilges, he expanded on that. 'Well, you're ready for step two.'

We tried the oil nut. Beaten again.

'You need a 22 on an extension,' Mark said, and left. I rewrote the definition of marine engineering: the art of doing a nut up so tightly that the next person won't be able to undo it, thereby establishing the superior strength of the first person.

I went over to Ian and Graham's boat and borrowed a 22 socket and extension. Their boat leaked like a sieve, had rot and needed new keel bolts. That cheered me up. I bounded back through the rain to remove the bleeding nut once and for all.

At 8pm, it was cold, wet and dark and still it wouldn't budge. I had worked hard all day and achieved only a sanding and recoat of the tiller, and filling the holes in the cockpit. I thought about crying, but there was enough salt water corrosion already.

As it happened, my boat was out of the water until Christmas – three months. I gave up on the oil nut and pumped the oil out of the sump. I chipped away the rotten marine ply from beneath the cockpit seats, and discovered the dreaded fibreglass itch. I painted the hull with purple anti-fouling and a bright blue stripe – I loved it. I polished the topsides. My tiller with its sixteen coats of varnish shone like a Stradivarius violin.

Finally, we were sailing again but every outing brought more problems, usually with the engine. It was time to do my diesel course.

At first the only girl in class dutifully took notes and didn't dare speak. That lasted until one of my classmates asked about the spark plugs. In a diesel? Hey, even I wasn't that dumb! But cockiness comes before a fall and one day my engine refused to start. I worked my way through my tutor's suggested remedies but to no avail: the engine was seized.

Graham WKE was of course consulted. I wanted to buy the 15 horsepower Yanmar motor in his garage but he recommended fixing the engine I already had. As always, he knew just the person for the job. Me.

I knew what lay ahead if I fixed that motor. There would be bolts that refused to move; the right parts ordered would be wrong when they arrived. Worse, those lonely hours surrounded by an engineering jigsaw puzzle I had no way of solving.

I also knew if I didn't pull the bloody motor apart and put it back together, I could never look Graham in the eye again.

It seemed too drastic to remove the engine, so I went straight to Graham's second piece of advice: 'Keep taking bits off until you get to the head.' The tutor on the diesel course had taken the head off a six-cylinder motor so I had some idea of the anatomy. Besides, heads sit on top of people so I figured it must be the same for Yanmar engines.

A big screwdriver and a hammer soon had the oil filter out of the way. Next, I had to remove the chain cover and cursed the last person – me – who had rounded off the bolts. I hacksawed across them so they would think they were screws but they couldn't be tricked. I tried brute force with the vice grips. That worked.

Then I removed the head bolts, just like that.

Naturally I was pretty proud of myself. After all, even blokes have been known to struggle with head bolts.

Graham and Vivienne were impressed too and immediately inspected my progress. 'Beckie,' Graham said solemnly, 'that's not the head. That's the water gallery.' I knew it had been too easy.

Apparently my engine was horizontal so the head was where you'd expect to find a kneecap. What followed was what I'd dreaded: dismantling the quarter berth and struggling with sockets that had no might against the head bolts. Graham lent me a pipe to increase the leverage of the socket handle and make me as strong as a bloke. Such Goliath strength undid two nuts and broke one socket extension.

That was the night I got locked on the marina, got wet feet swinging ashore beneath the ramp, lost my car keys and spent a miserable night with sodden feet on a smelly, dirty boat. The nuts came out eventually, still clinging to their studs.

The other end of the engine, what I technically called the back door, was more co-operative. I took the starter motor and alternator off – drawing diagrams as I went – and the teeny weeny bolts on the back door came off as sweetly as the proverbial nut. The con rod appeared like the Holy Grail of marine engineering, looking exactly as it did in the owner's manual.

The head followed a few days later, with the injector still fixed inside it, and sea water – the culprit – trickling into the bilges, but the piston was stuck in the cylinder. Even the car jack couldn't budge it and only succeeded in wrecking the engine mounts. The remedy was what I should have done in the first place – remove the engine.

One Saturday I disconnected and labelled every wire and hose and two male friends lifted the engine into my car. Graham, a piece of four-by-two and a hammer soon had the piston flying out of the cylinder and into the garage wall.

With every part of the engine now accessible, I whizzed off the flaky bits and painted it with etch primer. The first time I sheared off a bolt I was lucky – there was enough sticking out for the vice grips to grab onto. The second time there wasn't and I learned another tool, an easyout.

I honed out the bore until it gleamed like a saucepan in the Sunlight ad, and started putting things back together rather than pulling them apart. I waited three days for a gasket kit to arrive and then discovered gasket kits do not contain head gaskets.

Although I started feeling like a real apprentice mechanic, I wasn't fooling anybody and most marine parts shops still assumed I was buying for 'he'.

Instead of painting my engine bright red, I grumbled to Vivienne, I should have painted it pink with flowers on it. 'Then they'd know it was a girl's engine!' Overnight my rocker cover sprouted a pretty folk boat-style flower. Graham WKE is also an artist.

The best bit was the click-click, click-click of the torque wrench as the head and rocker cover completed my Mecano set. The next memorable noise was the creaking of my boom as it lifted my bright red engine back to its proper home.

I deciphered my cryptic notes and replaced hoses and wires until there were none left over and soon came the sound of a starter motor turning a fly wheel and a crankshaft moving a con rod, the chugging of a piston at compression and water splashing out the exhaust.

I sailed to Islington Bay and scrubbed the boatyard dust from her decks. I ate lunch in the cockpit and patted the coaming of my boat. For the first time, I really felt like I owned her.

Rebecca Hayter, 'New boat blues', Boating New Zealand, **1994**

THE FOUNDING OF NEW ZEALAND: THE JOURNALS OF FELTON MATHEW, FIRST SURVEYOR-GENERAL OF NEW ZEALAND, AND HIS WIFE, 1840–1847

SARAH Mathew deserves better than to be known to history as the wife of Felton Mathew, New Zealand's first Surveyor-General. It was she, as a diarist and probably the only European woman present at the ceremony, who has given us the best description of the founding of Auckland on September 16, 1840, and the first regatta that followed, as well as accounts of her journey to New Zealand and life in early Auckland.

Prior to that September spring day, Sarah had made an earlier trip down the coast from the Bay of Islands. On April 18, husband Felton was despatched by Governor-elect William Hobson in the revenue cutter Ranger *to select a site for a capital. He was to look especially at the Whangarei, Mahurangi and Waitemata harbours. Sarah, not dissuaded by the thought of spending two wintry months aboard a small wet sailing vessel, went too. In the first week of the cruise she clambered to the top-most rock pinnacles of the Whangarei Heads. The next day, April 23,* Ranger *proceeded south towards the Mahurangi inlet ...*

Thursday, April 23rd. – We found ourselves running along the coast with a fine breeze; the shores are all high, rugged and picturesque and we passed a number of small islands apparently quite destitute of inhabitants. The weather is most beautiful. We are really highly favoured in this respect for stormy, wet weather in this little vessel would be truly miserable. As it is I enjoy the voyage much, if voyage it can be called, running from port to port in about a day or so at a time. The wind failed towards evening and we lay so quiet on the water, the tide just setting us towards the entrance of the Bay of Mauranghi, our destination.

Friday, 24th April. – At daylight entered the harbour and at about 10 a.m. anchored. In less than a quarter of an hour we were in our boat and away to explore the river at the head of the Bay. The shores in many parts thickly skirted by mangroves, that strange tree that lives only in or near the salt water, and there, in the mud flats it thrives so rapidly that dense impenetrable thickets are formed by it extending far into shoal water. In other parts the high wooded hills extended to the water's edge, and here I first saw the famed Koudi tree which is now so extensively used for masts and spars under the name of New Zealand pine. It is a magnificent tree certainly, but not at all like our ideas of Pine, as it has a fine branching head quite different to any of the fir species. The forests covering the sides of the mountains were full of these trees, the young saplings are spiral and graceful and the older trees are many of them 50 or 60 feet high without a single branch and then a large branching head surmounts it; the foliage is generally rather scanty, being principally in tufts at the ends of the smaller branches, and of a lovely yellow green. There are numbers of other fine trees in these forests and the brushwood is thick and impenetrable, consisting of ferns of very large size, a sort of grass tree and the same sort of fern tree, which I have seen in the brushes of New South Wales, like a feathery palm tree about 15 or 20 feet in height. In these woods there are numbers of pigeons exactly like those of Norfolk Island; they are very large, of beautiful plumage and easily shot, as they sit quite still in the trees and take no notice of anything. We saw numbers of wild ducks also, but these are so shy it is impossible to get near them; we shot one pair only; pigeons we breakfast, dine and sup on, as they are an agreeable change from the usual New Zealand fare, pork and potatoes, the latter very indifferent this season.

After proceeding five miles up this beautiful river we heard the sound of a waterfall, and turning an angle came to the head of the navigation at once, for a ledge of rocks extended quite across the stream, about 10 or 12 feet in height, over which the water poured in numerous broken masses. We landed just below the fall in order to examine the country. Leaving the men to make a fire and get their dinner, we set off on our walk, the ground everywhere so encumbered with brushwood and fern that it was a most fatiguing task. Sometimes the scrub we groped through was far above our heads and the long, tough stalks of the fern twisted round our legs and sadly and painfully impeded our progress. We toiled on, however, to reach a distant hill which commanded a fine view over the neighbouring country, and in about two hours' walking arrived at the summit. The prospect was very beautiful, a succession of undulating hills, the sides of some of them clothed with woods, the river winding like a silver thread along the valley, sometimes lost in the woods and again seen in the distance sparkling over another rocky fall. We returned to our boat tired and hungry and found we must hasten over the rocks as the receding tide was leaving a very shallow channel for our boat. We got her out safely, however, and reached the cutter about 7 o'clock.

Saturday, April 25th. – Started early to explore a branch which seemed to extend from the southern side of the river. We found to our disappointment that it was of no extent at all, soon lost in a mangrove swamp, so we returned to the river and again went up to the Falls, where we landed on the south side, and proceeded to examine the country on this side. We found it similar to that on the opposite side which we went over yesterday. On reaching the hills the view was very lovely, commanding a distant sight of the Bay of Mauranghi, and the islands off the coast. The land must be fertile from the rank luxuriance of the fern and brushwood which was almost impenetrable except on the very highest ridges, and even there the walking was very fatiguing. We passed numerous traces of wild pigs, which are said to be very numerous, the descendants of those left by Captain Cook.

I believe we have not seen a single Maori (or native) since leaving Wangari, nor have we fallen in with the least trace of inhabitants. The whole country as far as eye can reach seems in its most primitive state, scarcely a living creature to be seen, insect or bird or beast; one small lark and a little quail were all the birds I saw during our two days' excursions. Nothing can give an adequate idea of the utter solitude and stillness that prevails around, and I found that even our own voices were lost among these extensive hills; calling aloud to my companion, whom I could not see for the thick scrub through which we were scrambling, he did not hear me for several minutes, and as I hastily groped on I found we were not ten steps apart. We got back to the cutter before sunset, and then determined to take advantage of the fine weather and favourable tide to proceed, so weighed anchor immediately and got out of the harbour with the ebb tide.

Sunday, April 26th. – A beautiful day. We have hitherto been highly favoured in the weather which has been most delightful. All day we were running down the coast to the southward with a gentle breeze. There is, I am sorry to say, no attempt to perform divine service on board this little vessel. The sailors all appeared dirty as usual, although not much work was going on; indeed very little was required for the little vessel seems easily managed. We read the service on deck ourselves and then walked, observing the various appearances of the coast and the different islands we passed. The land seems to be much lower all along, and the cliffs are bare, and were composed of a sort of indurated clay or soft sandstone, which appears quite white at a distance, and reminded me of 'Albion's chalky cliffs.' I trust I shall one day have the happiness of seeing them; with what delight shall I watch them as we approach the shores of our dear native land. The wind was so light that it was quite dark ere we reached the entrance to the bay of Waitemata, and then falling calm we anchored about midnight to avoid being drifted in as the channel is quite unknown.

Monday, April 27th. – Weighed anchor about 8 o'clock and proceeded up the harbour of Waitemata, the shores still comparatively low but wooded. The birds were singing sweetly among the trees in the early morning; there is no variety of song, but a sweet liquid note resembling in a slight degree the song of the blackbird, is the most prevailing note. At about 11 a.m. we struck on a sunk rock in the midst of the channel, though we were proceeding cautiously and sounding all the time; it must be a point only for there is deep water all round. She was got off with some difficulty and our worthy captain was very apprehensive of her having received much injury. He anchored immediately that she got into deep water gain and one of our men who could dive went down twice and examined the vessel carefully. He reported that she had received no injury whatever, which I trust we shall find is the case. We had but little wind at the time so that she did not strike with so much force, though quite enough to cause a very unpleasant and alarming grating sound under our feet.

About 1 p.m. we started in our boat to explore what appeared to be the principal river debouching in this fine bay, but finding time would not admit of our getting far before dark, we turned into a beautiful creek thickly wooded on both banks. Numbers of wild ducks rose from amongst the mangroves, which everywhere fringed the edge of the water, in many places extending far out, forming extensive banks of sand at low water. We saw innumerable pigeons also and shot several. We reached the head of the creek or as far as was navigable, and then landed and climbed the bank to get a view of the country, but after walking some time we found the scrub so thick that it was impossible to see any distance, so returned to the boat and after filling our water casks at a beautiful natural basin of rock into which fell a stream of pure water, we pulled back to the cutter.

Tuesday, April 28th. – Immediately after breakfast started to examine the Waitemata river. It is as usual a very irregular channel, in some parts the water so shoal that we could scarcely get our light boat over, in others very deep water close into the shore. The banks are thickly fringed with wood, but the hills beyond are bare and undulating, the hollows green with rushes and coarse grass. About noon reached a fall of about 5 or 6 feet, a ledge of rocks extending quite across. It was now low water, so we could proceed no further. We landed and walked for about two hours over the hills to examine the country, found it barren and encumbered with fern and scrub, but not so high and luxuriant as at Mauranghi, consequently it was not so difficult to traverse. About half way we came to a narrow but deep creek and were obliged to wade through the rushes and rank vegetation on its banks to find a place to cross. At length we came to a very romantic little cascade, where the whole stream was collected into a narrow shower and poured over the rocks in a sheet of foam, which we managed to jump across. The view we obtained from the highest point we reached was as barren and dreary as can be imagined, undulating hills extending in every direction; here and there the valley and sides of one would be covered with fine woods, but in general the slopes are so trifling that they are only distinguished by the light green of the rushes which everywhere cover the swampy ground. Returning to the boat we found the tide had risen so as to cover the rocks and allow easy passage to our boat, so we resolved to explore yet further. The banks were now higher, thickly wooded, and the stream narrower but not so shallow, it being nearly high water. After proceeding about three miles, we came to another fall and ledge of rocks, not very high but sufficient to bar our further progress. We saw numbers of wild ducks, but they were so shy we could not get near enough to shoot any. We returned to the Cutter about 6 p.m., the river as we descended appearing a noble stream, being at nearly high water; the hills here making so great a difference.

Wednesday, 29th. – Left the cutter at about 9 a.m. to examine the lower branch of the river,[1] but were soon compelled to return for it being near low water the river had not sufficient water to float our boat, we stuck in the mud several times and with difficulty got her off; fully two-thirds of the river's bed was nothing but banks of mud covered with oysters and mangroves, the former literally growing to the branches of the latter. We then crossed to what seemed a sandy bay on the south side of the harbour,[2] found it nothing but shells, principally cockleshells, almost triturated to sand; these shells seem thrown up continually, forming large beds which each tide rolls backwards and forwards always breaking, always accumulating. After walking over the peninsula, for such it seems, being almost surrounded by mangrove swamps, we returned to our boat and found added to our party a chief and his slave, who had come down the river in a canoe. They were fine looking men; the chief, dressed in a bonnet rouge and comfortable coat like a coachman, seemed quite happy but for the want of a pair of trousers which he very earnestly begged us to give him. We could not any of us spare these articles, so he was contented with some biscuit and cheese and a glass of wine which he did not omit to drink with due ceremony. He talked incessantly, but all we could make out was that he had come from 'Kiapara,' had seen the Governor and had signed the Treaty. From hence we went up another deep estuary in the bay which promised a fine opening, but being nearly sundown and the weather very squally, we were obliged to turn towards the cutter, our little ark at present. We saw myriads of snipes in the shoal water and shot a dozen of these graceful birds. They rise in flights and skim round and round in close phalanx, like starlings. We reached the cutter about 7 o'clock.

Friday, May 1st. – Anything but like May day. It was, however, rather less unpromising than it was yesterday, so I accompanied my husband as usual. We explored about the southern part of the Bay and encountered several very heavy squalls of wind and rain. In the afternoon a new and interesting object was descried in the Bay, a large boat filled with people bearing down towards us. Amid these dreary solitudes such an object is quite an event, and I watched it approaching very anxiously. As it came alongside we perceived that it contained several white men and a number of natives. One of the former came upon deck and asked for the 'Surveyor General,' who, of course, made his appearance. The object of these gentlemen seemed to be to find out where the new settlement was to be, but as nothing is as yet decided they did not obtain the information they sought. They were a strange set of beings, settlers from the Thames and Coromandel Harbour – and such specimens of settlers; many degrees below those of New South Wales in apparent respectability. Truly the early settlers in a new colony do become most extraordinary beings, somewhat, I imagine, of the Kentucky style, 'half horse, half alligator, with a touch of the earthquake.' They were not welcomed with much cordiality, so they soon pushed off again and we saw the smoke from their camping place some few miles off, where they stayed the night and departed the next morning.[3]

Saturday, May 2nd. – Still showery, but the wind rather more moderate, and between the showers it was warm and pleasant. I have never seen so many rainbows as since the last few days; there has scarcely been a half hour through the day when the beautiful arch of promise has not been visible in one quarter or other, sometimes most vivid in colour and of a full and perfect arch. I have also seen several lunar rainbows, the colours almost as bright as those formed by the sun. We explored a creek today, which promised to lead through a finer country than we have yet seen in this southern side of the Bay, but our hopes were fallacious as to the country on its banks, and for itself, at low water, it soon becomes a mere ditch running between broad banks of mud. We were obliged to stop till the tide should rise sufficiently to enable us to return, and as we were desirous of ascertaining the character of the country inland, we made some efforts to reach the shore through the mud, which we at last effected by laying the oars down to give some footing to the first passenger, who then cut down branches and small trees and laid a causeway to the bank; we then had an almost perpendicular bank to climb, so thick with fern and underwood, all wet from the recent showers, that we were soon wet through. The long tough ferns, however, formed a very good sort of ladder, and without this help we certainly could not have attained the top of the bank on account of the wet, slippery ground, which afforded no other support to the feet. The top of the bank gained, we walked over the country for three or four miles bent on gaining an elevation to look over the hills, which in every direction rose all round us. This toilsome task we at length accomplished and gained a rather extensive view over the most dreary and desolate looking country eye ever beheld. I cannot imagine that the deserts of Arabia or Syria can be more miserable and monotonous; not a sound to be heard, not a bird or insect to be seen along the whole extent of dreary waste, and the eye became quite weary of seeking some green spot to rest upon. The surface of the hills is all bleak and grey, being only covered with dwarf scrub and half dead fern; their sides are generally clothed with the same sort of vegetation, but more luxuriant and consequently more difficult to traverse, the fern and scrub being often higher than one's head; the narrow hollows between the hills are generally marshy and covered thick with rushes; it is indeed a gloomy country, without flowers or fruits or birds or insects. I cannot but fancy it accursed, for flowers appear to me as the symbols and sign of the beneficence of the Deity, seeming to be solely created for the gratification of his creatures. No wonder that the natives of these islands are a savage ferocious race, their country possesses not any of those refining gratifications of sense which tend so materially to soften and ameliorate the heart and manners. After two hours of fatiguing research we got back to our boat and were glad to find there was at length sufficient water in this muddy channel to allow us to return; we reached the cutter again at about 6 o'clock.

Sunday, May 3rd. – A day of rest. I am sorry to observe our worthy captain does not read the church service, inviting his crew to attend; so we read in our cabin. The weather is still very squally and disagreeable, rainy at intervals and very cold. For the sake of a little exercise to warm us we landed on the rocks near the ship in the afternoon and tried to walk round the point. We scrambled over the muddy, slippery rocks for about an hour and then returned to the vessel.

[1] Probably Lawson Creek.

[2] Point Chevalier beach (?).

[3] This was almost certainly the party of J. Logan Campbell and his friends, Webster ('Waipeha'), the 'Yankee King of Waiou' and W. Brown, Campbell's partner. They had come over from Coromandel, or Waiau, to buy up land at the Waitemata in anticipation of the Government's operations. See J. L. Campbell's delightful narrative, *Poenamo* (1881).

J.C. Rutherford, The Founding of New Zealand: The Journals of Felton Mathew, First Surveyor-General of New Zealand, and his wife, 1840–1847, **1940**

POENAMO

JOHN Logan Campbell was a 23-year-old Scottish doctor and adventurer who in April 1840 arrived in the Coromandel area to buy land. It was rumoured among the few European settlers that the Waitemata harbour might very well be chosen as the site of the first capital of New Zealand. Campbell and his mate William Brown, a lawyer nine years older, both wanted to be there, at the beginning, owning land, trading, making their fortunes.

Four months later Campbell and Brown hadn't managed to buy land on the mainland but they had purchased from the Maori owners a small volcanic island at the entrance to the Waitemata Harbour – Motu-Korea. They loaded up with pigs and stores and set off. Anyone who has ever landed at dusk on one of the inner islands of the Hauraki Gulf, and cooked up a beach barbecue under the stars, will warm to the account that Campbell wrote nearly forty years later, of his first night on Motu-Korea.

It was on the evening of a lovely day in early spring that a small boat with two sprit-sails set, one on each side, could be seen towing a canoe over an expanse of water which more resembled a lake than what it really was – an inlet of the sea.

The breeze was fair but light, barely keeping the sails full – a tantalizing breeze, which always promised to freshen up, yet never did – a breeze which you would fain believe made the boat go faster than it would if you took to the oars, and yet you did not feel quite at rest on that point. However, there was nothing to be done but either to furl the sails and unstep the masts and take to the oars, or to be content to keep creeping lazily along and make the best of the breeze, such as it was.

Two of the occupants of the boat were evidently much more interested in the scenery around them than in the rate at which the boat was sailing. Little wonder if they were so engrossed, for the landscape was one of surpassing beauty. The boat had just rounded a promontory, in doing which the travellers had opened up an entirely new view.

A sheet of water lay stretched before them about fourteen miles long by about six broad. From the travellers' point of view it was landlocked. Here and there openings could be seen, but more distant land filled up the background. These passages appeared to wander round little islands, creating a desire to be able to explore them all.

At the western extremity of the inlet one of these little islands lay in mid-channel. The most picturesque of little rounded mountains reared itself, as if guarding the passage, and, proud of its own beauty, was not in the least ashamed that it lay right in the fairway, and blocked up the centre of the passage and the view beyond. It was quite evident, as the boat headed for the centre of the island, and not towards one of the passages on either side, that to the island the travellers were bound.

The right-hand shore of the inlet rose steeply from the water's edge, save here and there where little bays broke into the continuity of the coast-line. In these indentations – hardly to be termed bays – there always could be seen a little plateau of level land stretching from the shore to the base of the hills, which then rose abruptly.

The eye rested with delight on the evergreen foliage of primeval forest, wonderfully rich in the varied contrast of its colours. Although the season was but early spring, winter had laid its hand so gently on all nature that it changed but little the aspect of the woods, which ever smiled, arrayed in a garment of richest verdure.

And to Nature alone was due all the beauty of the scenery our travellers were revelling in, for as yet her reign here had been undisturbed and all but supreme.

As the boat skirted alongshore the eye was able to detect every few miles that one of these diminutive valleys nestling at the base of the hills was less rich and beautiful in the colour of its vegetation. It owed its change of appearance to the clearing hand of man, for there he dwelt in an uncivilized and primitive state. Canoes on the beach and low huts on the shore told our travellers that they were passing native villages, and they seemed to scrutinize more keenly those spots showing signs of life, as if they wished to impress the respective localities well on the memory.

The boat meanwhile had its head steadily steered for the still-distant island, and gradually drew towards mid-channel, and the opposite shore became more distinct.

It was not nearly so beautiful as that on the right hand: it was destitute of forest, and was of an open, undulating character, resembling uplands. In the direction of the island it opened into a deep bay, and at its head, the land being low, the eye failed to detect where the waters ended and land commenced. Fatigued with the search, the eye ran along the gradually-rising high land, which ended in a bold headland just opposite the little island. This promontory showed a face of yellow sandstone, and at its extremity it was crowned by a magnificent clump of trees, while smaller shrubs hung over the edge of the cliff, the green foliage thrown into startling relief by the yellow background.

As you gazed on this plumed headland of exquisite beauty you now and again laboured under the optical illusion that it was moving; you thought at one time it was nearer the island, and then again farther off. You imagined it was making obeisances to the little island, and endeavouring, with the most graceful and quiet movements, to attract attention towards its pretty plumed head and command admiration. It was in vain the eye wandered away from this plumed headland to the bare promontory behind to make certain of the perfect stability of the whole. You found yourself again looking at and believing in the nodding headland, and half feared, if you took your eye away, the next time you looked the headland – plume and all – would be found to have thrown itself into the arms of the little island's mountain, and hidden all its beauties in the shadow of that mountain's bosom.

The boat had now gained mid-channel, and had lessened the distance to the island by one-half since we saw it rounding the opening, now seven miles away. The travellers thought they had come at least two-thirds of the way, and that they were almost at the end of their voyage. The island looked close ahead of them, not more than a couple of miles off, for they had not yet become accustomed to calculate distance correctly in that clear Southern hemisphere, and their impatience was bridging over too quickly the yet intervening space.

And now, to add to the deception, the sun sank behind the little island's little mountain, throwing its shadow over the water and illumining the outline of the whole island so vividly that it seemed close at hand, and that a few oar-strokes would bring them to its shore.

There is still time, however, before the shore is reached to pay a visit on board the boat and see in what manner it is freighted.

There were seven persons on board – three Pakehas, and four of the crew, who were Maoris; the Pakehas occupied the stern-sheets, one of them steering. Of the Maoris two were in attendance watching the sails; but as this did not entail much attention, one of them was dreamily smoking a pipe, whilst the other was cutting up some tobacco ready for his turn at the said pipe, for they had only one between them. The other two of the crew were wrapped in sleep in the bottom of the boat, one of them having pillowed his head on a grindstone, the other having selected more wisely and chosen a bag of salt. In the bottom of the boat could be seen in strange confusion the poles of a tent and the tent itself rolled into a bundle – why this was not preferred to the grindstone Maori ideas alone can say. Then there was a sack of flour, which would have made a nice comfortable pillow; then the bag of salt, some large and small three-legged gipsy pots, a frying-pan, a spade and a grubbing-hoe, a hatchet, some kits of potatoes, *kumara* and maize, and one of corned pork, as the head and jowl sufficiently demonstrated; a large and very capacious wooden chest, half a keg of negrohead tobacco, and a bundle, through the corners of which could be seen striped cotton shirts, blankets, &c., and there has now been summed up pretty nearly what constituted the ballast of the boat on that voyage.

And truly it was but a very primitive and scanty turnout with which to make a first settlement, as was evidently the intention of the occupants of the boat, because with no other could any one be wandering so far beyond the limits of civilization with so large a stock of commodities. No huts on the shore or canoes on the beach had been seen by the travellers for some time. These seemed to have been all left behind; and the boat, slipping quietly through the water before the gentle but fair wind whilst nearing its haven, increased the solitude of the surrounding scene.

Hark to that sharp, quick bark! A noble dog, half bloodhound, half mastiff, which must have lain concealed till now, bounded from the bow of the boat, and, smelling land, thus proclaimed the boat's near approach to it, and rushed to the stern sheets to tell the news to his masters, and then away again to place his paws on the boat's gunwale at the bow and bark again.

The boat was now under the shadow of the little island's little mountain. The sun had nearly set; the breeze no longer filled the sails; they began to flap against the masts. The steersman summoned the crew to their oars, and two sleepers were aroused, the luxurious grindstone and bag of salt pillows can no longer be indulged in, the pipe of lazy peace must be put aside, and the four natives twisted their mats round their waists, and having first furled the sails and unstepped the masts, took their seats, and their naked bronze shoulders soon strained to the oars.

The canoe towing astern made it a heavy pull, but they gave way with a will. We had only to look at the hound in the bow of the boat to know that the island was all but reached; he no longer went jumping along to expend his impatience in barking visits to his masters; he only changed his paws from one side of the bow of the boat to the other; his whining had changed into shorter and quicker barking; and at last, unable to restrain himself, he jumped on the gunwale, prepared himself for a spring, and plunged into the water, and by the time he had reached the shore the keel of the boat grazed on the beach – the island was gained.

The Maoris adroitly slipped out of their mats, and *puris naturalibus* they were over the boat's side in a moment and dragged it up as far as they could, just sufficient to keep it on even keel. Three of them commenced at once to carry the things on shore, the fourth started off in search of fresh water and drift-wood, and before his companions had finished their work of emptying the boat he had returned and had a brisk fire burning and a pot of water nearly boiling.

The Pakehas meanwhile had chosen a spot on which to pitch their tent; they had not been over-fastidious in their selection, as the shades of evening were rapidly closing, for there twilight has but little more than a name, and but a short interval elapses after the sun sets ere night prevails.

The stars were already shining brightly, telling the travellers to make the best of their time.

The tent was soon pitched, and whatever was wanted for the night, and anything that would have been damaged had a shower fallen, carried into it from the boat. It was only the elements that had to be feared, and the beauty of the young night forbade much apprehension in that direction.

From the intrusion of either man or beast everything was safe – of the latter the land was destitute, as has already been stated. Of the aborigines none were likely to intrude on that lonely spot, and if they did, what matter? They would not steal, and as to safety of life, why there was not a firearm amongst the whole party!

A lovely night succeeded what had been a lovely day. And such nights! Who can know their beauty and brilliancy but those who have seen them? The Southern Cross was brilliant in its beauty. There was no moon, but it was as light as it is at home when the moon is half at the full.

The Maoris sat around a blazing fire, variously occupied in the preparation of supper. The Pakehas were arranging the tent, spreading their beds of fern, of which a sufficient supply had already been brought to carpet the whole surface, and nothing could look more comfortable. A little lamp burned on the top of the big sea-chest which came out of the boat, and which served as a table for the coming supper, which was very soon afterwards partaken of in a very primitive manner. On the top of the chest was placed the inevitable three-legged gipsy pot, with the inevitable pork and potatoes inside it, and not far off were the inevitable tin pannikins with tea. Some woefully brown-looking sugar, some equally brown-looking ship's biscuit, such as was used in those days, and which Jack would turn his nose up at now, comprised the evening's banquet. But the supper was discussed with no small relish, and over it the plan for the morrow decided. We were to make the circut of the island in the canoe, and find out the best place to pitch the tent permanently, for on the morrow two of the three Pakehas were to be left to their own resources on the island, with the hound for company; while the other Pakeha, with his boat and Maori crew, proceeded still farther on their journey.

All was darkness now within the tent, and its curtain doors were drawn together, but Maori curiosity peering between them saw at the farther end of the tent two of the Pakehas endeavouring to court sleep; at the foot of the tent the Pakeha steersman was already in the arms of Morpheus, which arms the peeping Maoris wot not of!

The boat's crew then settled down comfortably around a blazing fire to thoroughly enjoy their pipes. Occasionally they heard a low murmuring in the tent, but the voices grew fainter and fainter; and to the two courters of sleep in the tent it appeared that the Maori fire blazed less and less brightly, and the soft Maori language fell softer and softer on their ears.

But the fire still blazed as brightly as ever; the Maori *korero* was not in less loud voice.

It was the sweet oblivion of sleep stealing over the travellers in their fern bed.

The fire flickered more and more – it went out. The voices died away – they ceased.

In reality the fire still burned brightly. The *korero* was still in audible voice.

But the two Pakeha wanderers from their far-off home now lie tranquilly sleeping in their new home in the land of their adoption.

But the spirit of their dreams on this night hovered not over their fern couch nor under their tented roof, but travelled afar to their fatherland.

There they trod the mountain heath and explored the rocky glen, they gathered afresh the wild flowers and berries with the companions of their youth, they mingled once more in the sports of the field with the friends of their riper years, they lived over again many bygone days, bright and happy with the near and dear under the parental roof.

Ah! Are there not as exquisite moments of happiness in our dreams as are ever enjoyed in our waking hours?

The Maoris no longer fed the fire; one by one they drew their mats around them, stretched themselves on the ground with but scanty sprinkling of fern underneath, and dropped asleep.

The hound moved closer to the tent-door and lay down so that no one could enter without stepping over him, and pillowing his head on his own body he too slept.

The night continued as serene as ever – not a breath of wind moved the leaves, now drinking the early dew-fall.

The stars shone down without a cloud to obscure their brilliancy, and were reflected from the smooth sea that girt the little island.

The ebbing waters receded from the gravelly shore without a ripple.

Not a sound, even the faintest, broke on the universal stillness.

All Nature slept.

And thus it was that the two Rangatira Pakehas of the good old Kanini took possession of their new home.

For had he not sold to them that lonely and far-away spot, the little island of Motu-Korea?

John Logan Campbell, Poenamo, *1881*

PERSONAL LOG OF THE COUNTESS OF KINTORE

WHEN the 186ft, three-masted ship Countess of Kintore *anchored off Napier on June 8, 1875, her non-stop passage from Gravesend was typical of the voyages of the many emigrant sailing ships of that period. It had, however, at 82 days from land to land, been the fastest to Napier on record.*

On board was a thirty-one-year-old sea captain Augustus Philip Samson *and his pregnant wife Mary, also about thirty and hailing from Jersey. They made the passage to New Zealand, as did thousands of others, as assisted emigrants seeking work and a better life. In Napier he could find work only in his former trade, as a plumber, and died in 1888 after a fall from a roof. None of the following generations of New Zealanders went to sea, but great-great-grandson Pete McCurdy, whose love of boats began as a toddler aboard his grandparents' Norwegian launch at Stewart Island, was the founding curator of the New Zealand National Maritime Museum in Auckland.*

A non-stop voyage of 82 days at sea with some 150 other passengers can scarcely be imagined now. Samson kept his diary like the seaman he was, even, from about ten days out, taking sights with his own sextant on the long journey into the South Atlantic, rounding the Cape of Good Hope, passing south of Australia and eventually turning north towards Cape Palliser, the southern tip of the North Island. But he also noted down, with shrewd precision, the most basic human elements of crowded shipboard life: the quarrels and fights, the domestic chores, the killing of animals for fresh meat, the vermin and the sickness, the storms and the deaths.

Wed: March 17th: Winds N.E. First part very cold, with hail showers. At 6 a.m. weighed the anchor and towed as far as the Downs. Set all sail and tugboat let go the ship. Weather turned out beautiful. Most of the women seasick and many of the men. At 4 p.m. passed Beachy Head with square yards. Today for dinner soup with too much salt, boiled beef and potatoes.

Thurs: March 18th: Easterly. Pleasant breeze and fine weather. Most of the women still sick. Today's dinner salt pork and spoiled rice. At 8 a.m. pilot left the ship off the Start Pt., and took all the letters with him. Ship going along nicely.

Fri: March 19th: Winds northerly. Pleasant breeze and showery. Nearly all the emigrants sick. Today for dinner preserved meat and potatoes. In the evening petty quarrels about the watches, the men being obliged to keep watch in the married people's compartment during the nights to keep the light burning, and to keep everybody and everything in order.

Saturday, March 20th: Winds N.W. Throughout pleasant breeze and fine. Most of the people alive again. Dinner salt pork and suet pudding. Crew securing the anchors and stowing away the cables. During the night a little Irish girl was taken sick, and the parents crying out for the bottle of Holy Water, which soon cured it.

Sund: March 21st: Winds easterly. Pleasant breeze and fine weather. After breakfast all beds made up, and people washed and clean. At 10 a.m. all hands mustered on the poop for inspection. Captain and doctor went down in the emigrants' places to see if they were clean and in order. At 1 p.m. dinner – preserved boiled mutton, preserved potatoes and plum pudding. Everybody in good spirits. During the night ship rolling very much. Mary sick yet. Lat 37° N.

Mon: March 22nd: Winds east. Throughout this day pleasant breeze and fine. One child sick in the hospital. Dinner boiled salt beef and preserved carrots. Had a jolly row with the baker about the bread not being good. Today killed a pig.

Tues: March 23rd: Winds easterly. First part light breeze and fine, latter part fresh breeze and squally with showers. In the afternoon most of the luggage was brought up for getting ship's stores. We got some things out of one of our boxes, and the other two boxes were stowed away for good. The child still in hospital. Plenty porpoises about the ship.

Thurs: Mar. 25th: Wind N.E. Pleasant breeze and fine weather throughout this day. Ship rolling heavily. Yards square. Crew shifting the fine weather sails. Three vessels in sight right ahead. Most all the people well and hearty. Two children in the hospital. I went in the hold and got my sextant from the box. Noon lat. 28°42' N.

Good Friday: March 26th: Winds N.E. Light breeze and fine. At 1 a.m. Sarah Harris died, age 4 years, disease inflammation with dropsy. At 1 p.m. dinner – preserved meat, potatoes and boiled rice. Had such a row between Green and Cook, our mess-mates, about the bread being bad. At 6 p.m. tolled the bell for the funeral. The boatswain, carpenter and some of the sailors went in the hospital to bring up the corpse, laid it on the planks and brought it on the poop to read the service. The Captain, suspecting the body very large for a child, examined it and said it was yet warm and very bulky, and opened one end and saw some clothing. He asked the doctor if he ordered the child's clothes to be buried with it. While the Captain was gone for the father of the child, who with his wife kept below, I went round to see the bundle, which was under the Union Jack. To my surprise it was our large clothes-bag, full of linen weighing over 100 lbs. Everybody was amazed at it. The boatswain took it down and brought up the child, which was quite different. You may suppose the ship was not stopped, going at the rate of 7 knots per hour, when the service was read. They rose the planks, but the body did not slide off, so they pushed it off. It made a heavy splash, falling on its face. All the sailors told us that they never reverenced an old sailor's bag, taking off their caps, before. However it was a near touch losing our bag. Remainder of the evening fine. Lat.26°42' N.

Sat: March 27th: Winds N.E. by E. Light breeze and fine weather throughout. Decks cleared up at noon. Mr. James' child not expected to live, having the bronchitis and inflammation of the lungs. P.M. – killed a sheep. Lat.obs.24°22' N.

Sun: March 28th: Winds N.E. Light breeze and fine warm weather. At 10.30 a.m. all hands mustered on the poop for inspection. At 11 a.m. had Church service in the saloon, Captain and doctor officiating. At 1 p.m. dinner – soup, preserved meat, potatoes, and plum cake. At 3 p.m. served out the stores. While opening a cask of molasses Jimmy Ducks trod on the head and fell in the cask. While going forward to shift himself, the sailors got some feathers and flour and decorated him. Lat.obs 22°44' N.

Mon: March 29th: Winds variable and light and fine weather. Ship very steady. Mary feeling more herself again. At 10 a.m. commenced schooling – 12 girls and 11 boys. School kept on deck near the poop. For dinner salt beef, potatoes and rice. At 2 p.m. school till 4 p.m. Sighted a steamer steering like us. Lucy Belshaw put in the hospital, being very sick.

Tues: March 30th: Winds N.N.E. Light breeze and fine warm weather. For dinner pea soup and fat pork. Some complaints to the doctor about some Irish people having Jerusalem crickets on them. At 4 p.m. Mr. James' child died, 15 months old. During this day most of the married people washing clothes.

Wed: March 31st: Winds N.E. Pleasant breeze and fine weather. At daylight the island of St. Antonio, one of the Cape de Verdes in sight, distant about 15 miles. At 10 a.m. buried the child. I took care of our bag this time. Several vessels in sight. In the forenoon had up all the passengers' luggage. We got out two jam pots and some clothes. In the evening put away all the luggage in the hold.

Thurs: April 1st: Winds E.N.E. Pleasant breeze and cloudy throughout. Several vessels in sight. Had a regular row about the schoolboys with their parents for beating them. Dinner – salt beef and potatoes.

Fri: April 2nd: Winds easterly. Pleasant breeze first part, showery middle and latter part. At 4 a.m. Mrs. Robt. Aplin gave birth to a boy, mother and child doing well. In the afternoon all married people's bedding turned out on deck to air. Our mess had a sea-pie for dinner. During the night had several flying fishes.

Sat: April 3rd: Winds easterly. Pleasant breeze and fine throughout. Sun's altitude 87°30'. This afternoon no school. One of the single women found to be covered with vermin. Brought up her bedding and threw it overboard, being alive. Lat.obs.7°43' N.

Sun: April 4th: Winds N.E. Pleasant breeze and fine. At 10 a.m. all hands on the poop to muster. At 11 a.m. Church service on deck. Passed the sun during the morning. Dinner sea-pie and plum pudding. At noon a pig died; threw it overboard. Lat.obs. 4°28' N.

Mon: April 5th: Winds N.E. Light breeze and hot sultry weather. Several large black fish, bonitos and dolphin, about. One large dolphin took the hook, but broke the line and lost it. One shark swimming round the ship. There was a quarrel between two families about their mess. Today's dinner salt beef, potatoes and rice. School continued. A large ship in sight, steering S.W. Lat.obs.1°30' N.

Tues: April 6th: Winds variable. Throughout this day light variable airs and rain. Plenty bonitos under the bow. Two were hooked and three grained, but all escaped. No school kept, being too wet. Crossed the Line during the evening – a general washing amongst the passengers! ...

Sun: May 16th: Winds NNE. First part fresh breeze and hazy. Took in the royals. No muster today. Our dinner spoilt through neglect of the cook. He should have been discharged off his duty at the commencement, being not competent. Last Sunday dinner spoilt the same. Whilst at table four or five of the sailors came down with ropes to hoist up Jim Aplin, pretending to throw him overboard for one of the sailors to have his wife, making to be in love with her. (The Aplins are two brothers married to two sisters, and they quarrel amongst themselves like cats and dogs, especially the sisters. The men are a little touched on the brain; they were sent out by the Union). While pulling him up on deck he yelled out awful with fright, he really thought they were in earnest. In the afternoon breeze freshening, evening strong breeze. Vessel going 12 knots an hour. While I was on deck I perceived that some of the head gear was adrift, reported it aft, and found the martingale to be unshipped. Stowed the jobs, and made a new bolt. At 8 p.m. all hands about the martingale – a nasty job to get it to rights. Took in all light sails. Ship tumbling about fearfully. During the night stowed all sails but the three close-reef topsails. Blowing a gale of wind. Lat.obs.44°30' SE long. 93°30' E. Distance to the Snares 3030 miles.

Mon: May 17th: Winds N.N.E. to S.S.W. First part strong gale and heavy sea running. Ship under close-reefed topsails and fore top mast staysail. At 10 a.m. wind shifted suddenly to the southward, with rain, large seas beating on board. Our breakfast was spoilt with salt water, tons of water coming in our place, even wetting the lower bunks, and drenching the beds. Several of the passengers got wet through. The steward was knocked off his feet and went swimming along the decks. Noon moderating a little. Set the upper topsails and main top gallant sail to keep the ship steady. Wind falling and weather clearing up. Today we had to get our dinner the best way we could, ship rolling so much. Mary kept in her bed all day, and I had to wait on her. After dinner the Aplins' slop pail capsized all over the place, and gave us such a fine perfume. Over that the sisters and brothers had such a jolly row, using such indecent language. Everybody down on them for their filth and dirt. The doctor was called down, and had a court-martial on them both, and had their provisions stopped for a week, except water biscuit, tea, coffee and sugar. Mrs. Robt. Aplin dressing herself and baby, a month old, to drown herself. The husband would not let her come out of her berth. He was crying and said what would he do with the children? It was quite a pantomime. During the afternoon weather getting fine. At 5 p.m. Cooper, an apprentice, 16 years old, whilst sweeping the poop, the mizzen top mast staysail struck him on the back of his head, and threw him overboard. Whilst he was floating on his back, by all appearances insensible, Chandler, an apprentice, threw him a life-buoy quite close to him, but he could not swim, so he sank under water. The life-boat was soon lowered with seven hands in her. They were half-an-hour away, and could not see any signs of him or the life-buoy. Hoisted up the boat, and proceeded on our journey. Long. 99°E.

Tues: May 18th: Winds N.E. to W. Throughout this day strong breeze and thick hazy weather. Vessel shipping heavy seas in the gangway. Large quantities of water rolling in our place, everything wet and miserable. Part of our dinner spoilt by the sea coming in through the skylight. At 6 p.m. wind shifted westerly, and a little rain. Vessel rolling fearfully. Set more sail. Ship made 250 miles this day. Steward killed a pig. Lat.obs.44°50'S., long. 105°13'E. . . .

Sun: May 30th: Winds variable. Throughout this day pleasant breeze and fine weather. At 11 a.m. all hands to muster. Mrs. Green still laid up; Mr. Green seems quite offended yet about the bird – he has not spoken since. The Captain and doctor said that we should muster again during the week, as we expect to land before Sunday. The mates went up aloft to see for land at 4 p.m. but the ship was too far off yet. Lat.obs.48°38' S., long. 164°28' E. Distance to Snares 86 miles.

Mon: May 31st: Winds northerly. Light breeze and cloudy throughout. After breakfast the crew getting up chain cables and putting the anchor over the rail ready for harbour. Afternoon had up the passengers' luggage so as to get their good clothes for shore, and put down all their boxes which they had in their bunks. Crew had up some provisions same time. No land in sight. At dinnertime there was a fight in the single men's place between Harry Smith and Concertina Jim. Lat. 48°29' S.

Tues: June 1st. Winds northerly. First part light breeze and cloudy. Steward killed a pig. No land yet in sight. Crew washing the paintwork. Towards evening wind favoured us a little. Lat. 47 51' S., long. 172°E. Distance to Napier 540 miles.

Wed: June 2nd: Winds northerly. Light breeze and weather overcast, with drizzling rain. Crew employed scrubbing ship outside. Tried to catch albatrosses but no chance, so the Captain amused himself shooting at them. In the afternoon picked up some seaweed. Evening calm. Everybody in hopes of a fair wind to send us in harbour, being so near. Lat.47°S., long.175°48'E.

Thurs: June 3rd. Winds variable. Light variable airs, and calm at times. During the forenoon little Lotty Grigsby fell halfway down the ladder, and hurt her chin and nose. Also Molly Quin, two years old, fell in the mess tin and hurt herself very much. Mary washing sheets and handkerchiefs. Captain caught five fine albatrosses. He gave me one, and to the matron, and some of the passengers. Ours measured 9 1/2 feet from tip to tip of wings, and weighed 14 lbs. In the evening skinned the bird, and stretched the skin to cure. Latter part light breeze and drizzling rain. Lat.obs.46°17' S., long 175°20' E. Distance to Napier 400 miles.

Fri: June 4th: Winds N. to S. Throughout strong breeze and cloudy. After breakfast took in all light sails, reefed the mainsail and slowed upper mizzen topsail. Everybody anxious to see land, but too far off. At 4 p.m. wore ship. At 5 p.m. wind shifted to the southward. Vessel going about 8 knots an hour. Mary very sick all day, in bed. Latter part strong gale and a light sea. lat.obs.45°15' S., long.173°20' E. Distance to Napier about 380 miles.

Sat: June 5th: Winds S.W. to S.E. First part strong gale and high seas running. Much water coming on deck. Crew getting 90 fathoms of cable on deck each side. All emigrants washing and scrubbing the fronts of their bunks, tables and forms and getting the place clean for inspectors. At 2 p.m. sighted land, Cape Palisser, for the first time since the Cape de Verdes Islands. Mary much better today, and up to see the land. At 8 p.m. strong breeze and rain. At midnight all hands up to shorten sail. Ship under three close reefed topsails. Wind S.E., and blowing a furious gale. Lat.obs.42°10' S., long. 175°45' E. Distance to Napier at noon 180 miles.

Sun: June 6th: Winds S.E. Throughout this day blowing a furious gale, and drizzling cloudy weather. Ship tumbling and labouring heavily. Everything flying about the place every time the ship lurches, even the charlies capsizing and leaving us a sweet scent! We had to get our breakfast and dinner sitting on the floor and taking it the best way we could. At noon no sun and the lee fore topsail sheet carried away. Crew rove it again and set the sail. The emigrants' water-closet was washed away. The decks half full of water all the time. Many of the emigrants very frightened. Mary stopped in bed all day, and a bit sick – the best place for the women this sort of weather. Some of the single women going in fits with fright. Towards evening weather moderating, stars and moon shining beautifully. The ship would have been at anchor today but for that gale. We were only about 40 miles from the place. Last night we were only about 15 miles from shore, so we can't be very far off now. No observations today. Sun obscured.

Mon: June 7th: Winds S.E. to S. First part fresh gale and squally. Bore off and made sail for shore. At 9 a.m. just sighted land. Gale increasing. Took in canvas, wore ship, and hove to. At noon had observations; ship 30 miles off Cape Kidnapper. Bore off again, and set all possible sail. Ship going about 10 to 11 knots. At 2 p.m. sighted land again. At 2.30 p.m. Cape Kidnapper right ahead. At 4.30 p.m. passed the Cape, and at 5.30 p.m. came to an anchor about six miles from Napier, in seven fathoms of water, with the port bower anchor. Stowed all sails, put up the anchor lamp, and set the watches. Everybody seemed quite excited at the sight of shore. Thank God we can sleep quiet tonight in hopes of landing tomorrow. Mary's sickness left her now she can see terra firma.

Captain Augustus Philip Samson, Unpublished personal log of the Countess of Kintore, **1875**

PART TWO

Working on Water

PHANTOM FLEET – THE SCOWS AND SCOWMEN OF AUCKLAND

AFTER Percy Eaddy, as chronicler of the Hauraki Gulf scows, came Clifford Hawkins with his classics Log of the Huia *and* Out of Auckland *and then Ted Ashby, whose 1975 book* Phantom Fleet *is also a classic of nautical literature. Raised on a farm near Auckland, where the only way to transport timber and other produce to market was by scow, Ted Ashby became a bushman and from around 1923 on, a scowman.*

Already, though, the scows were a dying race, with maybe only about fifty of the estimated 155 built, by the twenties still trading. But no-one has written better first-hand accounts than Ted Ashby of the day-to-day grind aboard the scows which ran themselves up on Hauraki Gulf beaches to take on shingle and sand. A good westerly blow could quite suddenly put the ship, her cargo and crew into danger . . .

'I wish to God we were on the other side of the Pond, Frank!'
Strange how I can remember a phrase like that over a period of nearly fifty years and can so clearly recall the conditions that existed at the time. I had just tipped my barrow and was trimming the shingle to the required height as John McKinnon ambled up and tipped his. He always called me Frank.

Jock always wheeled in sandshoes with his trousers rolled to halfmast and generally with a cherrywood cigarette-holder in his mouth. He had given me the inside deck to load and he, being the better wheeler, had taken the outside, with the tricky turn to negotiate between the mizzen and the after-end of the centre-case.

We had beached the old *Rimu* well with her bow a little bit further down the beach than her stern to give us an easy run directly we came through the gangway. The wind was coming down off Moehau in nasty gusts, each gust mixed with rain, and the rain dripping off Jock's sou'wester had long since put out his cigarette; it was just a soggy stump stuck in the holder clenched tight between his false teeth. I had no hat and was barefooted, with an old blue seaman's jersey and dungaree trousers, and the rain had plastered my hair down and mixed it with sweat till it kept getting in my eyes as I came up the plank. It was blowing from a warm quarter and though summer wasn't really with us yet, it was warm despite the rain.

Jock picked up his shovel but, instead of starting to trim his barrow, he paused and looking away again to the westward, where big dark scud clouds were already starting to move towards our vulnerable quarter. And again, 'Yes, I wish to God we were on the other side of the Pond.'

We had left Auckland the afternoon before with a light south-west breeze, a fair wind to Waiaro on the Coromandel Peninsula, to load shingle for Craigs. Ernie Deeble, the owner of the beach, had kept the beach open and anyone could load there. On account of this the big companies hadn't worked it much, as they had to pay higher royalties than on their own beaches.

This meant good shovelling and a short wheel, and we needed every bit of help we could get, for we'd had a couple of minor mishaps earlier on – a broken boom, etc. As we worked on shares, any mishaps that held up the ship paid finish to our incomes. We carried this light sou'wester through Emu Passage out past the D'Urvilles and into the Gulf till finally it died to a flat calm, and then later came away light from the north-east. I had the 12 to 4 watch, made coffee and called Jock. We had a third hand with us, a new chap who answered to the name of Andy Lind at this time, though I found out later he answered to the name of Arthur Lennon and a few other aliases.

(The reasons I remember him so well was that when we finally got back to Auckland, he borrowed a couple of quid off me, stole my overcoat and vanished.)

When they called me for breakfast we were slogging into a fresh nor-easter but making quite a lot of ground, as the Coromandel Peninsula was like a huge breakwater to windward and the closer we got to it the calmer the sea became. I can remember Jock saying as I came down the steps, 'If we can make the beach in time to lay on, we should get loaded easily tonight and carry this wind up our tail back home.'

We made the last board into the beach and dropped anchor at 1 pm with about a quarter of an hour to spare. Got the boat out, ran our shore lines to a couple of pohutukawas and hove on.

The *Rimu*, like a lot of other scows of that vintage, had a Heath Robinson power device for heaving in the anchor cable, for the hand-windlass was a slow back-breaking affair with which to wind in forty to fifty fathoms of cable with sore hands after six or seven hours on the shovel and barrow. There was a gipsy wheel on the little petrol engine that drove the winch, and a corresponding gipsy on the lowgear shaft of the anchor windlass. There was a slack, half-inch, endless chain that meshed these two gipsies and a crude snatchblock through which the chain ran. The idea was to drop the chain over each gipsy, take up the slack on the ship's burton which was hooked to the snatchblock and, when the right tension was reached, fasten the burton off, start the engine and with a lot of creaking and sparks from the slipping chain, in came the cable, *clunk, clunk, clunk.*

On the previous trip we had broken one of the cast-iron gipsies and sailed before a new one could be procured, so this meant heaving in the cable on the hand windlass. I recalled Jock saying, 'We'll only lay out about twenty fathoms this trip. Directly we start to lift with this swell coming round the Cape the wind will blow us off and we won't have to heave in all that chain.'

This was our second mistake; the first one was misjudging the weather.

Just after low tide the wind chopped to the nor'west in a nasty squall and really started to blow, and later it went to the west and never eased up, bring in a heavy sea. With the short wheel and good shovelling we had the gangway near enough to close up by dark, and didn't bother to light flares for the last few barrows as they wouldn't show much light in the wind and rain, even if they didn't blow out.

We got our planks and spreadings aboard, took in the shore lines, hove the cable tight and went aft to a good tuck-in of hot stew. We didn't bother to change as, by this time, though the tide was only about half in, the big seas were starting to thump on our weather side.

A couple of hours before high water, the big fellows were really starting to smash against the weather side, burst high in the air and then cascade down on our hard-won cargo. As they drained away they carried part of our shingle with them. With the heavy impact of the sea, and as we were sitting on soft shingle, the *Rimu* soon began to move and work down the beach. We stood by the windlass and every time she moved we worked her bow seaward, one cog at a time.

We knew we were in a tricky position, for Waiaro is bad holding at the best of times, and with only about twenty fathoms of cable out we knew with the sea running the anchor would break out early. There was too much sea to try and get a kedge anchor out, so all we could do was to heave in a cog at a time and hope the anchor would hold till we got enough water under us (as the wind was still a little to the north of west) to make a bit of sail and perhaps get into Cabbage Bay, which was good holding and a fair anchorage. But we only cleared the beach by a few fathoms, with a big list on, when the anchor started to come home, and back on the beach we went.

We started to set along the beach with the flood tide and drive of the seas, and were really thumping with every swell, though the bed of shingle took part of the impact. We paid out cable till the drift halted, and as the lee side was on the beach with only a couple of feet of sheltered water there between the swells, I hopped overboard with a coir rope and got it around one of the trees to keep us on the beach, then Jock and Andy hove it taut on the windlass end.

When I got back aboard, Jock had a hurricane light in one hand and an old plumb axe in the other. He knew I'd spent a lot of time in the bush, so as I climbed back aboard between swells, he handed me the axe with the remark, 'We've got to chop a couple of holes in the weather bulwarks so the seas will sweep the load off her and we can heave her as high up the beach as we can. Then as the tide drops we'll miss a lot of the pounding. Now let's see how good a bushman you are, Frank.'

We worked our way across to the weather side, which was really nasty now, waited for a break and one after another made the fore rigging, Jock above me with the hurricane light. We would wait for a lull then down I'd go with the axe, stand on the caprail and belt into the bulwarks with the axe. Jock would keep an eye out to seaward and directly he saw a big one coming he'd give a roar and up I'd go beside him. One thing – there was no trouble to hear Jock!

Didn't take long to make a breach about four feet long, then we worked our way aft and did the same thing there. In between each swell the *Rimu* would list out, as the inside chine was on the hard, and as the huge seas crashed aboard they would sweep through the forward breach and sweep aft out the other breach, taking our hard-won shingle with them. We were pleased to see it go, for we knew the only chance to save the *Rimu* was to get her as high up the beach as possible.

Time passed very quickly, and as she lightened and moved up the beach, we took in the coir rope, gaining every precious inch we could on the winch end. We soon began to realise that there was less movement, the list was more permanent, and the seas weren't belting quite so hard as she was taking the bottom. After she settled we went aft towards the cabin.

There had been a 200-gallon square tank on a low stand near the corner of the cabin. It had broken away from its moorings, brought up against the steering wheel, smashing off a couple of spokes and wedging the cabin doors shut. The *Rimu* was about three parts full of water as the forepeak hatch cover had gone, but owing to the list on the beach there wasn't much water on the cabin floor and what there was was on the downhill side. We managed to slide the scuttle back and climb down into the cabin, which was a shambles, but the lamp was still in the gimbals high up and undamaged. We found some dry matches in a cupboard and lit it and then sat down and settled our elbows on the table, tired and wet.

This must have been about 2.30 a.m. and the rain had eased off, though the wind was still blowing hard and had shifted to the south-west, square on to the beach. There was no chance of getting a cup of coffee as the galley was a mess and everything soaking wet, but how well a cup of coffee and toast would have tasted then. So we sat around the table, our elbows resting on it, and Jock remarked, 'Yer know, Frank, it's "me own blame." I shouldn't have trusted that damned nor'easter. Kept saying I'd bring my weather-glass from home and each time I forgot. Wonder what the hell Jack Hanna will say now?'

Jack Hanna was the manager of J. J. Craig, who owned the *Rimu*, and Jock had had a couple of minor mishaps a short time before, and had to go up and 'beard Jack Hanna in his den.'

Incidentally, when we did get back to Auckland with no freight and a battered ship, we all went up to see Jack Hanna, looking a bit scruffy and weather-worn, but ever after that interview we had a very warm regard for him, one of the early seeds sown in human relationships between employer and employee.

I woke first, cold and stiff in every joint. Andy was coiled up in the top bunk on the upper side of the cabin, which was fairly dry, and Jock was hunched over the table with his chin resting in his hand, sound asleep. Wet as we were, we must have dozed and slept for about four hours. The cabin lamp had long gone out through lack of kerosene and the early sun coming in through a porthole cut a swathe of light across Jock's face. A strong, rugged face in sleep, but tired out. I let him sleep awhile.

We worked a bit of action back into our joints and then up through the scuttle to survey the damage. There were still a few yards of shingle in corners around the deck, but most of the deck was swept clean. Except for the tank and the wheel and the galley, there appeared to be no serious damage topside, although there was water squirting out of a few leaks on each chine. We turned the tank tap on, lugged all our blankets and clothes ashore and spread them on the stones, lit a fire, got a saucepan of water from the creek, and had a royal feast of bully beef, bread, butter and tea. What a feed that was! There was an old farmhouse up the flat with a caretaker in charge and he let us camp in the spare room and cook on the wood stove till we got the *Rimu* mobile again.

The swell had eased a lot, the sun shining, but a nasty sea came back with the flood tide, and at its height as every sea hit the old *Rimu* one could see the topmast jumper-stay slacken and then snap bar-tight as she buckled on end. I don't think any other type of vessel could take the buffeting and pounding that these old tubs could take and live to freight again.

As the tide dropped we borrowed a two-inch auger from the caretaker and bored several holes on the lower side of the *Rimu* and later in the evening made wooden plugs with the axe, wrapped sack around them and belted them in the holes. At high tide we hove her as high up the beach as possible, and as the wind was easing she had a much quieter time. The wind eased overnight and next morning we trudged over the clay track to the Colville post office and rang Craigs to report the disaster. We waited there for a couple of hours and then they rang back to say they would send the AHB *Te Awhina* down to tow us home next day at high water.

That must have been about the fastest trip the *Rimu* ever made to Auckland, but we had little time off the hand-pumps. We spent about three weeks on the slip, and even when we came off were in a very leaky condition. We stopped the worst of the leaks from inside with a caulking iron and oakum, did a couple of trips to Marsden Point for silver sand, a few to Waiheke and Chamberlains for shingle, and then we were in trouble again.

We never seemed to be very far from trouble in the *Rimu*, though I rate Jock McKinnon as one of the best scow skippers I ever sailed with. We were back on the Coromandel coast again, but this time after shell sand at Kirita. Shell sand was a very pleasant, clean cargo to work both loading and unloading. It was easy shovelling, light, and there were no stray pebbles to get under the wheel or under the feet. We had carried a fresh sou'wester from Auckland, but the weather was fine and, we thought, quite safe to lay on even though we were on a lee shore. We got loaded.

As the tide came back in the afternoon, the wind freshened with it, but we weren't unduly worried as we had about 45 fathoms of cable out and were on a soft beach! We hove off the beach about 5 pm. The sun was shining hot and though a few seas came over our weather side and took a little shell sand with them, we came off almost on even keel. We hove in till we could see the fifteen-fathom shackle and were setting the foresail when the cable parted at the shackle. In minutes we were back on the beach again with the set of the tide working us along the beach with each swell.

We got a line ashore as quickly as we could but, before we could halt the drift, had fouled a low rock aft. This caught us at the rudder and after-end of the deadwood, although we checked just in time to stop it busting through the hull. The tide left us with the after-end of the deadwood smashed off and the rudder hanging on the top gudgeon, the one that was bolted to the sternpost. To brighten the outlook, there was a big blackfish about thirty feet long lying diagonally across the top of the beach, and he had been there for some weeks in the hot sun. All the beach near him was saturated with putrid oils and bits of blackfish, and the stench was almost unbearable. She was an unlucky ship that *Rimu*, even in the company she kept.

While there was still water round her to float the boat, we got a kedge well out to sea in the opposite direction to the rock and hove the coir tight. There was too much wind and sea to run the kedge line from the scow, so we coiled the 120-fathom kedge line in the dinghy, placed the 120 lb kedge in the stern with the flutes over the transom, battled our way out to windward until, at a guess, we would have enough rope to reach the ship, tipped the kedge over and ran in before the wind and sea, paying out line all the while. We took our tea ashore, well away from the whale that evening, but somehow our appetites weren't so good.

The wind swung a bit to the south during the night and blew hard and clear as it does sometimes in the Gulf at night. We didn't try to get off on the morning's tide as a sharp sea was coming in on the beach, but winched ourselves clear of the rocks and hung on till the tide left us. The wind died away in the afternoon and we hove off about 3 pm, bade goodbye to the whale, and squared away for Auckland with about a half a load of shell sand and the rudder trailing behind swinging on one gudgeon. Although she took a lot of wheel, with a light easterly behind us we could steer her and again arrived at Craig's yard, discharged and back on the slip.

There wasn't much Jack Hanna didn't say this time, but I think he realised we had worked like niggers, lost half our freight and, what is more, were a sober crew.

Ted Ashby, Phantom Fleet-the scows and scowmen of Auckland, *1975*

NEATH SWAYING SPARS

PERCY Eaddy *learned his seamanship in scows, the sailing craft that, derived from the trading vessels of the American Great Lakes, sailed around the New Zealand coasts from the 1870s until the 1930s. They were handsome, flat-bottomed, schooner-rigged vessels capable of carrying stock or huge loads of logs, timber, sand and shingle. In their heyday they graced the Auckland regattas with great spreads of sail.*

On a summer day in 1904 Percy Eaddy signed on for a coastal voyage in the Hawk, *139 tons. His shipmates were typical hardened scowmen — skipper, mate, cook and three able seaman. They included a sober-minded Dane, and a giant cook named 'Dargo Bill' who was 'the best all-round sailorman aboard' and boasted of being one of the last men in the British Navy to be flogged.*

Their six months together would take them from Auckland to the little Coromandel port of Tairua, there to load saw-milling machinery and plant for delivery to the Port of Hokianga. Then on to the Kaipara, and four days loading 180,00 feet of sawn timber, so that only twelve inches of freeboard of hull remained . . .

We had nearly a week to wait at the Kaipara Heads before we could venture seawards again. The wind had blown in from the west and sou'-west all of that time, and so strongly too that it had raised a very considerable sea on the bar.

However, one morning after it had eased down a little, and hauled round more to the south, the signal went up from the signal station — *Bar Workable!*

During the time that we had been lying there awaiting our chance several other outward-bound timber-laden vessels had joined us, and towards high-water the musical clink of pawls could be heard from them as they hove short on their cables in readiness to work out over the bar.

Our 'old man' stood in his companionway gazing out to seawards through his glasses, and at times strumming with his fingers on the cabin slide. On the top of the tide he seemed to make up his mind all of a sudden.

'Right oh! you fellows,' he said. 'We'll give it a go! I think. Get the rags on to her!'

With the aid of the steam winch we soon had all sail set and rigging a 'messenger' chain on to our windlass from the steam winch, we soon had the cable 'up and down'.

'She's hove short!' called out Frank to the skipper who was standing aft by the wheel.

'Alright! break her out as she cants to starboard!' replied the skipper.

'Shall we give her the jib topsail, Barney?' asked Frank.

'Yes! give her all she'll carry, there's not much wind and we'll need to chase her along to get her out clear of the break before the flood tide begins to set us in again.'

So, under the three fore-and-afters, three gaff topsails, and four headsails, we set off, with the ebb tide increasing in force under our lee as we proceeded on our way.

Passing the signal station on Pouto Point, on our starboard hand, we worked seawards tack for tack, with our centreboards down and sheets flattened well inboard.

As we passed the 'Graveyard', that well-known last resting place for many a fine vessel on the North Spit, the wind commenced to freshen, and the seas breaking across the bar to seaward of us took on a more ominous appearance as they crashed with monotonous regularity.

The old man kept the wheel himself with his hefty henchman, Dargo Bill, in close attendance, in case he needed a hand. The remainder of us stayed for'ard tending the head sheets each time we tacked.

'Just keep a weather eye lifting for'ard there, you fellows, we'll be in the break on the next tack,' shouted the skipper.

'Lee oh!' he called a few minutes later, and round we came on to the port tack, and headed straight out over the bar.

'Masthead those two topsails!' called Barney, indicating the fore and main gaff topsails, which had been lowered down on the head on the last tack, to save dipping the tacks and sheets.

We had them hoisted in a trice, and, bowing and curtsying gracefully, we slid out to meet the oncoming rollers.

'Look out for that fellow!' yelled Barney, pointing out to seaward, and, glancing in the direction in which he pointed we saw a great Pacific greybeard gradually rise and tower in all his majesty right in our track.

'Jump for the rigging!' yelled Frank.

We all jumped for our lives, and from the safety of the weather fore rigging we viewed the oncoming mountain of water.

On and inward it swept, irresistible and awe-inspiring, till suddenly the great crest of it began to curl, and, just as we were about to rise and let it pass underneath our hull, the whole length of it, for half-a-mile on either side of us, toppled forward in a seething, roaring mass of white foam.

For a few moments the *Hawk* seemed to be on the point of annihilation. Her hull, deckload and everything below the great straining booms, was completely submerged in a swelter of boiling foam, but, shaking herself clear, like a great Newfoundland dog after a dip, she shot through it and surged onwards ready for the next encounter.

Looking aft from our perch in the fore-rigging we could see the skipper and Bill shaking themselves and wiping the seawater out of their eyes. Luckily for them, the sea was well spent by the time it reached aft, otherwise it could easily have taken them overboard in its stride.

We repeated the performance once or twice in a lesser degree as we worked seawards and as the final breaker passed in under our lee we heaved a sigh of relief to be quit of the dread Kaipara Bar, and easing our sheets, we set our course nor'-west for Cape Maria van Diemen.

'To hell with the Kaipara trade!' said Old Bill, as he set the table for dinner. 'I don't like it, and that's telling you straight.'

We were all of the same opinion about the Kaipara Bar, but there it was, the timber had to be freighted out over the bar and that was the end of it.

With a strong sou'-west breeze on our quarter we made a splendid run right round to the North Cape and then the wind fell away altogether to leave us rolling and slatting in a long ground swell about five miles off-shore.

During the night we lowered the sails to save them from bursting all the seams, with the continual banging and slatting.

After breakfast next morning our skipper decided that this would be a fine chance to grease the mast down.

'A nice warm day,' he said, 'with no sails set, and therefore no hoops round the masts to keep running foul of. You boys shouldn't take long to grease her down from the trucks to the deck-load.'

We rove three long brand-new two-inch manila gantlines through each gaff-topsail halliard sheave aloft, and making fast a bo'sun's chair to each, Walter, Billy and I each went aloft with a large tin of grease and a wad of old rag.

Each man helped to hoist himself aloft, though with old Dargo Bill and Frank hoisting on the gantlines hand over hand on deck, we all three were soon 'mast-headed'.

The grease was one of those foul smelling mixtures of old slush from the galley, kept for this purpose for months on end in an old drum in the forepeak. Generally speaking, sailors have pretty strong stomachs, but this particular brand of mast-grease very nearly upset my equilibrium for the rest of the day.

The aroma must also have been sensed by the denizens of the deep, for presently, on taking a look down into the blue depths around us I could see sharks of all shapes and sizes. Some big fellows just cruised lazily around, while others shot vigorously here and there, with vicious evil-looking eyes that betokened ill for any prey that came their way.

'Good job we're not out here in a small boat in this calm,' called out Billy to me as I stood viewing these ferocious looking fellows from the safety of the main-cross-trees.

'They would attack you quick and lively, boat or no boat, in this weather,' continued Billy.

'Yes, I believe they would, especially that great wicked looking blighter in the shade of the starboard bow there,' I replied.

'Of course they would,' assented my mate. 'I knew a chap once who was attacked in a scow's dinghy by one of those cows; it would have got him too, only he had a rifle with him and he settled him with a couple of bullets.'

Meanwhile, down on deck the skipper, cook and Frank were busy getting shark lines and hooks ready, and as we started to come down the lower-masts with the greasing-down process, old Dargo Bill let out a yell as he hooked a monster about nine feet long.

'Never mind the greasing-down, come and give us a hand to land this fellow aboard!' called the skipper, and very willingly we hastened to oblige.

We hooked our bo'sun's chairs into the lower rigging and slid down the backstays to join in the fray.

And what a battle it was! We would never have landed the shark on deck at all if it had not been for the skipper putting a few bullets into its carcase, as it threshed and fought about alongside.

We dropped a running bowline over it when it had quietened down a bit, and tail on end we hoisted it aboard on to the top of the deck-load by means of a double purchase.

Even as it lay on deck its great jaws snapped viciously every now and then, behoving everyone to keep well clear. We settled it at last, and it lay like a great prone log upon the timber.

Nothing delights a crowd of sailors more, especially a sailing ship's crowd, who have time to observe the creatures that live in the deep, than to get a shark on board and destroy it.

'They'd have no pity on you,' said old Dargo Bill, 'so why pity them when you get one. Knock the cow's brains out! And dump it over to the others! That's always been my motto since I've been going fishing,' he concluded.

Seizing a great carving knife, he opened up the shark its whole length, and in a twinkling the deck-load was littered with dozens of young sharks about the size of a sprat.

Frank drew a bucket of water from overside, and threw half a dozen of the youngsters into it. They swam vigorously round and round the bucket till Old Bill seeing them, called out, 'Don't throw them back into the sea alive, settle them first, boys, they're all sharks.' And settled they were.

When we dumped the dead carcass overside there was a mad wild rush for it, and in no time it had disappeared from sight.

Half an hour later, as we finished the greasing-down of the masts, not a shark was to be seen anywhere near us.

That same afternoon, as all hands were gathered round aft, spinning yarns and whistling for a breeze, our attention was caught by a commotion across the face of the sea away to the sou'-west. At first it looked like a breeze on the surface, rippling the sea into a line of white-capped foam, but as it approached us we could see that this was not the case.

The whole ocean in that quarter was alive with porpoises. Dancing, jumping into the air and turning somersaults, diving and swimming at the speed of torpedo destroyers, they came towards us.

They presented a most remarkable appearance, as in massed formation they charged ahead. Evidently they had scouts out in advance of the main body, as suddenly we saw several shooting, lithe forms pass ahead and astern of us, and one or two dived right underneath our hull. Turning right about, they darted back to warn the main body of our presence.

Then a smart manoeuvre was executed, their ranks parted in the middle, one-half going ahead of us, and the other half passing astern. Several, more curious than the others, turned, and came back for a more close scrutiny of us, and then, helter skelter, jumping like playful children, and splashing and diving, away they went in the wake of their fellows.

'Porpoises,' said old Bill laconically. 'And where they're heading for is where the wind is going to come from,' he added, going into the galley to stir up the fire in readiness for the evening meal.

He was right, too, for at four bells, ten o'clock in the first watch, we picked up a good fresh breeze from the north'ard, which carried us to the southward of Cape Brett.

Here the wind headed us again, coming up strong from the south-east, and close hauled, with the sheets well in and centreboards right down, we tacked and tacked until we were heartily sick of it.

We were very nearly run down by an outward bound passenger liner from Auckland the night after we passed Cape Brett. We were standing out to sea on the starboard tack. The time was nine o'clock, and with both side-lights burning brightly, we were jogging along comfortably with one man at the wheel and the other handy on deck.

Frank and I, who were below, suddenly heard Walter the Dane call out to the skipper to come on deck, as a steamer's lights were approaching from the south'ard.

We heard the skipper say, 'Go and have a look at those side-lights, especially the starboard light, that one should have been visible to the steamer's lookout.'

'Lights are burning brightly,' said Walter, as he came aft.

'Alright, but by —! he is going to cut it pretty fine,' said the skipper.

Suddenly we heard the skipper call out hurriedly 'Lee oh!' and a rattling of wheel chains, and slatting of canvas, told we who were below that the scow was in stays.

Jumping up the companionway to see what was happening, I looked astern, and there about fifty yards off was a great passenger liner, slipping along at about fifteen knots.

The decks were a galaxy of shimmering lights; passengers were walking up and down the promenade decks arm in arm, some even pointed out towards us and waved.

What a joke it was to be sure. A great lumbering timber scow nearly under their bows, and yet the fault did not lie with us. They could not have been keeping much of a lookout from that steamer otherwise they should never have passed too close to us. Rather, by all the laws of the sea, they should have given us, a close-hauled sailing vessel, the right of way.

But there, we were only a despised timber scow, so why should the big aristocratic liner alter her course, even by a hair-breadth?

Two days after this episode we hauled the *Hawk* alongside the sawmill wharf at Auckland, thereby completing a round trip in one of the largest of the trading scows.

I left the *Hawk* and shipped away in an intercolonial barque shortly after this trip.

I might add that the *Hawk* was rather an unlucky ship, as just before I joined her, her skipper, Captain Irvine, was fatally crushed by a log whilst unloading. She broke a man's leg by the kicking of the great-wheel as she wallowed in a roll one night, and another had his wrist broken by a centreboard handle taking charge while it was being lowered.

A few trips after I left her, the skipper I sailed with, whilst in her, was washed overboard by a breaking sea when crossing inwards over Hokianga Bar, and drowned. I don't think they even found his body.

Percy Eaddy, Neath Swaying Spars, *1939*

PERSONAL LOGBOOK OF THE NEW ZEALAND GOVERNMENT STEAMER HINEMOA, 1906

THE only New Zealander ever to win a naval V.C. was Aucklander Lieutenant-Commander William Sanders, as commander of the Q-ship Prize in action against a German submarine off south-west Ireland in April 1917. Too few now connect his name and exploits with the prestigious Sanders Cup yachting trophy or a University of Auckland memorial scholarship, or a street in Takapuna renamed in his honour.

Willie Sanders, raised in Takapuna, had been at sea round the New Zealand coasts and the trans-Tasman run since he was 16. By thirty, he was Mate on the Joseph Craig (wrecked on the Hokianga Bar in 1914). When he joined the RNR's piratical Q-ships fleet in 1916, he was 33, an Extra-Master (Hons) with plenty of experience under sail, unmarried, a natural leader of iron nerve.

A Q-ship's job was to lure German subs within range of her hidden guns by displaying false colours or feigning distress. Prize was a three-masted topsail schooner, and on April 30 Sanders, displaying the coolness under fire that won him his V.C., withstood 25 minutes' shelling before opening fire himself. Unknown to him or anyone, U-93 was not destroyed, but struggled back to Germany. Four months later, now also a D.S.O. and soon to receive his V.C. from King George V, Sanders, along with Prize and all hands, was lost at night, blown clean out of existence by the revengeful torpedo of the stalking U-48, become wise to Q-ship tactics.

Sanders was apparently not a writing man, though a hundred postcards from his travels survive, neatly handwritten but revealing little to his family in New Zealand. The only extensive manuscript in his hand, offering a glimpse into the rugged training and experience that he was to bring to his later Q-ship exploits, is the logbook he kept during 1906 as 23-year-old seaman aboard the Government steamer Hinemoa. On February 23, having worked its way south from Auckland, the ship is in Bluff, preparing for a summer voyage to the remote southern islands.

Saturday February 24. We left the Bluff Wharf at 3.30 pm for the southern islands which comprises of the following islands; Snares, Auckland's, Campbell, Antipodes and Bounties, which are situated westerly apart, southward of New Zealand. The most distant lying about ( ) miles from the Bluff. At 6 pm we ran into Paterson's Inlet, Stewart Island for shelter from heavy S.W gale and anchored for the night.

Sunday February 25. We left Paterson's Inlet for the Snares at 2 pm, but the wind and the sea being very heavy, we put into Pegasus Bay and dropped anchor in smooth water at 6.30 pm.

Monday February 26. At anchor in Pegasus Bay sheltering from heavy S.W. wind and sea.

Tuesday February 27. We hove up the anchor and left Pegasus Bay at 4.30 am for the Snares where we arrived at 12.30 pm. After a rough passage we landed in the surf boat and visited the Depot which was surrounded by Sea Lions. Before we could open the door we had to chase away the Sea Lions which in turn chased us. Sometimes finding the provisions in the Depot had not been touched since the Ship's last visit. We took an account of the stores and closed the door again. When we were on the Island we saw hundreds of Mutton Birds and Molly Hawkes and Penguins which kicked up a terrible row when we approached them. Having finished all we had to do we returned to the boat and left for the ship. As we left the shore the Sea Lions followed us biting at the oars and stern oar and uttering calls of rage when they saw they could not do us any harm. We arrived on board the steamer at 4.30 pm and hoisted the boat on board. We then cruised all around the group of Islands blowing the siren all the time and seeing no sign of anybody we set our course and resumed our voyage to the Auckland Islands. It is still blowing and a pretty big sea resuming.

Wednesday February 28. On our way to the Auckland's at 6.30 am we sighted a large Bargue about north east running before the wind and she signalled to us, but the weather being pretty thick we could not make out the flags, and so we changed course a little, but could not make out the signal on account of the vessel running away from us all the time, and so we hoisted the flags K.B.K. and then resumed our course to the Auckland's. We made Port Ross at 1.30 pm landed the carpenter and some men to build a new provision Depot. The steamer then visited Enderby Island and the launch went ashore with the Captain and three passengers who returned to the steamer at 4.45 pm. They saw the mast of the French Bargue *Anjou* wrecked on the Island in the year 1905 and rescued by the *Hinemoa* in May the same year. They also got some pieces of Teak of the ship *Derry Castle* wrecked on March 20 1887 of which 15 men drowned and the surviving 8 were taken to Melbourne in the Schooner *Awaroa* (15 Tons) on July 21 1887. They saw the graves of the men who were drowned in the wreck with the figure head of the vessel for their tomb stones. Some of the skeletons are now showing out of the ground owing to the constant rain. We arrived back at Port Ross at 5.30 pm, had our tea and then went ashore again at Port Ross. We saw the flagstaff supposed to have been erected there by the crew of HMS *Blanchi* which had visited the island in 1869–1870, they put a notice on the flagstaff that they had visited the island and searched for castaways and left provisions behind. I carved my name and date in the notice and also in the Depot. We also saw carved upon another tree when the Victoria Commander Norman had visited the Island in search of ship wrecked people having been dispatched by the Governments of New South Wales and Queensland. This was dated October 13, 1865. On the same tree there was a slate fastened in leaving the following inscription:

Sacred to the memory of
Bart Brown CO
William Newton Scott AB
Andrew Morrison AB
Peter McNiven AB
Who started on the 22nd January 1867 for New Zealand in boat without chart, compass or nautical instruments. Blessed are those that Die in the Lord.

We also saw the frame of an old mast head lamp nailed on the same tree just above the slate. It now being dark we returned on board the steamer arriving at 8 pm.

Thursday March 1. Went ashore at 8 am and finished building the Depot and painted it. We then shifted stores out of the cottage into the new Depot and shut it up having our names inscribed inside it in the following order:

BUILT 1/3/1906
A.M. Ashill Carpenter
D McLeay A.B
W Sanders O.S
J Ryan O.S
Of GSS Hinemoa

We then visited the boat shed and everything being in order we closed it up again and returned on board the steamer and left for Enderby Island at 11.30 am. Arrived there at 12 noon and sent the launch ashore with the Captain and passengers. The launch returned to the steamer at 1.30 pm having captured a young Sea Lion which they bought on board. We then hove up the anchor and left for Norman's Inlet where we arrived at 3 pm. We then cleaned the Depot where the French crew had slept when they visited there from Camp Cove in search of more provisions and before they left they wrote the following inscription on the beams inside the Depot:

Crew of French Bargue Anjou at Camp Cove provisions Depot March 15, 1905 Help.

We then put some fresh stores in the Depot to replace those used by the Frenchmen. We then returned to the Steamer leaving at 4.15 pm for Carnley Harbour and Camp Cove. Arrived in Carnley Harbour at 6 pm cruised all around the Harbour blowing the siren. Also passed the wreck of the ill-fated schooner *Grafton* wrecked there in January 1864. All that remains of her is a few ribs and planks, there is also a small flagstaff erected there by the crew of the *Grafton*. There are also the uprights of the hut they erected out of planks of the *Grafton*, but the scrub and bush has grown over everything else. Also we dropped anchor in a pretty little bay called Camp Cove where the Frenchmen had lived when they were upon the island.

Friday March 2. We are sheltering in Camp Cove from a very heavy nor-west wind and sea. The boat went ashore and cleaned out the boat shed and provisions Depot. 11 pm the wind still continues to blow very hard and the ship is straining very hard at the cable, so we have to let another anchor go.

Saturday March 3. We left Camp Cove at 8 am and visited the boat shed at Adams Island and everything being in order we went and visited the place where the French Bargue *Anjou* crew first landed and returned with flag pole of Vessel. We then returned to Carnley Harbour and sent boat ashore to have a look at the life boat from the Bargue *Anjou*. The boat returned at 3 pm having on board some tanks, the rudder and boards out of the lifeboat. We then hove up the anchor and bidding goodbye to the Auckland's we headed for the Campbell Islands.

Sunday March 4. We sighted the Campbell Islands at 6.30 a.m. through the fog. Steamed into Penguin Bay blowing the siren all the time and seeing no wreckage or any sign of anybody, we proceeded on to Perseverance Harbour where we arrived at 9 a.m. and dropped anchor. The topsail schooner *Jessie Niccol* bound from the Bluff to the Macquarie Islands, she is now 23 days out from the Bluff and has her fore topmast and jib-boom sprung. We went ashore after dinner to have a look around the Island, saw the ruins of a house supposed to have been occupied by a crew-woman who was exiled from Scotland. We returned on board at 5 p.m.

Monday March 5. At anchor in Perseverance Harbour, Campbell Islands, we went ashore at 8 a.m. and built new provision Depot and painted it. The Captain and Carpenter went on board the *Jessie Niccol* to see if anything could be done to repair the damage, but having no spare spars on board the Captain decided to return to the Bluff. We were supposed to sail at 6 p.m., but the main steam pipe having to be repaired we did not heave up the anchor until 9.30 p.m. when we sailed for the Antipodes.

Tuesday March 6. At sea S.W wind and very heavy swell, sighted a large school of Cow-Fish.

Wednesday March 7. Arrived at the Antipodes Islands at 11.30 a.m. went ashore at 12.30 p.m., painted the Depot and cleared the track. Bought some Penguins, Albatrosses and Parrots on board and at 7 p.m. left for the Bounties.

Thursday March 8. Arrived at the Bounties at 8 a.m., sent boat ashore to visit the Depot and everything being in order we left for the Bluff at 10 a.m. S.W wind and very heavy sea shipping water fore and aft, only averaging between 5 and 6 knots. Lost a lot of Penguins overboard.

Friday March 9. 6 a.m. very heavy sea running averaging 2 knots, shipping big seas. 4 pm sighted a large Bargue running before S.W wind. 6 p.m. weather moderating we are now going at full speed, we have hoisted all sails.

Saturday March 10. Fine weather, ship rolling a little, we arrived at the Bluff at 9.30 p.m.

Sunday March 11. At the Bluff Wharf, blowing hard.

Monday March 12. At the Bluff Wharf, fine weather.

William Sanders, Personal logbook of the New Zealand Government steamer Hinemoa, *1906*

SUBMARINER IN THE MED

CON Thode is something of a legend in the Hauraki Gulf. As crew since boyhood and later skipper on innumerable Auckland racing and cruising yachts, as volunteer master of the Spirit of Adventure Trust's two square-rigged vessels, he has built up a long life's knowledge of the gulf and a wide circle of sailing friends. Currently he is sailing master on Sir Gordon Tait's magnificent Viking.

That early Hauraki Gulf experience was to form the background to his meteoric rise during six years of World War II service – from a relatively lowly Yachtmaster ticket gained in Auckland in 1938, to sub-lieutenant (Royal Naval Volunteer Reserve) of a Flower class corvette on convoy duty in the Atlantic, to Commanding Officer of a brand-new S-class submarine, the Scythian, *in 1944. His eight submarine postings took him on lengthy and dangerous patrols around the Mediterranean, into the North and Irish Seas and, towards the end of the war, east into the Straits of Malacca.*

Shortly after joining HMS *Medway*, mother ship for the First Submarine Flotilla, based at Alexandria, I was appointed Navigating Officer of HMS/m *Proteus*. In her small wardroom the First Lieutenant, George Hunt, introduced me to the Commanding Officer, Lieutenant-Commander Philip Francis, Torpedo and Gunnery Officer, Jeremy Nash and Engineer Officer, Peter Scott-Maxwell. After we had shaken hands the Captain turned to the First Lieutenant and said 'All right Number One, off with his shoes.' I was taken aback but realized from the barely hidden smiles that I was being tested. Then it was explained that they wanted to see if I had suckers on my feet so that I could hang on in the upside down part of the world in New Zealand. And so my nickname while in *Proteus* was usually 'Down Under', although sometimes called 'Pilot' and even 'Vasco'. Sometimes I even got my real name.

Proteus was one of the O P & R Class s/ms built in the '20s and early '30s and most of them were on the China station when war broke out. *Proteus* was in Singapore and among her patrols during the early months of the war was one off Vladivostock. In April 1940 she headed for Alexandria and after patrols in the Mediterranean, she returned to the UK for refit. Refit in Portsmouth dockyard was cut short by the Luftwaffe and *Proteus* eventually returned to Alexandria in September 1941 with extra engine-room artificers appointed to cope with defects. We had two H.P. air compressors and usually one was undergoing a strip-down and rebuild. Compressed air, of course, was vital as it was used for blowing out main ballast for surfacing, and firing torpedoes and various other jobs including blowing the heads.

Preparation for patrol was in full swing when I joined. Torpedoes were being loaded, also ammunition for the 4' gun, plus fuel, stores, battery water, fresh water and so on. The torpedoes were loaded into the six bow tubes and two stern tubes plus six re-loads secured in racks and trenches in the torpedo stowage compartment forward – fourteen in all.

Our fresh water supply was limited so we did not wash on patrol – Mediterranean patrols were usually 21 days – later in the war in the Far East, we did 30 day patrols. As we all had the same smell we got used to it. Incidentally, on returning from patrol there was a scramble for the depot ship bathrooms. The bathrooms were quite large spaces with several baths in the one room – there were no showers. If lucky enough to find an empty bathroom the lark was to run two or three tubs and after leaving a scum of diesel oil in one bath, hop into the next one.

On our last day in harbour fresh stores were loaded. Fresh food did not keep long inside a submarine so we were soon onto tinned foods and dehydrated vegetables. We had some frozen space for meat.

Batteries and air bottles were topped right up before departure so we were able to use both main diesel engines to speed us through the channel swept through the minefields and so into the Mediterranean by dark. We stayed on the surface all night travelling at around twelve knots but not making that over the ground because of constant zig-zagging. In the morning, as navigator, I took star sights as soon as I could make out a horizon and we then dived. On my first patrol in *Proteus* we headed for the eastern end of Crete and into the Aegean Sea.

We searched various areas and then received a signal that the tanker *Tampico* had left the Black Sea bound for Italy. The Captain studied the chart and decided that the most likely route would be through the Doro Channel, so we established a patrol line across the channel. Sure enough the tanker appeared, but escorted by two destroyers and four aircraft. Despite the heavy guard our Captain moved into an attacking position and fired torpedoes. Only one hit but it produced a tremendous explosion.

Our Captain, Lieutenant-Commander Francis, considered that 180ft was the best depth to be safest from the depth-settings used on the enemy depth-charges, so down we went. The destroyers were quickly on the counter-attack, probably guided by the aircraft sighting our torpedo tracks. The first pattern was very close and we suffered some minor damage. The destroyers then moved around the area using their listening devices and we crept along as quietly as possible. Then our Asdic operator, listening on hydrophones, reported a destroyer increasing speed and closing for another attack. With his speed drowning his listening ability, we increased speed and altered course but down came another close pattern of depth-charges. As soon as the water noises subsided, we resumed silent routine. At about this stage I found I was shivering although I wasn't cold, so I asked to be allowed to get my woolly submarine jersey. The wool was comforting and for the rest of the war I always wore a jersey when the alarm bells rang. I found depth-charging very frightening.

The hunt went on but eventually, after 43 depth charges, the destroyers lost contact and we crept away to safer waters.

At the end of January 1942 we left Alexandria for patrol off the west coast of Greece and while patrolling on the surface off Cape Dukato the alarm bells rang in the early morning of 8 February. The R.D.F. (radar) had picked up a contact and the officer of the watch turned stern on and called 'Captain on the bridge'. Peering through their binoculars in the darkness both the Captain and the O.O.W. decided the target was a U-boat so the Captain decided to fire the stern tubes before turning to bring the bow tubes to bear and away went two torpedoes set to run at 10ft but they failed to hit. We then started to alter around to use the bow tubes and the Captain decided to go to gun-action stations realising that our full silhouette might be sighted during the turn. Watching the target carefully through their binoculars both the Captain and the O.O.W. realized that the target's bow wave was increasing and the vessel was turning towards; the target was a destroyer rushing towards us to ram. Too late for a gun action the guns crew were ordered below again. The Captain ordered the main engines stopped and started making violent course alterations on the main motors to try and meet the destroyer bow to bow and fired two bow torpedoes which again missed.

Down in the control room we were very much in the dark as we still though we were attacking a submarine – my own thoughts were that we were dodging torpedoes being fired at us by a U-boat. The First Lieutenant's thoughts were for our precious battery power with *Proteus* being thrown around at full speed. He went to the voice-pipe to remind the Captain that our nightly battery charge had not been completed and now he was flogging the batteries. The Captain replied 'If you knew what was going on up here you wouldn't be worrying about the battery!' Then came the order 'Collision Stations.'

Shortly after that there was a terrific crash forward and we heeled violently to starboard and then the klaxon sounded twice for the diving signal. As the Captain came hurrying down the conning-tower ladder he said 'Bloody destroyer'. He ordered the boat down to 180ft ready for an expected depth-charge attack. The forward hydroplane operator reported he had no control and then a call from the fore ends reported water coming into the tube space. The Engineer Officer went forward and soon phoned back to get the boat back closer to the surface to reduce the pressure of water coming in. Solid bars of water were flooding the tube space.

In the meantime our Asdic operator reported that the destroyer propellor noises had stopped so, as a depth charge attack seemed unlikely, we returned to periscope depth to reduce the sea pressure and allow the Engineer and his team to plug the holes.

Being in a patrol area with the likelihood of a hurried dive we had had our forward hydroplanes turned out ready. With the inevitability of being rammed, our Captain had met the onrushing destroyer as nearly as possible bow to bow. The brunt of the collision was taken on the port hydroplane which was sheared off, and the hydroplane housing on the hull was twisted and this sheared off rivets through the pressure hull and also jammed the starboard hydroplane. Plugs were driven into the rivet holes and wedged to keep them in against the sea pressure but later, on the surface, we were able to take out the internal plugs and put them in from the outside so that the sea pressure kept them in.

We still had a steady leak forward while dived and of course no hydroplanes to control our dived progress. As we were no longer in a condition to carry out an attack, we headed back to Alexandria where we arrived five days later after battling south-east gales while on the surface at night time and having a difficult time while dived. We kept a substantial bow-up angle while dived until the leak forward steadily settled the bow down, then we would pump to lift the bow again. The sailors called it a 'penis trim'.

Crossed tin-openers were sewn onto our Jolly Roger but we heard later that the destroyer managed to get back to port. It transpired that we had attacked the torpedo-boat *Sagittario*, a vessel drawing only 7ft so our torpedoes had run under. Fortunately for her she rolled towards us as our hydroplane ripped her side open so the hole was above the waterline. However, she had to stop to prevent the sea washing into her hull so was unable to counter-attack. A year or so later our First Lieutenant, George Hunt, by then commanding the submarine *Ultor*, met the *Sagittario* in Algiers (the Italians were on our side by then). The engineer invited him aboard and gleefully explained that the destroyer had been in dock for six months carrying out repairs and he had enjoyed a good spell ashore. He also proudly displayed a part of the *Proteus* hydroplane which had been imbedded in the *Sagittario* and which had been mounted on a plaque on the quarter deck.

Con Thode, Submariner in the Med

FLOOD TIDE

HEATHER Heberley found herself a best-selling author when, in 1995, she published Weather Permitting, *and later* Flood Tide, *warm and highly readable accounts of her extended family's colourful life on Arapawa Island in the Marlborough Sounds.*

Right at the entrance to Tory Channel, with the Cook Strait ferries passing regularly several times a day, lies Okukari Bay, home bay of three families of Heberleys. Together they earn a living as farmers (sheep and cattle), fishermen (of live crays for the Japanese market, groper and shark), and in grandmother Heather's case, as author.

The sea dominates their professional and family life. Living at the entrance to Cook Strait, one of the most feared stretches of water around New Zealand, has inevitably involved the family in many dramatic searches and rescues over the years. But between times, day by day family life goes on, even if Heather's unusual mode of transport and her unique island environment do bring their own special problems.

My car is a 14.6ft Haines Hunter fibreglass runabout with a 90HP out-board motor. Joe had brought the speedboat in 1983 when he was elected to the Maritime Parks Board. 'It'll make it easier for me to attend meetings,' I was told. No longer teaching school I found myself using it more than Joe did. What joy in my independence. I wouldn't have minded had it taken me two hours to reach Picton instead of the actual 40 minutes. Just being able to leave the bay, if I wanted to, opened up new doors for me. But many times since then I've wished my car had four wheels and was parked in a garage so that when I wanted to go out I'd only have to jump in, turn the ignition key and go. I have to admit some people are never satisfied. But there it is. My boat is not a car, and I am governed by a list of considerations.

The most important is the weather. There have been incidents when the wind has got underneath small boats as they've come off a big sea, and overturned them. Only once have I really thought we might flip as I felt the speedboat lift in the wind when we came off the waves before crashing down in the troughs. But I wasn't scared. Not even when Joe told me to crawl up underneath the for'ard deck and lie flat on the bunk so my weight would help keep the bow down did I feel fear. I was with Joe. So I jammed my feet against the roof to stop myself being thrown around, and each time the boat lifted off the waves the screaming of the propeller spinning in the air warned me to brace myself for the thump that would follow when we hit the sea and slid down a wave into a hollow.

That was one trip when I arrived in Picton needing a shower, a hair dryer and a complete change of clothes. Once we were in Picton and I looked back up the Sounds to where we had come from, and saw the white water lifting off the tops of the waves as they scudded over the harbour, I attacked Joe for bringing me through such weather. His, 'Well, we're here, aren't we?' reply only made me more furious. It took a withering glance from a stranger as he walked past us in the marina where Joe was tying up the boat – just listen to that fishwife of a woman – that shut me up. It's always the same whenever I've been really worried or scared. I try not to do it, but the moment the pressure comes off and I know things are going to be fine I have to take it out on the one I love. And knowing about it doesn't make me feel any better.

When I take the speedboat out myself I choose my days with care. A westerly wind is deceptive. At Okukari it can be flat calm but at Dieffenbach, where Queen Charlotte Sound and Tory Channel meet, the tides plus the westerly wind blowing straight across the Sound and into Tory Channel turn it into one of the worst stretches of water in the Sounds. Thirty-four years of living here have made me weather-wise. I have learnt to gauge the strength of the westerly by looking out my kitchen or lounge windows, down Tory Channel as far as Wirikarapa, where the channel turns and disappears from view. The westerly wind can build up a huge sea in the stretch of channel from Dieffenbach to Wirikarapa and when I look through the binoculars and see white-topped waves I stay at Okukari. I know what it will be like at Dieffenbach.

When it blows a strong southerly it is not only the wind that keeps me from using the speedboat. A southerly swell built up by the wind rolls in the bay and crashes up the beach. Any attempt to launch the speedboat would fill it with water or wreck it as it sat on its trailer on the beach.

And nothing in this world would put me in the speedboat in fog.

If I'm thinking of going into Picton, any sign of fog in the channel keeps me with my feet firmly on my island ground, and my mind floods with memories of that particular trip, early in the morning, when I was going in to play the organ for the 8am and 10am services at Picton's Holy Trinity church. I can still taste the fog, and shiver as I relive the coldness of that day, when my face ached as if I had severe toothache. I can still feel the numbing pain in my hands, even more intense when they began to warm up, and I can feel again the cold tentacles of fog as they slid beneath my Swandri and sank down in my gumboots.

On that day the first shafts of light were beginning to fan across the sky as I skimmed down the channel in the speedboat. The grey waters of the Sounds melted into the shoreline. Stands of pine trees and native bush not yet emerged from night shadows grew blackly against the hillsides and on the skyline the tops of the trees stood out in sharp relief against the grey sky. There was no one to hear me and I laughed out loud with the sheer joy of being alive and the feel of the wind as it rushed past my face.

Closer to Dieffenbach I noticed pockets of fog in the gullies, and low cloud flattened the hilltops. 'She'll be right,' I told myself as I turned the wheel and swung around Dieffenbach into Queen Charlotte Sound. Here the fog was lower on the water, swirling around in patches, but I could still see occasional stretches of land. I'll steam from point to point, I imagined. Then without warning I was enveloped in thick fog.

No way was I going to attempt to go any further so I turned around to head back to Chum and Mavis Thomas's home near the power line crossing. From there I could phone the vicar and tell him I wasn't going to make the 8am service but I'd try for the 10am one.

When Dieffenbach didn't come into view I realised that I couldn't be heading in the right direction, and I felt panic. Then there was a lift in the fog and I was able to get my bearings again, and turn into Tory Channel, and reach the Thomas's home. I phoned to explain why I would have to try for the 10am service.

I waited an hour and once the sun started to shine through the clouds a lot of the low lying fog lifted. 'I'll give it another crack,' I told Chum. 'Surely it'll be better down the Sounds by now.' Once out of their bay I was soon passing Dieffenbach for the third time that morning. Ahead I could see the fog had thinned, but the land on my starboard side was still shrouded in it. Again without warning the fog bank rolled over the water and for the second time that morning I couldn't see a thing. This time there'd be no turning back. There wasn't enough petrol to reach home. Picton would have to be my next stop.

I kept steaming in the same direction but then I remembered how disoriented I'd become earlier, so I slowed down. All I could see was the boat I was on and the ripples that fanned out from the bow on the water's surface. I stopped. I was scared I might run ashore or might be going round in circles, and I reasoned with myself that if I stayed in one place I'd burn less fuel and be more likely to hear any boats coming towards me.

I was wrapped in silence. The years peeled away and I remembered the deafening silence of my early days at Okukari when the quietness was so loud it sang in my ears before it built up to a crescendo that had me screwing up my eyes and covering my ears with my hands, in pain.

Imagination had me rushing to the side of the boat to see who or what was making the heavy breathing I could hear, only to see the tail feathers of a shag sink beneath the water. Then I heard what I'd been dreading – the muffled thump of the Inter-island ferry. I strained my ears to try to catch which direction it was coming from. A trickle of perspiration felt warm as it ran down my back, and as I turned the key to start up the boat again I looked at my wristwatch – no ferry was due at this time. This was my imagination playing tricks, making sounds in the silence of my mind. I left the motor running. At least with that going, I thought, I'd have more of a chance to get out of the way of any boats.

While my heart thumped, slowly fragments of the shoreline appeared and as I recognised them I was able to head towards Picton. After tying up the boat I walked to my friend Mary's place where I could change my clothes. Each step echoed in my head and when I spoke it sounded to me as if I was talking through a long tunnel. I stood, dripping with water, letting Mary bustle around and strip off my clothes. As I sat with my feet in a bowl of hot water she chafed my hands to bring them back to life and pain. A hot drink warmed me inside.

By 10am I felt human although for the first two hymns my fingers fumbled over the keyboard. By the end of the service I was feeling myself again and when I saw a friend in the congregation who had recently had a hysterectomy I waved out to her. I hadn't seen her since the previous month when I'd been playing the organ and afterwards we'd discussed hormone replacement therapy. Then I'd laughingly told her if she wasn't on it she might grow hairs on her chest.

As soon as the service was over I packed up my music and hurried outside. I could only see her husband and I thought she must have already left. I tapped him on the shoulder and asked him if his wife had a hairy chest yet? A stranger turned around with a stunned expression on his face. Oh my God, I thought, I've done it again. Muttering an apology I rushed back inside the church where I saw my friend. When I told her what I'd done she said no, her chest was fine, but after hearing my story her stomach was sore from laughing.

All the way home laughter kept bubbling up when I thought of how I'd asked a stranger about the state of his wife's chest. No wonder my father so often used to quote to me that 'Fools rush in where angels fear to tread'.

The sparkling sea and cloudless blue sky made it hard to believe how inhospitable the Sounds had been less than four hours ago. It wasn't only the cold that had seeped into my innermost self that day. but fear. The fear of not knowing where I was and not knowing where I was going.

Mechanical problems make me realise my car is a boat after all. When it breaks down in the middle of Tory Channel I can't step out and ring up the garage for a tow. The trouble has to be fixed on the spot or perhaps a passing boat can be flagged down.

Joy with her two girls, and Lisa with Haydn were taking themselves out for the day with me to Dryden Bay. Fifteen minutes from our bay there was a clacking noise in the engine and as I stopped it I turned the boat in out of the tide towards the shore. My first thought was that we'd wound something around our propeller but when we lifted it out of the water it was clear. Next check was the fuel but there was plenty in the tank and I could see there was fuel to the motor. We wriggled the battery terminals before trying to start it again, but the engine was dead. Rather than put the anchor down we tied on to a thick piece of kelp to stop us drifting.

We weren't too concerned. The day was perfect with little wind and the sun was shining. We all agreed with Joy's comment, 'Surely someone will see us and offer us a tow,' so we sat back and waited for a boat to pass. Everyone complained we'd run out of things to look for in 'I spy' before a boat came in view and we all waved out. They steamed past, all waving back to us. A memory from my days of sitting my skipper's ticket jostled to the surface of my mind. 'We should wave something orange' – and so when we saw the next boat we waved a spare lifejacket. They didn't notice our distress signal.

'You could let off the smoke flare, Grandma.' But unless we were in serious trouble I'd already decided to leave it where it was. For me serious trouble would have been if Joy, with her diabetes, needed food. The weather and sea conditions were good and sooner or later our men would miss us.

Another boat steamed up the channel. Joy jumped up on the cabin roof, waving our international distress signal while the rest waved and yelled from the cockpit. They turned in, and came alongside. A call on their VHF marine radio explained to Joe where we were. I asked him if he could come and tow us home, but our rescuers told us they were passing our place and didn't mind doing for us what Joe so often does for other people.

The breakdown was serious, so when the big boat next went to Picton the speedboat was towed in and a new motor installed.

Thank goodness it's not as serious as that every time the motor stops. Coming home from town one day I heard the new motor cough and splutter. Then it kept losing its revs until finally it stopped altogether. Surely it can't have died already, I thought, as I quickly checked what I could. No fuel was getting from the petrol tank to the hose that led to the motor. It didn't take much figuring out that if I wanted to get home the motor needed fuel, so I ripped off the fitting on the end of the hose that clips on to the fuel tank, unscrewed the cap on the tank, and pushed the hose down into the petrol. Then I stuffed a piece of rag around the hose where it went into the tank, to stop petrol slopping out. It got me home, perhaps not safely, but at least soundly.

Fuel, in one way or the other, is the most common cause when the motor stops. I haven't forgiven Joe for the time he sent me off to Picton with only a part-tank of fuel.

It was summertime. As well as all the usual visitors we'd had in the house during the holidays, we'd employed two university students to cut scrub. I'd reached the stage where I felt as if I were running a boarding establishment. My life revolved around cooking, cleaning and washing, all essential jobs. One of the scrubcutting machines had broken down and Joe wanted me to go into Picton then drive through to Blenheim to pick up a replacement part. I didn't want to go. There was just so much to do. I told him I'd much rather stay at home. 'Go yourself!' I yelled as I picked up the clothes basket and headed out for the clothes line. 'He doesn't have to come home and cook dinner,' I muttered to myself as I plucked the pegs off the line and threw the dry clothes into the basket.

'Please, love,' I heard through the open window. It was when he said he'd cook the dinner for me that I began to listen. 'You get changed,' I was told, 'and I'll go and bring the boat in to the wharf.'

The last words Joe yelled out as I pulled away from the wharf were that he'd checked the fuel and oil.

The stiff nor'westerly wind blew my cobwebs away, and as I neared Picton the wind veered more to the west and blew straight on shore. The waves hitting the boat broadside on made it uncomfortable and I had to brace myself at the wheel. Then the engine stopped. 'Damn! Damn!' I said half to myself and half to an unhearing Joe as I slithered over the wet cockpit floor to change the tanks over. When he'd told me he'd checked the fuel I presumed he'd connected the motor up to the full tank. I unplugged the fuel hose from the empty tank and pulled the other tank closer to make it easier to clip the hose on. It was empty. 'Bloody hell!' I cursed to myself.

I took a quick look around. There were no boats nearby and these waves would soon have me rolling around on the weather shore. We always carry a spare oar – our auxiliary motor – and I bent down to remove it from the shelf where it is always kept. It wasn't there. I scrambled in the cabin and lifted up a squab to drag out the anchor which I knew was in a locker underneath the bunk. As I put my finger in the hole of the lid covering the locker I realised that I had a good paddle right in front of me. I left the anchor where it was and tried my hand paddling with my makeshift oar. It was only about four feet long and ten inches wide, but as long as I hung over the lee side of the boat and took long deep strokes, I managed to keep heading in the general direction of Picton.

My back was stretched, my knees hurt from jamming them against the inside of the boat, I was hot, my arms ached and I could feel a blister on my finger where I'd hooked it through the hole in the piece of wood. With every dig I made in the water I called Joe a few more names. My 20 minutes' paddling seemed more like an hour when a runabout came close and told me they were going in to Waikawa and if I wanted a tow to throw them a line. I was able to fuel up there, and soon I was on my way to Picton.

Picton to Blenheim was nothing compared with what I'd been through but all the time the words I was going to say to Joe were building in my mind. By the time I arrived home in the bay I had a full head of steam and I knew exactly how I'd greet that husband of mine for sending me off with not enough fuel for the journey. A strange boat was tied off the end of the wharf and I wondered who was visiting. I saw Joe strolling down the track with someone each side of him and I recognised his aunt and uncle. 'You look like you've got a bodyguard!' I called out, trying to be lighthearted about my trip. He needed one. Words I wanted to say would have to keep until later.

Picton is a small town and news of my running out of fuel had already reached Joe. Before I could say anything he told me he'd thought there'd be heaps of fuel, he was sorry, and he'd invited Rex and Eileen for dinner. By the time they left, my fury had evaporated. How could I stay angry when everyone laughed about it? But it taught me two things. I have a very devious husband (one who could make sure we had visitors around), and now I always check the fuel for myself.

It took a midwinter swim to teach me about tying a boat up. Once again I'd been in Picton playing the church organ, and I was bringing out some friends for a few days. Instead of tying up the boat I threw the bow-line up on the wharf while we unloaded the gear. I decided to tie the boat off the end of the wharf and come back down after lunch and put it out on a mooring in the bay. As I climbed up the tyre I reached out and grabbed the rope. Visitors are always struck by our beautiful white sandy beach and we all stood looking at it as I explained how the currents make it so cold you can't even swim. I pointed out places where the bank had fallen away, exposing indentations in the fresh soil where there had been Maori pits. Okukari was once the site of a fortified Maori pa, and over the years we've picked up many adzes both in greenstone and obsidian.

History was forgotten when we noticed our boat drifting out of the bay. I'd picked up the wrong piece of rope. The dinghy was out on the mooring, there was no one else at home, and I'd let the speedboat float away.

The first thing to come off was the string of Mikimoto pearls that Joe had recently given me, followed by my town clothes, stockings and petticoat. The gap between the wharf and the speedboat was widening rapidly with the nor'westerly blowing out of the bay.

A big gulp of air and I leapt off the far end of the wharf. The cold took my breath away and I was still trying to catch it when I reached the speedboat and clambered up the ladder over the stern.

My humiliation wasn't over yet. As I brought the boat alongside the wharf to climb up on the tyre again, another launch came in and tied up on the other side. I had to greet them in my now see-through underwear as if I did this sort of thing all the time. I was delighted when I discovered they were friends arriving for a Sunday visit. A hessian sack found in the boatshed sheltered me until I got up to the house and warmed up under the shower before getting dressed in my usual Okukari clothes.

Heather Heberley, Flood Tide, *1997*

WAITEMATA TALES

NO, the woman in the wheelhouse on the Waitemata ferries is not the skipper's girlfriend on a day's outing. She's the skipper.

Sally Fodie, a high country girl from North Otago, was 25 before she learned to sail. She joined the North Otago Yacht and Powerboat Club. A few years later, she was in Auckland on her first professional job, crewing on the ferry to Pakatoa Island, and studying to be a ferry master. With the necessary tickets and sea-time under her belt, she became the first female mate of the Kestrel *and was eventually appointed master of various Auckland harbour identities, the* Glen Rosa, *the* Island Princess, *the* Baroona, *the* Iris Moana, *the* Ngaroma *and, most recently, the* Seabus Kea.

Established as a skipper and thus something of an identity herself, Sally began collecting stories of the Waitemata ferries and those who travel and crew in them. Many have been passed on by passengers, old salts, old crew; others are very much from her own unique perception and experience. These two give a tiny glimpse into the challenges of driving passenger ferries.

If only the sea would open up!

As masters, we all have different ways of coping with boat-handling methods that have gone wrong. When the wind and tide take over, the planned berthing falls asunder, and the audience of passengers add to the irritation, coping can be difficult.

Some masters scream and shout abuse at their crew, no doubt relieving their own frustration, but adding to that of others. Some become deathly quiet, ensuring that no-one will speak or approach them for the duration of the shift. Most of us, I like to think, handle it with a sense of humour.

A very trying time, berthing the *Kestrel* at Devonport, necessitated one master taking the vessel back down the line of approach yet again. Finally alongside, he went to lower the gangway. As the gangway hit the deck, he turned and bowed to his audience: 'Next performance in an hour's time, ladies and gentlemen!'

One of my most embarrassing experiences occurred not coming alongside, but trying to leave the berth. I was running launch trips from Devonport to Kelly Tarlton's Underwater World at Orakei Wharf. On this particular morning the wind was easterly, and I was master of the small, twin-screw launch *Island Princess*. I was not particularly familiar with the vessel, having spent most of my time on the sturdier steel launch *Glen Rosa*.

I brought the launch alongside the eastern steps at the outer end of the Devonport wharf as the tide was flooding. I was pleased with the passenger turnout. There was an Australian submarine at the naval base, and it appeared that the entire crew were having an outing. I collected money for tickets as they came aboard.

The problem occurred when I went to leave the wharf. I had the launch lying alongside and secured with a spring line. Efforts to spring it out were unsuccessful, owing to the lack of power and the wind and tide conditions. Missing piles on the wharf prevented the obvious retreat, sliding along the face of the wharf.

After considerable time, I managed to get the boat around far enough to enable me to steam the bow ahead on the steps, bringing the stern up into the tide. Full astern and at last enough sea room to clear the wharf! The enjoyment which my predicament had given the Australian Navy was obvious. As they left the boat at Orakei, I jokingly asked for an extra dollar each from them for the entertainment I had provided!

I have heard tell that, within the ferry company, there is a society called The Stern Post Club. Membership is not gained until the unfortunate master has knocked the stern post out of a vessel. Thus 'blooded', he has proved himself a fully-fledged Devonport master.

Bulwarks damage can sometimes qualify one for 'honorary membership'!

I've not become a member yet . . .

No ray, Jose!

The fisherman landed the stingray as I eased *Kestrel* into the Devonport berth. The huge sea creature thrashed in torment, as an excited crowd gathered to watch it dragged up the wharf steps.

As passengers boarded the ferry, I watched a Polynesian man dragging the ray around the wharf. It was a big one, around one and a half metres across. The man ran down the wharf towards the *Kestrel* gangway, as my mate and I watched in disbelief. With the giant fish still thrashing in his hands, he approached us.

'Can I bring it on the ferry?' he yelled.

'No you cannot!' I replied, amazed that he should suggest it.

'You f . . . g bitch! Get the boss man!' he yelled back.

'I am the boss man,' I replied, 'and you can't bring that on the ferry. Perhaps you should try a taxi?'

'You f . . . g bitch! I have a ticket!' he shouted. Marching aggressively towards me, he dropped the stingray by the gangway. 'Put f . . . g bitches in charge and this is what you get!'

The large contingent of passengers watched with interest.

'You are not travelling with us, either,' I said, as I tried to raise the electric gangway. The man ran up the gangway and leapt aboard, continuing his tirade of four letter words.

'Please get off the boat, I will not sail with you aboard.' My apprehension began to mount. He moved forward, fists clenched. I ran to the wheelhouse, closely pursued by the enraged man.

'F . . . g bitch, I will do you!'

'Get the Takapuna police!' I instructed the engineer. He arrived, to be greeted with, 'F . . . g bitches, get the boss man.'

'She is the boss man,' insisted my loyal colleague.

There was now no placating the Islander and, as the passengers and crew watched, he marched around the vessel and back to the wheelhouse screaming obscenities, whilst I remained behind locked doors. The police finally arrived and – after much difficulty involving four officers – the man was arrested.

This incident posed a huge dilemma for me. Should we let stingrays travel on the ferry? What rate should we charge? A dog rate? Or maybe a bicycle rate? Or would it be fairer just to charge a flat rate?

Sally Fodie, Waitemata Ferry Tales, *1991*

THE FLOATING WORLD OF THE RICH AND FAMOUS

LIZ Light is an Auckland journalist who left New Zealand for a complete change of scene. Though inexperienced with boats, she found herself working with her partner Sam in the professional crewing scene, in the Caribbean and Mediterranean. Crewing the super-yachts of the rich and famous on the French Riviera may have its glamorous side, but it also has a darker one, as Liz found out when she and Sam signed on as skipper and cook/housekeeper of a 34-metre motor yacht called Wolf, *owned by a wealthy 48-year-old American businessman.*

We met Miles in a bar in Antibes, and were instantly attracted to him inthe way fellow countrymen are. He spoke with the same accent, and viewed the world from a similar perspective; he was comfortable to be with. Miles was running a boat called *Wolf*, thirty-four metres long, eight years old, a Huisman of Holland with two MTU V8 engines. It was a luxury motor yacht and the queen of its style and size. It was the best. Miles had been in the Mediterranean boat scene for five years and wanted to get out of it. He wanted to go back to New Zealand and live a normal life and meanwhile he had saved a bundle of money, enough to put a sizeable deposit on a house back home. Sam wanted Miles's job. To run a boat like that was his dream. The timing was right too, because *Windsor* wasn't going to Brazil in the foreseeable future, and neither of us wanted to stay working on her without the compensation of interesting places to go.

Miles arranged an interview with the owner and we went to Antibes in our hastily concocted best clothes, feeling nervous. Sam was interviewed for some time while I turned the pages of a magazine in the saloon and sipped a glass of fine wine. Eventually I was called in and got my first thorough look at Tom, the owner. He was in his late forties with the nondescript appearance of a person you could pass in the street a hundred times without noticing. He was balding, overweight but not obese, and myopic with strong spectacles obscuring small eyes.

He had a small jaw and a fleshy neck without being overtly double chinned, and a set of pearly white teeth that were all crowns. Fortunately he was reasonably tall and his large stature helped him look vaguely impressive. He wore an excessive amount of gold jewellery to signify that he was rich and seemed especially fond of chunky chains one of which dug tightly into his thick neck. His arm was weighed down by his sizeable bright gold Rolex. Tom had a beautiful voice, which, to my mind, was the only sexy thing about him. He had an underlying American accent softened by years of living in Europe, and the tone was deep.

The interview took the form of him saying what he wanted and expected of me. When he asked questions, which he did occasionally, he interrupted when I was three words into the answer and finished for me, or went on to the next topic. It didn't take me long to figure out his attitude to me; I was a woman, and also an employee, therefore I was next to nothing, never to be heard, and seldom seen. It was my responsibility to keep the inside of the boat spotlessly clean, do the men's laundry, make the beds, tidy up after his girlfriend, do the marketing, keep the books, and cook a hot meat meal for him every night and a vegetarian one for his girlfriend. I was to keep the galley immaculate, and prepare lunch and breakfast when he felt like it. I was to do anything he asked immediately.

After the interview he took us to a restaurant for dinner. The party included Sam and me, Miles, Tom and his girlfriend. It was a most uncomfortable evening. Tom constantly pawed the girlfriend, and told her how beautiful she was, she laughed and looked slightly embarrassed but said little. The conversation was carried by Miles and Tom. Sam is very good at telling jokes and he gallantly attempted to lighten the air with a few but they fell flat. The girlfriend's English wasn't good enough to understand the nuances of jokes and Tom never laughed. He never smiled either.

We knew if we wanted it the job was ours. The advantages were simple. A very impressive salary for Sam, paid in US dollars, and a reasonable salary for me. It was Sam's dream to run a boat like that and a long distance from running fishing trawlers in the Hauraki Gulf of New Zealand. This was what he had been looking for in his twenty months of nautical roaming so we were delighted when Tom rang to say we could have the job. We gave two weeks notice to the skipper of *Windsor*, and then the stories started coming in. Stories of sex parties on *Wolf*, stories of Tom firing people in a rage and not giving reasons, and stories of him, gun in hand, threatening to shoot people who annoyed. Engineer Paul had worked on a boat next to *Wolf*, and he maintained that he would never work for Tom no matter how good the money was. Miles, the man on the spot, agreed the rumours were mostly true, but said it wasn't quite as bad as it sounded and depended on how one gauged each situation. It wasn't without some trepidation that we started working on *Wolf*.

For the first month Miles was there; he eased us into the position, ever patiently answering the millions of questions we asked, and was a lovely person to have around. For me there were instant and unforseen advantages; Sam and I slept in the same room, had our own bathroom and no other people in the area. We didn't have a double bed, that would have been too much to wish, but we did have the space and privacy we longed for.

Wolf was the biggest and the most valuable boat we had ever worked on. It was Dutch-built with Italian finishing in the interior and German engines. There were two engines, each worth one and a half million dollars, and the size of a small car. They were MTUs, which is very significant because when boatmen chatted about engines they all became respectful, even reverent, when MTUs entered the conversation. I have tried dropping MTUs into various appropriate conversations in New Zealand but it only works in Europe; here no one has ever heard of them and in our society no one is rich enough, or silly enough, to spend that much money on engines for a pleasure boat.

The engine room looked like Dr Who's secret laboratory on a grand scale. The engines were the centrepieces and neatly placed around them were three generators, transformers, compressors, pumps, stabilizer systems, air-conditioning units, water systems, plumbing systems and electronic switchboards. At first sight it was a huge, spotless technological nightmare and Sam was stunned by it all. It was almost too horrifying for him to look at and he wondered if he was ever going to figure out the intricacies of all the complex systems. He constantly carried around a book to make notes in, and listened carefully to Miles for every piece of information he could glean. That engine room was Sam's biggest challenge.

The galley was delightful with teak floor and cupboards and walls of varnished pine. It was warm and golden. The galley was large, and doubled as the crew's saloon, with a table and three comfortable chairs. It was nice to be cooking dinner and have Sam and Miles lurking about with their after-work beers in hand. It was well set up with an electric oven, a microwave, a pizza oven, four gas elements and two electric, and a grand collection of pots, knives and cooking utensils. It was a lovely space for me to base my day's work.

The other rooms tended to be dark and broodingly self-consciousness. There were five bedrooms each with an attached toilet, shower and bidet; they were below deck level and were dark because the only natural light came through small portholes. To add to the sombreness they were finished in mahogany, which is a dark red-brown, and had heavy brocade bed covers and curtains. The bathrooms were dark mahogany and gruesome swirly imitation marble, coloured brown with gold flecks.

Upstairs, forward, the dining room was almost entirely taken up by an enormous oval mahogany table and the sixteen chairs around it. Below the windows there were cupboards which Tom liked to keep full of wine; he only drank Budweiser beer, so the wine was for his guests, his girlfriend, and as we got cheekier, for us. Behind the table a large dresser held the china; two complete dinner sets, one plain white bone and the other simple black. These sets included all the attached serving bowls and side dishes imaginable. There were two cupboards full of glasses, with at least ten of every possible size for every wished-for type of drink. The cutlery was simple and silver with twenty-four of each utensil. We always kept a fine linen cloth on the table because not even Tom was comfortable with its stern wooden magnificence. Unfortunately we couldn't cover the room's central light fitting; the light emerged from behind the stiff muscular mahogany neck of a rearing stallion's head. The Italians really went over the top on that one but luckily most people never look up.

The saloon was rather lovely; large comfortable couches hugged the walls around the main feature, a low glass table with a huge brass propeller as its central support. This was Tom's favourite piece and the propeller had special significance to him, maybe he identified with it as a driving force. A sizeable mirror accentuated the space in the room, and was shaded glass especially designed to make people look slim, tanned, wrinkle-free and beautiful. I happily grinned at myself whenever I passed. Tom loved brass, maybe because when it's polished it looks nearly like gold, and he had six large brass ash trays which I polished every day. He was a pipe smoker and I give him credit for only tipping his ash in to one or two of the ash trays at a time. The coffee table's propeller was fortunately protected from touch by the glass top and I only polished it every couple of weeks. There were brass railings and all the doors and drawers had brass handles. Brass is the thorn in the side of a boat worker's daily life as it always needs to be polished.

Above the galley and the saloon was the third storey, with the bridge and skipper's cabin. The bridge was bristling with technological navigation equipment; it had radios, screens, radars, satellite navigators and switch boards which would, using technological terms, be described as thus: Lorrane, GPS, Sat nav, Weather fax, Radar, SSB Ham, and VHF. It only had one comfortable chair, which is silly because there are two people on watch usually, but perfect for Tom who saw himself as a loner. Aft of the upper deck, behind the bridge, the hobbie cat – twin-hulled fast sailing yacht – and the Boston Whaler – flat-bottomed speedboat – were kept. These were lifted on and off the boat by a crane.

I had great fun using the crane and, when there was only Sam and I on the boat, I had the good luck to operate it. It was such a feeling of power to press a button and have a whole boat rise out of the water, seemingly at my fingertips, and I had wicked thoughts about the havoc a seven-metre Boston Whaler would cause swinging wildly on the end of a crane.

In total there were eight bedrooms, nine toilets, eight showers, six bidets and one bath, all of which needed cleaning. I had windows to clean, brass and acres of mahogany to polish, the ship's laundry, the cooking and the shopping to do. When Tom was there I worked for at least twelve hours a day. He was happy when he saw his crew constantly busy and felt he was getting his money's worth. I enjoyed the cooking and made an effort to learn as much as possible about French cooking while we were there. I kept my eyes and taste buds open when we went out to dinner and acquired some French cookbooks. One of the tricks the French have is that of excellent and careful presentation; even if their meals do not taste superb they always look it. They use a lot of alcohol in cooking and, I suppose, in life in general. A dish is often flavoured with a generous slug of wine and finished off with quickly stirred-in cream. Tom was a serious meat eater, his girlfriend a vegetarian, and Sam and Miles liked eating anything so they had two dinners in one. It was time-consuming to cook two separate meals every night, although it was a good experience and a lesson in organisation and efficiency.

One of my chores was doing the shopping and every morning at exactly eight with hair undone and eyes sleepy I trotted off to get the bread, croissants and the morning paper. The town, Antibes, was a twenty-minute walk around the horseshoe shaped Port Vauban. Usually it was a pleasant way to start the day but when the mistral was blowing cold it was difficult to slide out of my warm bunk. Later in the day I went into town again to do the big shop; I fetched things Sam or Miles might want at the paint shop or the chandler and did the marketing for the boat. I had a favourite cheese shop, bread shop, cake shop, and lastly I went to the market for the fruit and vegetables. Shopping was fun most of the time, especially as I could buy the produce I wanted, for Tom had no limit on expenditure for food.

The non-fun part of shopping was carrying all the purchases back to the boat. The walk from town around the perimeter of Port Vauban to the boat was pleasant but carrying the supplies was exhausting and uncomfortable; I felt as if my arms were being stretched. The long walk to town and back, twice a day, gave me all the exercise I wanted. I felt fit and healthy and hadn't lapsed back into the Caribbean's languidly addictive smoking and drinking habits.

The first month on *Wolf* was a happy one. Wayne was a good companion for us both, Tom was seldom there, and the winter was late in arriving. Hanna, Tom's girlfriend, lived on the boat. She was a beautiful, intelligent woman and half his age. It was the usual pattern of big boat owner's relationships; that of the rich older man with the beautiful young lovely in tow. Hanna didn't quite fit into that picture as she was too smart, and being a pharmacist was quite capable of earning her own living, but Tom did have an eye for quality and when they met he made a calculated and all-out effort to get her. She was on a two week holiday in Mallorca with her sister, and he was tiring of the streams of young women who were obviously only interested in the good times his money could provide.

Hanna was from a normal upper middle class family in Sweden, and was initially completely dazzled by the money Tom threw around. After a prolonged holiday she went back to Stockholm to lease out her apartment and to windup her job. She had decided to stay on the boat and see what life as a zillionaire's girlfriend was really like.

Tom had another girlfriend in the mansion in Germany and after he installed Hanna in the boat he resumed his habitual life of two weeks with the business, the mansion and the Fraulein, followed by two weeks with Hanna in the boat on the Riviera.

After their initial few months of glamour and partying, Tom settled in to his two weeks on and two weeks off with the accustomed two videos and eight cans of Budweiser every night in the saloon. He didn't like going out and would only go reluctantly when Hanna insisted. I learned exactly what he wanted to eat and how he liked it cooked and this gave him even less incentive to leave the boat and risk a restaurant meal that might not be to his taste. Hanna soon found this routine to be dull and drank and smoked too much to get through the monotonous evenings.

Tom was a peculiar character. He was a brat, aged forty-eight, and as long as I humoured him in the way I would a child we got along fine. He was prone to bouts of anger and verbally abused Sam, Hanna or me, and because he was boss we had no choice but to take it.

The boat was his home and he was a private person, so private he said on a few occasions, that if any one came on to his boat without his permission he would shoot them. I became anxious about the safety of visiting friends and acquaintances and told them under no circumstances to set foot on the boat; if they wanted Sam or me they must stand on the quay and shout.

The weather took a turn for the worse; it had been cold for a few months and most mornings we woke up to frosty decks, but the sun shone, the sky was pale blue and the days were pleasant. After Christmas we were battered by weeks of strong winds which the French call the mistral. Always, when it's blowing, the crime rate increases. The wind is so constant and aggravating that people lose their tempers and their nerves, and go to pieces. If they are potentially violent types this is the time they let loose. I understood this because my walks into town and back twice a day, being buffeted and torn by that bone-chilling wind, nearly drove me crazy. The wind turned the boat harbour into a shrill cacophony; thousands of halyards clanked continuously against thousands of masts, an endless, high-pitched dinging of metal against metal.

Life on *Wolf* was not at all bad and in the two weeks Tom was in Germany we had a nice time. I got up late, and did my usual chores with the music going full blast, which helps to make toilet-cleaning and vacuuming fun. I did exercises to music, on the plush rug in the saloon, and danced with myself in the flattering mirror. At night I lay in Hanna's large spa bath luxuriating, with a good book and a large glass of wine. Sam and I sat on the comfortable couch and watched videos, sometimes, very wickedly, during the day when we were supposed to be working, and I wrote the first part of this story in the study, which was more comfortable for writing than the galley table.

We got to know Hanna slowly because the rules were standard – crew and owner's girlfriends were not to mix. Tom was strict about this and Hanna was just as unlikely to break the rules as we. She went to school to learn French during the day and sometimes socialised with her fellow students in the evening, if Tom was not present. She didn't know anyone in the area and it's incredibly difficult to meet people when a foreigner in France.

In the evenings Hanna ate alone in the saloon with the television for company, while Sam and I ate in the galley through the wall. It seemed silly that we lived in such close quarters and both craved company and friendship, and yet we were not allowed to fraternise with each other. One night when I was taking her meal in I asked her to come and join us, and said we wouldn't let on to Tom. She deferred a while, then brought her plate in and sat down at the crew's table, and after that she ate with us always when she was alone. We developed a firm friendship that lasted until Tom arrived and was picked up again two weeks later when he left.

My friendship with Hanna was the beginning of the end for me on *Wolf*. The lousy weather dumped a heap of snow on the mountains, and, being the beginning of March, it was probably our last chance of skiing that year. So when Tom was away Sam and I took a day off work to go skiing with Hanna. We had worked six days a week for Tom for three months and felt a day skiing was well deserved. When Tom found out that we had all been skiing together he was furious. I expect his anger was caused by us having fun with Hanna, whom he wanted to keep secluded for his pleasure only.

Towards the end of March Hanna told us she was leaving Tom and leaving the boat. She now loved it when Tom wasn't there but felt bored and restricted for the consecutive two weeks he was present; she was tired of his total domination of her, she was tired of watching two videos every night, and she was tired of his conservative and dull ways. Hanna was only in her late-twenties and wanted to live life and not be cooped up in a palatial boat with an older man and nothing to do.

In early April, before Tom came down, he rang to say we were leaving for Palma the next week He also said he had invited four guests to come along for the trip and he asked Hanna to be the hostess. Meanwhile Hanna's sister arrived from Sweden and a situation was set up in such a way she felt she couldn't get out of it. She told Tom she would stay for the trip to Palma but after that she was leaving and this gave him two weeks to do all in his power to persuade her to stay. He didn't like anyone to walk out on him as he preferred to make all the decisions relevant to his life.

The guests were a hotch-potch of deadbeats and bludgers. There was a small slimy Danish guy who called himself Spike. He fancied himself as a model and was oozingly charming. He had absolutely no money and so needed to hang about Tom or Hanna for everything. He had an Italian girlfriend who was long, lean, dark and very sexy. She was a pleasant woman and it was sad that someone of her quality had succumbed to the considerable charm of Spike. There were two men from Naples; Ronaldo and Dante. Dante was short and stocky, a pleasant, ordinary sort of fellow. Ronaldo had the face of Michelangelo's David, a tall body that was not in quite such good shape as that of the statue, and long, thick, black, curly hair. He was a good looking man and fancied himself as a lady-killer, his main aim in life being to take a different woman to bed every night. His next aim was not to spend any money, as he had very little of it.

The trip to Palma was to take thirty hours, so I got about three days supply of stores on the boat thinking that would account for any unforseen eventualities. There were ten people, including the English engineer who had joined us a few days before the journey. Food for ten people for three days seemed like a lot and the fridge and freezer were bulging. The first day of the journey we left late and went only as far as San Tropez. The big boat harbour in San Tropez is right in the middle of town and we berthed stern-to with a large audience of afternoon strollers. I was totally mortified and embarrassed to be a part of that huge ostentatious spectacle. I was used to the boat and didn't see it as being anything special, or even nice, and was momentarily stunned by the enormous crowd of onlookers it attracted. The more courageous members of the crowd were asking, 'Who's he? Who's he?' as if Tom was some kind of holy man or king.

I was working like a little Trojan, and there were so many demands on my time that I felt dizzy. The guests were constantly asking questions, 'Did I have this or that?' 'How did such and such work?' and endless barrage of hows, whens and whys. I was cooking lunch and dinner for ten people, and they were free-flowing for breakfast, which meant I was cleaning up after them until about midday. That night in San Tropez we stopped work at 10.30 and went out for a quick drink and walk around the town before falling into bed.

Next day I rose at seven and cleaned up the mess Tom and his cronies had left in the saloon the night before. At eight Tom appeared and said we were leaving in half an hour, and I had thousands of things to do to make the inside of the boat seaworthy again.

Tom is one of those people who has so much money and power that he forgot he couldn't control the weather. He listened to the weather forecast and heard about the gale force mistrals in the Gulf of Lyon but decided to go anyway; once out of the lee of the islands off the coast of San Tropez we were into the serious waves. They were steep and sharp as Mediterranean seas tend to be. I taped up all the cupboards with duct tape to stop them flying open and had every movable thing wedged against an immovable thing. When everything was safe I retired to the rocky aftdeck with a bowl and proceeded to be seasick. At midday when all the guests were lying about ill and so was I, Tom decided to jettison the trip. We anchored in a quiet bay off one of the islands and Tom and the gang spent the afternoon water skiing; I spent the afternoon cleaning up the havoc made by the morning's bad weather and cooking the evening meal.

Again I stopped working at eleven that night and started again at seven the next morning. Undaunted Tom decided to have another attempt at the Gulf of Lyon. Again the boat got bashed about and most of us were ill and even more reluctantly and furiously Tom decided to turn back. This time we went back to San Tropez. Another night of working late was followed by another early morning. We were low on a few stores so the engineer went out and got some for me while I again prepared the boat for sea. Luckily it was only horrible for a few hours. We were at sea for one night and upon waking the coast of Mallorca was off to starboard – by 10.00 we were in our berth at Puerto Patals, a ritzy marina fourteen kilometres north of Palma.

After I finished helping Sam put the ropes away I went into the galley to find Tom looking in the fridge. I asked him if he wanted me to make some scrambled eggs for his breakfast and he replied, 'No, you're fired.' I was stunned and asked him why. He said it was because we had run out of milk and Coke. We hadn't run out of milk, someone had put it in a different part of the fridge, and although the bludgers had consumed gallons of Coke there was still some Diet Coke left.

The real reason for firing me was that Hanna was leaving him and he was hurt and angry. He thought by getting rid of me and my influence he would somehow make her stay, and he wasn't far wrong. I never liked him, I never admired him, and I had little respect for him. He was nothing to me but a pain in the neck I had to put up with so Sam could have the job he wanted, and I don't blame him for getting rid of me with my reluctant servility. I hadn't been fired before though and that stung my pride. I had a momentary feeling of panic until I realized what a wonderful liberation it was. I was free again to start a new adventure.

Liz Light, 'The Floating World of the Rich and Famous', *1998*

PART THREE

Drama at Sea

THE PAMIR UNDER THE NEW ZEALAND ENSIGN

THE late Jack Churchouse, Wellington master mariner and museum curator, published his classic book about the Pamir under the New Zealand ensign in 1978. His research uncovered the diaries of the third mate Frances Renner, and not surprisingly Churchouse chose to use extensive passages.

In his forties, 'Bob' Renner was older than most of the crew who sailed on the Pamir during those years, 1941 to 1949. As a young man he had rounded the Horn in the barque Antiope and then sailed the New Zealand coasts, but when he went back to sea (able seaman on the Pamir being an attractive alternative to conscription in wartime New Zealand), he'd been ashore for twenty years. He quickly became bosun and by 1944, third mate. His diaries thus uniquely record the Pamir's voyages both as a seaman and a deck officer. Churchouse states that he was 'a sea lover of considerable depth . . . a romantic; intelligent.'

Certainly this account of the hurricane which befell Pamir on her fifth voyage, in February 1945, must rate as one of the finest descriptive passages of a sailing ship in extremis in all sea literature.

For his part in the ship surviving the hurricane, Bob Renner was commended in the official report by the master, Captain Roy Champion, who also dryly notes 'I have never in my career so far felt the wind blow as hard before.'

Pamir, a four-masted barque of 316 ft, was built in 1905 towards the end of the sailing ship era and represented, says Churchouse, a peak of their perfection. She was tragically lost with loss of 80 of her 86 crew, many of them sail training cadets, in a North Atlantic hurricane in 1957. Bob Renner's account of similar sea conditions in 1944 gives some insight into what it must have been like towards the end.

The strongest bonds of human associations are those woven by the threads of a common experience. Such bonds often come into being between men and inanimate things, particularly so as in the case of ships. A landsman can understand the seaman's love for his ship but few appreciate the intimate understanding of a ship's personality whereby her every mood and temper is comprehended and humoured.

Some ships are full of expression, responsive to the slightest change of wind and weather, conveying in their own peculiar way just how they feel. Much of this ability to respond in this way depends upon conditions. A vessel which is taut and tuned like a violin is loud in her discordant notes and sweet in harmony. The *Pamir* is such a ship, the product of man's skill and ingenuity handed down from generation to generation, inanimate yet full of living quality, a vibrant personality, wise in the ways of the sea to whom wind alone is the breath of life.

I have seen her always mistress of the seas except during four terrific hours one unforgettable night when an unbridled fury of the elements had her fighting for her very life against appalling odds.

We left San Francisco that voyage ... [10 January 1945] and made an excellent run down as far as 10° south latitude. Here, the steady drone of the south-east trade wind died to a fitful murmur. Black rain squalls hung in heavy folds breaking the south-west sky with curtains of rain. The clear days, the starlit nights, were gone. It was the hurricane season in the South Pacific. Hot steamy days followed as the *Pamir* worked the backing squalls to the best advantage, sneaking south past the Tongan Group towards the open sea beyond Aitutaki and Rarotonga. Each twenty-four hours the barometer rose and fell with a reassuring regularity of the diurnal range. In spite of the fickle wind and the wayward sea, the black impenetrable nights and the humid sticky atmosphere, the good ship made grand progress towards home and beauty. But, the finger of fate was stirring a brew there to the southward, an indescribable mixture of fury.

Just after we cleared Aitutaki all the flood gates of grey heaven opened in a deluge of rain, sometimes lashing around the ship as the wind came hot and gusty with the strength of half a gale, then falling in a steady roaring cascade, flooding the decks ankle deep and churning the sea white.

For three weary days we hauled the yards from tack to tack, took sail, made sail, tacked ship and wore ship in a seemingly endless effort to catch the wind which flew about in fitful puffs from all around the compass. Between the squalls, the deluge roared its dreary dirge around the *Pamir* whose sails hung drab and lifeless, moving only to slap their sodden cloths against the masts in a gesture of exhaustion as she lifted in the swell. The heavens closed in, grey, impenetrable and menacing. We watched the barometer closely. There was nothing to indicate anything unusual yet the forces gathered, stewing around her, unseen and brooding.

By Saturday afternoon, 16 February, we had worked clear of the Islands, our position being about 25° south latitude, a little south and west of Rarotonga. We were almost through the most hazardous part of the voyage. We had had a hurricane warning during the week but the storm referred to was many hundreds of miles north and so far as we knew had filled and dispersed. The deluge ceased. A light south-west wind came away and the *Pamir* stood south and east under all sail. The heavy grey pall of the previous three days lifted. The sky brightened, giving every indication of better weather. There was no heavy swell, nothing to indicate anything other than normal weather.

I had the 4 to 6 p.m. dog watch. Captain Roy Champion, who had kept an almost continuous watch for three days, came up on deck just before 6 o'clock. I well remember him standing gazing to windward for a few minutes before he went below, as fine a seaman as ever paced the ship's deck. There was just a little something about his watchful attitude which suggested suspicion. With his customary word of warning to call him immediately there was any change in the weather, he went below for a much needed sleep.

All was well when I resumed my watch at 8 pm. The wind had switched into the north-east, freshening somewhat and the *Pamir* was buzzing along with yards squared and a good 7 knots on her course. The glass had not risen as much as usual but we were out of the tropics where the diurnal range is greatest and there was nothing unusual in the small rise. The night was intensely dark, the horizon only just discernible. The wind came in noisy puffs worrying at the rigging then slinking away muttering and whining as it prowled over the ocean. By 10 o'clock the *Pamir* was racing along south and west at 10 knots. The wind was growing aloft full of anger, yet, except for the thick black night around her, there was no indication of the fury lurking just over the horizon.

Just after 10 o'clock I called the Captain. A heavy rain squall came whipping out of the north-east hauling the wind around to a point on the port quarter and the breeze freshened. The barometer had fallen very slightly but, except for the eeriness of the night and for that indefinable something that warns the seaman, the weather did not look bad. However, Captain Champion acted immediately giving orders to strip her down to lower gallants. We took the crossjack, mainsail, the gallant staysails, royals and upper gallants, thirteen sails in all, leaving her with good sailing canvas ready for anything up to a hard blow. The lads streamed away aloft to make the sails fast. They had barely reached the royals when the wind came away in a terrific burst. The *Pamir* took it well, roaring along in a belt of foam spreading from her sides in a hissing mass. At first we thought it was just a hard squall but as the wind came harder and harder and the glass commenced to fall rapidly, we knew that something pretty tough was ahead. By this time all hands were out, one watch aloft struggling with the canvas; the other standing by and waiting for a lull to take in the lower gallants. The lull didn't come.

About 11.15 a blast of unbelievable wind simply tore the clewed up sails out of their gear; shaking the ship like a toy as she tore along. I could just see three of the boys on the fore royal. They were flattened against the yard, unable to move. They were fighting their way out on the upper gallant yard when Captain Champion gave the orders to get the men down from aloft. They could have achieved little in any case. He decided it was better to lose the remnants of sail than to risk the lives of men. Meantime, other sails had commenced to go. Some of them just burst and disappeared as though wiped out by an invisible hand.

The *Pamir* charged madly on before the livid fury which roared in hot blasts out of the inky murk sweeping over the sea. The three men at the wheel did their utmost to control her wild sheers to windward, hard up and then hard down, swinging desperately about to escape the horrible pressure of the inescapable wind. With each tearing squall seeking to overwhelm her the intensity of the storm grew and grew. The boys could not get down from aloft. She became unmanageable, burying herself forward when a great wave of foam crashed and broke in boiling masses around the knight heads.

In those moments the *Pamir* nearly sailed herself under. She was nearly beaten and staggered with a sick stride of a labouring ship. Through the welter of the elements she spoke in her own way, 'I can do no more'. Captain Champion acted with precision. 'Let fly your mizzen sheets,' was his next order. As those fine cotton canvas topsails thrashed themselves to ribbons amidst the sparks of madly lashing chains and the thunder of loose gear, the *Pamir* took heart; lifting herself again and fighting back with all the indomitable courage she possessed. She tore away again before a shrieking squall which came clutching at her with hot fingers, ripping the heaviest cloth to threads, in a paroxysm of elemental fury.

I read the barometer. It had fallen an inch in two hours. At midnight the centre of the storm must have been close to the ship. Where no increase seemed possible, the tempest grew until the *Pamir* could run no longer. Although she only had the main [lower] topsail, the huge foresail and one staysail left, it was impossible to keep her off. Captain Champion had the fore yards braced up and let her lay to. As she came round, the roar of the wind changed to a high pitched scream. The *Pamir* lay over, taking the blast abeam. No one heard the main [lower] topsail go. Then the huge foresail, the strongest sail in the ship, burst into shreds. She was hove-to, fighting for her life, all hands standing by amidships.

The two squalls which followed about a quarter to one when the glass rose and the centre passes, came with an appalling fury, seeming to lift the whole ocean and hurl it at the ship. She lay over until the bells clanged. Breathing was impossible while facing the wind. I was standing at the weather rail amidships and as she went down and yet further down, my feet left the deck. Under bare poles she buried the lee rail feet deep. Huge breaking combers, streaming long manes of flying spume ahead of them, drove down to burst on the curve of her bilge and surge over her in an endless wind driven race of spindrift. She lay inert and helpless just holding on with all her strength.

As the first tearing squall passed a damp roll of mist like cold steam writhed in the wind, whilst far above it with the remoteness of another realm a lone star dodged in and out of a flying rack. There was a comfort in that star, a reassurance difficult to define but very real in those dire circumstances.

During the momentary lull the second mate reported that the main topmast cap backstay had parted. We had one staysail left on the mainmast. The captain told me to get it down to relieve the pressure on the mast. With all hands at the down haul ready to pull for their lives as soon as the halyards were let go, I eased the sheet about 6 inches. The huge sail, nearly twelve hundred square feet, just disappeared, swallowed with hardly a sound.

Then the second squall leapt out of the night, flattening the sea and driving before it a wall of spume which rattled like hail. As her brave spars heeled over to an incredible angle, those of us who knew about that parted stay had but one thought, would the mainmast stand. It didn't seem possible, but thanks to Captain Champion's insisting that the *Pamir* be kept thoroughly seaworthy, everything held.

Slowly the wind eased. She lifted her spars gain, the tattered remnants of her canvas streaming like battle pennants in the gale. What a magnificent ship. I felt her take courage again and begin to handle the huge cross seas with all her consummate skill.

Dawn revealed a shambles aloft, whilst we set up the 5-inch towing wire in place of the parted stay. Tattered rags, twisted gear and haggard faces with bloodshot eyes greeted the day, Sunday, 17 February. Unforgettable. Of the trials of that hideous night, the narrow escapes, the cuts and bruises, there would be much to tell, but the mere human experiences were overshadowed by the magnificence of the *Pamir*'s victory.

On the Monday, we commenced putting her in order. By 6.30 that night we had her on her course again under lower gallants, the next day under all sail. We still had a reasonable chance of making a fine passage but the elements, as though peeved with the *Pamir*'s defiance, held us up for nearly a week just a few hundred miles from Cook Strait. We eventually made Wellington fifty-one days out. Most of the lads went back to sea in the *Pamir* conscious of a new bond with the ship they loved but thankful that it was her they sailed in that night and not a steamer.

Francis Renner in *Jack Churchouse*, The Pamir Under the New Zealand Ensign, *1978*

THE ORPHEUS DISASTER

THERE *are several lengthy first-person accounts of New Zealand's worst maritime disaster, the loss of the HMS* Orpheus *on the Manukau bar in February 1863, notably those of deck officers giving evidence to the official inquiry and the reminiscences in old age of the 'acting bosun' Jimmy Mason told to author Roy Hetherington in* The Wreck of H.M.S. Orpheus. *Mason died, the last survivor, in Hokianga around 1935.*

No account, however, matches the poignancy of the short testimony given at the inquiry by able seaman Frederick Butler, who was locked up in the brig on Orpheus *as a deserter. He survived the shipwreck and was hauled in front of the inquiry to describe how he, who had visited the Manukau twice before, had tried in vain to warn Commodore William Burnett that the* Orpheus *was in grave peril.*

The loss of the 226ft Orpheus, *a three-masted 21-gun screw corvette commissioned only three years earlier, still stands as the worst of many hundreds of shipwrecks around the treacherous New Zealand coastline. Officially, only 89 of 258 men got ashore through the raging surf and survived, although some of 189 men posted dead may, like (probably) Jimmy Mason, have taken the chance to stay on in the new colony, with new names, identities and lives ahead of them.*

Frederick Butler being sworn saith I am a seaman belonging to H.M.S. Ship *Harrier* and was on board H.M.S. *Orpheus* when she was lost. I was present with the jury this morning and viewed the body of deceased. I identify that body as that of John Pascoe Chief Boatswain's mate on board the *Orpheus*. I know by the scar of an old wound in his left breast received in the Crimea. I saw also the 'Banners of war' on his left arm. I also saw his name on the waist band of his trousers. I last saw him alive about (3 1/2) half past three o'clock in the afternoon on Saturday Feby 7th instant on the quarter deck of the *Orpheus* as she lay on the Manukau Bar.

I have been twice in the Manukau in the *Harrier* before. The ship struck about (20) twenty minutes past (1) one o'clock in the afternoon of Saturday

February 7th instant. I know the signal station at the Manukau Heads. We first saw the land about 10 o'clock in the morning and went to dinner about (1/2) half an hour earlier than usual. The ship was steering about East when she struck but I do not know what course she was steering before. I do not know what signals were shown until a spy glass was put into my hands shortly before the ship struck. I steered the *Harrier* in the Manukau when I was Quartermaster of that ship. When the ship struck the bar she was not in the channel. Before we struck I perceived that we were going wrong and reported the circumstance to the 1st Lieutenant Mr Mudge who was lost. We were amongst breakers, which are not to be seen in the channel in fine weather. Mr Mudge took no notice of what I said, and subsequently, at the instance of the crew I went aft and mentioned the danger we were in to the Master Mr Strong. He asked me why I did not come to him before. I replied that I did not know that he was unacquainted with the place. Mr Strong said he was sailing according to his marks on the Chart. At this time he was on the bridge with Commodore Burnett and had the chart in his hand. I pointed out to the Commodore the situation of the channel, who then ordered the helm to be put to Starboard. Before this time the ship had touched the ground slightly. About a minute and a half after the order was given to put the helm to starboard the ship struck heavily. I heard the Commodore ask the Master if he had his marks on. He said he had. At this time Commander Burton was on dock receiving orders from the Commodore. When I was on the bridge a spy glass was put into my hands. I saw the steamer *Wonga Wonga* coming out of the heads.

This was after we had struck. The time was about (20) twenty minutes past (1) one o'clock in the afternoon. I looked once at the signal station through the glass after we had struck and saw the signal flying, which I recognise in the Book of Directions as nearly as I can recollect as denoting 'Come to an anchor'. There was an arm on each side and I think in an inclined position. When the ship struck there was a moderate breeze. The fore topmast studding sails were set, in fact all plain sail. We were also under steam. The rate at which we were sailing was between nine and ten knots an hour.

When we first sighted the *Wonga* we did not hoist any signal of distress the confusion on board being great. Such is my belief but I am unable to state positively. Before the ship struck there was a man at the mast head as is usual in a man of war. When the *Wonga* came abreast of us, after we had struck, I saw a signal flying at her masthead. She was about (2) two miles distant from us at the time, and could have easily seen that we were aground. This was about three o'clock in the afternoon. The sails were 'clewed up', after we struck, and afterwards set again. This was done twice. I cannot tell whether the *Wonga* could have come any nearer to us to lend assistance at this time than she did. I saw the *Wonga* returning the way she came viz. the South Channel. In about an hour and a half she returned. It was fortunate for us that she did retrace her course as above mentioned, as by doing so she fell in with our pinnace and cutter and brought them back to our ship to save our lives. There were I believe two hundred and seventy five (275) men and officers on board the *Orpheus*. Of this number (69) sixty nine were saved. John Pascoe the deceased was one of those who were lost. I have no doubt that he came to his death in consequence of the wreck of the *Orpheus*. I know Mr Wing the Pilot of the Manukau. I saw him on board the *Wonga Wonga* (to the Jury). When there is an ebb tide at the bar, ships are in the habit of putting on all speed. The lead was kept going but I do not know that information was reported. The lead may be thrown while a ship is sailing at 10 knots an hour.

Frederick Butler X his mark

Thayer Fairburn, The Orpheus Disaster, **1987**

TALES FROM SEA – THE ROYAL NEW ZEALAND NAVY IN THE SECOND WORLD WAR

ANY peacetime landlubber can only begin to imagine the heaving grey Atlantic in wartime, in winter, the fighting sailor's dread of being torpedoed.

In October 1940 Able Seaman Bill Black, of the Merchant Navy, left the US seaboard on the Pacific Ranger, *a merchant ship carrying a cargo of tinned salmon and Lockheed aircraft to Britain.*

There was a loud explosion which threw me against the bulkhead and the ship seemed to jump out of the water. A shudder went through the hull, then came a strong smell of cordite, followed by three strident clangs of 'Action Stations'. I quickly grabbed my life jacket and steel helmet and headed for the gun platform. Before I could reach it, 'Abandon Ship' was sounded and we headed for the boats.

On reaching our boat stations we found a problem with the starboard boats. The starboard side was our weather side, fully exposed to wind and seas, it was going to be difficult putting people aboard these boats. So with two volunteers aboard, and with great difficulty and some tense moments, they were launched. On reaching the water, two volunteers jumped from one boat and were hauled aboard the other one. The lifeboat they abandoned went surging off into the wild wastes of the Atlantic, leaving us with three boats for the entire ship's company. With a mixture of skill and good luck, we got the rest of the ship's company into the port lifeboats, and, as coxswain of one, I had my first command.

We pulled clear of the ship, and were making a head count, when someone said, 'There is still somebody onboard the ship'. Sure enough, there was a figure standing on the forehatch, waving his arms. A lifeboat returned and took him aboard. It was the Captain – true to the old tradition – the last man off. I had my last look at the old ship, which was settling by the head, then it was

DRAMA AT SEA **143**

'Oars way together' and we pulled away. Thus started the voyage of the *Ranger*'s port lifeboat.

We could see the other boats – one moment on top of a huge sea then disappearing into a trough. We were fortunate enough to spot the boat with the four volunteers, so we pulled to it and transferred some of our overload but not without a few ending up in the sea and having to be fished out.

We were a mixed bag – a few naval ratings who had never seen a ship until conscription – some stewards and engine-room staff, engineers, etc – thirty six of us, all thrust together in this boat, and all hoping that we had bought the winning ticket in the lottery.

Darkness was closing in, so we decided to ride out the night on the end of the sea anchor, and plan just what next to do at daylight. We had just finished rigging the sea anchor, and were streaming it over the bow when, like a huge whale, the U-boat emerged from the depths, the sea cascading from the conning tower as she shot to the surface. There was no sound from any of us in the boat, we were all transfixed. Then she started cruising among the boats. That, in itself was quite worrying. We were afraid that in the heavy seas that were running, the submarine could roll on top of us and, as you can imagine, there were all sorts of things to worry about. The U-boat circled each boat, then set course for us. The Mate said to me, 'I don't like the look of this – he could ram us'. So, just in case, we were all poised to go over the side. On he came and after what seemed an eternity, he skilfully swerved clear and brought up alongside our lifeboat.

So there we were, huddled in our boats, hands full trying to stay afloat and now, alongside, looking down from the conning tower, was the cause of all our trouble – the man who had just sunk our ship. For what seemed just a brief moment we looked at each other. Then he hailed us, 'Boat Ahoy. Do you have any wounded? Do you need any bread or meat?' We acknowledged, saying, 'No' to both questions. Then, standing in the conning tower, straight as a ramrod, he brought his arm up and saluted us, his voice ringing out as he called, 'Good Luck'. And so we parted.

I have never forgotten him. He left a lasting impression. He had sunk our ship – that was his duty – and in doing that he was not going to cause any more injury or harm than was humanly possible in the fortunes of war. With that salute he showed us respect – one seaman to another – and I have never forgotten him. I hope he survived the war.

Royal New Zealand Navy, Tales from Sea - the Royal New Zealand Navy in the Second World War, *1995*

CRUISE OF THE TEDDY

EARLING Tambs arrived in New Zealand on January 6, 1931, on his beloved Teddy, a 40ft, 40-year-old Norwegian pilot cutter. He and his bride Julie had left Norway three years previously with no destination, no sextant, no barometer, no money and no great sea-going experience. Going west-about, via Lisbon, the Canaries, Panama, the Marqueses, Samoa and Tonga, they acquired a dog, a son and a long list of narrow escapes. They made landfall in New Zealand with their usual luck, no charts or pilot books.

During thirteen months in Auckland, the family made many friends and acquired a daughter, Tui. Visiting an aunt in Napier, they experienced the great earthquake of 1931. Earling raced Teddy in the trans-Tasman event of that year, and cruised up to Tonga. Then they began to think of moving on, to Brisbane.

This is not strictly speaking a sea story about a New Zealander. But the fate of the Teddy is still remembered as yachts sail around the rocky southern coast of Kawau Island and still serves as a cautionary tale to mariners about when and how they stow their anchors.

The farewells were over.

We had cast off the last mooring rope and shaken the last friendly hand. Slowly, very slowly we glided away from the boat steps. A navy pinnace offered to tow us past the harbour wharves. When, after belaying the tow-rope, I again turned my gaze towards the landing stage, I saw that the crowd on the wharf was thinning out. Perhaps a score of friends still kept on waving: Mick – Jim – Nurse – Brownie – Cobs – Gibbie – Fred . . .

I suddenly felt a pang of regret, as I realized that I should probably never see again those lovable people who had favoured us with the rare and precious gift of their friendship. Yet, I could not stay. I am not made to live in a well-ordered community for long. I am a wanderer . . .

'It's like a book, I think, this bloomin' world,

Which you can read and care for just so long,
But presently you feel that you will die
Unless you get the page you're readin' done,
An' turn another — likely not so good;
But what you're after is to turn 'em all.' — KIPLING.

More than thirteen months had elapsed since we first entered the harbour. Many times since then had we sailed in and out, on the Trans-Tasman race, on our cruise to Tonga; many times. On the whole they had been thirteen happy months.

Now *Teddy* cut her furrow through the waters of the Waitemata for the last time. To starboard arose the well-known cone of Rangitoto, visible from seaward at great distance. To port the sunny splendour of Cheltenham Beach glided by. We tried to pick out the trees sheltering the little house which had been our home for four months. Bathing maidens waved their towels in farewell.

Rangitoto Beacon sped by. Three hours later we sailed through the tide rip in Whangaparoa passage, and as dusk settled upon the surroundings it began to blow from eastward. *Teddy* rolled heavily.

The cabin was flooded with farewell presents; in the galley paper bags and packages of stores tumbled about. They should have been emptied into boxes and tins and properly stowed before we went to sea. In the bustle of farewells we had found no time for such details. Truly, we were hardly ready for sea. Also we were tired. We decided to run into Mansion House Bay at Kawau for the night.

Kawau is a beautiful little island some thirty miles from Auckland and a favourite goal for week-end excursions. There is a little pier in Mansion House Bay, alongside of which I could moor the boat without going to the trouble of anchoring. This latter was an essential consideration, seeing that the anchor was securely lashed in the forepeak and the chain stowed away in the stern.

When, about ten at night, we made *Teddy* fast to the pier, it was pitchy dark. Kawau had gone to sleep.

Rising the next morning we found that the easterly had developed into a hard gale from NE. We were in no particular hurry to get to Brisbane, our next destination, so, instead of roughing it outside, we remained in the sheltered comfort of Mansion House Bay.

For three days the gale lasted, but by Wednesday morning, the 9th of March, it had exhausted itself and we departed. Leaving the shelter of the cove, we found a disappointingly light breeze of southerly wind blowing outside. The tides were at their maximum, running strongly northward and setting us backwards almost as fast as we could beat to windward against the light wind.

However, after several hours of sailing, we contrived to weather the reefs and thence lay south of Kawau, heading well to windward of the southern point of Challenger Island, a little rocky islet a quarter of a mile long in a north and south direction, which is separated from the south-east end of Kawau by a narrow channel.

The gale had left a heavy swell, which broke thunderously over the rocky ledges of the point.

The breeze seemed to freshen a little as we were approaching these rocks, but the tide was setting strongly to leeward, so that when we were within a hundred yards off the point, it was obvious that we could not weather it. The point then lay east of us, and *Teddy* headed SE. I therefore put the helm down in order to go about.

Strange! She wouldn't obey the helm.

The wind had suddenly died out.

However, *Teddy* was still moving ahead; she surely had sufficient headway to respond to the rudder, and there was no sea. Here, on the western side of the point the water was almost smooth. Smooth indeed, abominably smooth! Glassy, like the polished surface of a river, where it hastens towards a precipice.

I tried again – drove the tiller hard to leeward, again and again. No response! Consternation seized me: the current had *Teddy* in her power!

With accelerating speed we were driven towards the point, on the other side of which the swell rose into gigantic breakers, which, hurling themselves against the rugged obstacles with thundering fury sent rumbling waterfalls of foam over the rocky ledges. Sunken rocks off the point showed their frothy fangs, thirty, twenty yards away. The tumult was deafening. Oh, how I hated them, those rocks, those breakers, those snarling fangs, threatening, sneering, evil, inevitable . . .

I rushed forward and ran out the heavy sweep, tore and pulled and rowed with impotent rage. My wife cast off the halyards. The sails came clattering down.

Like a mill-race the current swept round the point.

Then the sweep broke.

I grabbed the spinnaker-boom in a foolish attempt to stop a weight of twenty-five tons driven onward at five knots' speed. A desperate man will do stupid things.

Now we were close against it. We felt the lift of the surge: cold breaths of a moisture-laden atmosphere chilled us. My heart shrank within me: *Teddy*'s end was near.

We struck the first time. I felt how the rocks crunched beneath our keel. *Teddy* heeled over, hard, then, righting herself, was lifted again and carried onward, past the point, right into the breakers . . .

I shouted to my wife to fetch little Tui from out of her bunk in the cabin. The same instant *Teddy* was seized by an enormous wave, lifted high, and with one big sweep thrown sideways against the rugged rocks. Then everything seemed to happen at the same time. Planks crushed, spars splintered. Rumbling – crashing – shrieking – rushing waters – and above it all the thundering roar of ten thousand unfettered demons of the waves.

Sometimes buried in foam so that we lost our breath, sometimes clinging to an almost perpendicular deck, when the sea was on the return, we needed all the presence of mind that we could muster. The main boom had come adrift. One of the topping lifts had jammed in a block sheave aloft, keeping the heavy spar suspended just over the cabin coamings and leaving it to sweep wildly from side to side, hardly twenty inches above the deck, whenever the boat rolled. The boom was like a huge club swung with deadly intent by a cunning giant hand. To dodge its shattering blows, we were continually forced to flatten out on the foam-swept deck.

Tony in his canvas harness, tied by a short rope to the rail, was in immediate danger. I succeeded in undoing his rope and then, in that fraction of a second when the main boom hung still, while gathering momentum for another sweeping assault, I ventured to leap on to the rugged face of the rock. It was a desperate chance. For one terribly long moment I hung by one hand, with the other attempting to support Tony, whose grip around my neck was gradually loosening, while the rush of returning water seemed to load insufferable tons of weight on to us. The next moment I found a foothold and climbed on to the ledge, where I left Tony with strict orders to grab a hold and hang on. Then I returned to the boat.

Again and again the receding surf would drag the doomed boat away from the cliff, brutally tearing her trembling timbers over an uneven rocky bottom, bumping her, ripping her with jagged teeth and leaving her heeling to seaward with the lower part of a precipitous deck submerged in surging foam and the mainboom-end swinging insanely about in the milky whirlpool. Then the next wave would pick her up and dash her against the rocks with the full force of her own weight. Oh, how I suffered!

I had taken Tui from Julie and told the latter to jump ashore, as soon as a chance offered. With my wife ashore to receive the baby, our chances of saving her would be all the better, I judged.

My wife slipped, or jumped short, or was washed overboard, none of us knows exactly how it happened. I only knew that I saw Julie disappear in the seething foam between the boat and the rocks. I saw my wife being whirled about in the churning, roaring surf amid countless jagged spikes protruding from the rocks. At intervals I saw her head, a foot or an arm above the seething waters, now close to the cliff, now away out. I saw her clinging to the rocks in a desperate attempt to climb up even while the next breaker came thundering in. I pointed seaward, shouting for her to try to swim clear of the surf. Then the breaker was upon her. I could do nothing until I had saved Tui. There was no place on the boat where I could leave the baby even for ten seconds without committing her to certain death. As it was, I had sufficient reason to fear that Tui would drown in my arms ere I could bring her ashore. But it is hard to see one's best friend fighting a desperate battle for life without being able to come to her assistance.

However, Julie had not been battered to death against the rocks. She came to the surface again and grabbed hold of the main sheet, but before I could tend her a helping hand, the boom ran out jerking tight the sheet and hurling my wife away.

Somehow I contrived to bring Tui ashore. Hurriedly I handed her to Tony, instructing him to look after her and not to leave her, no matter what happened. I then hastened to the rescue of my Julie.

But in the meantime she had achieved the seemingly impossible feat of swimming clear of the surging breakers. With infinite relief I saw her making for a large piece of floating timber on the sheltered side of the point, meantime using the broken sweep for support. A motor launch I had not previously noticed had put out a dinghy to go to her assistance. She called out to me in a voice which showed that she was very much alive. Well, she had certainly proved her mettle.

Tony, too, had behaved like a hero. Without a word he had taken his duties like a man, sitting on the rocks where I had left him in charge of Tui. He never budged, even when the breakers washed over them occasionally. In all my misery, I could not help feeling proud of him.

Spare Provisions had also been washed overboard. I had seen the poor dog fighting in the surf, but could do nothing for her. However, she had saved herself; limping and bleeding she joined our little group of castaways.

The fishing launch brought us back to Kawau. When the family had been put up at the Mansion House, I returned to the wreck to see if anything could be salvaged. It proved impossible; the seas were continually sweeping over the hull, which was waterlogged and badly strained. Her flag, the proud ensign of the Royal Norwegian Yacht Club, awarded her for her merits, was still flying, half mast, where it had jammed in the rush of events. 'As if *Teddy* bemoaned her own end!' said one of the fishermen. I felt differently. To me it seemed as if my noble boat mourned not her own funeral but the end of a beautiful dream and the misfortune of the master who loved her.

I turned away. I had seen her dear and pretty lines for the last time.

When I returned on the following morning, *Teddy* – my kingdom – had vanished.

Earling Tambs, Cruise of the Teddy, *1993*

CAUGHT IN A 60 M.P.H. GALE

RONALD Carter, through his books and magazine pieces, has left us a rich record of the Auckland yachts and yachting in the earlier half of the century. The date of this incident may be 1949, but anyone who has sailed regularly in or out of the Waitemata Harbour over the years will know of the 'great hills of water' that can roll down the harbour in a good north-easterly blow. Add to these the strong tidal flow, the intrusive reclamations of the port area and the traffic, and you have conditions that have severely tested many a skipper's seamanship.

There she lies, nodding to her moorings off the Royal Akarana Yacht Clubhouse, a pretty picture if ever there was one. Ever and anon she curtsies to a little wavelet kicked up by the light sou'wester. The sunlight glistens on the seas lapping her white topsides, and the truck of her slender 35-foot mast describes a swinging arc under the blue dome of a summer sky.

She's a mighty fine little ship, is Reg Langford's 18-foot, raised-deck mullet boat *Freedom*. Well designed, well built, good to look at, sails well, and above all, she's a fighter!

She looks so secure lying to her moorings on this summer's day; and yet I invariably think of how near we came to losing her that day – so long ago. I'm not quite sure how Reg feels about it, but in my heart I know that she was in very grave peril that afternoon. With a full gale from the north-eastward, and a white line of foam bursting on the black rocks of the retaining wall less than 200ft under her lee, her chances seemed very slim to me.

I still have a mental picture of Reg up on the weather rail, hanging on to her tiller and waiting for a 'smooth'. And then his voice suddenly rising above the sound of the rushing wind: 'Lee-oh!'

Up she came like a bird on the wing, her jib flogging violently, and then that wonderful moment as *Freedom* went about, and sailed away to safety. That moment will always be fresh in my memory. She was in peril – no doubt about it.

But I must go back to that day – Sunday morning, 10 December 1939, to be exact.

'What do you think about it?' said Reg. We were standing on the stone breastwork outside the Royal Akarana Yacht Clubhouse and looking out into the Gulf. It was not a very attractive picture. The short, lumpy seas were running grey under a low and gloomy sky. The wind was north-east, and coming away in fitful puffs, which we knew would get stronger and stronger; which would soon develop into a hard breeze, and eventually, most probably a 'blow'.

We were both feeling pretty stale. The pressure was on in our office; the first year of war. We had not been afloat for weeks, and we wanted to blow the cobwebs from our brains, and stretch our limbs again. 'It's not too good,' I said, 'but what about a run up-harbour?'

Freedom was bucking and rooting at her moorings when at last, after a double trip in the dinghy, the party of five were safely on board – Reg, his sister, the young lady who soon was to become his wife, my nephew, and myself. I think that Reg and I knew that we were doing the wrong thing. We both understood the signs, and the signs, we knew, were not good. A small crowd on the shore watched us leave under a single-reefed trysail and jib, and once we fairly got moving it was not so bad after all.

Off the end of the King's Wharf we spent some time salvaging a Z class yacht which had capsized, and whose owner had been taken off by a ferry steamer. We eventually towed her in between the wharves, and as it was now past noon we decided to lie in the lee of King's Wharf and have some lunch.

It was quiet there. The high wharf sheds completely shut us off from the wind. We did not even hear it in the shrouds. At least not then. It must have been about 2 o'clock when, in a lull in the conversation, Reg and I looked at one another across the cabin table. We had both heard it; a thin whining sound; the sound of heavy wind rushing through the thin steel standing rigging on *Freedom*'s mast.

We decided to have a look at the weather. After climbing up on to the wharf, we walked across to the other side. We were amazed at the sight which now lay before us.

As far as our eyes could see down the Gulf was a high running ugly sea, and it was feather-white! The wind was no longer coming in fitful gusts. It was streaming past our oilskinned bodies with a steady full-throated roar. This was not a blow; it was a gale!

We returned on board. It was warm and snug in the cabin, but we knew the cabin was not for us; we had work to do. First of all we carefully tied down three reefs in the trysail, and double-lashed the tack and clew. Next we took off the worker, and replaced it with a strong spitfire job. Then we worked out a plan of action. Our home moorings, we knew, were out of the question, being on a dead lee shore.

As an alternative we decided to slip in past the vehicular ferry landing and sneak right up into the little inlet immediately in front of the Lane Motorboat Company's sheds less than a mile away. We edged out from between the wharves and *Freedom* reeled under the heavy blast which took her on the beam. There was no doubt about it now; it was blowing. Reg was on the tiller, my nephew tended the jib sheets, and I looked after the main sheet and backstay runners, each time we went about. *Freedom* was new to us, in so far as bad weather was concerned, and we knew this to be her testing ground. We wanted an offing to clear the end of King's Wharf. Our first tack finished up off Stanley Bay. Not so good. However, she came round without any trouble under the lee of the high land.

Again we lay across the harbour. The wind which had been steadily increasing was now roaring in from the north-eastward, attaining (as we subsequently learned) a maximum velocity of 67 miles an hour. *Freedom* was lying down almost to the level of the top of her raised deck, but, apart from the seas which were exploding against her high weather bow and cascading over her foredeck, she was as dry as a chip down aft.

About midway across the harbour, a succession of hard squalls came down on us, laying the *Freedom* over until she was no longer sailing, but lying inert on her side like a dead thing. The time had come for us to nurse her. Very carefully Reg put the tiller down, and as she came up into the wind I inched in the last of the jib sheet until she lay almost hove-to on the port tack, with only her jib drawing. Barring one or two violent flaps, when she got a little too high, she lay very quietly.

During one of these pauses in our passage, I stood on the cockpit and watched the little *Freedom* climbing over the great hills of water which were now rolling majestically up the harbour, but fortunately were not breaking. Up, up would go her full bow until she almost seemed to be standing on her broad tuck stern, and then, as the wave passed under her, the whole procedure would be reversed until she seemed to be standing on her head. And yet, during these gyrations, no solid water came aboard.

At last we scraped past the end of the King's Wharf, and got her closehauled for the finishing post. But the heavy seas were wiping her head off, and slowly but surely we were being driven to leeward.

And so we come to that moment when I thought that we were going to lose her. Nearer and nearer came the black line of rocks shrouded in a mist of spray. I had no fears for our own safety; I felt that we could have got ashore all right. It was the ship. If we lost her it would be our own fault. We had made an error of judgment in taking her off the moorings. Her life was in our hands.

Twice we tried to put her round, and twice she mis-stayed. I was now getting terribly anxious; I know Reg was, too; we were getting perilously close to those rocks; if we missed next time, we knew in our hearts *Freedom* would be done for; she would not last an hour.

And then, above the sound of the wind, I heard Reg cry those magic words which mean so much in times of danger. Words of judgment! Judgment of good timing in a bad situation; judgment on ourselves, if we ourselves should misjudge.

I say I suddenly heard him cry 'Lee-oh!' and I watched him put the helm down. Up she came into the wind, and the violent chattering of her headsail as she hung there for a second before paying off on the other tack was a wonderful sound in my ears. It meant that we were round. One more short tack and we were lying for our haven. And, just to show that it was really blowing, I am going to state a fact which a number of yachtsmen will probably not believe.

For those not familiar with the little hole into which we had darted, I wish to state that perhaps at a distance of 100 feet, or less from where we finally fetched up, and immediately to windward of us, was a spit of land at least 20 feet high. Behind this spit, the *Freedom* lay to one light and one heavy anchor at the full scope of the warps, and she was dragging slowly but steadily all the time.

We were employed for the next hour or so in constantly hauling up on, and relaying the anchors in turn. The ship lay almost in calm water, and it was only the wind in the upper portion of her mast and rigging which was causing her to drag.

At approximately half-past five in the afternoon Reg was doing a spell of anchor shifting in the dinghy. He was in the act of dropping one of the anchors overboard from the dinghy, having just carried it out, when I, who was standing on the foredeck, suddenly felt heavy spots of rain hitting my face. I looked up to windward. The sky was as black as the inside of a seaboot, the clouds almost seemed to touch the water. Above the roaring of the wind I heard another roar – the roar of torrential rain!

I called loudly to Reg to come aboard; that heavy rain was coming. He understood and scorched back to the *Freedom*, throwing the painter to me as he came alongside. It was now raining heavily, and we dived below, slamming-to the sliding hatch after us. Reg sat on the port bunk and I on the starboard, just below the sliding hatch, and for perhaps ten minutes or less the whole skies seemed to be falling on the broad main-deck of the *Freedom* with such noise and violence that we found ourselves shouting to one another across the 7 foot space which divided us.

And now for the last remarkable incident in the course of this eventful day.

Without the slightest preliminary warning of any slackening, the rain stopped. It stopped as suddenly as one might turn off the water in a tap, by giving it a quick turn of the wrist. We were amazed; we were still talking in loud voices and the ensuing silence was so great I almost burst out laughing.

We pushed back the hatch, and, gently wondering, climbed out and stood side by side on *Freedom*'s maindeck. Not one drop of rain was falling from the sky; but, more amazing still, there was not a breath of wind. No, not a breath! In one final fierce outburst of Nature millions of gallons of water and a gale which had risen in the squalls to 67 miles an hour had in an instant gone screaming away to leeward, leaving the *Freedom* rocking gently from side to side.

'Now is the time to switch the anchors round,' said Reg. 'Likely as not it will come in from the north.' We shifted them, tired though we were, and, just as we had them nicely laid out, and while Reg was still in the dinghy, I noticed a gleam of sunshine piercing the black clouds in the north. Sure enough the wind was coming in from that direction; but this was no return of the gale. It was a gentle sea breeze. Every minute the sky was clearing, getting lighter and lighter. It was time for us to go home.

At about 6.30 p.m. we rounded the tide-deflector, and ran slowly in to our moorings with the lightest of airs behind us. *Freedom* sailed gently forward, with only a slight rippling at her bow.

Just before we rounded up, we passed a mullet boat lying at her moorings. Her owner was on board, standing in the cockpit, with his folded arms resting on the cockpit rail, and as we sailed slowly past I heard him say quietly: 'You chaps knew something when you got out of here this morning'. I felt myself blushing, but said nothing.

The man was under the impression that, with good judgment, we had taken the *Freedom* away from a very exposed and dangerous anchorage – just to be on the safe side. He little knew that we had nearly lost a fine little ship through an error of judgment.

Or was it? Could it be possible that we had unwittingly done the right thing? For in that treacherous corner up by the Royal Akarana Yacht Club lay the mangled remains of Arthur Bone's 26 foot yacht *Calypso* smashed to matchwood. Just one weak link in her mooring chain – just one had been enough.

Ronald Carter, Caught in a 60 m.p.h. Gale, ***1980***

TASMAN TRESPASSER

IN the Maritime Museum of New Zealand, on Auckland's Hobson Wharf, you can see the 20ft orange Yorkshire dory in which Colin Quincey became in 1977 the first and only person to row across the Tasman Sea against the prevailing winds and currents. No-one's yet done it the 'easier' way, either. A former British naval officer and experienced square-rigger sailor looking for a new challenge, Colin took sixty-three days to row 1730 nautical miles across one of the world's most unpredictable stretches of water. Averaging 27 miles a day, he ran into storms, sharks, killer whales, self-doubt and depression. His back went. Eventually he ran into Australia, at Marcus Beach on the Queensland Coast, where incredulous locals took some convincing.

Meticulous planning, however, lay behind this seemingly crazy enterprise. The Tasman Trespasser *was especially fitted out for the task, and Colin had carefully researched the weather patterns, Admiralty charts and other epic passages made with oars alone. He set off from the Hokianga harbour on February 6, 1977 – New Zealand Day. The first task was to clear the notorious Hokianga bar, the second to clear the land, fighting forces which drew him back towards the dangers of Cape Reinga and the Three Kings islands. On day four, he was still uncertain as to his exact position.*

The WNW wind which greeted my still sleepy eyes when I crawled out of the tunnel at 1800 was warning of the approaching gale. The sky was ominous to the west. How much ground had I lost while asleep? I wasted no time in further contemplation and was rowing hard to the west within five minutes of waking.

At 2015 I took a short break to get the forecast. 'Winds west, backing south-west and freshening.' As far as I was concerned this was the most dangerous weather of all, as it would set me towards the endless breakers of Ninety Mile Beach, or the rocks and cliffs of Cape Maria Van Diemen to the north-east. But perhaps more deadly than either would be the steep seas and breakers thrown up by Pandora Bank, a steep-sided shoal area about seven miles off the coast and now directly downwind from me.

Clearing the land had always been the biggest gamble of the voyage. I had reckoned the chances no better than 50/50 of achieving it first time. (The possibility of being forced back and starting again from further north than Hokianga had been considered.) Now the Tasman was putting its cards on the table – but which of us held the trumps? Why the hell hadn't I taken a second sight in the afternoon? At least that would have told me the amount of sea room I had to play with.

Dusk was approaching fast as I prepared for a wet and windy night. I had a good tot of rum, turned TT's sturdy little bow towards Australia and rowed into the night and the freshening west wind. Progress was painfully slow as time after time the boat was stopped dead in its tracks by the opposing seas. It was impossible to know at the time, but I suspect I was only just holding my own. Further ground was lost when I had to stop rowing and bail out the spray and wave tops that came over the bow.

By 2200 I reckoned I was losing more ground during the increasing bailing sessions than I could make up rowing and decided that sea-anchors would once again be the best action. As I secured the oars I caught the faintest glimpse of a light over the stern. Was it a ship or a lighthouse?

I stood up and clung to the mast. Five minutes passed before I detected it again as we rose and fell to the waves. A definite flash this time – a lighthouse! A quick glance at the steering compass to get a rough bearing. It was desperately important to know which one it was and thereby determine my approximate distance from the land. I had to work fast as the brief gap in the weather which had opened to the north-east would not stay for long. I heaved the small sea anchor over the bow, strapped the watch outside my jacket sleeve, and dug into the canvas deck bag for the hand-bearing compass. I had already memorized the lights' characteristics. Cape Reinga – flashing every twenty-six seconds – height about 540 feet – nominal range twenty-six miles; Cape Maria Van Diemen – flashing every fifteen seconds – height about 300 feet – nominal range ten miles.

My thoughts briefly centred on the many nights I'd spent on other coasts searching for lights, and was grateful for the experience it had given me, for assessing ranges across the sea is – at best – a dubious occupation and only by experience can one become even remotely proficient. I needed three hands – one for the watch, one for the compass and one to hold on. With my weight high by the mast the rocking motion was increased. Another flash as we crested a wave, but this time spray hit my face and the compass, so no bearing. I prayed the light would be Reinga – a flash every twenty-six seconds, as in this visibility and with the light low on the horizon, my range was likely to be about twenty-five miles. Van Diemen was lower and smaller and the maximum range fifteen miles, probably less.

I dispensed with the compass – identify the light first.

I climbed on the pitching foredeck, my feet wedged against the sea anchor cleats, and wrapped my arms around the tiny mast. A squall obscured the view for precious minutes, followed by another clear patch. A good sighting on the next flash, I started the second hand – at fifteen seconds I was deep in a trough so still didn't know. My knuckles were white against the red paint of the mast.

Again I started the watch as I just caught a glimpse . . . Eleven, twelve – I was counting out loud as we began to climb upwards – thirteen, fourteen . . . flash, then another stronger slightly to the left.

The first had to be Van Diemen – I was within fifteen miles of land, probably less, and Pandora Bank with its vicious breakers was right in my path – dead downwind.

Somehow I had to stop my progress towards land. The wind had in fact reduced to about twenty knots and was again veering to the west. A brief spell of moonlight was sufficient to show heavier cloud approaching from the north-west. If that was a trough then a reversion to southerly winds would possibly follow. That was a gleam of hope – I had to buy enough time to keep off Pandora Bank until it had passed.

I decided to put both anchors out f'ard, get the radar reflector down to reduce windage and row into the seas as well. The large sea anchor was still rigged aft, the small one streamed f'ard. I had to crawl to the stern to take off the anti-chafe hose and, inevitably, I got soaked in the process. I was concerned that with both anchors streamed they might tangle, so rigged a short line and a flotation bottle to the slings of the large anchor to get maximum vertical separation. The small anchor set quite deep because of the iron band at the mouth. With both anchors streamed we really dug in, but with the adverse effect of increasing the relative speed of the waves past the boat.

'Nasty seas – not big but vicious little devils thumping the boat quite hard!'

I fought the bolts holding the radar reflector for half an hour before giving up and resorting to the hacksaw. With only a quarter of one bolt left to cut a larger than normal wave enveloped me and the foredeck. I ducked. When I looked up any future problems with the radar reflector had been resolved – it had disappeared. Visibility had closed in again with the arrival of the gusting winds and associated squalls. Any thought of assisting the situation by rowing was rapidly shelved after having the oars knocked from my hands by the passing waves. At 2330 I got another bearing of the light. It was impossible to tell whether I was nearer or not and the bearing was much the same – 050. As I reckoned my accuracy was only within 10 degrees, this really gave me no indication of which way I was moving.

Having bailed the boat out, there was nothing else I could possibly do to improve my precarious situation. My attitude was philosophical – I literally cast my fate to the wind – made a cup of coffee, lit a fag and waited.

Day 5 – *Friday 11 February*

Throughout the night and the following day wind and seas increased. Visibility remained bad. I had no further indication of where I was or in what direction I was moving. My log tells the story:

'Wind and seas increased. Time 0810 – only just writable. Another one inboard and into the tunnel – 12–20ft seas – steep and confused – two sea anchors out – lee shore – dangerous – no sleep – humming rigging – baling, baling, baling! Log now floating in the tunnel as I write. No land in sight yet – TT may have really dug her claws in, but it is very wet. Glucose – hot drink – change – the motion vicious – snapping and heaving – makes me dizzy.

'Squall line close to the North West. Barometer dropping faster. Winds up to 30 knots – then warmer – rain, sunny to SW but still blasting away. On my last dry clothes. Baling every 1/2 hour – dry breakfast. Incredible how confused these seas are and how many TT manages to avoid – a longer warp on the sea anchor would be better, but I don't possess. Roaring as waves go past – pause as we come through – 'swim' out of the tunnel – bale away – then back in.

'These conditions now for 9 hours – with I suspect at least another 6 to come. It is not the size of the seas that is dangerous but their speed and strength. A bloody day with winds 20–30 knots and some 20–25 foot seas, with other waves like steps on them – baling half-hourly. No sign of land – the forecaster is now catching up with the weather! Re-rigging large sea anchor frequently to keep the turns out and avoid chafe. Forecast at 1515 – SW 15–25 possibly backing SE, then 10–15 knots, fine, seas slight to moderate. The wave that just filled up the cockpit had other than 'moderate' written on it.

'Worried – but what else can I do? Eating non-cooked breakfasts. Resting as much as possible. No really dry clothes left. Taking glucose doses, tots of rum and hot coffee. Regular search for lights/land. Barometer now creeping up again but so is the wind.

'Time 1700. Estimate my position about 5–10 miles west of Cape Van Diemen, but don't know how good and what effect the anchors are having. Quite frankly I don't know if the next problem will be 90-mile Beach or Three Kings!'

The steps referred to were the result of one wave climbing another. Although I did not record all wind direction changes, I remember them to be quite frequent, thus providing one reason for the confused waves. The steep seas were almost certainly caused by the shoaling of the sea bed to the west of Cape Maria Van Diemen and possibly Pandora Bank – I shall never know whether I passed over it or not.

I bailed, kneeling between the footbrace and the rowing sea, using Tupperware pots or the bucket, depending on the depth of water. Pumping was impractical as the water was sloshing rapidly from one side of the boat to the other and I could not achieve a vacuum. My position estimate at 1700 could, at the time, have been nothing more than a guess; however, having now re-plotted my probable course for this period, it seems a fairly accurate assessment.

By the evening of Day 5 only the glucose and snatched dry meals were keeping me going, my actions had considerably slowed, but morale was still good.

'Generally OK, apart from worry of land. TT riding most of the waves brilliantly – I have to be careful not to alter her trim too much. Down aft is probably the best place for me. Tasman is having another bash tonight. I pray I got enough offing before this lot, and that the wind shift to SE arrives in time.'

The night passed in a sort of haze, I was dizzy from the motion. I knew I had to rest as much as possible for, if a landing was to be made, I would need all the strength I could muster – but bailing took up much of the night. At some time I thought I caught a glimpse of land to the east, but can't be sure. When I wasn't bailing I'd creep into the tunnel or curl up in a corner of the cockpit. The sea anchors required frequent attention.

Day 6 – *Saturday 12 February*
By dawn I must have been north and west of Cape Reinga, though I didn't know this at the time. Nor had I fully appreciated that disaster had been averted by a timely backing of the wind to the south-east. Later in the day I wrote:

'I have no record nor can remember the wind shift to the SE. This was the most important factor and I can only assume my alertness was inhibited to the extent that it simply did not register with me.'

During the forenoon there was a little cheering sun, but no relaxation. The waves steepened as the great mass of water squeezed between the northern capes and the subterranean mountains capped by Three Kings Islands – thirty miles to the north-west. I was a very insignificant little speck in this racing, magnificent panorama of sea and spray – one cannot help but feel humble in such surroundings.

'1500 – approx. Still the same conditions but wind back to the south – some sun – thought I saw the outline of land to leeward – still dizzy of the snatching movement created by sea anchors – so on both counts, with the hope of establishing my position by dusk and to ease the boat's movement I took in sea anchors. Going forward to get them in was quite interesting even though the crawl was only about three feet.'

Without the sea anchors the full advantage of the boat's design and buoyancy was gained. She rode beam to the seas, careering along to the north. The motion was still bouncy but blissfully quiet compared with the snatching created by the anchors, and the amount of bailing required was greatly reduced. I spent long periods standing at the mast seeking any sign of land but with no reward. An easing of the wind about 1800 allowed me sufficient time to throw a mixture of dried meat and vegetables into the pressure cooker. The meal made a great difference and I could almost feel it bringing some life back into my weary limbs.

At about 2030 my hours of searching were rewarded. As the sky darkened, the powerful beam of Cape Reinga light cut the sky to the south-east. After twenty minutes of clinging to the mast, the small compass pressed to my watering eyes (I was facing the wind and spray), I got a reasonable bearing. I dug out the very soggy chart from the tunnel, rested it on the hatch cover and, between bailing sessions, I plotted the bearing line and my assessed range. I was certainly within range of Three Kings light. Taking up the compass I returned to my perch by the mast, looked down the probable bearing and was immediately greeted with three bright flashes. For the first time since leaving Hokianga I knew exactly where I was – ten miles due south of Great Island in the Three Kings group. But once again danger loomed right in my path in the form of the smaller islands to the west of Great Island. The lull in the weather earlier in the evening had passed and we were soon being driven towards another lethal lee shore by twenty-five-knot winds and steep seas.

'Oh, no – not again!' Sea anchors and the consequent violent motion and bailing faced me once more as the logical solution but I didn't put them out – I would allow myself to drift until such action was absolutely necessary.

'Time 2330. Shattered now after little sleep for two days – aching and feeling old. How does one describe looking at a seascape of waves of twenty feet or more careering along towards shore, blown by an angry thirty-knot wind – not knowing really where you are, slightly dazed by the bashing and rapid motion. Wondering how much longer you can last in this and how TT manages to climb these bastards. Living on nervous energy and fags. Took 2 hours to get dry clothes on – hyperthermia symptoms were becoming evident. Took 3/4 of an hour to make up coffee. Trying to rest in 2in of water. Baling-out to near completion and then 'crash' – start again. Reminded of Kipling's 'If' – perhaps a source of strength on this occasion.'

When I was about ten years old, I think, my father had shown me the poem 'If' by Rudyard Kipling and I had never forgotten it. As I squatted in a soggy, dispirited ball fighting desperately to stay awake, fighting maybe for my life for the third night, I muttered the powerful lines to myself, over and over again.

If you can force your heart and nerve and sinew
To serve your turn long after they are gone
And to hold on when there is nothing in you
Except the Will which says to them 'hold on!

Day 7 – *Sunday 13 February*
By 0100 visibility had reduced.

'Now blowing 20 knots from SSE – but where are the Kings? Dozing in cockpit f'ard – daren't sleep – 2in water in the boat. I'll wait until the next wave comes in – my knees ache with bailing and holding me steady in the boat.

'0315 – got a clear sight of Three Kings Light – quite high up – the light is situated on the peak of the island – 934 feet above sea level – and the outline of South West Island lurking with it to leeward in the gloom.

I crammed myself in the tunnel with the *Pilot* and relevant chart – what a hell of an uncomfortable hole this is to do anything. Still, who designed it! Be OK if it was dry, but it isn't. Check my position, rate and speed of drift, assume my range from the light and hence the range of the nearest islands. We're OK but only for a bit. I turned to the Pilot to find out what I could about these dangers to the North. They were named appropriately enough by Tasman, who discovered them on the Feast of the Epiphany, hence the name; and are now uninhabited and a wild-life sanctuary. Fine for hermits and ornithologists but what about tired rowers? There was a simple message for me later in the entry: "Tidal Streams – The tidal streams between these islands attain rates of from 3-5 knots and the races frequently give an appearance of shoal depths. The tidal streams, strong currents and races between these islands and the mainland must be guarded against . . . Landing is always dangerous and uncertain".'

At that my bravado deserted me. It was a reasonable risk to pass through one of their many channels by day, but not in my condition at night. I streamed both sea anchors, made yet another cup of coffee, lit a fag and continued my vigil, now interrupted by the necessity to bail. Only an hour of darkness to go.

'0520 – dawn and three grey lumps sneak from the veil of night and reveal themselves about 2 miles dead downwind! These are the three western islands of the group, lying roughly East-West, the tallest 600 feet high and all covered in rich vegetation. They stretched for about 3 miles right across my path.

'It appears we are being set to the NE but that may be an illusion – Do I go for a gap between them or for the western end? Wind continues SSE 20–25 knots, but sky clearing – we are getting closer, maybe a mile and a half now – I can see many birds.'

I wrote to myself in the log:

'Well Q, if you're going to go, go now – you might not get another chance to escape the coast. You got this far by a mixture of luck, seamanship and, I suppose, tenacity. The road to Aussie is there – take it! Take it!'

But all I wanted was sleep – my eyes kept closing, but finally:

'0610 – cleared the decks and prepared oars. I'd go for the western end. The oars didn't appear to be interested, my back protested quite a lot and the surface waves careering along made proper rowing impossible. The first two hours rowing resulted in little or no progress.

'I cursed, stopped rowing and made a cup of coffee.'

I hadn't bothered to re-stream the sea anchors and we were closing the islands fast. Then I noticed that TT appeared to be slowly creeping to the west on her own, her bow facing Australia. I wasn't steering.

I watched and waited as transits passed on the islands – it was right – this marvellous little boat had found herself a counter-current and we were being set clear of the western end. Taking heart from this and a glimpse of the sun, I took to the oars to help her. Together we clawed around the end of West Island and then there was only the empty ocean between us and Australia.

We had made it – we had escaped the trap!

I noted: '1200 – position 3 miles due West of Three Kings Islands – left New Zealand to starboard! – one week exactly!'

Colin Quincey, Tasman Trespasser, *1977*

'MAN OVERBOARD!'

THE name of master mariner Captain Barry Thompson will long be connected with the New Zealand Coastguard movement, specifically as long-serving committee member and historian with his book Deeds Not Words, *the story of the New Zealand Coastguard published in 1995.*

After service in the British Merchant Service and Royal Naval Volunteer Reserve, he came ashore and became a respected marine insurance assessor in Auckland. As a founder trustee in 1972 of the Spirit of Adventure Trust, he was largely responsible for the decision to build a ship with square rig, setting up the challenge of 'going aloft' for thousands of trainees.

In 1947 he was eighteen, an indentured apprentice serving on Port Line ships on the New Zealand run. It would have taken only a mouthful of water, or a shark, or a crippling spasm of cramp for his career to have ended almost before it begun, in the middle of the Pacific on a warm December day.

During the era of the commercial square-rigged sailing ship, the cry 'All hands on deck!' would see the crew scurrying aloft, often at the onset of heavy weather and in pitch darkness, to battle with the elements on an upper yard while they struggled to shorten sail. Too often an unfortunate seaman, restricted in movement by oilskins and sea boots, fighting with the heavy, wet and sometimes freezing canvas, would lose his footing and plunge to his death a hundred feet below.

There was little chance of recovering him and little more to mark his disappearance than a formal entry in the official logbook. There would probably be a brief period of sadness amongst his shipmates but he would soon be forgotten.

But once the steamship replaced the sailing ship on most of the world's trade routes, the cry 'Man overboard!' was heard much less frequently. The improved manoeuvrability of steamships often made it possible to recover a seaman from the water.

About the last thing that a young man expects now, on going to sea for a career, is to find himself joining the ranks of those who have 'gone over the wall.'

The dawn of Monday 15 December 1947 heralded yet another typical, uneventful day at sea in the tropics as the Port Line motor vessel *Port Fremantle* headed across the Pacific Ocean. She had cleared the Panama Canal ten days earlier outward bound from England and was not due in Auckland for another ten days. The crew had settled into their usual routine and were enjoying the 'flying fish weather,' the sailors' name for fine, calm, tropical conditions. Each crossing of the Pacific tended to be very much like any other at this time of the year. We were eagerly looking forward to the prospect of perhaps ten weeks or so on the New Zealand coast over Christmas and the holiday period.

As an eighteen-year-old apprentice life had yet to impose its responsibilities upon me. I was single and greatly enjoying the career I had embarked on about two years previously. Life was good and the world was treating me very kindly.

On that Monday morning most of us were giving little thought to anything more serious than what we would be having for breakfast and what job the mate would expect us to carry out today.

I was the senior of the two apprentices in the ship and the mate, Mr Dunn, with whom I had previously sailed in the *Port Adelaide* a year or so earlier, gave me the job of painting the starboard accommodation ladder (gangway) which had been turned out horizontally over the side at main deck level for the purpose.

The job was quite a pleasant one for that cloudless fine tropical morning. I really enjoyed painting and when I turned to after breakfast and started work I was comfortably dressed in a pair of old painting shorts and shoes. I did not have to concentrate too much on the job in hand. I was accompanied by two quartermasters and two spaniels which were part of our cargo en route to their owners in New Zealand and under my tender care for the passage.

Somewhere around 10.30, and with the prospect of 'smoko' coming up, I had painted my way to the end of the still horizontal accommodation ladder. It had an adjustable, small hinged platform at its extremity and, as it was going to be easier for me to stand there to carry on with my painting, I did so, cautiously at first. I saw no reason for not putting my whole weight on it.

Whoosh! Before I realised what was happening the platform tilted and I was on my way. Little did I know that when the accommodation ladder was overhauled in Liverpool before sailing, its bottom platform had not been refitted properly. Ah well, it was a little too late to be worrying now.

I fell feet first, still upright, and must have covered about twenty feet by the time I reached the water. Although I had only a second or two in which to think, I made up my mind that I was not going to allow myself to be sucked into the dreaded propellers. The ship was deeply laden and making about fourteen knots. Apart from my entry into the water I never felt anything untoward and did not become conscious of the pull towards the propellers that sometimes puts an early end to the saga of man overboard. I did not go very deep and I was soon well clear of the ship and on the surface again.

Until that moment there had hardly been time for any thoughts other than those of getting clear as quickly as possible. Now, well clear of it, I was able to stop and think again. I was alone, very alone, and, unlike me, the ship was by no means stopped. She was still continuing on her way on her customary fourteen knots. There was no point in trying to swim after her.

This was suddenly the moment when I was facing stark reality. Utterly alone in the water, I felt very insignificant and very humble. There was not very much that I could do about my predicament. Many thoughts flooded through my head but above all I simply felt stupid. So very, very stupid. Why on earth did I not have the sense to hang on to the gangway rails with at least one hand and try that platform more carefully before trusting my full weight to it? How could I have been so irresponsible?

The real question now was how long before they rescued me? I was pretty certain I had been seen by the two quartermasters working near me. I had certainly given a pitiful yell as I fell. Someone must have heard it. I did not then know, but was told later, that the two dogs nearby became very agitated. I like to think that even if the quartermasters had not been able to give the alarm then my two faithful long-haired companions would have done so.

It was not long before the ship responded and I could imagine that Captain Hazlewood must have been on that bridge mighty quickly as he heard the officer of the watch raise the alarm.

I could so vividly picture my cabin on board with all my clothes hanging exactly where I had left them when I had changed into my working gear little more than an hour earlier. If only I had been more careful I could have been back there now, enjoying a cup of tea during 'smoko.'

Then the thought of sharks occurred to me. Fortunately I did not know until later that the fourth mate had seen sharks the previous day. Anyway there was not much point in dwelling on that subject for long and I soon dismissed it from my head. I was more intent upon watching the ship.

It was not long before she responded, to my enormous relief, and turned around to retrace her course to where I fell. But then the ship passed by me not very far away and apparently without anyone seeing me. My heart sank. Back down her original track she steamed for a mile or so until Captain Hazlewood realised that they had missed me and should turn round again for another look.

For all my previous optimism, things were not going too well for me. The wind was just strong enough to raise a few 'white horses' and the sea was sufficiently choppy to make swimming difficult. From high up on the ship's bridge, the officers must have thought I was fortunate the sea was so calm, but from my perspective it was far from calm. Fortunately, having only a relatively loose pair of shoes on my feet, I was able to kick them off and this helped me to stay afloat. I could at least tread water without too much difficulty

I must have been in the water for about twenty minutes by now. Although my common sense reactions told me that my chances of being seen, let alone being rescued, were diminishing as each minute ticked by, I never really let that worry me. I just did not want to think that way. After all, I could see the ship and she was doing all the right things, so surely I would soon be found? Or so I told myself.

How slowly the ship seemed to be returning. And how inconspicuous I knew my small black head must be in that huge ocean. I needed something to draw attention to my presence and soon I had my shorts off and was waving them frantically. Suddenly, I felt much less encumbered in the water. Not long afterwards they were snatched from me by a wave, but that was about the least of my worries.

Now the seconds began to tick by slowly. Although my plight was steadily becoming more desperate, I still managed to find a peace and calm. Throughout my ordeal I never lost faith that I would be rescued for I have always had strong religious convictions. I was alone in one sense but I knew that I was never really alone. I could understand how self-professed atheists, confronted by the horror of trench warfare on the Western Front in World War One, had acknowledged that they felt a presence, at times far stronger than themselves and their comrades.

As I waited for the ship to get back to me I found myself compelled to call out the necessary helm orders to the Captain to enable him to find me.

'Starboard ten. Ease to five. Midships, then steady!'

I knew, of course, that he could not possibly hear me but somehow I just had to call out these orders. It gave me some comfort, and kept my mind busy too.

The ship was getting close now but her course would still take her a little too far to starboard of me.

'Port five,' then, 'Midships,' I called, and a moment later 'I am dead ahead. Steady as you go.'

Then someone did spot me and waved back. At last I had been seen and could hope to be rescued quite soon. But after the long time in the water – I suppose it must have been half an hour or so – I was getting cramp in my legs and stomach. I was always prone to attacks of cramp when I swam and only the warmth of the water on this occasion had delayed its onset. But I had to keep going and stick it I would.

The ship stopped. She was not very far away now and although I was keen to keep moving to ease the cramp I did not at first feel inclined to try to swim to the ship. I decided they could come and get me! Then, after a short while, I became conscious that someone else was in the water besides me. I could not possibly have seen what was happening when a starboard lifeboat was being lowered as I was a hundred yards or so off the port side of the ship, out of sight of the events occurring on the other side of her. Somehow I just knew that I was not alone in the water. Telepathy or what? Who knows.

The *Port Fremantle* was quite an elderly ship and by modern standards she had old-fashioned gear for launching her lifeboats. I did not learn till afterwards that as the boat was being lowered the rope falls were not paid out evenly. Someone held on to the forward fall instead of lowering the bow of the lifeboat. With the after end of the boat continuing to drop and with the bow hung up, the unfortunate mate, who was in the stern, fell out of the boat. I had to await my turn to be picked up. Even in the middle of the Pacific it was necessary to queue for some things!

Meanwhile the motor lifeboat, on the port side, in charge of the second mate, had been lowered and a rope ladder was put over the side for me. Although this second lifeboat was now ready to rescue me, I decided to swim to the ladder and climbed up to the deck above, stark naked, to the horror of the lady passengers who had been watching the drama unfold.

Arriving on deck exhausted the doctor greeted me and took me up to the Sick Bay.

'Give me a massage please, Doc,' was all that I said. I think he was almost disappointed that I did not wish to avail myself more fully of his professional skills and equipment. I needed little more than to have my cramped muscles relieved, otherwise I was little the worse for my experience.

I soon recovered and went up to my cabin which I had last seen a couple of hours earlier. Everything was just as I had recalled it while in the water. Oh, what a fool I had been!

The ship was soon under way again. The 'Old Man' and the mate came down to see me shortly afterwards and not surprisingly they were very relieved to find me looking so hale and hearty. Surely somebody should have made sure that I was wearing a lifeline. There is nobody more precious than an indentured apprentice as far as the Company is concerned and to have lost one at sea would have been a very 'black mark' on their careers. The last time a Port Line apprentice had gone over the side, he was lost at sea.

With my ordeal over I was looking forward to a quiet afternoon after my morning's exertion but the mate sent for me after lunch. He had other ideas.

'I want you to varnish the woodwork on the wings of the bridge.'

No doubt I went away muttering about 'bully' mates and the woes of being an apprentice, but it did not prove too arduous a task. Later in the day he sent for me again and said, 'You probably thought me a right b . . . making you work this afternoon?'

Leaving that remark to sink in, he said, 'I did the best thing for you. I didn't want you to lie in your bunk and have time to brood over your morning's adventure.'

He was quite right of course. And Dicky Dunn was certainly not the proverbial bully of a mate. Quite the reverse. Nor was Captain Joe Hazlewood a hard man either. The *Port Fremantle* was a happy ship and both of the men responsible for me were gentlemen, even through the eyes of an apprentice!

Ten days later it was Christmas and on Boxing day we arrived in Auckland. I was mighty glad to see Auckland and by then I had almost forgotten all about the incident. But this was not to be for long. A young reporter from the local evening newspaper, the Auckland Star, managed to ferret out the story from the crew and the newspaper ran a front page account headed 'Fall Overboard and Pacific Rescue.' If the story had to be told, well, at least it was told correctly and not too sensationally.

Perhaps now I really could begin to forget about the incident. But no, not that easy. I thought that one day I might possibly tell my father as he would be interested and would tell me what a fool I had been, but I certainly did not intend to tell my mother, who would only worry for as long as I remained at sea. But I had not reckoned that newspapers syndicate their copy. There was an account of my swim in a Wellington newspaper. It was read by the girl friend of my nautical college chum, Peter Johnson. She wrote to Peter telling him of his friend's exploit. Then on leave from his ship and at home in Liverpool, Peter promptly picked up the telephone and rang my mother.

'Did you know that Barry had fallen overboard in the middle of the Pacific?' he said.

It was several anxious moments before my mother managed to get out of him that Barry was now safe and sound on board his ship in New Zealand. As I learnt to my chagrin, even fifty years ago global communications could be pretty effective.

Even today I can not keep my experience entirely to myself. On board, at the time of my rescue, was a young ordinary seaman working his passage back to New Zealand after a couple of years in England. I hardly knew him then, and it was to be many years later before we met again by chance in the street in Auckland, by then my own adopted home city.

That young seaman was Alan Haddock who later, in 1974, became the founding President of the Royal New Zealand Coastguard Federation at just the same time that I was the President of the Auckland Volunteer Coastguard Service. Our interests were now closely interwoven in the Coastguard movement in New Zealand, twenty-seven years after we had been involved in our first search and rescue operation together in the South Pacific Ocean! Just occasionally, and in the nicest possible way, Alan reminds me of my indiscretion as a young apprentice many years ago.

Captain Barry Thompson, Man Overboard! unpublished memoirs, *1999*

BOATS AND BLOKES

MOST *amateur yacht races on coastal passages happen without major incident or public awareness. Occasionally, though, around the notorious New Zealand coast, a race runs foul of unforeseen weather, tragically making headlines and maritime history.*

George Brasell, an experienced Christchurch yachtsman, fisherman and boatbuilder, set out as navigator in the yacht Joy *on the 1951 Centennial Yacht Race from Wellington to Lyttelton.*

Along with others who read the warning signs of an approaching 'stinking southerly gale' more accurately than the weather forecasters, the crew of Joy, *with the owner's family aboard, decided to retire from the race. But for what happened next, George Brasell was to win a gold medal from the Royal Humane Society of New Zealand. He hastily flew back to Christchurch, where his 58ft trawler* Tawera, *a sturdy vessel he designed and built himself five years earlier, was standing by . . .*

There was no sign of Kaikoura Light or anything else except windswept water that night in January 1951. With the wind blowing 80 mph and our steering veering up to 20 degrees on some of the seas, our position was just a wild guess. Soon after daybreak, with visibility nil and the gale unabated, we judged the distance steamed to be far enough. Some time after we have hove-to, about 20 miles offshore north of Kaikoura, through a gap in the clouds Archie Childs spotted a plane circling. Our radio frequency was different from that of the aircraft so we contacted the fishermen's shore station at Kaikoura. They phoned the plane's base and the pilot was informed that we had spotted them. Although they could not see us from the plane we were able to communicate by this roundabout system. We were told the plane was circling over the dismasted race yacht *Astral*. They had found her the day before but could do nothing to help because of the force of the wind and the terrific seas that were running, and had returned to base. They had sighted the yacht again on the second day while heading for their base after a search in weather which was really too hazardous for low flying. We gave *Tawera* all she could take and steamed towards the spot where we had seen the plane circling. Within fifteen minutes *Astral* was occasionally visible to us on top of the heaving sea. The pilot was so jubilant at being able to hand over to us that he spontaneously swooped down and took a photo of us before returning to base. At one time I thought we might have to rescue a plane as well as a yacht. I heard from the pilot later that when he arrived back at base the old Anson had holes in the fuselage from the force of the wind and was nearly out of fuel.

The breakers were 50 to 100 feet apart at times and nearly as high. Our 58 ft trawler appeared small and helpless when we were down in a trough peering up to the top of a cracking wave which seemed impossible to ride. Having designed and built her myself, I knew that everything of the best had been put into the construction of *Tawera* and for that I was very thankful.

We had no worry about our vessel – the problem was how much the crew could stand. I was fortunate to have with me men who would not scare easily and were prepared to put up with any hardship.

We quickly assessed the position. The weather forecast (wrong again) was for the wind to ease. We considered it our first priority to get the men off alive so we decided to secure *Astral* with a long tow line and hold her head to sea until the wind abated. I realised later that this was the wrong decision because after a hell of a night we had to take the men off in conditions that were just as bad.

Securing a tow line was a major job. Positioning *Tawera* to throw a heaving line across the yacht without a collision seemed almost impossible. After a lot of manoeuvring, our anchor rope, 60 fathoms of heavy manila, was hauled aboard by *Astral*'s crew and securely fastened, with chafing gear wrapped around the rope where it would rub on the yacht's bow. We then paid out 100 fathoms of our trawl wire and headed as slowly as possible into the sea.

Darkness was approaching by this time. We were tired and very conscious of the fact that we would pull the yacht to pieces if we put on too much power. Our tow wire was long enough to lie in a deep bight in the water without ever stretching out straight, which would be fatal to anything on the end of it. Nevertheless they had a hell of a ride on the end of the tow. Finally, in the middle of the night, and in spite of all their efforts to prevent it, the rope chafed through where it passed over their bow and they were adrift again.

Astral had power left in the battery and the crew had rigged a small light on deck. One of our men was on lookout. He was lashed to the mast, with the sole object of watching for their light which only showed like a glow-worm when Astral occasionally bobbed up on top of a huge wave.

Precious time had elapsed before we noticed that their light was no longer showing. We then had the job of hauling in our trawl wire and tow rope. The belt drive to the winch was wet like everything else and it was some time before we could get the winch working. Our crew were very despondent when we eventually steamed back over the course with *Tawera* trying to tie a knot in herself and visibility very poor. Luckily they were able to keep the light showing on *Astral* and there was great excitement when we spotted it right on our course.

All we could do now was attempt to keep their light in view until daylight. This was a major job as it was impossible to keep *Tawera* on a steady course. Every time the light showed, which was only when we were both on top of a wave at the same time, it appeared in a different direction. Our lookout was having a hell of a time on deck finding their light and passing the direction back to me at the helm. We then noticed they were trying to send a message by morse code with a torch. At first we thought it was SOS but we finally translated it as OIL. We realised then they were in real trouble and wanted oil on the waters to smooth the tops of the breakers.

Up to this time we had been manoeuvring to leeward to the yacht, but to spread oil we had to steam to windward and zig-zag our course. Our spare twelve-gallon drum of lubricating oil was brought up from the engine room, lashed to the trawl davit, and punctured enough to allow a small flow of oil.

Tawera had a steering wheel which was three feet in diameter and fairly heavy to handle, being linked by chain to the rudder quadrant. We were all weary and aching all over from our constant battering and I had been at the helm for about 30 hours relieved occasionally by my cobber and mainstay in this rescue operation, Archie Childs. Anything we had to do was a major job, but we managed to hold *Tawera* to windward of *Astral*, spreading oil in a zig-zag course for the rest of that long, unforgettable night.

Working on deck was hazardous. The force of the wind blew your voice back into your mouth and the only way to talk to your mate was to yell right in his ear. At one time Archie reported to me that the engine room hatch was off. All hands were called to the job while I eased her into the gale as quietly as possible.

Seas were rolling aboard green and occasionally carrying the men bodily across the deck. At one time Archie was hanging on behind the mast as though he was in love with it. Cecil Welsh yelled in his ear, 'Wrap yourself around the weather side, you silly fool, or the sea will tear you away.' Nevertheless the work was done by sheer determination, in spite of every difficulty.

Brian Millar, skipper and owner of *Astral*, explained to me later that the seas were breaking so heavily aboard the yacht that water was coming through the cabin top which had been damaged when their mast broke and they were having trouble keeping up with the bailing and pumping. He assured me that the oil spreading was well worthwhile.

By daybreak we were exhausted. The wind force was still about 80 mph with no sign of the sea moderating. We decided there was no option but to take the men off the yacht by means of a heaving line, a full coil of manila rope with a heavy shackle attached.

Our first try was from the leeward side of *Astral*. This was unsuccessful as it was impossible to get close enough to throw a line without the risk of collision. Our next try was to run down wind and throw the line across the bow while passing. *Tawera* went past with a flurry of breaking seas and there was no time to throw a line. We circled again for the third try and came in bow to bow, slightly to windward of *Astral* on the same sea, and the line was thrown across the bow.

In the meantime *Astral*'s crew had held a conference and decided there was little chance of being hauled aboard *Tawera* alive; they could see right down to our keel at times and *Tawera* was really cutting capers. Their skipper had hurt his back so they decided to send him first as he was not much use to them!

He wrapped the rope around his waist, hopped in the drink and my crew started hauling him aboard. *Tawera* had cocked her stern into the wind and was bearing down on *Astral* so I was forced to put her full bore astern to avoid a collision. She went stern first into the gale and bowled one over the stern right to the wheelhouse. The rudder was bashed across from one side to the other. The wheel spun out of my hands and nearly threw me out the door. Thank God the steering gear was designed to stand this treatment and nothing broke.

My crew in the meantime were sitting back in the breeching, hauling Brian Miller alongside. They had the sense to bring him in only when *Tawera* was rolling down with her gunwale under water. They knew that if he was allowed to fall under the bilge, one roll would probably be the finish of him. He had taken in quite a lot of water but apart from that he was okay, so we circled round again and came bow to bow as before, but with her stern this time slightly down wind.

My man on the heaving line, Cecil Welsh, had been a seaman. He was expert at throwing a heaving line and it landed right across the bow of the yacht. The next man was brought aboard with less trouble and *Tawera* was positioned again for each man, the last one arriving with his kitbag under his arm which contained dry clothing and a bottle of rum. We then sadly left *Astral* to her fate, put on the kettle and a pot of savs, took a nip from their rum bottle to warm us up and headed in the general direction of Wellington.

When I say 'general direction' I mean just that. We had been floundering around for two days with no sight of land, being pushed here and there by the wind and waves and just guessing our position. Although the wind had eased slightly, conditions were still bad and we still had the problem of finding Wellington Heads and entering them. *Tawera* was a champion in a running sea and steamed away before the gale beautifully. The crew set to work making everything shipshape and attended to the engine which had purred away all this time with practically no attention.

Land showed up but we had missed Wellington Heads and were heading in towards Island Bay on the west side of the entrance. Several yachtsmen and fishermen had received news that we had missed the entrance to the harbour and were in broken water to the west. They motored around to where they had a view of us battling offshore. One fisherman told me later that he saw *Tawera* perched on top of a huge breaker with both ends showing clear of the water.

Just when I was thinking we could relax as we were passing Barrett Reef, a huge sea came from nowhere, lifted her stern and she started to broach. I hauled her back on course again and yelled to Ray Clark on the gear lever and throttle to put her out of gear. He looked at me with surprise and said, 'She is out of gear'. The old tub was racing along on top of a breaker with no power.

About this time we noticed a yacht entering the harbour under small jib only. It was the *Ruawhaka*. She had almost reached Cape Campbell when she was submerged in a terrific sea which tore the bolts through the side of the cabin. The crew had been forced to make temporary repairs by stuffing blankets and clothing into the seams and cracks to keep them afloat. They had taken a terrific battering off Cape Campbell and had averaged eleven knots under bare poles back to Wellington from Banks Peninsula. As we came into calmer water in the harbour we went alongside *Ruawhaka* for a yarn and passed them a line to tow them into the boat harbour. What a relief to be tied up at last alongside the breastwork. The only problem was how to cope with the scores of visitors, friends and reporters wanting first-hand information.

The ill-fated race, which saw us out rescuing *Astral*'s crew, had been put on by the Banks Peninsula Cruising Club as part of the Canterbury Province centennial celebrations and the course from Wellington to Lyttelton took the entrants down 200 miles of exposed coast with virtually nowhere to shelter in an emergency. I had been approached by Claude Smith, the owner and builder of the yacht *Joy*, to navigate her in the race. As we were busy fishing in our trawler *Tawera*, and making arrangements for a regatta at home in Lyttelton, I decided to fly to Wellington and join the *Joy* there.

Just before the race was due to start, the organiser, Lt Commander Arthur Lambert, came to me for a yarn about the weather and we decided to ring the meteorological office and get the latest forecast. The official forecast we received at 0900 hrs on 23 January 1951 was: 'Light to moderate northerlies in the Wellington area; moderate easterlies across Cook Strait; moderate to strong north-easterlies on the Canterbury coast.'

The weather sounded so good that Arthur rang his club in Lyttelton and told them to expect us to finish early as we would have the wind up our tails. Even at this stage a stinking southerly gale was approaching the South Island but we were given no warning of it. Harry Kingham, an old yachtie friend of mine, was working in the Met Office in Timaru and he rang Wellington to warn them of the change down south and advised them to change their forecast but they were either too pig-headed or too ignorant to make any change. Even the evening forecast which we received during the race stated: 'Fresh easterly winds, overcast weather and mild with periods of rain. Further outlook dull and mild. A deep depression over North Island moving southwards.' With this sort of forecast there was no reason to postpone the race.

We were late across the starting line in *Joy* and tailed the fleet to Wellington Heads where we were becalmed for some time until the weather came in from the east. As we approached Cape Campbell the weather deteriorated and visibility was very poor. We were reduced to a jib and mizzen and everyone was wet. The owner of *Joy* had his wife, daughter and son aboard and they were battened down below. After a discussion between Ossie Wilks and Claude Smith we decided to turn back to Wellington and were pleased to be back in Oriental Bay boat harbour before the approaching gale from the south really got going.

Several of the yachts returned to Wellington early in the race. *Restless* retired early, taking water seriously. *Nanette* retired because a crew member had hurt his back. *Caru* also retired early. Arthur Lambert with Les Taylor and John Doleman, in *Banika*, were south of Cape Campbell, reefed right down and plugging into the freshening southerly. They also decided to head back for Wellington, but while crossing Cook Strait *Banika* was knocked down and completely submerged. Arthur and Les were fortunate enough to be able to cling to the mizzen mast while she was submerged. *Banika* came up just long enough for them to get their breath before she was submerged again by seas running across the direction of the gale. John Doleman (Dauntless John) was preparing a meal below and he found himself collecting food off the inside of the cabin top. Luckily the companionway was securely fastened and very little water went below. About this time Arthur spotted a yacht to seaward of them which he considered would be the ill-fated *Argo*. The cross seas which overwhelmed *Banika* could have been the downfall of *Argo*.

The next day those of us who had returned to Wellington were receiving bad news of the race. Realising that I might be needed in Lyttelton with *Tawera*, I booked a berth in the inter-island ferry. In the meantime I received a telegram from my wife Olive: '*Tawera* out searching for yachts. Stores and fuel ready. Expecting you, Olive.' I hastily cancelled my ferry booking and caught the first available plane, arriving home in Lyttelton that afternoon. Archie Childs had just arrived back in *Tawera* and was standing by with my crew. The local yachties were at the Banks Peninsula Cruising Club, gloomily listening to reports when I arrived. The news was not good.

The only yacht still battling through was *Tawhiri* from Nelson. She was a beautiful boat for ocean cruising and although hove-to with very little sail she had gradually made slight headway through the gale. Much to their surprise, the crew found that they were approaching Banks Peninsula and went on to win the race.

There was no word from *Argo*. Her crew were: Skipper Jack Young, Alan Baker, Malcolm Mace, Alan Henderson, A Feilding and C L Pickering. *Argo* had run on the stern of *Annette* just after the start of the race and damaged her bobstay. Temporary repairs were carried out but several of the yachtsmen were of the opinion that this might have given her trouble in the full gale when she would be hove-to. Nothing was ever heard of *Argo* again and it is presumed that she foundered while hove-to well offshore. Jack Young, her owner and skipper, was an experienced yachtsman who had sailed extensively in the Hauraki Gulf and off South Africa. He had been granted a post entry after his yacht had been slipped for examination and found seaworthy.

Tawera, with my old friend Archie Childs in charge, had just returned from her search off Lyttelton heads in company with a navy launch. Further reports were coming in and *Astral* was reported with a broken mast somewhere north of Kaikoura. No word of the little *Aurora*, the smallest of the fleet and no word of *Husky*, skippered by my friend Arthur Clements who had sailed with me in the Navy during the war. Many of the yachts were sheltering in Kaikoura and planes were out searching in weather which they should not be flying in. The wind force was about 80 mph and seas were running at about 30 feet.

The Lyttelton Harbour Board and the Navy could do nothing, so I decided to leave immediately in *Tawera*, which appeared to be the only boat suitable to put to sea and stay out and work in this weather. Some of the yachtsmen thought I was wasting my time and that the position was hopeless. I decided that, by leaving at once, with the southerly gale up our tail, we could be in the search area off the Clarence River by next day, so I called for volunteers to boost my crew and several immediately offered their services.

Tawera was a beautiful hull in a running sea, her deep bow and full shoulders keeping her up and easy to steer. She rolled like a son of a bitch side on, but in a head sea she just kept pegging on without having to push the throttle down. If you did, she only took more water for'ard. The harder it blew the better she liked it. There was no chance of her falling to pieces. Neither the boat nor the crew let me down when the pressure was on.

When we finally got back to Wellington with *Astral*'s crew, the magnitude of the race disaster was just hitting home – Wellington yacht *Argo* was missing with six men aboard and the Lyttelton yacht *Husky* was missing with four men aboard.

Wreckage of the unfortunate *Husky* was later found in Owhiro Bay. She had evidently been forced off her course to the west while heading for

Wellington Heads as Arthur Lambert and I had been. *Husky*'s crew were Arthur Clements, Kelvin Hopkinson, Kevin Clark and Harvey Mason. Kevin Clark's brother Ray was one of my crew in *Tawera* and the early reports of the missing *Husky* made things very hard for him. *Husky* was slightly under the minimum length for yachts allowed in the race but was given a special permit as she was very heavily constructed and rigged. I am sure that Arthur Clements would have survived the storm if he had not missed the entrance to Wellington Harbour.

The only other yacht still not accounted for was the smallest of the fleet, the little 22 ft *Aurora* from Dunedin. Skipper and owner Neil Brown, a very experienced yachtsman, had just completed a cruise in Aurora from Dunedin to Suva and Rarotonga. Although she was under the specified length of the race, Neil had received special permission to enter because of his previous ocean cruising experience. This dispensation proved justified when it was found that *Aurora* was hove-to away out in deep water, well clear of the land. While riding to a sea anchor, *Aurora* drifted as far north as Napier. We learned later that a large vessel approached them with an offer of assistance but Neil and his two young crewmen, sixteen and seventeen years of age, just waved them on cheerily, saying that they were okay.

On looking back on all incidents such as this I often wonder, did I do the correct thing at all times? Should I have taken the men off *Astral* when I first found them although the risk was great. Then there was the possibility of their small yacht breaking up when we had her in tow, and when we lost them from the tow line in the dark we might never have found them again. They were a very resourceful and experienced crew and might have survived without our help. We were very fortunate that we hove-to only a few miles from the helpless yacht, when we were not even sure of our own position. I was fortunate that my crew members were so loyal and never hesitated to act on any decision I made no matter what the conditions were.

There is one thing I have learned over the years: the captain of his ship, be it ten foot or whatever size, is in command; anything happening while he is in command is his responsibility, especially if he makes the wrong decision.

George Brasell, Boats and Blokes, *1991*

THE 1994 PACIFIC RESCUE

THREE times within the last twenty years, yacht race fleets have dramatically found a place in maritime history – the 1979 Fastnet, the 1994 Pacific cruising race from Auckland to Tonga, and the 1998 Sydney-Hobart classic.

Of the three, the challenges facing the rescuers of the 1994 Tonga-bound fleet were undoubtedly the toughest: how to rescue nine distressed yachts caught in the middle of the south Pacific by a Force 12 weather 'bomb' that raged unabated over a vast area, more than 234,000 square miles, for four days.

Over 72 hours, twenty-one people were rescued from seven disabled and sinking yachts. Orion aircraft crews and professional merchant seamen recorded mountainous waves 100ft high, surface winds reaching up to 90 knots.

Only one boat (Quartermaster, with three aboard) was lost – testament to the skill and stamina of the New Zealand-based rescue services with ships from the New Zealand and French navies, a fishing boat, two freighters and the Royal New Zealand Airforce; not forgetting the courage of the amateur sailors involved and the luckier others of the 60-strong fleet who escaped the very worst of the storm's path and successfully battled through to Tonga.

Commander Larry Robbins was in command of the Royal New Zealand Navy hydrographic survey ship HMNZS Monowai that Queen's Birthday weekend. A Kentishman, he had joined the RNZ Navy in 1974 with a British Merchant Service second mate's ticket. He'd had his share of storms at sea, hurricane conditions once before, in 1973 in the North Atlantic, when a ship had been lost.

For his part in the 1994 operation, Commander Robbins was to win the O.B.E. and the crew of the Monowai a Chief of Naval Staff special commendation. Commendations also went to Leading Seaman Abraham Whata, Able Seaman Linton Hemopo and Leading Medical Assistant Michael Wiig.

178 SALT BENEATH THE SKIN

When I took command of *Monowai* at the end of January 1994 more than half my naval service had been in the ship. On May 31 we sailed from Auckland for a planned three-month deployment to the South Pacific Islands. Our intention was to undertake surveying work in Tonga, and around the Northern Cook group, especially at the atoll of Penrhyn.

Because of the planned length of the deployment the ship was carrying an orthopaedic surgeon from Christchurch, John Talbot, a surgeon commander in the Reserves. Our first call was to Raoul Island, initially to re-supply the weather station, but where an injured Conservation Department volunteer needed medical assistance. It was about 1100 on the Saturday morning, June 3, when we finally headed away from Raoul Island. It was a beautiful day, everything you could wish for a South Pacific deployment, the sun coruscating across the calm sea, just a very gentle swell and the ship heading purposefully north.

While we were at anchor on the Friday, I had listened to a VHF conversation between a yacht in the other anchorage at Raoul and the weather station discussing the likely forecast. The guy on Raoul Island had indicated that the weather looked reasonably good, although he did call attention to a depression that appeared to be forming over Fiji. I had not previously noticed this system forming, so watched our fax records as they came through. I noted that the depression was deepening and moving steadily towards the south east. That did not concern me at all, as it was clearly going to pass south of *Monowai*'s track.

Indeed, I recall saying to one of the watch-keeping officers as the fax came in, 'Gosh, I would not like to be in the way of that lot,' pointing to the depression. Prescient words indeed.

Around midday that day we received a signal asking us to alter course to the south west and proceed to a position where a yacht was experiencing difficulties. This yacht, the *Mary T* was reported to have four people on board, two of the crew disabled due to the motion, and she was taking on water. She had thus issued a PAN warning indicating that she was requiring some assistance but was not actually in a full state of distress. I was somewhat puzzled by the request as the position given for *Mary T* was some 420 miles from our current position. We altered course anyway while we sorted the matter out. It later transpired that our position had been wrongly transmitted that morning (we were close to the dateline and our 'west' longitude had been wrongly transmitted as 'east') and so it was believed that we were within 70 miles of the yacht. However, by the time it had been established that another vessel was closer, various yachts were reporting themselves in distress down in that part of the ocean. We carried on our southwesterly course.

As we did so the sea conditions slowly built up. As the depression was on our starboard beam, that is to the north west, the seas were also coming in from the beam and the rolling of the ship built up as we moved towards the reported positions. By the evening time the sea had built up such that the ship was rolling about 35 degrees either way. My impression was of the old sailing ships rounding Cape Horn. The ship would roll one way, water would sluice along the main deck (6 1/2 metres above the waterline), the ship would give a bit of a shudder and then roll the other way and water would then foam down the other side of the deck. It was particularly impressive at night as the back-scatter from the navlights caught the phosphorescent foam.

The ship was in no immediate danger and I felt that it was important that we maintain our course directly towards the yachts. We had some problems from scuttles (portholes) leaking. These scuttles were normally above the water line and are perhaps best described as 'water resistant'. They certainly were not designed to be submerged for a number of seconds at a time. We also suffered the ingress of water from around the main doors from the accommodation out onto the main deck. As she rolled the ship was being hit with the occasional wave and water was seeping in from around the wooden edge of the doors. Under normal circumstances this was not a problem. However that night it made for slippery and dangerous conditions inside and we had junior ratings working through the evening mopping up. Indeed at one stage, about 2200, I did a glorious cartoon-like slip coming out of my pantry and landed heavily on to my wrist and arm. I remember thinking 'that is all we need in a situation like this – the Captain with a broken arm!' Fortunately, although the wrist still troubles me, it was nothing serious.

There was not much sleep to be had that night. The heavy and continuous rolling of the ship made it more than a little tedious and the wooden joinery and the partitioning inside the ship creaked and groaned somewhat alarmingly. My cabin, as I recall, looked something like a train crash. The loose furniture, the upright chairs, had all been laid down on the deck under the table as was our normal practice, but with the considerable motion of the ship these were sliding around the cabin. My steward secured them in the corner of the cabin using a couple of heaving lines. The armchairs in the corner and the table were attached to the bulkhead so they were not a problem. In my sleeping cabin I found that no matter how well one tried to stow one's gear there seemed always to be something to roll around to keep one awake. It took me several goes to get to the stage where any mobile items such as cans of Coke and the like were sufficiently jammed by towels, jumpers and so on. Around midnight with the ship rolling 35–40 degrees either way I ordered an alteration of course about 40 degrees to starboard to put the sea more on the bow and to ease the rolling of the ship.

The senior ratings' beer cooler, installed in the ship some seventeen years earlier, pulled away from the bulkhead and other fixed equipment was showing similar signs of strain. The only cargo or non-ship fittings to carry away, a couple of drums of cleaning liquid down in the forward hold, had sprung their lashings and destroyed the PTI's bicycle. It occurred to me that we would be no use to anyone if we arrived in the position having destroyed ourselves in the process. We had only been able to make about five knots with the sea on the beam and our speed increased to at least 6 1/2 knots with the sea on the bow. So the penalty of longer distance was ameliorated slightly by the small advance in speed.

There was, however, still a lot of motion! I lay on my bunk trying to get at least some rest although my efforts were thwarted. Having finally secured the drawers, the magnetic stays gave way. The drawers would open and shut as the ship rolled, with a suitably loud clunk each time. I ended up with all of my cabin drawers laid out neatly across the deck after copious applications of masking tape had failed to equal the strain.

Shortly before 4 a.m., I was phoned by the officer of the watch, Lieutenant Andrew Saunderson, who advised me that he had seen a bright light in the sky which he considered might have been a flare. He asked that I join him on the bridge. It was pitch black with no sign of any moon and raining heavily. There was a large sea running, a huge swell. The ship was still rolling a great deal. Andrew described what he had seen as a 'bright white sudden flash of light.' We decided that it did not sound much like a standard distress flare because those are normally red; if a white flare is fired, it is normally a parachute flare and thus of long duration. It was probably a meteorological phenomenon of one kind or another. I had seen something similar once when I was on watch on a lovely still evening-a meteor had ended in a flash which lit up the ship as would a camera's flash gun.

However, as Andrew did not seem totally convinced, I said that we would put out a call on the VHF, a radio system that has a relatively short range of perhaps 20–25 miles. If there was anyone around in that part of the ocean-which I thought doubtful-then we would be able to discuss the nature of their problem. So I picked up the VHF radio and put out a blind call on channel 16 saying 'This is warship *Monowai* in position ... Any vessel sighting or firing a white flare is requested to communicate. Warship *Monowai* listening – Out'.

I turned to Andrew and said, 'There we are. Nothing.' Suddenly, the radio crackled into life. An Australian yacht *Ramtha* indicated they too had seen a bright light – albeit that what they saw was green or orange. The position they gave was some fifteen miles ahead of us. It was obvious that no flare would be seen over that distance, which reinforced my view about it being a natural phenomenon. We discussed the situation with *Ramtha*. I was speaking with a female on board the boat who indicated that they were having a pretty dreadful time. She indicated that her husband said he was 'having a pretty bloody time of it' and if 'someone could take him off he'd go'.

I was a bit flummoxed by this because it did not sound like the standard call of distress that one is trained to expect. After a couple of moments thought, I said 'Yes, I know exactly how your husband feels madam, if someone could take me off here I would go too'. That rather served to keep them quiet for a while, but, essentially, I indicated that we were on our way to a vessel which had issued an urgency call and that if *Ramtha* was not in any immediate need of assistance I would report their position, course and speed to the Rescue Co-ordination Centre in Wellington. I told them we would keep a listening watch should matters develop.

There was not much sleep to be had down below. I propped myself in the Captain's chair on the bridge to gain whatever amount of doze I could. Around 0430 the radio again came to life and it was *Ramtha*. They indicated that they had taken a very large roll, lost the little bit of mainsail that they had out, their steering had been damaged and they now considered their situation to be dire. They asked if they could be taken off. This was very much more what I expected from a distress call but, given the conditions at the time, I said that I would stay in the area until daylight, about two hours later. We could perhaps assess the situation at that stage. We therefore continued our slow progress towards *Ramtha*'s position.

It was somewhat worrying to know there was another small vessel out there. We could see very little on the radar screen due to the incredible amount of clutter from the wave tops. At 0600 we called the hands early, advised them of the situation and put them on standby. As day dawned the actual weather conditions became clearer. The height of eye on *Monowai*'s bridge was a little over eleven metres and the mountainous seas at times towered over the bridge wing, with the crests of some waves breaking well over our heads. At other times we appeared to be sitting upon a mountaintop in a manner akin to the ark on Mount Ararat and could see for miles. The rain was horizontal. It was grey and grim. The anemometer showed the true wind to be a steady 60-65 knots with gusts over (sometimes well over) 80 knots. The air was full of wind driven spume.

It was readily apparent that there was absolutely no possibility of bringing *Monowai* alongside *Ramtha* in such conditions. The traditional rescue method is for the ship to bring herself alongside the yacht upwind, with cargo nets, ladders etc rigged on the lee side. The yacht crew would then climb nimbly up the nets to safety.

Monowai, though, was still rolling violently and ship handling was somewhat variable – to say the least. So this option was very quickly dismissed. I discussed the situation with my Executive Officer, Lieutenant Commander Hugh Aitken. We considered the possibility of floating a life buoy attached to a line across to the yacht. Ultimately, and I have to say that it was not my idea, we decided that a more certain method was to use our line-throwing rifle to pass *Ramtha* a line to which would be attached two rescue harnesses. We would pass these harnesses across to the crew of *Ramtha* and instruct them that on our signal they were to enter the water. We would then pull them across to the ship. We briefed the Chief Bosun's Mate (CPOS Nathan) and the ship's Petty Officer Seaman (POS Jackson) accordingly. They mustered the seamen and surveyor ratings in the forward vehicle deck and prepared the equipment.

We had great trouble keeping sight of *Ramtha* from the bridge due to the sea conditions. Indeed, on more than one occasion we had to ask *Ramtha* for an approximate compass bearing of us from the yacht so that we could reverse the calculation to eyeball the yacht. We could often only locate them by seeing the mast break the horizon. We had all our deck lights turned on so that *Ramtha* could see us. The radar was totally useless in such conditions. A complicating factor was the very slow speeds required to maintain our position and manoeuvre towards *Ramtha*; the rolling caused the main engine cooling water intakes (which are well down towards the keel) to come out of the water. The consequent intake of air would cause one or other of the engines to overheat momentarily and to shut itself down. I endeavoured to remain calm and phlegmatic under such trying circumstances, though that was far from the way I was feeling. We made our first approach to *Ramtha*. It was about that stage that the enormity of the task ahead came to me.

When we were a few minutes away from the yacht, we called the fo'c'sle crew up on deck to prepare the recovery lines. The deck crew were wearing life jackets but we felt that additional lifelines would be more of a hindrance than a help, except for the two gunners who needed to position themselves at the rail. The deck crew were quite stoic; as they prepared the lines on the starboard side, *Monowai* would take a large roll, fall off a wave, and we were then lining up for a port side approach. So they would quickly unshackle the line and move it over to the other side in time to for the operation to be repeated in reverse. My earlier view, that putting *Monowai* alongside *Ramtha* was not a viable option, was well justified.

We made our approach and ended up with *Ramtha* close by our starboard side at about twenty metres off. The line was fired and taken in hand by Robyn Forbes but to our great chagrin we saw the line break. By the time the gun line had been recovered the two vessels had blown a considerable distance apart despite my best efforts with engines and bow thruster. We lumbered around in a large circle and made a second approach. The fo'c'sle crew were called on deck and the earlier processes repeated. The manoeuvring and the slow speed caused the ship to roll considerably and at one stage our instruments recorded a roll of some 48°. I was never terribly concerned for the safety of the ship as a whole. *Monowai* was only four days out of port and thus had an almost full complement of fuel and water in her double bottom tanks low down in the ship. I was aware from the ship's stability information that her angle of maximum stability under such conditions was 58° whilst in theory her stability does not go negative until 88°. Theory, I reflected, is a wonderful thing; given my experiences with the cabin furniture, and the senior ratings' beer cooler the night before, I felt that long before 88°, everything on the high side of the ship would be joining all of us on the low side, and the equation would be rapidly changing.

I was more concerned for the safety of the deck crew because had any of them slipped and fallen through the guard rails, I doubt that we would ever have seen anything of them again. However, they too had obviously been well briefed or had a well developed sense of self preservation – I noticed that they were all holding on incredibly tightly.

Life for those not immediately involved, however, appeared to be proceeding below as normal. I had one report that there had been an accident to one of our female sailors who had fallen over in the shower that morning and had unfortunately broken her front tooth. I was somewhat amazed that anyone would even be trying to shower in those conditions. I also received a more troubling report that one of the radio operators had had her foot crushed by the communications office safe that had come free from its mounting. It later transpired that the safe – which everyone believed to have been attached to the ship's structure for the seventeen years – was actually just slotted into a cavity in the deck. The safe had actually leapt forward for a distance of about two feet. Fortunately the rating's foot was just a little bruised. Frankly, I did not need these distractions.

We made three more approaches to *Ramtha* firing lines each time, either drifting apart as they missed, or on one occasion became entangled in the yacht's rigging, needing to be cut loose. We commenced our fifth attempt at around 0950 on that Sunday morning June 5. I well recall that it was a Sunday as a number of my junior officers were appropriately dressed in their good uniforms in accordance with our Sunday routines. I was dressed in whatever the rating, who I'd asked to go down to pick up my clothes, could find lying around in my cabin.

The fifth line fired across was fortunately taken in hand by *Ramtha* and the deck crew, who'd seen the first line break, were taking no chances. The line was kept slack at all times. The gun line was attached to a couple of thin heaving lines attached to a slightly thicker line, and the harnesses paid out on a line which was a little under 25 mm in diameter. Unfortunately, this array took a considerable time for Robyn Forbes to haul in. With my twin controllable pitch propellers spinning at around 220 rpm and the bow thruster similarly running constantly, I was considerably agitated about the line in the water. At one stage I believe I shut down the port engine from the bridge, in fear of becoming entangled.

However, we saw Robyn finally bring the harnesses in board. We had earlier briefed them that they should put on wetsuits and bring with them any money and passports and other personal documents that they could. When they donned the harnesses, they should ensure that the toggle was very securely fastened in order that they not slip out. My recollection is that Bill placed Robyn's harness over her shoulders first and then his. We saw him reach up to tighten the toggle on her harness. As he did so we lost sight of them. *Monowai* took an extremely large roll to starboard and they disappeared from sight. As we rolled up and back the other way we could see the tension coming out of the line between the ship and the yacht almost in slow motion. We saw the line jerk tight like a rubber band, and Bill and Robyn Forbes were pulled together. They fell. I just watched, appalled, as they bounced about four times on the deck towards the bow of their catamaran.

It is surprising how quickly all the dire consequences can run through your mind. If Bill and Robyn Forbes had fallen through the guard-rails or had fallen between the twin hulls then we would have been faced with pulling the catamaran towards *Monowai* using them as a toggle. It was with some relief that we saw Bill and Robyn fall into the water just off their starboard bow. I recall hearing an epithet from the fo'c'sle followed by POS Jackson's exhortations to pull them in. And we watched as the couple was pulled through the foaming seas for a distance of about 150 or 200 metres to *Monowai*. They spent quite a lot of the time actually under the water, especially Robyn. I remember remarking to someone at the time that she was obviously under water a lot of the time but we would 'just have to pump her out' when we got her on board. That is one of these throw-away remarks that one makes and which keep coming back to haunt one! But I knew that John Talbot and two medic assistants were standing by with resuscitating equipment which they would have used if necessary even while the two were being dragged out of the strops.

After about a minute and a half by the navigator yeoman's notebook, Bill and Robyn were alongside the ship close to the portside under the torpedo davit, being hoisted up towards willing arms reaching out to drag them in board.

I was told later that Bill's first words on being brought over the deck were 'Bloody hell, you guys are great.' One of the female crew members said, 'Welcome aboard. Come and have some good kiwi hospitality'. Certainly a spontaneous cheer went up as the couple were landed in board, clearly reflecting the tension at the time. We had other yachts to go to, so I re-entered the bridge. Uppermost in my mind was that I had been up since 3:30 a.m. and had not had a cup of tea in the whole of that time-so things were not totally normal. I was also mindful of the fact that I had not had breakfast. Indeed very few of us had, but that was the only meal that most of us missed during the five days of the operation. My pangs of hunger were being activated by the smell of curry being wafted onto the starboard bridge wing by the galley exhaust fan. I recall being amazed that the chefs were able to keep cooking in what must have been indescribable conditions below.

As I entered the bridge one of the crewmembers, an engineer rating said 'Oh, well done sir.' I was somewhat surprised because the gentleman in question was usually quiet and one would not expect such a quiet rating to be so bold to his CO. I was also greatly heartened because this was a guy I had reluctantly punished with reasonable severity in the preceding weeks. Barry's words moved me immensely and demonstrated the crew's total involvement in what was going on. It was the Ship's Company of *Monowai* who endured the danger, discomfort and difficulty, and I was very proud of what they achieved that day.

Without too much ado, though, we set course for the next group requiring our ministrations.

The weather conditions were variable as we weaved our way around this little part of the Pacific. 'Pacific' though was never a word I would have used to describe the situation. I was in frequent touch with the naval liaison officer at the Rescue Coordination Centre, (RCC), and with the naval authorities by either Inmarsat (satellite) telephone or naval signal. The telephone rang either in my cabin or in the radio room annex. Sometimes I felt that modern communication methods were somewhat too immediate as our target was frequently changed. I recall at one stage fighting my way across the cabin to the satellite phone about 2200 one evening having been roused from a deep slumber to be greeted with 'Oh, glad you are still up.' I think I just grunted! It was a very fluid situation.

Inmarsat is a great communication medium though a little expensive at times. We were to build up a large bill over the six days in which we were ultimately involved in the operation, but a large part of it was in telephoning the many Press, radio and TV stations who had requested that we call them. There was a lot of interest from stations around the world. The navy (thankfully) would not give out our Inmarsat number but instead agreed to telephone me with a request to return the call on the understanding that we would bill the station later (there was no way we knew of by which we could call collect). To give them their due, every bill we sent was honoured very quickly.

Bill and Robyn were very eager to (as they said) repay us for what we had done by speaking to any of the media people who asked and they beat a regular track to my door. It cannot have been easy for them but they were great!

On one occasion we were asked to chase a liferaft which had been sighted by the Airforce and which was an important target as contact had been lost with the NZ yacht, *Quartermaster* after she had put out a 'Mayday' call. The principal interest was in checking whether anyone was in the raft and, indeed, whether there had been anyone in the raft at any stage. However, I plotted the positions given for the raft and calculated that it was scudding across the ocean at about seven knots. In the conditions we could only make about four knots so I suggested that perhaps we could be more gainfully employed. We were re-diverted towards the main body of yachts.

During the early hours of Monday morning (6 June, Queens Birthday) an Airforce Orion asked us to investigate an unknown yacht which they had spotted, by an incredible stroke of luck. Nothing was known about the yacht, although people could be seen in the cockpit. No radio communications could be had with it and there had been no EPIRB beacon signals from its position. We were asked to assist the crew and, as quickly as possible, to determine whether they had ever had a liferaft and if so whether they had lost it, since they were immediately downwind of the errant liferaft. If it seemed likely that it had come from this yacht then the search for *Quartermaster* could be refocused.

We made our way towards the position. Knowing nothing of the yacht, and having no means of communicating, a *Ramtha* type of rescue – which required close coordination between the two parties – was clearly out of the question. The weather had improved somewhat – to a 'mere' 35 to 40 knots with about a four to five metre swell, and we felt that a boat could be launched. The duty crew – Leading Seaman Whata and Able Seaman Hemopo – was briefed along with Sub Lieutenant Bradley Tong who was briefed to quickly ascertain information about the yacht so that it could be passed to the Orion in order that the aircraft need not be unnecessarily detained from more pressing duties.

All hands on the bridge peered forward as we approached the given position. Nothing could be seen until suddenly, about two cables (400 metres) ahead, a small white dismasted yacht was suddenly spotted atop a large swell. Then we lost it again. I later found out that the yacht's crew had been sitting in the cockpit, feeling all alone but comforted somewhat by the presence of the Orion. They saw a rainbow a little way off and suddenly saw (to them) a large ship appear in the middle of the bow heading towards them!

I altered to my launch course and the deck and boat crews were warned out. I altered course several times in an effort to find the best approach. The boat was launched from a HIAB crane on the starboard boatdeck level with the bridge and it was necessary to reduce the ship motion as much as possible since with the boat at waterlevel there was a sixteen metre long pendulum to cope with. It was very difficult at the best of times (and usually impossible after a certain point in the proceedings) for the deck crew to control the boat with

DRAMA AT SEA

the lines due to the almost vertical angles. No course seemed very satisfactory but I ultimately decided to launch 'down sea' (i.e. with the sea and swell on our port quarter) as the sea and swell were confused and coming from different directions.

The launch was achieved successfully though not without some anxious moments–and this was only from those of us looking safely on from the ship! The RHIB (a rigid-hulled inflatable boat) was frequently out of sight as we hovered in the general vicinity. Occasionally the bright orange clothing of the crew could be seen through the foaming sea.

They reached the yacht and Bradley boarded. The crew of the yacht, which turned out to be the American yacht *Pilot*, were apparently somewhat bemused to be faced with a number of administrative questions in the middle of the seething ocean before their rescuers would do anything. (We later explained the reasoning to them and they seemed satisfied.) The tension in Bradley's voice was evident as he radioed the details across to us including the tortological statement 'two POB on board.' He also advised us that the vessel had never had a liferaft (which we found astonishing at the time, but later accepted the crew's rationale and explanation of their alternatives) and had no radio callsign. The Orion then sped off to other matters requiring their ministrations. *Pilot*'s crew boarded the RHIB after the skipper had opened the toilet valves in the boat so that she would not remain a hazard to surface vessels.

The recovery of the boat was far more gut-wrenching than the launching. Though I steamed the exact same course, the twenty minutes since the launch had seen a change in conditions which seemed even more confused. Faced with five people in a boat for which I was responsible I was not terribly happy!

Whata brought the boat skilfully alongside though it looked at one stage as if he had lost control, the boat ending up perpendicular to the ship at about a foot off, and filling with water from the main engine cooling discharge. The boat's manoeuvrability and his skill saved the day and she quickly lined up under the fall. Hooked on and jerked from the water, the boat came into contact with the hull several times as the ship rolled. The boat would swing away from the ship and then come thudding in despite the deck crew's best efforts. The pinched faces of those in the boat were obvious from the bridge and one could discern that the yacht's crew were wondering whether their current situation was preferable to their original one. Everyone was holding on very tightly indeed!

The boat was eventually recovered inboard and we met the people. 'Low budget cruisers' who were not actually part of the regatta but who were on their way to Tonga, Greg Forbes and Barbara Parkes had been sailing for around seven years in their small vessel. Greg's surname caused some comment but he was, of course, no relation to our other yachtsmen! Apart from being somewhat weary, and a little cold, they were fine and very quickly became a vital part of our crew, throwing themselves into the ship's life and work.

The operation continued and we struck off towards the south west and the *Silver Shadow*. We were told that this New Zealand yacht had been rolled, and the skipper had suffered a broken shoulder. The Orion crew told us that they had been speaking to the yacht and gave us a good position. The weather was again variable. We had recovered *Pilot's* crew a little before 0900 on Monday 6 June, and as the day drew on, the wind was again increasing, though fortunately not to the same degree as during the *Ramtha* operation.

We continued to receive reports about the *Mary T*, and were reassured (as we were now heading away from them) to hear that their crew were coping.

The injury to the skipper of *Silver Shadow* and the worsening weather caused us come concern as we discussed methods by which we might effect the next rescue – if, indeed, they required a rescue. We were told that the yacht was able to motor under emergency steering, though she only had enough fuel to get (as the Air Force puts it) 'halfway to anywhere'. We had some empty 44-gallon drums which could take diesel but there were only a couple of jerry cans onboard containing petrol for the outboard. With the ship still rolling some 20 degrees either way in the large swell, we couldn't see how we could pass them to the yacht; we could throw them overboard for the crew to pick up, but we knew this would be difficult. Likewise, to lift the injured man off using the crane or a davit, we didn't consider it wise to bring the yacht alongside. Conditions were still too severe for a helicopter launch.

Clearly the recently invented '*Ramtha* Rescue Method' would be unsuitable for an injured man. Though the weather was worse than in the morning, a boat launch was the only possibility.

It took us all day to make our way towards *Silver Shadow*. Soon after lunch, when clearly we would not reach them before sunset, they suggested (through the Orion overhead) that they could motor towards us. We gave them a course to steer to intercept our course; the sea conditions prevented us steering directly towards them. The boat crew were warned out and relieved of other duties for the day. The medical assistant, LMA Michael Wiig, was also put on standby and the helicopter's lightweight stretcher (the only piece of the helicopter used in the actual rescues) got ready.

A little after 1600, we finally came within VHF range of the *Silver Shadow* and discussed their situation. I offered to take the skipper off and pass them some fuel as best we could, or take the entire crew off. I told them what I could not do was take the yacht in tow, since we were still required for the rescue operation and I could not expect a successful tow anyway, nor could I transfer any of my crew to them. They agreed to discuss it as we motored the last few miles towards each other. Within twenty minutes they came back and said that 'if one went, they all went.' They asked if we would take them off. I understand that a significant consideration was that they had lost their liferaft and only had a small VHF radio and emergency steering. It seemed like a sensible decision to me.

Monowai bucked and heaved as we came up to the yacht and launched the boat. The sea was very confused but the launch went surprisingly well. We watched as the RHIB, though difficult to spot and often lost in the troughs, approached the yacht. They bucked about considerably and it wasn't possible for the RHIB to lay alongside. Instead we saw it nose up to the yacht's stern and I saw LMA Wiig leap across. He gave the skipper, Peter O'Neil, a morphine jab and lashed him firmly in the stretcher. We saw the stretcher literally thrown from the yacht into the rescue boat. Then we lost them from sight for several minutes as the rest of the crew transferred.

The RHIB made its way back to us, and came alongside the port side just forward of the bridge where the torpedo davit used to rescue the Forbes was again utilised. Though I gave the boat a good lee, the sea was still very sloppy. I could see the stretcher in the bottom of the RHIB with Wiig concernedly ensuring that Peter O'Neil's face was clear of the water. The boat was taking a lot of spray.

My heart was in my mouth as I watched the operation from the bridge, issuing the occasional engine or helm order. The boat and deck crew were magnificent and the stretcher came up onboard and Peter O'Neil passed into the care of the doctor, John Talbot, in a remarkably quick and smooth operation. The same was not quite true for the rest of the operation.

As the boat lay alongside and the others prepared to disembark, a considerable amount of water slopped into the boat, about a foot of water at one stage. The other three yachtsmen were taken out by sling, two coming out together in a most friendly fashion — a photograph which since been the subject of much ribald comment.

As they came aboard, the RHIB engine started spewing out volumes of thick black smoke. The coxswain reported that his alarms were sounding. I passed the order to keep the engine going and I would accept any damage. From the bridge we looked directly down into the boat. As the final yachtsman was lifted out, the order to 'get the crew out of the boat and abandon it' formed on my lips. I was very conscious that if the engine failed I would have a dreadful time trying to recover the boat and could well lose the crew. A quarter million dollars' worth of boat didn't seem very expensive compared to my people's lives.

Something said by Hugh Aitken caused me to withhold the order. The crew were told not to delay but to get round under the davits as quickly as they could and to stay as close to the ship as possible. As I worked the ship around to provide a lee, they motored round, leaving a plume of black smoke. Again, the boat deck crew were splendid and the fall went down soon after the boat came alongside. Unfortunately the block had been somewhat strained during the other recovery and the thin plate which prevented the fall from slipping off the sheave had been bent. As the crew tried to hook on, the block flipped and jammed. It was too dangerous for them to sort it out in the boat. The falls were describing an arc of many metres through the air and jerking taut. They would, at best, have lost fingers. So the fall was recovered into the ship.

The very worst place for a boat to be is alongside a ship at sea. It was always my aim to have the boat wait off until all was ready and to keep it alongside for as short a time as possible. However, in the situation we kept the boat there. It bucked, filled with water, jerked the lines and contacted the ship's side. I felt every jolt as I am sure did the crew.

The block was sorted out temporarily and lowered down with Petty Officer Donsellaar holding the standing part of the fall to stop it swinging. This was very effective and Hemapo hooked on in very short order. The boat jerked out of the water. Though it contacted the ship's hull several times, it was soon at the boat deck. Wiig leapt out just as the ship started to roll so that the boat moved away, but the seamen timed their exit beautifully and stepped daintily onto the deck. We recovered the boat just before 1800, and sent a signal indicating that it was now subject to an 'operational deficiency'.

That the ship's doctor, John Talbot, was an orthopedic specialist was a great boon to Peter O'Neil. He was soon up and about with his injured arm firmly in a sling. The others soon could be found on the bridge and in all parts of the ship 'mucking in' as best they were able. The senior ratings mess took the team to their heart as only senior ratings could and I expect there were a number of evening sessions en route to Tonga.

Mary T cancelled her Pan message that evening, but the search for the crew of the *Quartermaster* went on. We were able to launch the helicopter on Wednesday and located a considerable amount of floating debris though this proved to have come from the scuttled American catamaran *Heartlight*. The formal identification was made from the label of a small pill bottle that we found floating in the middle of the Pacific.

We were released from the operation at 1700 on Thursday June 9 and set course for Tonga. I had the option of returning to Auckland but since the yachties were going that way anyway, the thought of returning for a couple of days and then heading off was not an attractive one. Anyway, we had a survey to do.

We reached Tonga at the weekend and got a tremendous reception from the other members of the Regatta. The New Zealand and Australian High Commissions and the US Consul were very efficient in looking after their respective nationals. I needed a rest and am not a great party person in any case, but the crew was regally entertained. They deserved their place in the limelight. Of course, we had a number of repairs to effect. A new inflatable collar for the RHIB was sent from Auckland, along with a variety of spare parts. Phone calls from the press continued. We managed to get our video of the three rescues, later to be extensively used in the television documentary *Pacific Rescue*, back to New Zealand care of a friendly Air New Zealand flight attendant.

Greg and Barbara from *Pilot* had very few resources and had lost everything. I turned my Nelsonian eye to the fact that they lived on board in Nuku'alofa but did insist that they should disembark as we sailed. Greg particularly would have happily stayed.

Frankly, I was surprised at how much it took out of me and I still get very moved when I see the video. I talk about it all, though, at the drop of a hat. I learned much about the ship that I had not picked up in the previous seventeen years and became a real 'safety' martinet when it came to lowering boats and in the wearing of lifejackets. I don't think this is necessarily a bad thing.

I was conscious all the time of having to lead and make the decisions, though very conscious too of the considerable part that all 136 people on board (including two surveyors from DOSLI and the Airforce flight crew with the helicopter) played in the operation.

We were deflated by the lack of success in finding any sign from *Quartermaster*, later confirmed lost at sea, but pleased to have been able to rescue eight people – who all became good friends.

Commander Larry Robbins, 'The 1994 Pacific Rescue', *1999*

AN ISLAND TO ONESELF

AFTER thirty years of roaming the Pacific as naval apprentice engineer, odd-job man and storekeeper, 50-year-old Tom Neale got an inter-island trader to drop him off on an uninhabited coral atoll in the Cook Islands. Suvarov, half a mile long and three hundred wide, its great lagoon circled by nearly 50 miles of reef, was to be his home for the next twenty months.

After being taken off the island ill, followed by six restless years on Rarotonga, in April 1960 Tom Neale returned again to Suvarov. During this second spell, of three and half years, a dramatic capsize in the lagoon nearly ended his dream. He left in December 1963, disliking the prospect of sharing his island home with occasional pearl divers, or (now approaching sixty) the thought of a lonely death.

I have never in my life encountered any natural force more relentless than the Pacific Ocean. Sometimes it almost put me in mind of an enemy biding its time, awaiting the one moment when I might be off my guard.

Consequently, I never took a chance and never took my boat out should the barometer show the slightest sign of impending bad weather, because I knew only too well how swiftly the Pacific can change her moods; one moment calm and tranquil, the next a cauldron of titanic force. Nor did I ever let a week go by without examining my box of tools, which would be my only insurance against survival should a hurricane sweep over the island.

And yet – through no fault of my own – I suddenly found myself one morning, in July 1961, struggling for my life when my boat capsized in the middle of the lagoon.

I didn't know it then, but I was to be in the water for five hours.

There had been no warning. We had been experiencing a short spell of bad weather, but this was over now and we were well out of reach of the hurricane season. The barometer stood high, and that morning, which dawned as placidly as any I can remember, there seemed nothing on earth to prevent me sailing the five miles to Bird Island on one of my 'tours of inspection' to see if anything of value had been washed up on the beach.

I reached the motu aided by a good breeze, collected one or two useful bits of flotsam and by midday I was on my way back to Anchorage. I was in the middle of the lagoon, in about a hundred and fifty feet of water, when a squall rose right out of nowhere and hit us. Within a few seconds everything had changed. The sun had vanished, the clouds grew horribly black and the wind started screaming. Plainly we were in for a sudden sharp squall – the sort which could be on one in a few minutes. I did not even have time to lower the sail, but simply rapidly pushed up the boom and sail, making sure the main sheet was free to run. Next I lashed it to the mast, a trick I had long ago learned for getting sail off quickly. Altogether the whole job took less than a minute, so that I had the boat trimmed before the squall had a chance to reach its height. I still had the jib set. I would be able to sail it out, and was quite confident. Obviously the next hour or so looked like being thoroughly rough and uncomfortable, but perfectly safe so long as I resigned myself to being tossed about like a cork.

But as the storm gathered force – and I could see it sweeping towards me across the lagoon – I began to have doubts.

It was astonishing how rapidly the sea rose with the force of the wind. Suddenly shivering a little, I remembered a description in one of Frisbie's books of how heavy seas tearing through the pass would meet a comber inside the lagoon and explode in a cloud of spray.

This was exactly what *did* happen. Within a few minutes the coral ring had become a cloud of spume and the waves inside the lagoon started gathering ever-increasing force and size. Over above Brushwood and Turtle – the nearest motus – I could see clouds of black frigate birds being blown all over the place despite their four-foot wing span. The great waves hitting each other far out across the reef were forming gushers which curtained off every speck of land.

I was still not really worried, for the force of the heavy seas roaring through the pass was still well south of me, so that the combers came rolling in from east to west. In actual fact I was only getting the backwash, so that, though drenched, I was able to stand the buffeting well until unexpectedly a stronger gust overtook us. What happened next ought, by rights, never to have occurred. I had stowed the sail carefully away when I tied the boom to the mast, but this freak gust seemed to bite into it and sneak inside so that before I could move, the sail was bellying out above the mast.

I knew immediately that I must act swiftly since otherwise I would be in real danger of capsizing. Cautiously, but as rapidly as I dared, I clambered on to the forward thwart, where I stood, hugging the mast with one arm, and trying to secure the wildly flapping sail.

I almost succeeded when another gust caught us and the sail bellied out right into my face. Without warning, the boat gently keeled over. I couldn't do a thing. One moment I was standing there helpless, waiting, as my twelve-footer slowly turned right over beneath me – so slowly that the next minute I almost stepped into the water.

A wave caught me, forcing me under the warm water. When I surfaced, eyes smarting with the salt, gasping, spitting out sea water, I found I had been swept several yards away from the boat. Everything was so confused – the big waves were charging at me all the time – that at first I thought I'd lost the boat, for it was all so dark – the darkness of storm clouds covering the sky. Then I saw a patch of white and knew the boat at least was safe – even if upside down. I struck out towards her, and tried to grab her for support but it was impossible to obtain any hold on that smooth bottom.

Luckily I was thoroughly at home in the water, a legacy of my old Tahiti days. I knew that somewhere under the water the mast must be pointing downwards, and felt confident that if I could only get a grip on it, give it a sharp jerk and a heave, I might have a chance of turning her upright again. It was not so much a question of strength; given a well-placed shove, a capsized boat with a mast will naturally tend to move upwards in the right direction.

I took a deep breath and submerged. But I had under-estimated my task. Time after time I had to dive before I was able to grab the mast by its tip. I knew that once I caught hold of it I would have to swim under water and push it with one hand whilst I kicked out with my feet. Fortunately the water at midday was warm, but I think I must have had to dive ten or a dozen times. The struggle seemed never-ending. Each time I shot to the surface for air, I had no support on which to rest and was forced to dog-paddle whilst getting a breather. Finally I managed to reach the mast and give it one enormous jerk. Immediately it seemed to give, to slip away from my pushing fingers.

I followed it up until I could feel the wind on my face, and as I gulped in air and spray and trod water in the violent chop, I felt something brush my leg. I knew at once that if it were a shark there was nothing I could do. But the solid feel of it told me that this was no shark. It was the mast.

It was horizontal at last, just under the waves, and I grabbed it and had my first real rest, leaning across it, indifferent as wave after wave swept over me, just hanging on grimly, half submerged, wondering what on earth I was going to do next. For a moment I toyed with the idea of trying to push the mast out of the water. But I abandoned this plan since I knew that were I to let go of it for long the waves would sweep me away.

However, now the mast was level on the water, it was acting in the same way as a spar on an outrigger canoe, and now the boat was on her side I had at least a sort of floating platform to support me. If I wanted to right her, however, there was only one thing to do – get the mast out. And this was impossible until the wind went down. Hanging on there, I tried to open my eyes between the waves that kept coming over me. I wanted to see the sky, the clouds. It seemed – from the brief glimpses I could manage – that the sky was growing lighter. I knew from experience that these storms are violent but short-lived. And so I prepared to 'sit it out' hanging on to the mast, waiting until the waves were smaller, more infrequent, so I could tread water without fear of drifting away from the boat.

The squall must have lasted an hour or more, and curiously enough – or perhaps, on reflection, it was natural – I do not remember ever being afraid of sharks during all that time. I never saw one, and I suppose I was too busy holding on to my boat – and my life – to think about them. I suppose in fact that all this time I must have been acting instinctively.

The wait seemed interminable – so long that when finally I found myself waiting for the next wave to fill my eyes with stinging salt water and it didn't come, I could hardly believe my good fortune. Raising myself slightly in the water I looked around. It was still choppy, but the sea was definitely beginning to quieten. Waves still hit me from time to time, but failed to push me under. The sky, too, had lightened from black to grey, and as I floated, one hand clutching the mast, I noticed a sliver of blue in the sky – and knew the sun must be trying to struggle through. All at once life seemed much more cheerful!

Fortified with the new energy this realisation seemed to summon up, I now set about the major task of getting the mast and sails off the boat. It took at least an hour. I remember later, when I told somebody how I had managed this job, he told me flatly that it was impossible, but in fact, given strength and patience, it wasn't so difficult as one might imagine.

But it certainly seemed to take an age. First I had to free the rigging – the two back stays and the fore stay. These were made of wire, but were fastened down with rope lashings which had swollen and were difficult to free when I dived under for short bursts. However, I managed to undo them. Next I had to dive to free the jib sheets – a similar job because they were only fastened to the cleats. I had to take several rests, clinging with one hand to the mast to support myself and give my legs a rest.

My next job was to haul all this gear I had dismantled into a sort of state where I could wrap it round the boom and then try to lash the whole unwieldy lot roughly to the mast, which was still lying a little under the water. I managed this by wrapping the loose ends of the ropes round everything until I had boom, sails and all attached in a rough bundle to the mast.

Now I surveyed the mast itself which had been stepped by being passed down through a half loop of brass fastened to a timber which in turn was made fast to each gunwale. It was a simple design, so that the foot of the mast fitted into a notch in another piece of timber fastened to the keelson. I had deliberately designed it this way so that, though it was strong, I could easily step the mast unaided by merely lifting it up, dropping it through the half-loop and into the notch. It was not, of course, permanently fastened.

Getting it out, however, proved much more difficult than I had anticipated. Since the boat was lying on her side, the weight of the mast – encumbered by its bulky burden of sail and boom – made the butt jam in the loop.

I couldn't budge it at first and though the wind had fallen a lot by now, and the chop was not too bad, I had been in the water for some hours and was beginning to tire.

Each fresh attempt seemed more wearying. Every time I held on to the boat with one hand and tried to free the mast with the other, I found I was too close to get a proper leverage. Finally I decided I would have to use both hands, so after clinging to the boat to regain a little strength, I swam to where the tip of the mast lay just under the waves, and grabbed hold of it, kicking as hard as I could with my feet, and violently jerking and pulling it up and down to get it free. To my delight my efforts were almost immediately rewarded. At the first attempt I could feel it had left its step at the bottom of the boat.

But in its wake this victory seemed to conjure up a new hazard. For almost at the moment I felt the mast loosen, it started to swing. I clutched at it, endeavouring to keep it steady, for I knew that were the loop of soft brass to bend under this pressure, the mast would jam irretrievably. If I were ever to get it free, it was now no longer a question of brute force. What was needed was a gentle, coaxing pull and a pretty constant maintained pressure in order to keep the mast as straight as possible while I slowly tugged it free through the loop.

Treading water all the time, I used one hand to balance and swim and held on to the mast with the other, kicking as I carefully manoeuvred it inch by inch through the loop.

And at last I managed it, too exhausted now to experience anything but a profound feeling of relief. I didn't have to worry about it floating away; it lay, with all the sails attached, a soggy mass in the water.

After that it was fairly simple to right the boat. I swam round, climbed over the opposite side and put my foot on the centreboard. She righted herself immediately and I let go and fell back into the waves before my weight sank her, for amidships she was barely an inch or two above water.

I had lost my bailer when she capsized, so after hanging on to the gunwale until I regained my breath, I tried to start scooping some of the water out of her with my hands. The wind had eased up considerably by now but the seas were still rough enough to slop into the boat, until, holding on with both hands and kicking with my feet, I managed to turn her bows into the wind. Gripping one gunwale with my right hand, I began splashing out water with my left. For over an hour I was forced to keep on bailing madly with intervals for rests. Every so often she would swing broadside to the waves and the water would start to slop in again so that it seemed as though I would never make any real headway. Amidships she was still barely two inches above the water, but I kept on doggedly in the knowledge that the wind was continuing to drop.

Nearly an hour later – it may have been longer but I had lost count of time – I suddenly began to realise that she was imperceptibly rising in the water. And the sun was breaking through! From then on I took great care to keep her head on to the seas and frequently had to swim away from my task to slew her round. Even today, so long afterwards, I still only remember one particular moment during this long-drawn struggle, as I hung on to the gunwale, getting my breath back, crying out loud, 'Neale! You're not going to let this beat you.'

And I didn't because, simply through sticking at it, I kept on bailing until eventually I had three inches of freeboard at the lowest part of the sheer. By now I was so tired that this seemed like the promised land and I decided I would try and get into the boat. I knew it would be fatal to try and clamber in over the side so, having made sure her bows were well into the seas, I summoned up what strength I had left and swam round to the bows where I climbed quickly and carefully inboard. To my relief, I found she was just able to bear my weight without going down. But it was a near thing and I didn't dare to rest, not even for a second. I sat down on the midship thwart and bailed like mad with cupped hands. It is amazing what a lot of water you can shift this way; before long I had four inches of freeboard and only then did I take a brief rest.

Now at last I felt safe and all I had to do was go on ladling out water until it was low enough for me to haul in the bundle of mast, sail and boom, and make for home.

I did not have the strength to try and set the mast to sail home, but fortunately the oars had been well stowed and had remained in the boat all the time. I dragged them out and wearily started rowing for Anchorage.

I reached Anchorage at dusk, and not until I was rubbing myself down in the shack did I notice that all the skin on the inside of my left arm had been rubbed off. Each time I had scooped out the water, I must have rasped my arm against the gunwale.

I was too tired to bother about it, for as I wrote in my journal that evening, 'There's no need for a rocking chair tonight.'

Tom Neale, An Island to Oneself, *1966*

DOLPHIN, DOLPHIN

IN 1965 *diving mates Wade Doak and Kelly Tarlton burst into the news when they rediscovered the wreck of the* Elingamite, *lost in 1902 off the Three Kings group of islands north of New Zealand. Three years of meticulous planning and research later, Doak and Tarlton, with a team of New Zealand divers, recovered much of the* Elingamite's *sunken treasure, mostly silver.*

Tarlton went on to develop Auckland's world-famous underground aquarium, and Doak to become a notable writer, film-maker and marine conservationist. In 1976, following an encounter a year earlier with a group of bottlenose dolphins off the Poor Knights islands, he and his wife Jan returned to the Poor Knights for the first of many occasions of 'dancing with the dolphins – swimming with them, playing them music, gambolling, "interlocking".' They began to use the dolphin kick and specially designed wet suits: black and white with fins and a single flipper. Their task was to explore the notion that dance, music, mimicry, familiarity and above all, respect, might remove the cultural communication gaps between humans and dolphins.

16 November 1976: It was weighing heavily on me, such a long lapse of time since my last contact with dolphins – months of research and writing about them – all based upon that initial cavort, the day we danced. With this ticking over in my mind Jan and I headed the Haines out of Tutukaka Harbour for the Poor Knights this morning – a rare day of good weather in a bad year.

The inshore water was green with plankton. Over to the north of our path a cloud of seabirds hovered, wheeling and plunging into the sea – gannets and petrels working a school of baitfish. We veered over, my heart surging with expectancy. This time in readiness I was wearing my snug-fitting, farmer john wetsuit pants and all my gear was close at hand.

Dolphins leaping. Common dolphins. *Delphinus delphis.* Our bow was flanked with curving shapes. We slowed and headed towards the school activity. Jan took the wheel while I got the cassette player going: something to interest them, the message tape, side two. Cetacean sounds, *Tursiops truncatus*.

The boat circling slowly, we cheered and drummed on the hull while through the fibreglass came the sounds of their big cousins. I was scrambling into my gear – the dorsal fin on my weight belt all set to don. The dolphin sounds ended so we switched over to the song of the humpback whale. I slipped in with the movie rig to record anything odd that happened.

While I was in the water and Jan was steering the boat round me in circles she could see the dolphins passing me from all sides and knew that I couldn't keep track of them all, my field of vision being so small wearing a mask. She noticed that the dolphins were coming in and riding on the front of the boat for a while; then they would peel off and go back to feeding where the birds were continually plunging in from great heights. Some would then leave the boat to have a look at me, diving under and around me.

There were dolphins weaving everywhere, around me and below. Silver black bullets in the green haze. I could see only twenty feet because of the plankton bloom but groups of dolphins kept whizzing by within ten feet of me, twisting on their sides, or leaping out of the water and plunging back. When one made a shuddering burst past me, I managed to keep within range of it a while before, just on vanishing point, it whisked around and returned to circle me. From time to time the numbers around me would disperse, and eventually, after about fifteen minutes, contact was lost. Jan pointed to the bird activity a few hundred yards away – the dolphins had all resumed feeding.

I climbed over the stern and we moved nearer to the feeding frenzy – again the dolphins responded to our presence with frolicsome behaviour, leaps and tail slapping. I slipped back in and began diving down and circling about. They seemed to react even more when I descended but I needed more weight on my belt to do it with ease. The damned camera housing was buoyant.

I was surprised at the frequency with which they were defaecating right in front of me. Was it a signal? Dolphins swallow each other's faeces, I had read, but the way the emissions break up in clouds of tiny particles, all they would get is the taste – a form of chemical communication. Did they expect me to respond in the same way? The least I could do was grab at a cloud as if in acceptance of their gesture.

As a dolphin passed me I heard an extra loud whistle and saw a string of bubbles emerge from its hole just afterwards. I took the snorkel from my mouth and screamed 'ruuaark' at the bunch as they headed directly at me. They veered slightly and passed at close quarters, turning on their sides to eye me as they zipped by.

This session was much longer and more intensive than the first. Jan had stopped the boat and was drifting nearby. It was full interlock in that no other stimulus than my presence was now keeping the dolphins from their feast. The birds working the fish school were some distance away. How I wished I had some comparisons to reinforce gamesplay, the exchange of body language. After about twenty minutes the numbers around me diminished. For another ten minutes I played with a pair of the largest in the group, while others came and went sporadically. Were these the oldest in the group? They seemed very curious about my performances with the fin. Whenever I put on a good demonstration of swimming and diving there was a noticeable surge of vigour. I had improved greatly since my session with the rock band but I wished they were here. The more I increased my activity the closer the dolphins came.

I yelled out for Jan to get in but first she had to make sure she had a rope over the side to hold the boat. As she got ready there were two dolphins that kept coming over to the boat looking up at her as they turned on their side and then returned to me.

She was just about to enter when they disappeared. They must have satisfied their curiosity and resumed feeding. I got back in the boat at a quarter to eleven and we headed for the Knights. We didn't take the time I was actually in the water with them but the whole period they were in contact with the boat was forty minutes.

About two miles from the islands a string of leaping dolphins passed us on a parallel and opposite course. Careering along at top speed in a series of arcs like a rippling rope, they took no notice of us. I have often seen this leap-swim progression when schoolfish are about and on all such occasions the dolphins have ignored the boat, intent on their rapid passage.

During the day we hunted for signs of paper nautilus shells, and tested the underwater loudspeaker again. This time I'd filled the housing with thin brake-fluid oil retained by a rubber diaphragm. It worked about as well as the speaker had, pressed against the boat interior, but it was only half the size so the sound transfer seemed to be quite good. At least it would be a pressure-proof component for the submersible tape replay unit my friend Allan Kircher had built me, slicing the end off an old scuba tank and fitting it with a three-quarter-inch plexiglass port.

In Rikoriko Cave we sat and listened to the song of the humpback whale. In that huge echo chamber even the twelve-volt car stereo could set the echoes ringing. The deep notes were most effective in producing resonant echoes that filled the island interior with sound colour.

At the entrance a gannet plunged into the interface between light and dark to bob up with a tiny maomao in its beak. Swallows flitted across the light and bird calls wafted in from the surrounding cliffs to blend with the whale's song. I was hopeful we could set up another rock music session in this cave, playing the whale songs for the Hazemen to emulate.

Homeward bound we were skittering over the crests of a rising easterly sea twelve miles out when we saw birds working near the Pinnacles. Closer in dolphin fins appeared. I'd left my wetsuit on for the return journey, just in case another opportunity arose. It was much quicker this time to approach the dolphins. Our tape was transmitting the humpback song and in no time we were with the nomads again. Out there the water was oceanic blue and the countershading of their bodies looked quite startling against the backdrop.

With the whale sounds playing we approached and I leapt in. One dolphin sprang out and thwacked the water with its tail as he re-entered. He seemed excited at what he heard. There was a baby with its mother. The mother leapt out of the water and there beside her in mid-air was the baby. Only about twenty-four inches long, a miniature of its parent.

It was incredible to think that such a tiny thing could not only keep up to the speed of its mother, swerve and dive in perfect time, but it could leap out of the water at the same level as its mother too. It seemed to be glued in place by two invisible rods. Its position beside her never altered a fraction as far as I could see.

Jan was circling me in the water with the boat, yelling over and over 'Too much! Too much!' as she watched the activity around me and knew I must be out of my mind. From the boat she had a much better view of how many dolphins there were. She could see them circling me at times when I couldn't. She was not sure whether it was the same ones that kept going back to the feeding frenzy and then returning to circle me or ride on the bow wave or whether they were different dolphins each time.

In the end there was no need to keep the motor going to attract them. They were coming in anyway and seemed very curious about my dorsal fin. Down below I found the schoolfish activity was frenetic: a white line of foam zipped across the surface hotly pursued by birds and crisscrossed by dolphin fins. I felt honoured at the attention they gave but was not surprised when they hurtled back towards the melee only to return for another series of circuits.

After fifteen minutes of such antics I left them to it. I felt I was encroaching. What creature would abandon a high feast to play games as they had done? Schoolfish activity has been very lean this season with all the lousy weather and low temperatures (only 15 degrees C inshore this week). I was glad the dolphins were having such a picnic.

Why didn't they snap up the odd seabird? From below I could see webbed feet and feathers all over the surface – sitting target for a poultry-minded dolphin. But I never saw any attacks, drifting feathers or injured birds. Maybe the fish herders have a partnership. Nor is it likely that a common dolphin could swallow a seabird.

In her excitement Jan forgot to time this interlock but it was longer and much more intensive than the morning's one.

22 November 1976: One week later we met the dolphins again. This time Jan had her first experience of playing with them, and Claude, our neighbour, too. Another day of calm, a brief break in the weather following a southeast blow, we set out for the offshore islands, hopeful that the stormy weather might have brought the nautilus in. The ocean seemed deserted – there were no signs of activity until we were within three miles of the Knights. Then to the north of our course we sighted gannets wheeling and plummeting. We homed on dolphin fins. Soon they were gambolling around our bow. While the boat circled I leapt over wearing the dolphin fin. The tape was playing dolphin sounds (*Tursips*) at half normal speed, decreasing exponentially until they were as slow as human vocalisations. Once I was accepted, Claude joined me. We tried to stay together in a pair like the dolphins but it was difficult to match their synchronised swimming. For a while we tried towing each other with a special yoke arrangement in hope that the dolphins might follow suit, giving us a high speed ride. But we have not yet won such acceptance and they divided their interest between us and the schoolfish activity in the vicinity.

By now the plankton cycle had progressed from the initial bloom of tiny plants to the animal stage: mauve jellyfishes, translucent, wriggling larval fishes and pink krill, all heading into the gentle current which, at this distance offshore, flows warm from the north. Somewhere beyond the verge of vision kingfish, kahawai and sprats would be raiding each other and the plankton.

With my Pentax camera and 35mm lens I was trying to get pictures of the group in hope that we might find body marks and scratches from which to recognise them in future encounters. The concentration on taking photos wrecked my relationship with the dolphins. (It was much more demanding than the super 8 movie rig which is automatic and doesn't even need to be sighted.) Squinting through the viewfinder and adjusting the aperture I lost the spontaneity of play and failed to respond to many of the cues they offered, the body language gestures which, if I took the trouble to imitate, heightened their excitement and demonstrativeness.

Claude decided to slip on his aqualung. By this time the boat was playing mood music which Ian Briggs had sent me because he thought it stimulated cetacean sounds. Perhaps because of my camera the dolphins' attention had turned more towards the boat than me. As it cruised around slowly I could see Claude forty feet below and 300 feet above the seabed, the centre of a dolphin circus. Later he told me he agreed about the faeces signal. It was a definite gesture, he felt. From down there he had a three-dimensional uninterrupted view of the situation compared with a surface-oriented snorkeler. He saw two dolphins peel off from bow-riding and spiral down to his level. At ten and thirteen feet distances respectively they both released faecal clouds and rejoined the group.

Claude and I were exhausted after forty-five minutes' frenzied activity. We climbed out. The dolphins resumed feeding nearby. We were adrift with the music playing and Jan was getting into her gear when over the calm sea came what seemed to be the entire tribe – some thirty or more dolphins, lolling about slowly in groups, a playful indirect movement towards the boat about which they sported, occasionally lifting their heads out of the water briefly.

Jan hurried into her gear and leapt in. They were immediately all around her. She didn't know how many there were altogether but was mainly conscious of a group of five that stayed with her.

She dived down and dolphin-kicked. Straight away they mimicked her with exaggerated movements. She couldn't believe her eyes. This was the first time she'd been in the water with dolphins. Surfacing, she stuttered with excitement to us in the boat and then took a deep breath and dived down. Again she did the dolphin-kick and again they responded with an exaggerated version. Round and round they circled. There were two pairs and a single one. Every time it was the loner, perhaps lacking a mate, that came closest. She extended her arm and it seemed only a foot away from her outstretched fingers.

The dolphin wagged his head at her and seemed to want her to dive deep and follow his antics. She had to go up for a breath for the next dive. She could see them faintly far below, their white undersides flashing as they turned, so she knew they were still there. As she dived again the five dolphins came hurtling up from the depths like five spaceships taking off, with all their noses pointed straight at her. It was a cylinder of dolphins. They were close together, almost touching it seemed. Just before they reached her they peeled off. The pairs reformed and the loner spun around her very close, defaecating as he swept past with his exaggerated dolphin-kick and wagging head. She rolled over and over. One couple slapped each other with their fins and let out a shower of faeces as they streamed past her. They seemed to want her to copy them. She felt they were disappointed because she had to keep breaking off for air and was unable to dive deep. So it went on for half an hour; every time she descended they would come rushing up vertically to frolic around her.

These dolphins came in of their own accord. The boat was not running to attract them. When they arrived the music was playing and nobody was in the water. That lone dolphin sticks in her mind very clearly. He seemed to want her to be his playmate and she will never forget looking into his eye as he made his slow, close passes. 'It was a friendly intelligent look; understanding, playful and wise all at once.' All the time she was conscious of other dolphins circling at a distance. Towards the end of her dive she played with the dolphins just under the bow of the boat so we could see what was going on. Then she began to feel seasick and it impaired her performance – most frustrating for her! All she had wanted to do was forget everything and swim away with the dolphins, copying all their actions.

Afterwards it seemed like a dream. Jan wrote in her journal: 'I'd listened to others raving about their experiences but hadn't really believed them – I used to think silently to myself that they were exaggerating because they were excited. But honestly – this was no dream – it was *very real* and I feel humble that I was able to have such an experience during my lifetime.'

Wade Doak, Dolphin, Dolphin, *1981*

TARATAI II – A CONTINUING PACIFIC ADVENTURE

PHOTOGRAPHER/WRITER *James Siers had dreamed and planned for fifteen years when he set out in 1976 on the first stage of an epic Pacific adventure. In* Taratai I, *built by village craftsmen of traditional materials, he sailed 1500 miles from the Gilbert Islands to Fiji. In* Taratai II, *a similar traditional design and Micronesian rig but built of modern materials, he and six crew, including his ten-year-old son Conrad, would venture 6000 miles into the eastern Pacific to see where such a craft 'would fetch when attempting a west to east crossing.' Only in their nightmares would they imagine they'd fetch up spending two weeks adrift in a cramped inflatable life-raft, praying for deliverance.*

From Suva at the end of June, they had safely reached Tonga, and then Niue. On August 3 they set out for the Cook Islands, voting to continue on despite the loss of their mast two days later. On Monday, August 8, at 9.30 a.m., about 200 miles east of Nuie, disaster! In rough seas and driving rain, Taratai II's *outrigger broke off with a loud report 'like a great gun going off in the midst of the roar of battle.' Instinct and basic seamanship told Siers to stay with the hull, but at 2 a.m. the next morning, fearful of it being flipped over in the conditions, they cast off in the life-raft.*

They should pass beneath commercial airliners going to Niue, and be able to alert them with their radio beacon. They see and hear nothing. On August 13 they hold a prayer meeting. On the 14th they calculate they are probably drifting into a patch of ocean with no land for a thousand miles.

Thursday, 18 August. Watch 6 seconds fast. Beacon used for sixteen hours. This is our critical day. Two flights into Niue. Rob gets a sight which puts us 20 miles to the east of the flight path from Niue to Samoa. We must connect this time. The aeroplane will be almost directly overhead. The beacon is turned on at 10 o'clock in the morning. By 5.30 we have had no response. It seems almost certain now that the beacon is not working. How can this be possible when the agent in Fiji found it to be in 'perfect' condition?

We take stock. There is still plenty of food. Our water ration is down to about twenty days with careful usage. Probably, it will last a fortnight, I calculate. We seem to be cursed. All during the night and day, rain squalls march around us but we get none of the precious water. The wind is still from the south-east. We are heading for the great gap between Samoa and Vava'u. This seems to be the most depressing night. Tarabo complains of a sore back and does not want to nurse Conrad. I try sleeping on my stomach so that the boy can sleep on my back, but it is painfully difficult.

The only bright note is Tarabo talking about what we shall do when we got back to the Gilberts.

Later, I warn the men that water must be conserved at all costs. I tell them I know that some is being taken and that this is irresponsible and may jeopardise our chances of survival. I tell Rob I know that it may come to drastic action, but I have already planned what should be done.

Friday, 19 August. Watch 6 1/2 seconds fast. Beacon used for twenty-three and a half hours. I wake late after a sleepless night and listen to Fia begin the morning devotions. Tarabo, Conrad and I spend the morning making plans for our visit to Ribono in 1979. We agree that Tarabo will come and spend a year with us in New Zealand and then we will all go back to the Gilberts. There are gorgeous moments as we contemplate the compound we shall build on a point of palm-fringed land facing the trade wind; the fishing canoe we shall put together which shall be pre-cut in New Zealand; the days we shall spend outside the reef in search of tuna, shark and kingfish and the marvellous times we will have diving in the lagoon to shoot fish and recover clams.

In the early afternoon there is pandemonium. We hear an aeroplane. There's a frantic rush to get the beacon out. The plane is flying low. If only there was no cloud cover the pilot would probably see us. What luck. We turn on the beacon. Nothing. At 2 o'clock the aeroplane returns. Again there is no response. The sky, which had opened, is closed when the plane passes. It is one of the worst moments of my life. The compass tells us that this is the Pago (American Samoa) Niue, Pago flight and that Rob's sights, despite extreme difficulties, have been remarkably accurate. We know also that on this basis we shall be dead on track for the Apia (Western Samoa) Niue flight tomorrow and very close to the line of the Pago-Niue flight. We pray for the cloud to lift so that the pilot might see us. There is little hope in the beacon. The rain squalls are still passing to the left and right and the wind is still driving us for the open space between Samoa and northern Tonga.

Saturday, 20 August. Watch 7 seconds fast. Beacon used for twenty-four and a half-hours. Disaster again. Hard on the heels of yesterday's disappointment, we wake with a start at 1.30 in the morning to the sound of water rushing into the raft. The floor has opened again. There are three new holes, but they will be extremely difficult to plug. I bless Rob for his foresight in making up extra bungs. One of the holes is so big that even a king-size bung will not plug it. He builds it up. The rushing flow is stemmed, but now the seepage is such that we have to bail constantly. We are convinced the rubber floor is perished and cannot understand why. The raft is new and only one year old. It was surveyed by the agent in Fiji prior to our departure but obviously, there was no test applied to the rubber floor. We now reflect on the state of the inflation tubes. The prospect is too horrifying to contemplate. In the midst of our frantic scramble to stem the flow, we all think the floor has gone irreparably. Rob grabs one of the containers of water and drinks. By the time it has done the round, nearly 4 litres of water has gone.

The day is partially overcast with rain squalls which invariably miss the raft. At times the sky has large open windows and we pray that such a window will be there for the afternoon flight from Niue to Apia. According to Rob's sight, we are directly on track. He is right. Just after 4 o'clock (our time) we hear the turbo-prop jet slightly to the west of us, but almost directly overhead. As usual, the clouds have closed in and there is no response to the beacon which we have had turned on since 2 o'clock. We are crushed again. But this time with certainty. The previous day's flight, we had reasoned, was run by a small private company in American Samoa and possibly did not carry a distress frequency monitor. Today's flight was Polynesian Airlines, run by the Government of Western Samoa and subject to New Zealand Civil Aviation regulations. It would certainly carry a distress frequency monitor and it would be turned on.

It is as if our very last chance has gone.

The night comes on inevitably, but now there is the additional burden of constant bailing. We divide into two watches: Rob, Fia and I in one and Jope, Paea and Tarabo in the other. The water comes in at just over 5 litres a minute. We can cope with the flow, provided the bailing is constant. If for some reason it is not, then everyone has to turn to, to get the excess out. The worst problem is to change the teams round. Those who are going onto the bailing shift have to change places with those who have just finished.

Sunday, 21 August. Watch 7 1/2 seconds fast. Beacon used for twenty-four and a half hours. The night was bitterly cold again. The early hours before dawn especially bad. The wind kept on from the south-east, gusting up to 15 knots, but much milder than before. After morning devotions I notice that our water bottles are loose on the floor. nearly 4 litres is missing, confirming that it is being taken during the night and that the rate at which it is being taken, is accelerating. I tell Rob. He did not want to believe it before, but now it is obvious and the fact cannot be denied. I tell him that our situation is absolutely desperate. The wind is still taking us for the gap between Vava'u and Samoa. The next land is the northern Lau of Fiji some 400 miles away. Because of the water we had drunk in a frenzy when the floor ripped the second time and because of the water which disappeared during the night, our supply had diminished from twenty-five days to fifteen days. The time had come for drastic action. I suspect that most are taking an extra sip, but some are drinking it uncontrollably. I suspect two people particularly.

'Rob, you and Tarabo are appointed keepers of the water,' I announce in the morning.

'There are those among us who are drinking water at night,' I continue. 'It is the most precious thing we have. Without it we cannot live. By taking a little each day we can survive for a long time. When it is gone, we are dead. I want to say now that if the water continues to disappear the most drastic action will be taken.'

I had already told Rob my decision to kill if necessary. He knows that I am very weak and no match for the others, but he does not know that it is strength of mind, which would make such an act possible. I don't tell him that it can be done easily with the thrust of the point of the brass dividers through the eye socket and into the brain while the other person sleeps. Death would be instantaneous.

The day grows warmer, calmer, and the sea gentle. We attempt to sail the raft by letting the wind get inside the canopy. One man holds the flap as an extra sail. Another guides the raft with a paddle so that the course is west and not north-west. During the day the wind shifts slightly to the east and then to the north of east. If it holds for a few days we may reach Vava'u, or perhaps with luck, strike one of several small uninhabited islands which lie between Niue and Vava'u. We examine this possibility, Conrad setting off on the great Romantic dream and quizzing Tarabo. How would we build a house; what would we eat; how would we make tools; spears for fishing; fish traps; hooks from shell, stone and bone, as countless generations have done since time immemorial. It was such a lovely dream that we held on to it for most of the day. The dream's scenario eventually yields stone and shell adzes with which we cut wood and make an outrigger canoe. The canoe is rigged with rope from coconut husk and the sail is made from pandanus leaf. In this craft we reach Vava'u.

'Once there were people on that island,' Fia says, recalling an old story. 'One of the women was very sick and was going to die. Her husband got in the water and swam 40 miles to Vava'u.'

It is a story very much to Conrad's liking. As the wind continues to veer north, north-east, our hopes rise for the possibility of one of these islands or for Vava'u.

Monday, 22 August. Watch 8 seconds fast. Beacon used for twenty-four and a half hours. Rob and I had taken turns with the bailing during the night, our spirits buoyed by the fact that the wind continued to come from NNE. At noon, Rob shot the meridian and confirmed that we were approximately 40 miles north of Niue and some 30 miles to the west. This puts us some 140 miles east and approximately 30 miles north of Vava'u. The wind has died considerably, but it is the right wind. We continue trying to sail the raft.

I also notice that more water has disappeared during the night, and now resolve to take action. As the amount taken is generally reflected in the amount passed out, the suspicion centres on one individual.

On the positive side, Rob quotes various sources to say that a little salt water when taken with fresh water, will not do any harm. It is something we had experimented with before. Now it becomes a necessity. Rob, Fia and I have been taking about 115 millilitres of salt water for the past few days, getting rid of the after-taste by sucking vitamin C pills and then serving the first part of the 115 millilitre fresh water ration.

While we now have raised hopes of reaching Vava'u, I realise that unless the raft fetched up on the beach, my chances of survival are nil. I write a letter to this effect to Judy. Fia also knows that he had almost reached the end of the road. He tells me that if we are not rescued, he will be dead within two days. For my part, I know I will not be strong enough to fight through surf or to drag myself over coral reefs. But it gives me great heart to see Conrad in excellent shape and Tarabo still strong as a horse. If it is at all possible, I tell myself, Tarabo will save that boy.

There is an incredible number of dolphin fish around the raft. A barracuda has also been with us for two days and a small shark has kept station. Fia opened the canopy one morning to see a huge shark looking at him. It passed to and fro and under the raft but eventually went away never to come back. Thank heavens! We had very bad moments when the dolphin fish would go under the raft and bump the floor. Sometimes they would bump it very hard, causing pain and initially also fear, to the person above. I was kneeling most of the day and watched the fish, eventually making up a lure with coloured synthetic fibre. I tried this several times, streaming it behind the raft and pulling it in when the dolphin fish would come to look. They ignored it. Towards evening when Fia was again steering the raft towards the south-west, gaining valuable southing to put us on the same latitude as or even south of Vava'u, one of the largest dolphin fish decided to take the lure.

'Mahi mahi,' Fia croaked through parched lips. He grabbed the line which was attached to the raft's safety lanyard and held on with all his strength. The fish kept going, bent the hook, got off and went leaping away to freedom. When the excitement died down, I thought with regret about the food we lost.

'Never mind, Jim,' Paea said.

The significance of his remark; the way he looked at me and the way he said it, escaped me. But he would tell me again that night. The darkness came with a still, moonlit, calm night. The raft rose and fell on the peaceful swell. Rob and I took our turn to bail. We put Fia by the canopy and left him trying to sleep. Our discussion was again philosophical. Was there a God? Were we part of His grand scheme? Would He deliver us? Were we being presumptuous?

Then it happened.

'Listen,' Rob said. 'I can hear a ship's engine!'

James Siers, Taratai II – a continuing Pacific adventure, *1978*

SHIPWRECKED ON MIDDLETON REEF

ENGINEER Bill Belcher, aged 62 and sailing a modest 24ft yacht, had won the 1974 Transtasman single-handed race when, almost immediately, he decided to have a crack at the 1978 race from New Plymouth to Mooloolaba. He asked John Spencer to design a new and bigger boat, the Josephine 11, and built her in his back garden on Waiheke Island.

Belcher's remarkable story of that race centres not around a second win, nor even the achievement of a man in his mid-sixties completing the race at all, but on the events that followed the shipwreck of the Josephine on the notorious Middleton Reef off the coast of Brisbane. After headlines that proclaimed the apparent reluctance of race organisers to instigate a search, the Josephine 11 was found wrecked on the reef. Of Belcher or life raft there was no sign. He was eventually picked up by a Naurau-bound ship after drifting for 28 days, in astonishingly good health.

On Saturday 22 April he had been on the reef for seven days, beginning to wonder what, if any, attempts had been made to rescue him. He'd abandoned the Josephine, searched her for food and inflated the life raft. By the 24th he was beginning to reach some unpalatable conclusions about his chances of survival.

Tuesday 25th. It has been a lovely day all today, sun and only a gentle breeze. Measured the tide again, which gave high at 11 o'clock. In the afternoon got fed up waiting and did a recce for deep water. Found that it only slowly deepened and so decided to leave *Josephine* and set out on our own. Started about 4 pm in two feet of water, and ended up about half a mile away in clear water about 3'6" so there should be no trouble. I have both anchors and warps but together they are less than one good one. Found a bottle of beer in *Josephine*, so celebrated our parting by having a drink, but this is written before in case I get drunk on a very empty stomach.

Tomorrow will see if I can go out with the tide. I wore my shoes to pull the boat, they are a good idea, as I have no foot damage. Today's menu: breakfast – small piece of chocolate; lunch – tin of soup; supper – beer and a portion of cheese.

Wednesday 26th. A plane flew over at 0750 hours: 240° wind, which was north, now more to the west. Writing very difficult due to sea motion. Rearranged the cabin, with everything tied down ready for the open sea. If and when. The wind is still contrary and no sign of its going to the SE which is the prevailing wind. Shifted to a new position nearer the gap, but rather close to some coral patches. Had my third motion of the jaunt and some stomach upset after a tin of pears but seem OK now. Have had a little extra water to compensate. At present reckoning I can last out twenty-five days food, and rather longer for water, so if only I can get out of here there's a chance of being picked up sooner or later, but when will this wind change?

Thursday 27th. It rained last night, and now I have a full can, so am increasing the water ration to 1 1/4 pints.

Last night, after the rain, the wind went round to south (magnetic) which is nearly, but not quite, good enough to get me through the gap. I am getting better at looking after the raft, and last night I got about 1 to 1 1/2 gals of water into the can without getting the rest of the boat too wet. However, I had to use the torch, which is getting low in its first set of batteries. I hope the second lasts out.

It's funny, this survival business. One moment you think you will make it, and then the next not. But then you start thinking, how will I die? Will I just fade away – or what? I don't mind for me, but I have rather let Aileen down, although she should have enough to live on, and can presumably draw a pension in a couple of years' time. All told she should be OK. Perhaps, however, it will be better to try to get back myself. Incidentally I wonder what the search-and-rescue people really have done – if any. Is it the usual story of not having a yachtie to advise them?

Friday 28th. Last night low tide 1830, I again moved the liferaft, but not so far, as it was cold and a 15-knot wind blowing, which all made it very uncomfortable. This morning I find we are well placed for a getaway, but high tide is not until 1.15, so will have to hope the wind does not change before then. Food yesterday: 1 tin of bully beef. This morning had breakfast of about three finger-lickings of peanut butter and water.

Hurray! Hurray! At about 1320 we cast off. I kept one anchor aboard and jettisoned the other. At about 1340 we were through the reef and going nicely with a 12-knot wind behind us. Running with the wind is much more comfortable than being at anchor. Celebrated by drinking an extra ration of water.

Now all I have to do is to stay alive for the next twenty days or so, and keep a good lookout. I have plenty of rockets and so can afford to waste a few if I meet a likely proposition. I now have a chance again, but didn't rate my chances of leaving Middleton in one piece very high . . .

Saturday 29th. Had a good night last night. I am beginning to be able to sleep in the completely rolled-up position. It was a fine night, and this morning the ship on the reef was out of sight; allowing 15 miles this gives 1 knot over the time. I have constructed a speedo today, and have kept a record of time and distances. It has been a lovely day, wind about 8 knots and no cloud. Grub – one tin of bully beef.

Sunday 30th. No wind all night and this morning just the same, although there still seems to be a slight drift to northward. I still seem to be in good health, but slowing up a little. Do a lot of thinking. Will I be picked up – if so, by what sort of ship? The possibilities are endless, and all get indulged in, in turn. On the other hand, if I don't get picked up, what happens to the raft? Does it eventually reach shore and thus enable the authorities to declare me dead, or does it wander off, and almost sink and so become invisible?

All day long it has been fine with wind about 6–8 mph, giving me a speed of 0.4 knots. Grub today was one tin of fruit salad – very tasty. Otherwise 1 1/4 pints of water daily and a good look around every half hour.

I had my first signs of weakness today. I tend to black out if I get up too quickly for my look around. Also if I look into the sun. But still, this is after 15 days, so I suppose I can't complain. Most of the day made up thinking of all types of ship which might pick me up and their destination. Silly, but it keeps the mind amused.

Monday 1st May. What a day to have a procession! Last night was again calm with very little progress, but this morning the wind is up a little to about 10 knots, and we are sailing at 0.74 k in nearly the right direction. We have had quite a good day, about 10 miles at 310° which is all progress, but the wind is now dying for the night, I'm afraid. Food: a tin of herring, which I had no particular appetite for. It seems that if I go out through lack of food, it will be painless, as gradually you seem to lose the desire. Spent the day designing windmills.

Tuesday 2nd May. A good night's progress. My health seems good and I now sleep when I want it, and do not try to force it. Result, better nights but still plenty of wakeful intervals for watch-keeping. A good day's wind and good progress, a few showers but not enough to wash the cloth and get clean water, but I was able to drink some. Grub – one tin baked beans which were eaten bean by bean. Working out our speed and the time taken, it looks as if it is going to be an interesting race with time. I can still win without playing the overtime on no food at all.

Wednesday 3rd May. A good night's progress again with some showers, but not enough to clean the tent and provide water. Evening: Again a good day with plenty of wind for progress and we have made 13 miles today.

The present estimate is tinned food – 12 days. Liferaft rations – 12 days. Starve – 12 days – i.e. 36 days at 8 miles per day. This should see us on the beach, but am I going to be alive to tell the tale? Poor Aileen – it must be hell waiting and not knowing what to do, particularly as my time has already run out as regards ordinary search-and-rescue time.

Thursday 4th May. A good night's progress again, this time with no rain squalls. Calculations: to Mooloolaba, 420 miles on 315°. The distance to the coast if N and S 290 miles, allow a further 40 miles of curvature and total distance is 250 miles. We have come 78 miles, so there is another 170 to the shore, or 100 to 150 to go to the sea lanes. This looks like 20 days. Still possible.

The last few days the wind has slackened at dawn but picked up soon after. Velocity measured by a 20′ line on the end of a quoit – this is thrown out in front of the liferaft, and the time taken to overtake the quoit taken. 12 secs ± 1 knot. The raft has a maximum speed of about 1.2 to 1.3 knots at 18 k wind. At 12 k wind this comes down to 1 knot, while a very small breeze gives about .3 to .5 knots. Evening: quite a day – caught and ate a sooty black gull. It was the third bird which had alighted on the canopy since we started. It, however, was not fast enough, and tasted quite nice. It was very plump with plenty of flesh on the breast. Other grub – one tin of sardines. Had some pimples on my bottom, but with care these are not so bad today, will have to be careful however.

Friday 5th May. The wind died at 2.30 last night but came up again to give about 3/4 knot. The seagull sits rather heavy on the stomach. Trying to make a good fishing line. There are no traces, so trying to make one from the electric wire. No further excitement today, tried fishing but without luck. The only decent bite was before I had a metal trace. Wind is easing all the time, and we are now down to 3/4 k but still in the right direction.

Saturday May 6th. A peaceful night with a nice steady wind as far as I can tell. I seem to be OK physically with cuts healing up with no trouble. I get hungry but on about 1 1/4 pints of water a day do not get particularly thirsty. Fishing no good in spite of there being fish about. After a bit of a struggle had a bowel motion this morning, but I certainly must be using most of the food I am eating. Checked water – have used about 1 1/4 gallons in 9 days. This gives me still about another 32 days which (DV) should be enough.

Ornithology: till today we have had 2 or 3 black birds as eaten, and 4 small white birds plus a very occasional wave dancer. Today we have 4 birds, sooty on top, black patch near the eye, mostly whiteish underneath with a thin well-forked tail. Does this mean anything?

Evening. A good fine day with good progress. Am now left with 5 tins plus 2 of sardines. This seems enough if progress keeps up. It seems that the chances are now much better than they were when I started.

Sunday May 7th. A quiet night with little progress, however some is better than none, it seems to have picked up a little this morning.

Evening. A good day's progress and quiet. The tin which I opened thinking soup was baked beans and sausages. They were consumed bean by bean which took nearly an hour. Wonderful! Calculating today something should happen in 3-5 days. Grub still for about 20 days, so prospects are getting better all the time, as long as I don't get a week of contrary winds.

Monday May 8th. A wild night last night – was twice nearly turned over by big waves. I don't know how far we went but judging by last night and this morning, at least 15 miles.

Evening. A very quiet and uninteresting day with the wind dying soon after sunup to give no more than 1 knot. However better than nothing and we are now getting within a reasonable distance of our objective. 3 days should see land, if not 5 will. Accurate navigation! Longing to know what the liferaft rations consist of, but so far have been firm in my intention to use up all the tins first. One small tin of sardines is however rather a small day's supply, so my fortitude may break down. It probably depends on our progress as to whether I think it safe to muck about with raft rations.

Tuesday May 9th. A very wild night with rain squalls – calms – you have it. But could not get any good water. Everything inside a bit wettish; overcast but clearing.

Afternoon. Now the wind has gone round to the NE – annoying of it, just as we were doing so well. Also had a bowel movement (expand method). Also a dissertation on noise required after last night's effort. (The above references to bowel movements and the effects of noise were subsequently expanded) Today would have been our last day if it had not been for the wind shift. We started off at 1.7 knots at the end of last night's storm.

May 9th continued. My ornithology is all haywire as the same birds are here today. The wind settled to give a course of 225° – I hope it doesn't get any worse or else we will have to use the drogue. Today a fit of depression; first of all, with a easterly how do we land through the surf? Now that it has gone NE how do we get there? A real fit of depression. We have to watch the wind tonight and decided what to do about it. Incidentally – bowels opened. Reading back there is too much tautology in this diary, as it is not written up at one time, but every morning and evening, and sometimes in between.

Wednesday 10th. A peaceful night with a further wind shift at 5 am, which brings us on to 195m, which gives us very little useful progress. Have had to construct a sine table to enable me to work out distances. Very approximate, but so is everything else.

By 10 am we are going due south so streamed the drogue and have been like this all day, but with rough seas which make writing very difficult. Have decided to start on the raft's rations tomorrow, and keep the last 3 tins, 1 sardine, 2 small fruit, in reserve. Due to the wind and rough seas, no progress, so morale is low.

Thursday 11th. The morale of the troops is up. Everything got wet last night and all is misery, but I collected enough water to nearly fill the jerrican, and have started on the rations, which are good and more than I have been having. Also with the rain the wind has swung, and we are now going 045° – not where we want to go, but not so very far off.

Evening. Wind still giving course 045° and rain off and on all day, so no chance of drying. Am trying the space blanket as it, at least, cannot get wet.

Friday 12th. Still raining – everything wet. Have put on wet-weather gear. Writing is hard as cannot put book on my knee, as it is damp and will wet the book. Wind still gives 045° perhaps the rain will go when the wind changes. 2.30 got swamped, now everything completely wet. I nearly resigned.

Saturday 13th. Last night I was quite prepared to give it all away because of cold, wet and *fear*. This morning I have survived and the wind has gone round to due south which is hopeful. Everything is sopping wet but I think I can cope.

Midday. Everything is much lighter. The sleeping-bag is half dry, so am I, and I have just stolen a day's rations from the last few tins, and it was baked beans – a lovely lunch. Have just heard an airplane's engines, but could not see it. We are now on a reasonable course for home again 315° but only making slow speed as the wind has died. This however is good for trying to get everything dry again and provided it picks up again we can afford the distance for the comfort . . .

So ends the log kept in the margins of the survival handbook. Some comments on it, written subsequently, follow.

I reported that the sumlog packed up on Friday evening, but references to the tape transcript indicates that this took place on Wednesday night. It just shows how very easy it is to make mistakes even after only about a week.

When I was on the reef I thought that it did not dry out. This was due to the waves, which were very large, washing right over the reef. Later, when the wind and waves died down, the reef was well exposed at low tide.

I stated that it was nearly a week after we struck that I got out of the liferaft and examined *Josephine*. This seems a long time and indicates that I was suffering from depression induced by shock, and that I must have been pretty apathetic, waiting to be rescued and not worrying about much else. Later I either got over my shock; or the realisation that I was not going to be rescued made me pull myself together.

The last tape recording I made was around midday and it was only two hours later that we struck. At the speed we were going the distance covered in that time would be about twelve to fourteen miles, at which distance the two wrecks on Middleton Reef might have been visible in calm weather. Under the conditions obtaining, however, with thirty-five to forty-knot winds and pretty large waves, the visibility from a small boat is very restricted, and even if a very occasional glimpse had been possible I would have found it hard to identify what I saw.

The log kept on the margins of the survival handbook was not started until the following Saturday, that is to say a week later. I would have started a record earlier, but for the first day or two I was not interested and anyway had no writing materials. It was not until my second or third trip to the boat that I found the two pencils and was able to do some writing. There are inconsistencies between the tape and the diary, particularly as to the timing of my resetting the sails, but at even a week away the mind is not to be relied upon to be very accurate.

I think I realised, by the time I started to write the diary, that I had a story on my hands. Either that, or perhaps I was trying to leave a record behind in case I came unstuck. At any rate, considering the difficulty of trying to write very small letters on a far from stable platform, I seem to have really spread myself.

My training has been that of an engineer, factual rather than philosophical, so that when left alone with a pencil and paper I may try to record the tides or the wind strength or even nature notes, but cannot get my mind up in the clouds and write pages of guff which may not mean much but do fill up volumes.

In a small liferaft there is little fact or event to comment upon, hence my rather inconsequential references to fish in the lagoon and birds in the open sea. The reader should treat these references not as the work of a trained observer but rather as objects which presented themselves and on which I could hang my thoughts. The interest is not in the objects described but in the state of mind of the person who tried to make the description.

Of the aids that I carried to alert the search-and-rescue, the radio was the first I tried. As, however, the aerial was broken my first Mayday was not effective. After I had seen the aerial was missing I switched on a New Zealand-made Osbourne bleeper. This has no indicator light and I had no means of finding out if it was working. As, however, the set was new and had new batteries fitted before the race it should have worked. As no one picked up any signal I can only assume that it was defective in some way.

The batteries of these sets are supposed to last seventy-two hours. After this time I switched on the American-made bleeper which I had packed in the liferaft. This instrument had a new battery obtained from the importers and fitted about two months before the start of the race. When switched on, the indicator light showed only a slight glow and after about three hours did not light up at all. This seemed to indicate that the battery, which should have lasted a further seventy hours or so, was defective.

As far as I am aware it is just possible that the unexplained signal picked up by an aircraft near Norfolk Island and thought to be sent out by Lloyd George was from my set. The times seem to match, but the distance seems excessive unless Hurricane Hal was playing tricks with radio reception.

As far as the race organisers were concerned the fact that they got no radio signal from me was no cause for worry as radios are known to be unreliable. And when no bleeper signal was received this suggested to them that I was OK, as otherwise I would have used one and they would have heard it. It is a possible argument.

This diary, like the first taped log, has been left unedited, hence the lack of polish in the writing. However it seems that the diary gives a more vivid impression of my mind and physical state than attempts afterwards to write up the whole incident from my memory of what I think happened. The diary was used however by a journalist to write up my experiences in a series of articles. These made good reading, with eerie voices, and spirit companions, and myself holding on to my sanity with both hands. All good stuff, and it filled up the newspaper, but it had no connection with the truth of what actually happened.

Bill Belcher and *Aileen Belcher*, Shipwrecked on Middleton Reef, *1979*

SATAN'S EYE

ROBERT McIntyre *came from a dairy farm at Flat Bush, north of Auckland, so* Flatbush Man *was what he called the brand-new 44ft cutter he flew to Taiwan to buy in May 1975. Aged 34, he was newly separated from his Canadian wife, and the rebellious 'Flat Bush' lust for freedom and adventure was upon him. After his planned voyage to Guam and Hawaii, New Zealand for Christmas and then back to the Canadian seaboard, the yacht would fetch a good price in Vancouver. Why not?*

With his old Flat Bush mate Gary Green, two other younger crew, and very little sailing experience between them, the trip to Guam was 'a piece of cake.' But heading north-east towards Hawaii, the conditions deteriorating, they avoided a collision with a passing ship by just twenty feet. The wind increased to 80 knots, then to over 120 knots; the seas became mountainous as the full force of Typhoon Winnie struck. McIntyre was swept overboard but the crew managed to winch him back aboard. Worse was to come: the capsize, the dismasting, the abandoning ship, the thirteen days in a life-raft before they were spotted by a Russian trawler. Rarely in nautical literature has a capsize such as that which doomed Flatbush Man *been described in such hair-raising and minute detail.*

Flatbush Man suddenly lurched to starboard again, only this time without the preceding crash against her hull. Down on her side she went, throwing Jim off the bunk and pressing Sarah and Gary against the starboard settee. My arms shot out for support in the confines of the passage. We were still going over. Then, suddenly, the mast must have hit the water, for the momentum decreased and we very smoothly began to roll upside down.

There was a terrible crashing as sharp-edged floor hatches dislodged themselves, plummeting dangerously to their new locations. Drawers fell out, spilling their contents. Cupboards opened from the pressure of bottles and cans which were now smashing on the opposite wall and ceiling. There was the sound of rushing water and the engine starting to race. Bodies desperately clambered around the inner periphery.

My mouth said the first thing my brain told it to, 'Christ, what an experience!' From the corner of an eye I saw the others flash a glance at me from their new floor, incredulous at such a casual statement in this moment of horror.

The rolling action stopped and we were perfectly balanced upsidedown. My legs were straddling the locker lid where sails and other equipment were brought into the boat. The lid had wrenched open and I was looking into a void of beautiful phosphorescent green ocean. The water lay in the hatch smooth as a mirror; air pressure caused by the sea rushing into the boat through the door hatches, which were lower down, was stopping it from bubbling in.

The engine was screaming protestations from its new suspended position, the volume amplified by the resonance of that section of hull now out of the water, like a dome soundshell.

The cabin and engine compartment lights were still working; I didn't have time to think of the consequences had they gone out. Looking up at the engine which was racing itself to death, I noticed the oil pouring out of the breather and filler caps. Reaching up I grabbed the stop lever and held it back. There was no difference, for the engine was dieseling on the lubricating oil being forced past the pistons in its inverted position. I held on to the stop lever for a good one and a-half minutes before accepting the fact that it would have to burn itself to a halt.

Gary, picking himself up, had noticed the water charging in through the door hatch louvres in a boiling torrent. Grabbing one of the displaced cushions, he held it firmly against the louvres, managing to partly quell the flow. He needed more than two hands and yelled at Jim, who was lifting himself out of the accumulated foot of water, using the mast to aid in the struggle, 'Quick, help me, Jim!'

Jim, who at this stage didn't even know we were upsidedown, clambered over to assist Gary. He saw a cabin light shining up through the rising water and, suddenly realising the situation, yelled, 'We're upsidedown!' Triggered by the shock and misunderstanding what Gary wanted, he lunged at the hatch, viciously kicking at the louvres, thinking Gary wanted an escape exit formed.

'What are you doing!' Gary barked. 'I want the hatch sealed up, not fuckin' booted out!'

Sarah grabbed Jim's arm. 'Help us hold the cushion, Jim.' Jim sheepishly stopped kicking and made a grab for the cushion, helping to contain the water. Sarah backed into the cushion, leaning her weight against the centre while the other two held the outer edges.

The engine began to slow down with the harsh sound of seizure caused by lack of lubrication. It ground to a halt and we were plunged into deathly silence. The noise of the storm was cut off by the thickness of the hull; all outside exits were under water. A thin ringing sound could be heard as the outside waves pelted the shell held firmly by the mast in the grip of the moving water and the keel caught by the wind, both in perfect balance. Gas from the upended batteries began to affect nostrils and throats.

I peered around at the havoc, wondering when we were going to come back over, as the surging flotsam over the lights created changing shadows. There was no physical action we could take. Sarah kept her weight on the cushion as she watched the water level rising. 'What's going to happen? I thought sailboats had to come back up?' Her voice was thin.

'She'll come back up. Come on mast – break off?' Gary urged.

'This is too much. We have to come back up soon. Alex was right when he said "We make strong for you," about that mast.' I saw that the water had risen to two feet.

'What if it fills with water first?' Sarah asked quietly.

'Then we'll get out of here,' Jim replied.

'Where will you go to, Jim?' Gary's eyes quickly scanned the closed trap. Jim fell silent.

I cast my eyes up to the floor, now our ceiling, noticing the bare hull where the floor hatches had dropped out all the way up to the forward cabin. The foam rubber cushions and other floatable objects such as drawers and packaged food were swaying with the rhythmic movement of the boat. I thought of the mess that would have to be cleaned up. All the electrics would have to be replaced; the wiring and switch panels along with auto pilot and instruments; the engine rebuilt and its accessories replaced. My mind tired of the thought. I had salvaged swamped boats while in business and this one would be a major job. The will-destroying seasickness wrenched at me, and I thought, 'No, I can't go through all that with this boat. Come on, boat, flip back over.'

'Come on, mast – let go!' Gary growled again. Considering the circumstances, all remained calm. We were held by a powerful energy force in which panic was overruled. All we could do was wait for the next stage and react accordingly. All faces looked at the surging mass around them.

'Here she goes!' yelled Gary as *Flatbush Man* began to roll. 'Hang on!'

The roll began easily, then gained swift momentum as the keel fell off centre. There was no mast to act as a brake, for the mast had let go.

Water, floor hatches, equipment and a fresh supply of drawers and fixtures flew dangerously through the air. Bodies were in orbit, for the final speed of righting would not even allow a superman to hang on. There was an abrupt halt as the keel found its centre of gravity; we were the right way up again. My own position in the passage proved the safest, as there was nowhere to fly to in its limited space.

'Everyone OK?' I called.

'I'm all right.' Gary and Sarah answered, picking themselves up.

'How about you, Jim?'

'I think my arm's broken. I can't move it and it hurts like hell. I was thrown against the mast.'

The water was up to three feet deep now and, though I wasn't sure, it appeared to be rising. This had to be imagination; we were up the right way again.

Inside was inundated chaos. Anything that could have possibly dislodged had done so. The water level was over the bunks and settees. Drawers, floor hatches, bottles and cans, food and cooking gear were all bobbing around on the surface in the swaying mass.

'You'll have to wait, Jim. The mast has to be checked.' Gary spoke rapidly, struggling through the confusion and flinging the hatch open. The ladder had fallen, and he had to hoist himself up with his arms while propping a leg on the galley sink top. Once outside, he saw that the wind had abated to about eighty knots. Typhoon Winnie had satisfied her lust and was now moving on.

Gary checked the position of the mast and was relieved to find it lying parallel to the hull on the windward side, held by the collapsed stay wires. If the mast had been end on it would, somehow, have had to be chopped off, for it could have driven through the side of the hull like a pile driver, eventually sinking us.

The end of the boom was still attached by the main sheet and was flailing back and forth in the air like a giant scythe as the hull pitched and rolled. Gary waited for it to reach the lowest point in its arc, then rapidly winched in the sheet.

Flatbush Man was steadier without the long lever of the mast to assist in the rolling action. Her movement back and forth was at a faster rate with less arc as the keel carried out its job more effectively without the competition of the overhead spar. Gary, seeing there was nothing more that could be done at the moment, sprang down inside again.

I had stayed beside the engine to keep the pump operating. There was no lying down as before, for the water level was now over three feet and was covering the engine exhaust manifold. The pump, which was mounted higher than the engine, was working heroically as I kept the strainer clear, but the water level was catching it up.

'How does it look, Robert?' Gary asked anxiously.

'Not at all good. The water is coming up fast. Something has happened. Better start cranking the gusher pump, fast! Better prepare to abandon also, just in case.'

'OK, Honkey.' Gary flew into action. 'Come on, Sarah, we have to start pumping.' Gary and Sarah headed out to the cockpit, then Gary stopped, calling, 'Anyone seen the flashlight?'

'It was on the chart table before we rolled. It'll be gone now,' Jim answered.

'Son of a bitch!' Gary muttered.

In the outside darkness, Gary opened the port cockpit locker and swept his arm around for the pump handle. His hand came across a round tube and he extracted the handle, then fitted it into the pump aperture on the port bulkhead. 'You pump, Sarah. I'll go down and help Jim out here.'

Sarah began pumping. 'Are we going to sink?'

'Shit no, get fuckin' pumping!'

Jim had moved with difficulty through the mass of floating obstacles to the hatch. It was almost impossible for him to balance with the use of only one arm. He gasped with pain as he shot his good arm out for support and the movement jarred his left shoulder.

'You all right, Jim?' Gary called down.

'Get me out of this place! The pain is killing me and I can't climb out.'

'I'll help you into the cockpit. Maybe it's just dislocated. I had that in football. Here, give me your hand.' Gary hoisted Jim into the cockpit. He eased him into a sitting position. 'Lie down, I'll have a look.'

'Just you be careful!'

'That's what it is, all right. I don't think it's broken. Your shoulder blade is sticking out because the arm has come out of its socket. Just relax and I'll try jerking it back in. It may hurt, but it'll be worth it.'

'Come on, you don't know what to do!'

'Yes I do. I used to pop my own arm back in. Relax.'

Gary put a foot under Jim's arm and with both hands he jerked violently. There was a scream of pain. The arm was no better.

'Sorry, buddy. Let's try one more time. Relax.' There was another cry as Gary wrenched on the afflicted limb. Still no success.

'That's enough!' Jim yelled. 'I'll put up with it the way it is.'

'Right. Stay there while I see what's happening down below.'

I had to keep two strainers clean now as Sarah worked the gusher pump. The one and a half inch pipe from the gusher pump dropped down close to the electric pump pickup, which aided the task. The strainer on the bigger pipe was too small to allow the high volume of water Sarah was trying to pump to pass through. A vacuum was created, cutting down the amount of water that could be lifted.

'What's it look like now?' Gary came beside me.

'Bad! Still rising fast. Grab me a knife, Gary. I'll cut the strainer off the gusher. It won't plug with garbage going through it.'

Gary waded back to the galley and opened the only drawer that hadn't fallen out. Wrenching it open he found the large carving knife and forced his way back to where I was. With the sharp blade, I cut through the plastic pipe, now slippery with engine oil, and dumped it back in the water which was now climbing over the electric pump; not being the immersable type, this pump would soon give up from the dunking. The knife fell out of my hand.

'I'll check up front for a leak,' Gary said.

'Right,' I said. 'I'll check the aft cabin. We're going to have to move fast.'

Dragging open the aft cabin door, which was jammed with my diving cylinder and other floating objects, I waded into the cabin. Water seemed to be boiling out of the rudder inspection hatch in the aft end of the bunk and out of the locker in the front of the bunk. I bent down and pushed my right arm in through the locker, feeling around the fibreglass hull. I couldn't reach far enough, so I pushed my head under the water for more arm length. My worst fears were true. I felt the serrated edge and a cavity where the rudder skeg should have been. It had been torn off, possibly when we whipped back upright. There was no way to seal the huge aperture; no way the pumps could keep up if we tried to seal it.

A decision was required fast. Better to make the life raft ready now, forgetting the hole; then there would be at least a chance for survival.

Back in the passage I noticed the smaller pump had stopped and was smoking. The water was half way over the engine compartment light. 'Gary,' I yelled, 'it's time to abandon. There's a hell of a hole in the back. Nothing's going to hold the water off!'

'Where's the hole?' Gary shouted.

'The skeg's broken off under the bunk. We have to move fast. With a keel we'll sink sooner than a power boat would.'

'OK, that's it then.'

'Sarah, forget the pump! Come down here and throw food up into the cockpit! We're leaving!'

Sarah dropped back into the saloon and began collecting canned meats and other goods that had trapped themselves in various places, handing them to Jim who was lying in the cockpit near the door hatch. She never said a word as she carried out her task for she knew that speaking would only slow down the programme.

Gary and I edged to the aft deck where the self-inflating life raft was secured. We were cloaked in terrifying darkness and had to move carefully. The outboard motor was mounted on its bracket immediately above the life raft and restricted my access. Undoing the motor's clamps, I lifted it off the bracket and threw it over the side, thinking, 'Sorry, motor, you have to go.'

'We may as well take the inflatable dinghy with us too. What do you think, Honkey.'

'You'll have to inflate it first. Are the bellows around?'

'No, they fell out when we rolled. There's some air in it yet, so it should float well enough to carry some of the stuff.'

'Go ahead. I'll get the life raft ready.'

The dinghy was lying on the aft deck where, earlier, Gary had tied it with random twists and knots. Working in the restricting darkness he yanked and tore at the lines, inwardly cursing the secure job he had made. He had forgotten his fatigue, as had we all; no time, in a moment such as this, to realise the body had overspent itself long before. His hands worked fast, finger nails broken from wrenching at the fouled lines. A tremendous effort, and one of the ropes parted as *Flatbush Man* lurched in the ocean; the wind may have lessened but the seas hadn't abated in the slightest.

I yanked on the slipknots that held the life raft in its cradle and began sliding the canister forward up the lee deck. 'Careful! This is our only chance of survival.'

I was beside the gate in the lifelines and decided not to throw the raft over the side in case the inflation line pulled right out and allowed the raft to escape.

'Let's drop the dinghy in first, Gary,' I yelled above the din.

'All right. If we leave a line on both ends of the dinghy we can trap the raft before you inflate it.'

The dinghy was ready to be thrown over, and Gary and I stood at each end waiting for the stern to dip.

'Right, over!' I shouted. We both heaved outward. Unknown to us, a wave was coming over the top at the same time. It crashed down on us, knocking Gary over the side with the dinghy. He hit the water still hanging onto the line that had wrapped around his wrist. I threw the dinghy's forward line around a coaming winch, yelling, 'Sarah!' at the same time. We didn't have safety harnesses on. 'What is it?' Sarah sensed the panic.

'Quick, Gary's over the side!'

Sarah was beside me almost before I had the words out, and we began hauling the dinghy in through the gate, its lack of inflation allowing this. Gary clawed his way around the side of the dinghy and now had a hand over the mother boat's gunwale.

'Let go the dinghy, Sarah. Grab his arm!'

'Here, grab this first.' Gary gasped. He had brought the dinghy's stern line back with him thinking we would have trouble retrieving it with the storm holding it out straight. With the rope secured we hauled Gary back aboard. No words were exchanged.

Sarah headed back to the task of food finding, the water over her waist, surging debris trying to knock her off her feet. She would reach out for a floating can just as the boat heaved and the whole mass would move pushing her to one side. Her determination never let the situation gain the upper hand, however, as she doggedly passed the food up to Jim.

Gary and I now had the dinghy hanging out on the water by its two lines. The next stage was to drop the life raft inside the two lines. I was left to do this as Gary headed for the port cockpit locker to extract two five-gallon cans of water to take along with us.

I edged the raft canister over the gunwale, after tying the inflation line to a stanchion, and dropped it into the sea between the dinghy lines. The stern dinghy line was untied and held as I jerked the raft's inflation line, ready to let it go when the raft inflated, to allow room for the expansion. There was a loud hiss as the two clam shells of the canister dropped away and the raft speedily inflated. I let the dinghy line feed out as the raft grew to its full size, the orange canopy now rising. Both the vessels bobbed up and down, their lines taut against the fierce wind.

'OK, we're ready to put Jim in,' I called.

'Right, come on, Jim.' Gary bent down and lifted Jim by his good shoulder. 'You'd better come and get ready too, Sarah.'

'Here's a bottle of brandy for Jim,' Sarah called as she hoisted herself out of the hatch.

The life raft was held in close to the hull as we assisted Jim over the side. He leapt through the canopy opening at an opportune moment, stretching out to support himself in the dark interior as the raft hurtled around, slamming *Flatbush Man*'s side. The painter line was fed out a little to keep the raft from hitting the mother boat, but the angry wash still brought the rubber vessel back in.

'I'll go down and get the emergency gear,' I called to Gary, leaving him to watch the raft, and headed for the hatch. I stepped into four feet of water, my brain working at top capacity as I grabbed the compass and ELT transmitter off the bulkhead above the chart table, then forced the ELT into the left hand pocket of my pants. I smelled acid fumes as my hand reached into the locker above the batteries, groping for the flare gun and flares. 'Forget it, they've fallen out.' I moved into the saloon area and was bowled over by the force of water and solid materials. Now I stooped down, with head under water, reaching the drawer with the watermaker that had been given us by a friend in Guam. Yes, it was there; my hand came out with it.

Gary poked his head through the hatch. 'You get the watermaker, Robert?'

'Yes, I'll throw it up to you – catch.'

I threw the ten-inch square plastic container up.

'How about the sextant? It could come in useful.'

'All right,' I answered, stooping again. The drawer was jammed. The wooden box containing the sextant must have been floating in the drawer, jamming it against the frame. I straightened out, took another lungful of air, and tried again, shaking the drawer vigorously. It was no use.

'The sextant's stuck. We'll have to leave it.'

'Sarah wants you to grab some trousers.'

'All right. How's the raft?'

'Banging against the boat pretty hard but it should be right for a while. Sarah's watching it.' Gary called. Noticing some cans of ham jammed on a shelf he jumped inside to retrieve them.

'Christ, the water's high now! We'd better get going soon.'

'I'll just grab some stuff out of the aft cabin.'

I waded back toward the cabin. The light in the engineroom had gone out. I stooped where I thought the carving knife had fallen and my fingers latched straight onto it. I dragged open the cabin door and went in. Clothing was strewn all over the place and I threw trousers, woollen sweaters and various warm articles, including a down jacket, up to Gary who had climbed back to the cockpit and opened the door hatch. Noticing my wetsuit jacket floating on the surface I hurriedly stripped off my raincoat and shirt, and put the jacket on. This would stay warm regardless of the wet.

The tape recorder emerged out of the mess and I quickly removed the tape and stuffed it in my pocket. I grabbed my attache case with business papers and passports, and a case with tapes of a course I could give when reaching safety; the boat would be a complete loss but at least I had my business tapes and papers. I then climbed out on deck.

Gary had thrown all the food and water into the raft, and Jim pushed it to one side. Other items including the carving knife were put into the dinghy; a knife wasn't wanted in the inflatable life raft.

'That's it, we're ready to leave. Oh, let's just throw some items into the sea in case they search for us. It'll give them something to go on. I'll toss some stuff up to you, Gary.'

'OK, hurry. I don't like the way the raft is ramming the boat.'

I went down into *Flatbush Man* for the last time and my eyes took in the scene that had been our home for the past weeks. The feeling I had was strange. I didn't seem to have any sadness about the thought of abandoning this boat; in fact, there was a feeling of relief that it was all over, as if the whole episode was something that had to be – a phase of life ending when a new one started. Perhaps the seasickness distorted rational thinking. No, it couldn't have, my brain was working at full capacity as far as our safety was concerned. This boat wasn't a dying thing, it had always been dead.

I picked up floor hatches and handed them to Gary who then threw them over the port side into the ocean. I tried to lift a cushion, but it was too heavy, soaked with water. A drawer was handed up, followed by more floor hatches and other floating objects. That was enough.

On the way out my eyes caught sight of my guitar. It was half full of water and I choked back my emotions as I realised it wasn't practical to bring it along. The thousand-dollar classical instrument had travelled many places with me and was a reminder of many happy occasions. It now had to drown, and I felt a part of myself would go with it. My beautiful guitar! The lights suddenly went out, the sodden batteries finally failing.

'Come on, Honkey. Let's go.'

Out in the darkness of the heaving deck we helped Sarah into our new retreat. Then the dinghy line was tied to one of the safety handles vulcanised to the outside of the raft. Gary leapt in and held onto the painter line looped around a stanchion of *Flatbush Man*. As I jumped into the frighteningly dark pit he let the line go, saying softly, 'That beautiful boat – having to leave that beautiful boat.'

Robert McIntyre, Satan's Eye, *1977*

AT ONE WITH THE SEA

IN 1978 Naomi James became the first woman to sail single-handed round the world. Not only that, her time of 272 days in her 53ft yacht Crusader *was the fastest circumnavigation, by male or female, on record.*

Eight years earlier, aged only twenty, she had set off from New Zealand in search of adventure. With no qualifications to speak of, she found casual work in England and Europe. Then, a chance meeting in St Malo with the British yachtsman Rob James changed her life. Introduction to blue water sailing and marriage followed. She began to dream of her own venture: to sail single-handed around the world. Incredibly, despite her lack of sailing experience, she found support and sponsors, and set off from Dartmouth on September 9, 1977.

The voyage south was a rugged introduction to ocean sailing. Her navigation skills were rudimentary, her radio and self-steering broke down, her cat went overboard. Crusader *weathered several gales as she struggled towards Cape Town, turning eastwards on the long haul passing south of Tasmania and New Zealand bound for Cape Horn.*

On February 20, 1977, with about 2500 miles to go before Cape Horn, she was feeling 'fit and ready.' On the 23rd, with storm clouds gathering, she logged that she was much less confident. Then, near-disaster.

At six o'clock in the morning of the 24th there was a clatter on deck. Any new or strange noise usually brings bad news, but this was catastrophic. When I got up on deck I could do nothing but hold my breath and stare in horror at the mast. It was bending from side to side with each roll of the boat and on the deck, collapsed in a heap, were the starboard lower shrouds.

After a few seconds I ran to the mast and pulled down the mainsail. That left the storm jib set, and I let its halyard go. But then I saw that with no sail to steady it the mast's movement was even more pronounced, so I quickly hoisted the jib again. I stood back and looked. It was the leeward shrouds that were down and not the ones that had the weight – the ones on the windward side. This was strange but fortunate for if the windward ones had collapsed the mast would probably have gone.

After I'd watched for a few moments I decided it didn't look about to topple, so I climbed aloft to check the fittings which held the lower shrouds on the windward side. They seemed secure. I then looked on the other side of the mast to discover what had caused the shrouds to collapse, and saw that the fitting which held them had sheered. I climbed down and looked around for some immediate way to steady the mast, even if only temporarily. I thought the heavy rope spinnaker guys might do the job. They were in the cockpit locker, so I dragged one out and climbed back up the mast to make the end fast beneath the spreaders at the point of the broken fitting. Then I led the free end through a block which I fixed to the deck, and winched tight. I looked aloft and saw with relief that the mast had now stopped swaying. After that I went back to my bunk and assessed the situation. I couldn't sail with the mast in its precarious state, so the first thing was to decide how to strengthen it. Could I get the shrouds back up again?

The fitting which attached the shrouds to the mast consisted of a fork-shaped plate which, in turn, was held with a long stainless-steel bolt through the mast. Each shroud was fixed to the fork ends of the plate, and it was these that had broken. If I could drill a hole in each severed plate then perhaps it would be possible to fit them back by placing them over the bolt. That's if I could undo the nut....

Meanwhile, the overall situation looked fairly serious. I didn't know how long the mast would hold with rope, and I dared not put up more sail till I had repaired it more satisfactorily. I gave a fleeting thought to my position and then immediately put it out of mind – 2800 miles from New Zealand and 2200 from the Horn was not a prospect to contemplate. I stayed in my bunk for a little while to get warm while I decided what part of the planned operation to tackle first.

Breakfast seemed a good idea; going up the mast twice before eating had made my legs wobble like jelly. I heated some spaghetti but had to force it down. Then I hunted amongst the spares for tools and likely looking materials for the repair job.

At 1 p.m. I wrote in my log:

Things look black. I've been up the mast twice and, even though the wind has lulled somewhat, the effort of hanging on is exhausting. First, I tried to loosen the nut on the bolt, but it wouldn't budge – furthermore, it looks very much as if it won't be long enough to carry the two plates I want to put on. However, it's still worth a further try. I do have another bolt which is thinner and longer, and though not ideal it is better than nothing. I drilled a hole in one of the plates and then had to file it to fit the bolt. What a blessing I brought along a kitchen steel.

The barometer is still falling and it's raining. No sign yet of a wind change. Trying to sail with the prospect of a gale in the offing is pointless, but I've left the jib hoisted and I'm jogging along at two to three knots. I've rigged an extra spinnaker guy so now I have two replacement shrouds. I also have my bosun's chair ready which will allow me to sit while I work, and, if I tie it to the mast, this will also mean I have two free hands and don't have to use all my strength to hang on. The awful truth is that there's no chance of a flat sea in which to do the job; such things don't exist in these parts and when there's a calm, the rolling becomes worse than ever. A light wind with the boat close hauled would probably produce the steadiest motion, but I don't suppose I'll get it.

Now the reaction's setting in and what at first I thought would be easy I now realize to be very involved. Still, there has to be a way. If only the weather would be kind to me . . .

I'm going to try to have a little sleep. I feel so devoid of strength and I'm sure it's lack of sleep.

At 3 p.m. I wrote:

Couldn't sleep – too apprehensive. I'm going on with the drilling. I've just realized the barometer and weather are behaving in the same way that they did when I was off Tasmania.

As soon as it was dark I crept miserably into my bunk to wait for the night to pass. The weather was obviously brewing something horrible, but I tried not to let my mind dwell on the memories of the storm off Tasmania.

Then the following morning I wrote:

The weather didn't break in the night, but the barometer kept falling until it had reached 987 millibars. I thought of another way to fix the shrouds when I couldn't sleep so this morning I rose early, had tea and toast, and put on my oilskins. I got the bosun's chair out and put a spare harness round the mast to stop me from spinning. In addition I had a crescent spanner, mole grips and a socket spanner with ratchet – all tied to my harness with bits of string (a precaution after losing my best spanner yesterday). It was much easier to work from the chair tied in position, although I still suffered bruised legs from being flung from side to side.

My new idea was to overlap and bolt the broken pieces on to the original plate, but it was unworkable because there was too little material to drill. Still, after two hours of struggling I managed to free the nut from the bolt which was something I had been unable to do yesterday.

I was feeling relatively pleased with myself at the finish until I had a close look at the fitting on the other side of the mast and saw to my horror that it had also cracked. And it had cracked in exactly the place where the starboard side shroud had parted. As the port shrouds were in danger of coming down as well, I rigged guys on that side, too. There was absolutely nothing further I could do, and with so much else to worry about I simply carried on with the job of drilling.

The night of 25 February I wrote in my log:

Today seems to have lasted for ever. I spent the rest of the morning drilling and filing, then at mid-day, as there was still no wind and the barometer was more or less steady, I decided to go all out and see if I could get the job finished.

I climbed the mast to fit the new bolt and then found that it wasn't even as long as the old one! How could that possibly be? I was so absolutely certain that it was longer. I felt defeated, even cheated and so depressed I could have sat down and cried. I now had to go back to the original bolt hoping that it might just be long enough; it was already too late in the day to file the larger holes in the plates to the size which the thicker bolt required. As a desperate measure I fixed the shrouds with a snap shackle secured to the bolt – even that took me over two hours.

When I finally got back down to the deck the weather was breaking, and within minutes gale force gusts and rain were sweeping across the sea. I tied the sails more securely, removed all loose items on deck and stowed them down below. The barometer had risen several millibars in the last few hours, and I hoped it wouldn't begin to rise too fast. There was a deep blue hue all round the horizon which definitely wasn't blue sky.

It's now 23.00 and I've been trying for the last hour to make contact with Radio Wellington. I can hear them very clearly, but they don't seem to hear me at all. All this after I have made such an effort to hoist the aerial. It meant going up the mast yet again to free it from the temporary shrouds. I wanted to call Rob and let him know what had happened. Now it appears I can't even do that.

The starboard shrouds came down again at seven o'clock next morning. I couldn't see what had broken, and it was too rough to climb the mast. Still, the port shrouds with the cracked fittings were holding and so were my spinnaker guys; I only hoped the nut had stayed on the bolt. The weather was doing its best for me and the wind hadn't increased above force eight. The barometer, too, was rising slowly.

I began to consider the options that the situation presented: if I could make a reasonable repair, then I would press on to the Falkland Islands. If the repair was less satisfactory then I had to think of another plan, because the mast would be unable to stand up to the type of storms possible at the Horn. What about a port in South America? I wondered. I looked at the chart, but there seemed to be no suitable place south of latitude 30°. Besides, I had no large-scale charts with which to navigate along the coast. Then again the boat would probably not be able to sail satisfactorily to windward as often demanded in coastal sailing. I thought about returning to New Zealand, but was very loath to do that, as it would mean delaying my passage round the Horn until the following year. Also I would still have about 3000 miles of windward sailing simply to get there.

I concluded that the most favourable course was to make for the Falkland Islands, but to do so meant that at all costs I had to make a good job of repairing the mast.

In the meantime, the barometer had stopped at 999 mlb and was falling slowly again, and the wind had died away. I had spent the morning drilling holes in the shroud plate to fit the larger bolt, and while I was doing this I hit on an alternative idea. I wasn't certain that these plates would fit over the bolt so I decided to wind a wire strop around the mast and spreaders. At least it would be secure and hold in place even if it did obstruct the sail track and make it impossible to hoist the mainsail to its proper height.

By early afternoon the plates were ready with the holes now large enough to take a reasonable-sized rigging screw. I took the strop up the mast, having previously hoisted the shrouds on a halyard so that they would be in easy reach from my chair. I fixed the strop, secured the shrouds to it, and the arrangement seemed to go together quite well, except that I was disappointed to see it was impossible to tighten them sufficiently. The strop with its plates was obviously too long and would have to be shortened. However, I found myself with no time left to do this by then because the weather had worsened.

Another nagging fear, although it had lately diminished in comparison to my others, was the excessive play in the main rudder. The play appeared to be getting progressively worse and now – on top of it all – I had to consider the possibility that the rudder might fall off. What should I do? Go on . . . or go back? What would Rob have done? If only I could ask him. Even if I could have got a telegram to him, however, it would have taken perhaps a week to get a reply, and I had to make an immediate decision. I was very depressed and I ached badly from all the climbing.

My overall sailing time seemed to be of little consequence now that the fate of the trip itself hung in the balance, but by the evening of 26 February, two days after the rigging failure, I was seriously considering yet another alternative course. With the weather deteriorating rapidly, my fear and apprehension grew – then suddenly I had a brilliant idea. I would give up the plan to sail around the world via the Horn and go through the Panama Canal instead! It would mean returning to New Zealand where the rigging could be repaired, collecting more charts and then going on. It would add many more miles, but it was still worth considering. It was an exciting idea because it represented the possibility of turning defeat into something less than defeat. As I felt at the time I could no longer contemplate carrying on around the Horn and facing further punishment from the Southern Ocean.

26 February (Day 172)
6 p.m.: Goodness how I ache! I can feel every muscle and bruise acutely. Priorities now are: 1) to survive this weather; 2) to rig better shrouds; 3) to head north.

Fierce squalls pass every ten minutes or so, fifty-knotters at least. Each one builds up its own nasty waves and one of them has just broken right over Crusader. I saw it coming as I was looking out of the window, and I hung on. Luckily she didn't heel too far over. If only the barometer would rise. I've been lying-a-hull or just creeping forward with the storm jib for almost three days now, and I know that it could last a lot longer. I wish I had a way of cheering myself up. I've started re-reading one of the books in my library but haven't been able to concentrate at all.

Sometimes I lie in my bunk for an hour at a time, and to stop myself from staring at the barometer I gaze through the skylight at the rigging and sky, which doesn't make me feel any better. I can't sleep.

8 p.m. I'm soon going to be faced with the decision as to whether I should stay lying-a-hull and risk capsize, or steer down wind and risk personal injury from waves breaking over the stern. The thought of the way that wave bent the self-steering rudder gives me the shudders. There's a good force eight now with horrible squalls, and every now and again a wave bangs into Crusader with a shocking thud. I am running the engine in order to charge the batteries in case Radio Wellington try to contact me tonight. At least the diesel drowns the noise outside, and with the cabin light switched on the world seems quite friendly – so long as I don't look out.

I've made some re-arrangements down below and put the heavy things like boxes of tinned margarine and bags of sugar into empty lockers which can be fastened shut. Until now they have lain secured by lee-cloths on the top bunk: safe now, but hardly so in the event of a capsize.

Just before it got dark, I watched the effect of a squall coming over the sea. The waves were flattened, but the surface boiled under the furious wind. When a squall hits it shakes the mast and yet there isn't a shred of sail up. To drown the noise I am now playing the cassette, in place of the engine, and trying to deaden my mind with a glass of port.

On the 27th, that which I had always dreaded happened. Hours later I wrote in my log:

I capsized at 0.500 this morning. I was only half awake at the time, but suddenly aware that the wind had increased even beyond the prevailing force ten. It was just daylight, and I was trying to make up my mind whether to get up and try steering when I heard the deafening roar of an approaching wave. I felt the shock, a mountain of water crashed against Crusader's hull, and over she went. An avalanche of bits and pieces descended on me as she went under, and I put up my arms to protect my face. After a long and agonizing pause she lurched up again. I don't recall the act of climbing out of my bunk or even my sleeping bag, but I found myself well and truly free of them both.

As far as I remember, my first move was to look through the skylight at the rigging. It scarcely registered that the mast was still standing. I could hear water running into the bilges, so I quickly started to pump. For a terrible moment I felt that she was sinking, but as I pumped I could see the level going down. I pumped in a frenzy for a few minutes and then jumped on deck to see if the mast and rigging were all right.

I noticed one spinnaker pole had gone and the other was broken. The sails which had been lashed along the guard rails were dragging in the water. I hauled them aboard somehow and re-tied them to the rails. The radio aerial was flying loose, and the deck fitting from which it had been torn was now letting in water. As a temporary measure I plugged it with an old T-shirt and returned below to continue pumping the bilges. There was a strong smell of paraffin and milk. All the stores on the top bunk had been hurled out and the lee-cloth hung in shreds. My main concern was that she might go over again, so I left things below as they were, dug out some thick socks, gloves, hat and oilskins (all wet) and went to the helm to steer.

I secured my safety harness to the compass binnacle and faced the waves so that I could see them coming. The vision scared me stiff. The waves were gigantic, a combination of twenty-foot swells with twenty- to thirty-foot waves on top. One crashed near by, and it didn't need any imagination to realize what would happen if one of these monsters fell on me.

Suddenly *Crusader* started to surf, and I gripped the wheel desperately to keep the stern directly on to the wave and hold her straight. The next wave picked her up like a toy and wrenched all control from me. There was nothing but mountains of water everywhere, like waterfalls. The speed was impossible to gauge as there was nothing to judge it by, and the water all round me was at deck level, seething and hissing as if on the boil. Finally, the wave passed and she slowed down. I started to cry from a feeling of helplessness at being out of control and caught at the mercy of one of those awful waves. But I still had to leave the wheel to pump the bilges. When I got back to the wheel a wave broke over the stern, and I threw my arms round the binnacle as the water cascaded over me and filled the cockpit. Fortunately the volume of water wasn't too alarming. What was the lesser evil, I wondered: capsizing or being crushed by a wave? What would Rob do? Keep on top of the situation and trust to luck. I had to accept the dismal thought that there was only me here with my quota of luck; I steered numbly onwards and hoped that my luck would last.

On the fourth occasion that I went below to pump I saw the barometer was 1003 and rising slowly. I was confronted by a terrible mess, but the biggest things had held in place; there was no actual damage except for odd dents and scars on the roof of the saloon. My neck was very sore – somehow I must have pulled a muscle at the moment of capsize because I was aware of aches as soon as I reached the deck.

I steered on devoid of thought and incapable of feeling. At 10.30 a.m. I detected a lull, followed half an hour later by another. At last I began to feel better, and when on a trip below I saw a bottle of port rolling in a corner and took a swig. I also grabbed some water biscuits and ate them at the wheel.

At 11.30 the wind was down to force eight, but I kept steering until 2 p.m., by which time the wind had reduced to intermittent heavy squalls. It now seemed safe, so I left her lying-a-hull. The radio was drenched but it worked, and after an hour or concentrated cleaning up the interior was almost back to normal. However, there seemed to be a curious itinerary of missing items, including my fountain pen, the can opener, hairbrush and kettle. Most of my crockery was broken. A bad moment was finding my Salalite transistor quite dead; that meant no more time signals to check the error of my chronometer. Still, the clock was quartz and kept very good time, and there was no reason to think it might suddenly become erratic.

My bed was sopping wet, but fortunately I had a spare sleeping bag stowed away in a plastic bag. I hauled it out in triumph – bone dry! The cabin heater soon dried out my pillow. I had no dry footwear and on the floor was a slippery mixture of milk, paraffin and bilge water.

After clearing up I made myself a cup of tea and heated some tomato soup. I then slept for an hour but only fitfully as I could hear water dripping into the bilges. I finally stirred myself and found that the water was coming from the hole in the deck where the insulator had been. The best I could do was to fill it with more rags until the weather improved. At 5 p.m. the wind strength was force eight again, but the seas were settling down, and within two hours the barometer had begun to climb. The weather might have improved but I still felt very shaky.

My neck is still sore, and I have a lot of cuts on my hands which sting. I have no willpower to go out on deck and steer and yet if the wind increases to storm force again I shall have to make the effort. The weather must be on the mend even if it's taking a long time.

I awoke the following morning feeling sore and lethargic. I was still heading due north, but making a mere two knots. I didn't dare risk a bigger sail – not yet anyway. With the previous day's decision to sail back to New Zealand still in my mind, I studied the chart and felt an overwhelming depression. All those miles for nothing. Everything I had achieved so far would go to waste. It all seemed so wrong. I sat down and once again wrote out my arguments for giving up, or rather for not going on. The awful indecision was back. As *Crusader* was still in one piece after the previous day's storm, I wasn't sure that my earlier doubts about her seaworthiness in bad weather could still be used as reasons for abandoning my course to Cape Horn. I suddenly began to question my true motives for turning back, and all at once realized that the decision had been caused by fear. How then could I reconsider going on? The answer was that at the precise moment I also realized that by surmounting the storm I had almost totally eliminated the fear that had been dogging me for so long.

In my log I wrote:

a) If that rig can stand a capsize without the proper shrouds, then it should withstand ordinary bad weather when I fit a decent replacement; b) it's 2800 miles to the Falklands as opposed to 3000 to New Zealand against the current and head winds; c) surely there are not likely to be too many severe storms in the next three to four weeks.

Having written down these considerations the decision I had to make became clear: I turned around once more and set course for the Horn. My mood changed rapidly from depression to positive optimism – I was on my way again. I wrote down the priorities for the day:

Fix the hole in the deck where the aerial has broken off.
Make a replacement hatch-cover for the cockpit bin which is open and letting in water.
Fix the shrouds. Yippee! We're off!

Naomi James, At One With the Sea – alone around the world, *1979*

ICE BIRD

AT 2 a.m. on November 29, 1972, a monstrous breaking wave capsized the 32ft Ice Bird, *snapped off her mast and left her solo skipper, Dr David Lewis, on a wrecked yacht. He was at 60° S, a little over half way between New Zealand and South America; logic told him he was now doomed to a miserable and lonely Antarctic death. How one of the great navigators and small boat sailors of the 20th century coped with this capsize, and another, and then another in the course of two epic voyages into the deep south are related in a harrowing account of endurance and survival at sea.*

His plan had been to circumnavigate the Antarctic continent. By a miracle of seamanship, navigation and courage, through two capsizes and seven weeks of southern ocean hell, he made the first leg to the U.S. Palmer Research Station on the Antarctic continent, almost directly south of Cape Horn. While the shattered boat was repaired, Lewis flew off to journalistic commitments in America and Australia. In December 1973, he doggedly set off again in Ice Bird, *and by his arrival in Cape Town ten appalling weeks later knew that for many sound reasons the last stretch (Cape Town to Sydney through the Indian Ocean) would have to be abandoned. The miracle is that he set off on that second leg at all, given the earlier capsize and its aftermath . . .*

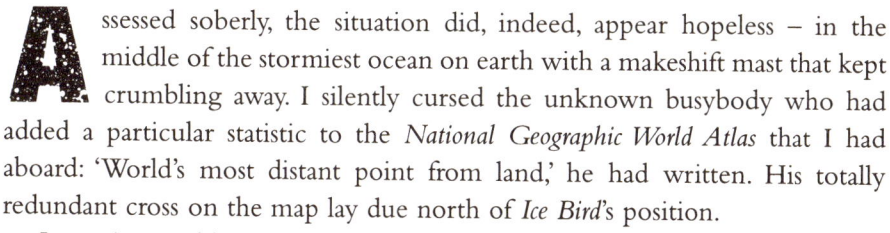

Assessed soberly, the situation did, indeed, appear hopeless – in the middle of the stormiest ocean on earth with a makeshift mast that kept crumbling away. I silently cursed the unknown busybody who had added a particular statistic to the *National Geographic World Atlas* that I had aboard: 'World's most distant point from land,' he had written. His totally redundant cross on the map lay due north of *Ice Bird*'s position.

It was impossible for me any longer to ignore the facts. 'A shutter has closed between a week ago when I was part of the living and since. Chance [of survival] negligible but effort in spite of pain and discomfort. These last are very great. Must go on striving to survive, as befits a man. Susie and Vicky without a daddy is worst of all.'

Next day, as blinding snow showers driving up from the south ushered in a new gale, I wrote further. 'Surprising no fear at almost certainly having to die, a lot of disappointment though.'

Would all I could offer the children be memories that would soon fade and the austere comfort of the words I had written in the will made before leaving Sydney? 'In the event of my death attempting to storm new frontiers at sea . . . I want Vicky and Susie to know that I expect them always to face life unafraid, with their heads up, and always remembering to laugh. My grown-up children already know this.'

To my own surprise, I realized that the intolerable thought of the little girls left fatherless did even more to keep me striving than did the urge for self-preservation. Also, surprisingly, the expectation of dying in such utter solitude, about as far from human contact as it was possible to be anywhere on earth, did not occasion me any special despondency; since every one of us must ultimately tread this road alone.

A kind of philosophy seemed to have taken shape about this time. The chances of crossing two and a half thousand miles of Southern Ocean in my leaking, battered boat, with its ludicrous mast, were too remote for serious contemplation and the far from welcoming blizzard-swept escarpments that were my destination promised no welcoming havens. I must just live for the day, therefore. The awful effort demanded by the daily struggle was worthwhile *in itself*, regardless of its hopelessness; despite its futility this striving would, in some obscure way, not be wasted.

I tried clumsily to express these thoughts in the log. 'Earning membership of humanity – must earn it every day, to be a man.' I proceeded to try for that day's quota by laboriously and painfully emptying out twenty-four bucketfuls of bilge water, clearing the jammed halyard in a snowstorm and hoisting another sail to assist the little jib. This was the storm tri-sail. The head had once again to be knotted so that it could fit the diminutive mast.

If it were not for my hands, how much more I could do, I kept thinking. But even after being outside only long enough to take a sun sight I found myself 'shouting with the pain in my fingers.' The morning of 11 December was relatively calm and I was able to get the stove going, for the first time in five days, to heat up a can of stew and make a lukewarm cup of coffee. I was depressed the greater part of the time, overtired but restless and unable to sleep soundly even when I did have the chance.

By the 12th I had become more obsessed than ever with my terrible hands. Time and again I postponed or put off altogether going on deck to carry out the most urgent and necessary tasks, all for fear of the endless minutes of torture that I knew must inevitably follow. 'Steering by yoke and line from the cabin all afternoon,' I wrote. 'Gashed and frostbitten fingers more painful now.

Are they healing? Worry over water [the supply of fresh water aboard was unlikely to prove adequate for reaching land at the present rate of progress], distance, time. Sometimes just get cowardly and whimper a bit in my sleeping bag.'

Then at midnight I concluded the tale of the day's tribulations. 'SW gale, force 8, *lower four inches of jury mast crumbled*. Lowered sail and lay a-hull. Hands stand less cold than ever.'

The grim reality behind these laconic phrases had been my clawing desperately about the deck, as always on hands and knees, smothering the flapping sails with my body until I could secure them with lashings and then tightening down the shrouds to secure the mast, as I had before – only this time even less of it remained. All this was in darkness out of which streamed volleying snow pellets and stinging half-frozen droplets of spray.

I could not know then that *Ice Bird* was on the eve of another new disaster.

Did I pray? people ask. No. I longed to be able to but, not being religious at other times, I had just enough dignity left not to cry out for help when the going got a bit rough. A higher power, should one exist, might even appreciate this attitude!

I am very often asked about loneliness and I have mentioned the subject previously. Even though my prospects had now changed so radically, I was at least spared this desolate emotion. My little drama was being played out on the vast stage of the Southern Ocean with death lurking in the wings, but my solitude, while full of anguish, was never lonely.

The last day of the eighth week out of Sydney Cove, 13 December (just a fortnight after the capsize) was not a Friday. But it dawned inauspiciously enough – and continued worse. The gale that at midnight had sheered off its four-inch quota of the spinnaker pole mast, had increased until it was blowing at force eleven by 7.30 that morning – only one point in the wind scale below a hurricane. The lashings I had tied so tightly round the sails the night before were totally inadequate in a storm of this intensity. Frozen snow-filled pockets of heavy sailcloth ballooned out of the ice-sheathed ropes that confined them and proceeded to flog themselves to pieces with the abandon of demented living things. I hastily hunted out more cord and braved the icy deck to wind the cord round the tri-sail and jib, in defiance of the screaming, snow-laden wind that strove to wrest the line from my numb hands.

'Dear God,' I thought, 'if only I could set even the smallest headsail to give the yacht steerage way and render her controllable in these terribly high, steep seas.' But I knew this was a vain ambition – doubly so, because the strongest sail would have disintegrated before it ever could have been sheeted home and, in my case, the frail jury mast could never have stood the added stress. I was left with no option but to try to make the yacht steer downwind under bare poles again. And I had already experienced the futility of attempting that procedure in these Southern Ocean seas (unlike in the North Atlantic) and the near-fatal consequences of failure.

Well, no more could usefully be done on deck. Down below I made sure that nothing had been omitted from the gale routine that bitter experience had dictated. I mentally ticked off the items. Hatches fastened, washboards in place. Yes, I had secured the table by spreading across it a piece of strong nylon fishing net, anchored on one side to the port bunk board and, on the other, tied down to the floor battens. This should keep not only the table itself in place, but also the current supply of canned food stored in three boxes underneath it, even if – I hated to admit the possibility even to myself – even if the *Ice Bird* were to be capsized again. One locker only was without a catch and this I attempted less successfully to net down too. A criss-cross of cords (seamanship basically boils down to having quantities of string of all sizes – impossible to have too much) tied down my cardboard files of letters, lists and photostats, many of these papers stuck together and part-pulped from their ducking a fortnight earlier. There were few suitable points to anchor the cord to, so the documents stood to fare little better than before. The heavy bundle of damp, slimy charts – there were so many that I could scarcely lift them – had already been stuffed into the plastic bag with the fewest holes. Now I pushed the logbook in on top, and after a moment's thought, added a few rolls of toilet paper.

What else? The vital watch, of course. I wrapped it in cotton wool and placed it in a box which I wedged among the plastic bags containing spare batteries and matches in the driest locker. Next the ventilators. I stuffed each one tightly with rags. Fresh air was not at a premium that day – neither was salt water. Finally, laboriously, at the cost of many a bruise and quantities of spilled water, I bailed out twenty bucketfuls from the centre well to leave the bilge dry. This done, I tried once more to steer, but, as in the hurricane that had turned her over, the yacht generally wallowed broadside on and refused to run off before the enormous wind-torn waves, which were becoming more formidable every minute.

By early afternoon the relentless, sustained wind of sixty knots or over had built up huge hollow seas, which differed in two respects from the mighty storm waves I had encountered in other oceans – the rapidity with which they increased in height and their extraordinary steepness.

'They are *jetting* forward,' I noted at 1.30 p.m., with horror. The streaming lines of foam driving across the frothing waste were scarcely distinguishable from the opaque white of the snow blizzard that swept over them. And here and there amid the general turmoil great killer breakers collapsed like tumbling waterfalls in thunderous ruin. Sooner or later one was bound to mark us as its prey. Could we survive?

After watching in helpless misery while the remains of the self-steering gear broke up and was swept away, I made one more attempt to steer. It was hopeless. We lay, helplessly, starboard side to, rolling the decks under. I cowered down on the port bunk, back braced against the cabin bulkhead – as if to seek companionship from the kangaroo and kiwi painted there – about as far into the depths of the cabin as it was possible to get.

It must have been around three o'clock in the afternoon that it came: the dreaded shock that exploded like a bomb: that heart-stopping lift again. Then the little home enclosing me whirled round in a dizzying arc and, for a fraction of a second that seemed an age, I was standing on my head on the roof of the upside-down cabin, before *Ice Bird* crashed over right side up once more.

My preparations had paid off. True, the sleeping bag was soaked through again and my already damaged typewriter, vaulting from its restraining cords, had been smashed into a shapeless tangle of twisted keys and festooned ribbon. Sodden ships biscuits plastered the sides of the cabin and the deck head (the roof). Sultanas, peanuts, cheese and chocolate had once again been liberally dunked in brine laced with kerosene and, in the case of the first two at least, rendered practically inedible. But the precious charts and the logbook were safe and the netted table had held down most of the cans in the boxes beneath it. Blocking the ventilators had kept the water intake down to a paltry twenty-one bucketfuls. More remarkable still: the little mast, I saw with astonishment, was miraculously still standing.

So far, so good. But we had not escaped unscathed, as I realized when I tried to open the main hatch. It slid back a foot, then jammed. No amount of straining would budge it a millimetre farther. Was I trapped in a steel coffin? My heart began to race unpleasantly until common sense came to my aid. There was always the fore hatch, and the difficulty there was to keep it closed, not to open it. In a calmer frame of mind I pushed and struggled and at length succeeded in squeezing through and locating the trouble. The frame of the pram hood, made of half-inch galvanized steel piping, had been so buckled when the yacht had crashed upside down into the water as to jam the hatch by fouling the Perspex dome. In no way, without the facilities of a machine shop, could I hope to straighten it again. Fortunately, I could just wriggle my way through in my bulky clothes.

The immediate problem of course, was how to bail. How on earth could I lift a bucket of bilge water past me when I was wedged in the hatchway, not to mention the far more delicate manoeuvre of lifting the toilet bucket out into the cockpit? The answer was found by trial and error. I was able to evolve a set of co-ordinated movements that, when I removed my parka and exhaled deeply, just sufficed to allow me to squeeze the bucket up past my chest and, balancing it precariously above my head, lift it out of the hatch. Bilge water could then be unceremoniously tipped into the cockpit, though the toilet bucket required further contortions before I could gain the bridge deck and empty it safely overside.

The canvas that had covered the twisted pram hood frame had been completely torn away, but this was of little moment. Far more serious, the steel framework had been bent over until it almost touched the steering compass, which was mounted on the main hatch (incidentally, the mounting was damaged). The proximity of the steel tubing must be deflecting the compass needle out of true. This much and the fact that the deviation was easterly was apparent at a glance. But exactly how great was the deviation was a question that could only be answered much later when I had the opportunity on rare fine days of comparing the compass with sextant readings of the bearing of the sun. It turned out to be a good 20°.

When *Ice Bird* turned over, the barometer had already started rising and, as if satisfied at having so effectively demonstrated its power, the storm now rapidly declined in intensity. The wind eased but, I noted with no enthusiasm, rogue 'killer waves' still continued occasionally to avalanche thunderously. During the night the gale finally blew itself out.

An incongruous note is truck by next day's log. '14 December. My paper is being read before the Royal Society in London today.'

This was an account of ancient Polynesian astronomy, a science that in the Islanders' maritime culture was virtually part of navigation. I would much rather be there than here, I thought, wistfully – even at the cost of facing intimidating questions from ranks of eminent astronomers.

No point in wishing. Fortified by ships biscuits and muesli, I pulled a soggy wool glove up over my right hand and a freezing mitt over my left (their mates had never come to light since the first capsize) and reluctantly issued forth into chilly blustery wind under a low, leaden sky. Dubiously eyeing the split and twisted base of the mast, I hoisted a rag of sail and found my forebodings realized when more shards of the aluminium broke away. Was there anything I could do? Seated on the deck, I stared intently at the mast, willing there to be an answer, oblivious of all else except this life and death problem.

I was not wearing my safety harness, for I often omitted it these days; after all, the precaution seemed rather pointless when the ship itself was doomed. The breaking sea caught me unawares, the shock catapulting me through the air towards the vanished starboard guard wires. Here I was brought up agonisingly, if providentially, against the tip of a stanchion. I felt my ribs go in a blaze of breath-stopping agony and my right arm went numb as the elbow shared the impact. I can't stand any more pain, I thought, as I writhed in the scuppers, gasping for breath. But there was also relief that I had not gone over the side, where five minutes in the -1°C water would have brought oblivion. Such is the mark of our humanity. There is no foreseeable way out of your predicament; you have come to the end of your tether; yet some unsuspected strength within you drives you to keep on fighting.

I dragged myself, moaning and groaning and making a great to-do, along the side deck and down below. As the wind was from the south-south-west there was no need to steer. Bilge water was overflowing the floorboards, though. Cursing mentally – drawing each breath meant stabbing pain enough without aggravating it by speech – I prized up the floor and scooped up twenty-two buckets from the well to tip them into the cockpit. The rest of that pain-fringed day and a restless, chilly night I spent on my bunk, increasingly aware of the vast difference between a merely damp sleeping bag and one still soaked from the recent capsize.

The morrow brought little relief. True this was the day I discovered the missing rum bottle projectile, which had penetrated the floor of the locker; but our poor progress, as revealed by two sun sights, gave little cause for complacency. I hoisted the tri-sail to give us a little more speed and was duly rewarded when the wire span that held the halyard blocks to the masthead parted and the sails came tumbling down. Three hours in snow showers relieved by intervals of fitful sunshine were taken up in lowering the mast and repairing the damage. I also took the opportunity of fashioning a pair of wire shrouds out of a spare inner forestay, to reinforce the rope stays.

The knife-stabs in my right side that had greeted any sudden body movement during this work on deck became less frequent once I had returned below where I could move with greater caution. But my hands! I rocked back and forth, tears squeezing out from under my eyelids. Would they never mend? Extravasated blood ballooned out each finger end grotesquely so that the finger nails were acutely angled. The bases of the fingers were, in contrast, pale but so swollen that my hands looked like flippers. On the credit side, there was as yet no sign of gangrene. The antibiotics must be taking effect, then, and the healing process beginning, though how complete it would be only time would tell – if time were allowed me. But the pain! The agony resulting from only the briefest moment of chill was worse, much worse than it had been and was lasting longer.

This was the day that my sheepskin trousers, which had shown signs of falling apart, finally disintegrated. Damp and smelly though they were, I was sorry to see the last of them; sorrier still to have to go through the awkwardness and discomfort of getting them off, then pulling over my shivering limbs the mildewed and half-frozen Dacron flying suit I had earlier discarded. How much more of this recurrent misery could I stand? Would it not be easier just to give up the hopeless struggle? And fresh trouble was in store: as I lit the hurricane lamp that evening, I saw with a sinking heart that the glass was dropping again.

I spent a sleepless night as the weather worsened. The number two storm jib, despite the knots that reduced its length to fit the short mast, was setting so badly that periodically it threshed violently. This was my best and strongest sail, a brand-new one, but because I could not immediately think up any way of saving it from the damage it was sustaining, I did not even venture outside to look. Had I done so, ways of dealing with the trouble surely would have become apparent. I would rather not record this, but the sorry fact of the matter is that I had become so demoralized and my dread of pain from fingers and ribs was so great that I did not once go on deck to experiment with the sail's sheeting for three whole days.

Meanwhile the wind rose, fell and rose again, varying between a modest force six breeze and a force eight gale. *Ice Bird* took some heavy buffets and the jib continued to vibrate. Lengths of shock-cord hooked to the tiller lines allowed me to leave them but not for long, so I sat for hours staring miserably out of the transparent dome at the happy-looking ice birds that fluttered around the cockpit. A careless one even flicked the backstay with its wing.

By 19 December a strong gale was building up steep, hollow, tottering seas. This was the third day of my shameful cowering below – I was aware of my own weak-mindedness; I even noted it in the log, but I had not will power enough to overcome it, taking refuge instead in escapist novels. At 11 a.m. one of the collapsing seas broke aboard, catapulting a volley of pots, aluminium plates and cutlery clear across the cabin.

It was five o'clock that afternoon when the much abused jib split, leaving a portion still drawing. I could have saved it had I only bestirred myself earlier. Now it was too late, so I left up the flapping remnants to give the yacht some steerage way to run before the gale, which had now increased until it was blowing at something like fifty-five to sixty knots with no sign of abatement.

Somewhat belatedly I set about the near hopeless job of trying to stitch up the first storm jib, which had been torn almost in two in the initial capsize. One vital item forgotten in the rush at Sydney had been a sail-mending palm. The best that could be done was to use a book to press the sail needle through the seams of the tough eleven-ounce Terylene, to execute a clumsy repair that I doubted would stand any strong wind. Meanwhile outside my tossing steel shell the south-east gale, fresh chilled from its passage across the polar floes, roared out ever more fiercely over the Southern Ocean, tearing off great gouts of water bodily from the wave crests and driving them horizontally before it.

'Trembling and fearful night,' I wrote, without exaggeration. 'Water washing over floorboards. Shriek wind in spite of blocked ventilators and full battening down washboards.' My thoughts can be imagined.

Blinding snow showers, sweeping across the ocean's face before even stronger squalls, heralded dawn around 2 a.m. The formerly hollow seas now seemed to have flattened a little by the very fury of the storm – but for how long, I wondered? Then, somewhere round 6 a.m., the stainless steel luff wire of the already split jib tore right through. Now I had to redeem as best I could the cowardice that had kept me so long in the cabin – now that it was much too late to save anything of the sail, unused until three weeks ago, which was now completely split in two, with even its bronze hanks fractured. I brought up the jib I had mended the day before and dragged it along the deck to the forestay, where I hanked it on. But no sail could be hoisted in that storm. Once again we were riding out a severe gale with no means of propulsion so that the ship was out of control and the seas tossed her from side to side at their will.

By now the cabin was well awash and fresh spurts of water were continually being forced under pressure through the split coach roof. It must be got rid of even at risk of swamping when unbattening the hatchway. Twenty-seven bucketfuls were lifted out, every one paid for in pain: pain in my right ribs with each gasping breath; in my hands as always; from a new bruise whenever a wave smashed me against the side of the cabin. At length it was done, though a worse task awaited me. For a record three days I had held off using the toilet bucket. Now it could not be delayed a moment longer. This was a dreaded chore and a difficult feat of balance at the best of times. In a gale it was a hundred times harder. I dreaded removing my flying suit and, even more, stumbling into my filthy tattered clothes again with one wary eye on the bucket. Emptying the bucket without spilling its contents all over the cabin, myself, the cockpit or the deck was the most delicate operation but, more by luck than otherwise, it was always successfully accomplished.

Afterwards I could not rest; no relaxation being possible while the heavy seas kept crashing on to the resounding metal hull. My morale was very shaky for no respite was in sight even should we survive this particular storm without further damage. Indeed, towards midnight the storm did begin to ease but I was little comforted.

'No progress. Near despair,' I wrote. A half-forgotten fragment of poetry from my schooldays flitted through my mind and was scribbled down in the log.

Though we are ringed with spears,
Though the last hope is gone,
– ? fight on, the – ? gods look on.
Before our sparks of life blow back to Him who gave,
Burn bright, brave hearts, a pathway to the grave.

Though I characterized this as 'corny', it did express a little of what I felt, though at times the implications of this bleak destiny would overwhelm me.

By the following morning, 20 December, except for an occasional last fling, the gale had moved away eastward. We had been nine weeks at sea. Going on deck I found that the rope forestay had parted and that several more inches of the spinnaker mast had crumbled away since the day before. When I hoisted the roughly repaired number one storm jib, the yacht had been forty hours lying a-hull without sail.

Back to bailing, only to find that the cockpit drains had become blocked, probably with pulped paper, so the cockpit needed bailing out too. Depressingly, no amount of poking about in the wet cockpit succeeded in clearing the drains. That job would have to wait for another day. I clambered down into the cabin, to discover that the socks I wore to protect my hands and keep them warm, and which were normally relatively dry, had got wet in the recent gale. All these trials and discomforts were getting me down. The perennial problem was the hopeless inadequacy of my attempts to escape from this fierce, lonely sub-Antarctic ocean.

Why was I bothering to write anything down, I wondered, as I drew the damp logbook out of its plastic bag, opened it on the bunk and scrawled painfully.

'How long will the 'mast' and stays last? What sail or gear can stand such gales?' Still less could my makeshift arrangements be expected to cope with them.

All in all, the urge to make a daily record in the log was basically illogical because, now that I was facing the issues squarely, there did not really seem to be a way out. Even should *Ice Bird* continue to ride out these repeated storms without mortal damage, we were for practical purposes getting nowhere and time was slowly but surely running out before the freeze-up would render unattainable even the grim shelter we were seeking. Water, too, would be running short before long, for I had anticipated a quicker passage. The fine rain of high latitudes had been more of a dank mist and impossible to collect. Certainly some handfuls of snow had been scraped off the Perspex dome and cabin top on 3 December and made into several cups of coffee but generally the snow had been too contaminated with spray to be drinkable. The last resort – to seek out floating ice – would probably take all summer in a boat so little mobile as *Ice Bird* then was.

Yet I did have vague hopes that someone, somewhere would read what I was setting down. Even if by then I was dead of thirst and privation, *Ice Bird*, floating half waterlogged or perhaps frozen in, might be found by some whaler or expedition ship. Such thoughts were often in my mind these days, as were speculations about how revolting it would be for someone to come across my decomposing body – unless, of course, time and birds had reduced it to an aseptic skeleton or, more likely, it had been deep frozen like a Siberian mammoth's carcase.

If only it had been possible to erect a stout, dependable mast I could have made it. I mixed a tot of rum (a large one, I see by the log), drank it down resignedly and squirmed into my sleeping bag, for it was night now, the evening of 20 December. This was my darkest hour. But some portion of my mind was far from resigned. All at once the idea, fully formed, burst into consciousness to set me bolt upright, trembling with excitement. The key to survival had come into my hand.

The ideal jury mast had all along been the robust eleven-foot, six-inch wooden boom. But it was far too heavy and unmanageable for me to lift upright by hand. Now I *knew* how it could be done. Would it work, though, in practice? I would soon learn the answer, for the very next morning, 21 December, the wind had miraculously dropped right away, though the sea still ran very high. There had been little sleep for me during a night spent elaborating the idea and I was early astir. By eight o'clock it was calm enough for me to begin.

The boom first of all had to be rigged with side shrouds, forestay and backstay. The wire shrouds I doubled for extra security with stout rope ones made fast to ringbolts that I bolted to the rail. The twin backstays leading to each quarter were retained and reinforced by a central wire stay improvised, like the forestay, out of a deck safety wire. This standing rigging must be doubly secure. Should this mast ever be raised, I was making sure that it would never come down again.

I would not have thought it possible to do all this, down to fitting and tightening the bulldog grips that locked the wire loops, with hands encased in a mitt and a glove. Yet that was how it was done. Halyards for hoisting the sails had next to be rove through blocks shackled to the future masthead – a double purchase for the jib, since it must be hauled up taut; a single block for the tri-sail. One end of the boom (the intended foot) was fitted into the mast step; the other, with its festoons of ropes and wires, was lifted into the boom crutch above the main hatchway.

Now for my inspiration. I detached the main sheet (the many-part tackle with sufficient mechanical advantage to haul in the mainsail against the pressure of strong winds) from the sliding horse over the rudder head and, on hands and knees, dragged it forward to the bow. Here I shackled its lower block to the forestay fitting and led the tail back aft to the powerful sheet winch. All these preparations, which had mostly to be carried out crouching or crawling to maintain balance on the erratically tossing deck, took from eight in the morning till half-past four in the afternoon – eight and a half hours without a single break. But too much – life itself – depended on the outcome for me to stop them.

Tense with anxiety, I began to turn the winch handle. Was the 15° angle at

DRAMA AT SEA   **249**

which the boom lay, hopefully pivoted at the mast step and supported upon the crutch at its other end, sufficient to give purchase? Yes. The boom rose a foot out of the crutch, then it slewed as the yacht lurched sharply to port and stuck fast. I could have cried. But, thank goodness, its foot had only jammed in the pin rail. One the second attempt the boom mounted steadily inch by inch to the vertical.

One hour later. An old cotton staysail folded in half along the centre seam to fit the strong, but still diminutive, new mast had been shackled on, hoisted and sheeted in. No matter that pus was now welling out of my right thumb where the bone itself had become infected. Never mind exhaustion and pain. We were under way with a reliable mast at last, one that could stand up to all the sail that I could string from it – the storm tri-sail and the lower half of a folded-over or divided staysail. That night I drank rum and condensed milk in celebration of hope reborn and, in the gentle yellow glow of the hurricane lamp, supped on corned beef that had miraculously taken on a new, delicious flavour. From time to time I peered aloft at the wind pennant streaming from the backstay and adjusted the helm with a pull on the tiller lines.

I contentedly dozed the night away, the tiller lines still in my hands. Next morning in a snow shower I hoisted the tri-sail to speed our passage. The tiller lines continued to demand my attention all that day, the following night and on into 23 December – forty hours or thereabouts – before the wind shifted into the south and *Ice Bird* could be trusted to pursue her way unaided.

How lucky I was to have reading matter, but how boring, I thought, referring to those long monotonous hours lately past. The boat had to be kept moving as fast as possible and on course. There must be a system of priorities, which I summed up that morning. 'Not concerned with sights – only to make the best time – other problems like my last jib with windward ability can wait until, if ever, needed! . . . Finger nails beginning to loosen. Tender, tender fingers vulnerable to cold [There was some necrosis of the terminal bone in my right thumb. Care of my fingers was certainly a priority.] . . . Fluid conservation . . . sea is not cruel, it is neutral. Depends on *me*,' I concluded.

David Lewis, Ice Bird, *1975*

THE SPIRIT OF ROSE-NOËLLE

THERE are two graphic accounts of the astonishing survival story of the Rose-Noëlle *and her crew of four. The 12.65 metre trimaran had set out from Auckland in June, 1989, on a two-week voyage to Tonga. Four days later, in huge seas, she had done the unthinkable for skipper John Glennie, and capsized.*

The crew survived in the upturned hull for 119 days. The story of how their watery home drifted inexplicably back in a huge loop towards New Zealand only to smash itself to pieces on the rocky eastern coast of Great Barrier Island was so incredible that it was only after an official inquiry that a suspicious media accepted the story.

John Glennie, the skipper and builder of Rose-Noëlle *and a life-long trimaran enthusiast, published his account of the episode a year later. Jim Nalepka, an American loner, one-time Outward Bound cook, followed three years on. Both accounts, unsparingly honest, tell how four very different men, virtual strangers, came together as some sort of uneasy team.*

By day 117, having learned how to catch water and fish, survive gales and accommodate each other's black moods, they were reasonably convinced that New Zealand was somewhere to the west and closing. They sensed their ordeal was nearing its end. But no one had yet spoken much about the possible difficulties of the landfall, although John Glennie was anticipating problems . . .

I wasn't really surprised when we spotted land. For days we had seen a long, low bank of pale cloud on the horizon, and I knew New Zealand must be out there somewhere. The Maori named their land Aotearoa – land of the long white cloud. There had been other signs in the past few weeks; we had seen the lights of two ships at night and then the yacht on Rick's birthday. Just a few days previously we had seen another large yacht heading towards where I suspected land lay, but it was too far away to signal.

However, it was the planes that gave me the strongest clue. Several weeks before we sighted land we were all up on deck early, watching the sun rise. It was a calm, clear Sunday and as I watched the pink rays of the sun warm the sky I noticed a thin white line just above the sun itself – a jetstream. I pointed it out to the others and we wondered where the plane had come from, where it was heading . . . Auckland to Tahiti perhaps?

The following Sunday I was up early again and there was another jetstream, and this time I could see from its position that we had drifted to the west. Both planes were flying northeast, which meant we were on an air route, but we still had no idea which airport they had come from. A week later the weather was overcast and cloudy, and though I searched as the sun rose, I saw nothing.

Then one day we saw a jetstream right overhead and I was able to get a direction of magnetic north with the hand-held compass. That meant we were somewhere north of New Zealand. The international airports of Christchurch, Wellington and Auckland are all roughly in line, and the plane was heading north.

On the afternoon of day 116 I was standing up holding onto the rigging ropes supporting the mast, relieving myself over the side, when I noticed a humming noise vibrating through the rigging. About an hour later I heard the same noise. I looked up to see a plane flying overhead, low enough to see and hear clearly. We estimated that it was about 15,000 feet up and still climbing. It flew directly overhead and I took a bearing. It was heading magnetic north.

We had a lengthy discussion about how long it takes big passenger planes to reach altitude, and decided the one we had seen was about 80 miles from the airport. I knew the plane could not have come from Wellington or Christchurch, because that would have put our position somewhere inland; it had to have taken off from Auckland, which gave us the longitude of the airport.

Most of the charts in the bin below the chart table had been soaked for months and were ruined. But there was one – a small-scale chart covering the east coast of Australia, the Tasman Sea and New Zealand – which I now spread out in the aft cabin. Although we could not see land, I was convinced we were close. The height of the northbound plane gave us the latitude from Auckland, assuming that was where it had recently taken off from.

We couldn't believe it. If our assumptions were correct, we were drifting towards the Hauraki Gulf, one of the most populated boating areas in the South Pacific. By rights we should have been well on our way to Chile.

It was like a script for a B-grade movie. A sense of the absurd took over and I chuckled to myself as I imagined us floating up Auckland Harbour to step ashore before an astonished crowd of weekend shoppers. Or maybe a local fisherman would discover us and give us a tow, passing us cold drinks and taking our photograph.

This was the first real indication of our position during the entire trip.

Although I had a sextant on board, I did not attempt to use it because the declination tables were long gone. The other tables were in the satellite navigation system, which was underwater. All the rest of my navigation gear was stored in the deep drawers which were pulled out, upside down, to use as packing in the aft cabin and the contents lost.

I went below and did a lot of writing that day. There was my log to write, 80 pages of survival notes and articles for multihull magazines and the letter to Geordie and Elizabeth. There was so much I wanted to say and suddenly there seemed so little time. I knew once we hit land, things would change. Now was my chance to purge my thoughts and feelings, to get it all down. I wrote for hours.

On the morning of day 118 the outline of the land was quite clear and the colour had deepened to a dark green. We were all up on deck early, eagerly checking to make sure that our landmark was still there and that we were still drifting towards it. After so many days of scanning an empty horizon it was hard to believe that we were nearly home.

As the day progressed, Rick and Phil became convinced that the mountainous shape ahead was Great Barrier Island, which literally forms a barrier to the Hauraki Gulf at its northeastern boundary, 53 miles from Auckland. Both Rick and Phil had grown up in Auckland, and Rick had spent time tramping on the island as a youngster.

I vaguely remembered visiting Great Barrier just before Christmas 1964, when David, Graham and I sailed *Highlight* over there and spent the day shooting rabbits. We had decided to cook our catch in the pressure cooker and succeeded in blowing rabbit stew all over the roof of the galley.

As we drifted closer I still hoped that someone would spot us and take *Rose-Noëlle* in tow. I began to collect a bundle of personal possessions in two airtight plastic containers ready to take ashore. The contents of these boxes would represent the most treasured and sentimental mementoes of my life to date, and I was determined they would not be claimed by the sea. In them I put the logbook, the pages of survival notes and articles for multihull magazines, sketch plans of the new catamaran, the letters I had written, my traveller's cheques, passport photographs, bank accounts, my boatbuilding apprenticeship papers from Morgan's boatyard and a collection of cycling medals won by myself and my father. In a locker beneath the dinette I had discovered some drawings Geordie had done some years ago when he stayed with Danielle and me on *Rose-Noëlle* in the Brisbane River. He had watched me updating the Hitchiker catamaran and had decided to draw his own boat. His design had an underwater observatory which he made his bedroom. I tucked those drawings in one of the containers with a lock of his hair saved after his first haircut when he was a year old.

That night, the last we spent on *Rose-Noëlle*, I became so angry over an incident involving Phil that I wondered later how close I had come to losing control. Phil and I had been arguing a lot in the past fortnight. I felt he had become intolerably big-headed and suddenly thought he knew it all. He started challenging everything I said and we seemed to be always bickering. All four of us were starting to lose patience with one another.

Late on the night of day 118 I crawled up through the cockpit to check for ships and noticed the mast lights of a big ship which had come from Auckland and was heading away from us out past the Barrier. It was several miles away and I knew it would be pointless trying to signal it. The only light we could use at such short notice was a small, rapid-flashing strobe, which was not nearly powerful enough and could not be used for Morse code. Even if a crewman happened to be on deck and spotted the light, it would only look like a tiny light on a fishing buoy. It was better, I thought, to save the precious battery power for something closer.

I went below to tell the others what I had seen, and Phil disappeared up on deck to see for himself. A minute later he crawled back through the opening calling out for the strobe light.

'I don't want you to use the strobe, Phil,' I told him. 'The ship is too far away and you'll just be wasting the battery.' He took no notice and once again we were arguing. His defiance was the culmination of four months of my opinion and knowledge being ignored or challenged. I felt the anger well up in me as Phil and Rick disappeared on deck with the strobe.

Jim, always the diplomat, sat quietly and listened as I vented my anger on him. Then curiosity overcame me and I poked my head through the cockpit to see what was happening up on deck. The sight of Rick sitting on Phil's shoulders, hanging onto the mast and flashing this tiny light at a rapidly disappearing set of ship's lights in the distance suddenly struck me as funny; the laughter bubbled out as uncontrollably as the anger. 'If you want a good laugh, go up and look at those two,' I said to Jim.

The incident was over as far as I was concerned. I knew we were near land; soon we would be back with our family and friends, no longer having to put up with one another's idiosyncrasies and irritating habits.

That night I needed to pass water and, not wanting to disturb the others while crawling out of the cabin, I searched around the darkness for the screw-top coffee jar we used as a miniature latrine. Before the jar, we used to kneel on the plank and urinate in the flooded main cabin if the weather was too rough outside. In the early days Jim and Rick were not keen on us urinating there, thinking we would pollute it, but as time passed, those sorts of shore-bound ideals became less important as practicality took over.

As I unscrewed the top of the coffee jar and began to relieve myself I noticed a strong smell of garlic. I thought it strange to notice an odour in my urine, as we had become immune to such things. Then it dawned on me what I had done. 'Oh no!' I exclaimed involuntarily. I had urinated in the remains of our pickled garlic! Rick couldn't let the opportunity pass. 'That,' he said with heavy sarcasm, 'says it all.'

It was just as well we were so close to land, for I don't think my crewmates would have forgiven me for the rest of the journey. I would have found it hard to forgive myself.

That night we slept fitfully, the atmosphere below tense, wondering what the morning would bring. Then there was the welcome sight of lush green bush, the white outline of breaking waves on Great Barrier's coastline and a northeasterly wind that was steadily pushing us towards the island. It was obvious that we were going to hit land that day and I scanned the horizon anxiously for fishermen or pleasure cruisers who might be in the area.

Phil, Rick and Jim began to collect together their possessions until we each had a separate bundle. Rick put his letters to Heather and his passport in a bag. I asked about the two rolls of film from my camera. He already had them with his things, he said. I took the white sail bag we had used for fishing and put my two plastic containers inside with a jersey and a pair of woollen socks.

We put four cans of food in a bucket with a yellow-handled diving knife Danielle had given me, and Phil retrieved the woollen blanket, the tent and a cooking pot from the aft cabin in case we had to spend a night in the bush.

Knowing that there was no longer any need to conserve food and water, we ate well that day. Jim caught a fish in the landing net and bent the handle in the process, but it no longer mattered. I made up fish soup using leftovers and we ate Jim's fresh fish, pan fried. The meal fortified us for what lay ahead.

Just after 12.30 p.m. on our final day at sea, an 18-year-old student pilot from Auckland Aero Club was flying over Great Barrier Island on a cross-country training exercise. Mark Hughston had just made a touch-and-go landing at Great Barrier's Claris airfield in his two-seater Grumman aircraft and headed out to sea, gradually climbing to 2,000 feet.

As Hughston followed the coastline south towards Whitianga, on the east coast of the Coromandel Peninsula, he caught sight of what looked like a long, yellow liferaft, the kind used by airliners in emergencies, about three nautical miles offshore. Curious, he altered course and began to circle around it. As he flew closer, Hughston decided the long liferaft was in fact some sort of multi-hull yacht.

At this height he could just make out a mast of some kind and flags, but he didn't notice anyone on deck. Assuming the occupants were getting ready for an afternoon's fishing, Hughston continued banking in an anti-clockwise circle and continued south to Whitianga.

I was below in the aft cabin writing my log when I heard a commotion on deck. 'John!' I heard someone yell. 'There's a plane coming. I think he's seen us!'

I scrambled up through the cockpit and saw a small red and white aircraft beginning to circle overhead. Jim was frantically waving a yellow quarantine flag attached to a piece of conduit pipe which we had rigged up that morning in readiness. Rick was waving a yellow raincoat while Phil and I leaped up and down, waving and screaming ourselves hoarse. We were convinced we had been spotted and that the pilot would radio ahead for help.

The four of us sat up on the keel clutching our bundles, waiting. Nervously I eyed the wild and rugged coastline looming before us and constantly scanned the horizon for any sign of a rescue boat. If help was on its way, they had better be quick.

I had often wondered what we looked like from the air, or what rescuers would think should they stumble across us out at sea when we were all below in the aft cabin. On fine days we looked like a cross between a junkyard and a Chinese laundry with clothing, the rug and sleeping bag, life-jackets and socks strung through the rigging to air. Towards the end I laid the charts out over the keel to dry; there was the Honda generator up on deck – which I gave a decent burial at sea shortly before we struck land – coils of rigging wire, cans of epoxy resin, the barbecue and crab pot lashed to the mast.

An hour and a half after the plane circled, it became obvious that once again we were on our own and that we were going to hit Great Barrier, probably in an unfriendly spot. Further out we had seen long, white beaches, but as *Rose-Noëlle* drifted closer we could only see cliffs and rocks.

High above on the ridge across a valley I could make out the pitched roof and television aerial of a well-built house, the first sign of life. I decided that would be a good spot to head once we got ashore.

Ahead of us lay a tiny cove with a strip of beach, and we hoped we would be lucky enough to drift ashore there. But the wind pushed us past to a neighbouring but much wilder cove, guarded by a reef about 75 metres offshore.

While the sea had been relatively calm offshore, the waves grew stronger and angrier as we approached land, and now they picked *Rose-Noëlle* up and pushed her towards those rocks. She hit with a sickening crunch; the waves lifted her firmly onto the reef and abandoned her, leaving the full weight of the upturned trimaran to grind itself over the remains of the mast and rigging.

Phil looked at me and said quietly, 'I'm sorry about your boat, John.' In the first few weeks after we capsized, Phil had been vehemently outspoken against multihulls, but as time went on, his attitude softened. Towards the end he had in fact talked of the possibility of buying the remains of *Rose-Noëlle* should she be salvaged.

I shook my head and told him it didn't matter. I had designed and built *Rose-Noëlle* to the highest standards of strength, and I had known all along she would hold together for as long as it took for us to find land or be rescued. She had carried us home safely and that was all I expected. If we escaped with our lives the spirit of Rose-Noëlle Coguiec would have guarded us to the end.

John Glennie, The Spirit of Rose-Noëlle, *1990*

CAPSIZED

JAMES Nalepka recalls those final days on the Rose-Noëlle...

I look at my shipmates and see in our flickering torchlight tattered clothes, haggard faces matted with grease-soaked hair, beards scattered with crumbs of food. All, but Phil, seem to move in slow motion. Just outside this dungeon is a beacon of hope that we may soon be free, but from within, our world is just the same, and progressively deteriorating. I hope, I pray that this is the real thing this time, that it is not the cruellest of hoaxes perpetrated by a sadistic power beyond our control. *Please let us drift ashore.*

Finally we decide to kill the flame and try to get some sleep. John slips out. A half hour or so later he re-enters our cell and says very matter-of-factly, 'A couple of months ago we would have been excited and jumped outside to see a boat.'

'What do you mean?' asks Rick.

'I just saw another ship, but it's too far away to signal. You can't even see its navigation lights.'

'*What?*' yells Phil as Rick rolls over unconcerned, accepting John's word. Phil practically bowls John over and scrambles to the deck. 'I want to have a look,' he says. Almost immediately I hear Phil stomping back across the plank to the cave. He scurries inside, shouting, 'Shit, John, that boat is really close! I'm going to signal her.' He starts rummaging through a ceiling locker in the dark. There's a clatter of gear flung about, the noise of some of it falling, a wrestling of bodies. 'John, John, where's that strobe? We're going to try to signal her.'

'No, you're not!' John orders sternly. 'It's too far away. You'd just waste your time and the battery. Damn it, Philip, chuck it in!'

By now Rick has joined the scuffle. He'll believe Phil before John any day. 'Come on, Phil, let's get to it! That ship is probably already getting away.'

'*Leave the strobe alone!*' bellows John.

'The hell I will!' answers Phil.

'Yeah, John, shift your carcass!' orders Rick.

'Get the hell out of the way!' echoes Phil.

'Who do you think you are? The skipper? This is *my* boat! *I* built her, not any of you. That's *my* strobe. These are *my* things. You've been helping yourself to the whole bang lot for four months! You have no business taking *anything*. I'm in command here! You do what I say!'

'Bloody hell with you, John! You need your head read,' Phil challenges. I hear a clutter of grabbing noises and feel bodies shoving and yanking. Phil must win the light somehow because he wiggles back out the hole with Rick on his heels.

John and I lay in the cave for about five minutes that seem like days. I remain as still as a root. I don't care if they signal the ship. I convince myself that we're too close now not to be saved somehow, even if Phil and Rick don't stop the ship. But what is John trying to do now, after all this time, trying to establish his command? But I dare say nothing. John's boiling anger is tangible, like the first light rumble in the ground before the volcano erupts. His body shifts in spasms. He is suddenly gone.

There's going to be a fight. I can feel it. Where is the diver's knife?

Rick and Phil's voices are muffled by John's position in the cockpit. In twenty or thirty seconds John re-emerges in the mouth of the cave making a noise that I cannot decipher. He's either chuckling or choking on tears. When he gets in on his back he begins to guffaw. His whole body writhes with sharp maniacal laughter that hurts my ears in this confined space. What is going on? What's with this guy? Is this man, this skin-covered bundle of sticks, about to snap? He struggles to emit sentences between fits of strange gaiety. 'If you want – ha, ha, ha -'

'What, John? What's so funny?'

'– see something really funny -' He shakes so with laughter that he cannot talk, but tries between gasps for breath. 'Ho, ho – you should see – ha, ha – take a look at those guys.'

As I poke my head out the cockpit, I see Phil straddling the keel and unsteadily weaving. On his shoulders, Rick perches, hanging on to the mast with one hand and holding the strobe aloft with the other. Off to the north the ship steams. It is alive with light, like a floating carnival. To me it looks only a mile or so off. I see individual port holes. But it is now moving quickly away from us. I have to wonder if John watched it coming all along and never told us until it began to pass by. Why? What is so funny about it? I feel guilt. Rick and Phil have vainly tried to signal the ship while I remained below, but in the confusion of changing relationships these last few weeks, I do not know what to do.

I return to our madhouse dungeon. 'Isn't that funny?' John manages to ask between raucous laughter.

'John,' I whine, 'it's not funny to *me*.' This sets him off into another joyous binge. I feel completely befuddled, lost on a carousel of blinding emotions in a circus that is about to be obliterated by the pent-up passions of four desperate men. My tense hope over the last several days intermingles with John's bombastic talk of records, his apathetic reception of a close-passing ship, his intense anger when Phil – who was once John's fledgling clumsy protégé – challenges, ignores, and then casts off his command, and now this unintelligible hysteria. What is going on? How can I get out of here? *When* can I get out?

Phil and Rick finally return below and lay down in the middle between John and me. They are keyed up, chattering between themselves.

'Boy, was that ever close.'

'Yeah, I was sure they'd see the signal.'

'That ship had to be no more than a mile off.'

Phil says, 'John, you're going berko, mate. We should have signalled that ship a long way back.'

'Use your block, Philip,' scolds John. 'We would have never been seen. It was too far away.'

'Crikey Dick, John, I can't figure you out. I think we could even see people on the deck. I just can't figure you out.'

Slowly the tense atmosphere in the cabin subsides. We begin to slumber. I get out once to look around. The lighthouse is quite bright now and I see another looming to the north. When I report this to my mates, there is no response.

We begin to drift off again when we smell garlic in the air. John has always emitted his long, ecstatic groan when the garlic bottle is opened. But there is silence now, then a trickle, then an 'Oh, shit, oh, dear. Oh, shit! Oh, dear! I may have just pissed in the garlic bottle.'

Rick chuckles. '*That* says it all.' As this bizarre sideshow closes for the night, it is our turn to laugh.

September 30, Day 119 Following Capsize.

I emerge from the brig to relieve myself and check out the dawn. Fish already swarm the surface, stirring the long, low swells. My eyes follow the waves as they roll away to the distance, where they merge with … Oh, my God! Broad shoulders of a monolithic folded island dominate my view. To the north, pencil-thin white beaches meet the oncoming waves. The distant gray landscape emerges from wafts of mist to stand close by in deep rich green. Colour! The colour of it! And the size of it! For fifteen minutes I selfishly gorge myself without alerting my mates. I am a glutton. I want the feast all for myself at least for a minute more. Through a carpet of woods, I see the cut of a road leading northward where the hills slope away and disappear into the haze. Behind beaches, the pitched woods are sprinkled with buildings. Dead ahead, near the top of the mountain's chest, I spy a lonely, tiny white box.

John comes on deck and sits next to me, cooing, 'Oh, my.'

I fell compelled to ask, 'John, are you all right?'

He gazes at the island. Waves of confusion roll across his face. 'You know, I'm the kind of person who holds things inside. I got kind of carried away last night. I wasn't sure what I was going to do. I'm sorry.'

'You don't have to apologize to me, John.'

We sit quietly for a while. Then John sighs. 'Oh, I've lost everything. I have nothing left. At least you three have something to go back to.'

John slumps on the keel like some worn-out scarecrow. He wears his black singlet. His legs are threaded through the arms of a dingy white sweater, the body of which is lashed around his waist with green twine. His ducky feet that paddled off to take a last-minute shower seventeen weeks ago are covered in tattered wood socks.

He looks beaten, vanquished by the sea, by us, by life. Maybe he thought that he needed only the uncontested command of a boat in the wide-open sea to control the path of his dreams. Perhaps we all thought that a masculine voyage to the islands would restore us and prove the integrity of our lonesome flight. It was to be a pure voyage without the complexities of our shoreside give-and-take relationships. But our quest was capsized and, like the boat, is now only a wreck that rests beneath us. We may have lived these last four months as if our survival was certain, but our voyage through life is not. Dreams, like desserts, are best shared, and in the sharing take on a life of their own. When we four men have shared, this voyage has transcended our mere survival and become much more, but when we have not, it has been much less.

I recall all the conversations I've had with John over the last month. He's told me that I have my whole life ahead of me, that I should use this experience to my advantage. His eyes would sparkle with enlightened fulfilment as if we knew something other people didn't know, that with the gift of this experience we would launch ourselves into a brilliant future. The wreck of the *Rose-Noëlle* would be a new beginning. It was what I wanted to hear, what I needed to hear. He was so confident.

'I'm really sorry, John,' I say now. 'I know that I've treated you like shit these last four months. But it doesn't matter now, John. It's over. This whole journey is over.' I remind him of his own words of confidence and rebirth.

He turns to me, his eyebrows lifted, a sparkle caught in those deep eyes of his. 'You're right, Jim. We're really lucky, aren't we?' For the first time, I actually feel like John and I have touched.

The fish boil in their pool as intensely as they ever have. I calmly unlash the net, make my way to the sidewalk, scoop, and come up with a fish. The net bends and collapses under the weight. 'That's just wonderful, Jim!' cheers John with a big smile on his face.

'I think we should all have a big meal together,' says John, 'because we're going to need it.' Rick and John may know what is likely to happen to us, but I have no idea. In my mind we're still going to float smoothly onto some sandy beach, carry a line ashore, and tie old *Rose* to a tree. Rick suggests that maybe a 'fizz-boat' will roar up to us as we get close although there's no reason for a small motorboat to be out here. Maybe a fishing launch will cruise by and we'll toss our gear and ourselves aboard while they take *Rose* in tow. I'm ready for a good celebratory banquet.

John doesn't even ask who wants which piece of fish this time; he just dices it and dumps it into the pot. I add the last can of baked beans, a can of corned beef, some water, and boil her up.

The food is warm and there is a lot of it. It helps calm our stomachs as we find ourselves closer and closer to the island. Anxious to return to the deck, we wolf the meal in fifteen minutes. We dream that we will drift to the south of Great Barrier Island and head into the gulf. We can now see details of the rocks and trees. We even see wild goats climbing the slopes. Waves crash into rugged cliff faces and smash themselves into fans of white.

'This isn't going to be a party, you know.' Rick's words hit me like an anchor on the head. We *aren't* going to drift south of the island. We're going to crash straight into it.

Ours is a fate met by sailors before. In 1922 the freighter *Wiltshire* smashed into the rocks just south of where we are now. Heavy seas trapped 102 men and the next morning snapped the vessel in half. The island's precipitous cliffs impeded rescuers' efforts, but after two days every man from the *Wiltshire* arrived safely ashore. No rescuers know we are even out here. We cannot call for help. Our fate will more likely be like the *Wairarapa*, a steamer of about eighteen hundred tons, which drove straight into Great Barrier Island at eight minutes past midnight, October 29, 1894. One hundred twenty-one people died and to this day no one knows why the steamer crashed ashore. Great Barrier devours the small as well as the large. All that was found of a sailing dinghy in 1984 was debris on the rocks. Booming waves dragged its two crew away forever.

Rose-Noëlle swings down the coast past ridges and seething backwash that serve as landmarks. Our speed seems incredible compared to the apparent stillness of 119 days surrounded only by rising and falling water. We slide south along the island but edge closer to catastrophe by the hour, just a mile or two away now. We will not clear the shore.

We begin to gather gear and put it into whatever we think will be waterproof. Without thinking about it, Rick and I find and share a small plastic container with a screw-top. Rick lists what we will need. 'We'll want our life jackets. Get your shoes, whatever you want to bring ashore.' I can see by the look in his and John's eyes that both men are tense. Rick pulls from his pocket two rolls of film. 'You think I should tell John about these?' I shrug my shoulders. 'Do you know what these are going to be worth if they turn out?'

Yeah, all our pikkies for the calendar. There's the one of Phil naked wrestling with his fish, one of us finishing our great net, and another of us looking depressed, John scratching his head and shrugging his shoulders at the great net's failure. We captured John and me cutting the hole through which we hauled the LP tanks and Phil's and Rick's faces, their eyes bulging in anticipation over fish frying in a pan. The camera caught Phil huddled over the generator with springs popping out and bolts falling in the water, and Phil gazing toward land like an Indian scout. I recall our laundry flapping in the wind, Phil gaffing while Rick waited patiently with the net, John filleting fish like a surgeon, the four of us around the barbecue like a campfire. In my mind John emerges from the deep with a smile and a handful of spaghetti; John leans against the corner of our cave with the flicker of a flame and an inferno in his eyes. I do not know which we have pictures of, but the images are burned into my memory, enough for a calendar of thirteen months. It was, after all, an unlucky year. Or maybe thirteen isn't so unlucky after all.

I grab the film out of Rick's hand and throw it into the container quickly. 'They'll be safe in here.' We scurry to gather essentials: 'Letters to Heather,' our passports, some money and plane tickets back from Tonga.

Rick takes my Buck knife from me and tosses it between his hands, feeling the balance. 'Sure is a cracker knife,' he says, then tosses it into the can. The container is full.

John and Phil have also gathered some gear, stuffing some clothes, food, and a couple more plastic waterproof containers into a sailbag. In the plastic jars John has secured the remaining treasures of his life: his notes, boat plans, logbook, articles he's already written for magazines, and his bicycling medals. Phil has donned his foul-weather gear and gathered a remaining half dozen cans of food in a bucket and tosses in the diver's knife.

A speck in the sky banks around the northern side of the island, seemingly stops, and expands. We hear a faint buzz that grows to the winding grind of an engine at high revolutions as the dot elongates into an expanse of white and red wings and tail joined by a slim fish-like body. I grab the PVC pipe that we've removed from the fishnet and to which we have attached a flag, leap up on the keel, and wag it around like a madman. Phil waves his arms, his white foul-weather bib overalls glowing in the sun that has burned off the haze. Rick grabs Martha's yellow raincoat to flag the plane down. John also waves. Waaaaaooooo, the plane roars above us, beyond us. He must have seen us. We wait for him to circle and make another pass, but he banks again to the west and disappears around the other end of Great Barrier. Would he even know we are in distress? From two thousand feet, with a mast rigged and all, we might just look like a normal boat.

We do not stop to worry about the plane. Maybe he saw us, maybe not, but it doesn't really matter because there's no longer enough time for help to reach us. We hear the breakers, see the smashed water swirl in and out of the rocks. *Rose-Noëlle* rises and eases down again on the swells that grow as the bottom of the sea emerges to meet the surface. As far as our eyes can see, only sheer cliffs drop to the sea. There is no place to land.

As *Rose-Noëlle* skims along, a rocky promontory slips back form view and exposes a bite out of the coast. We see a small beach in the cove. It's been the only break in the rock walls for miles. *Ah, my beach*, I think for just a moment. *Maybe we'll drift straight in there.*

Other than this distant hope, the danger of land lords over us. Even looking nearly straight up, all we see is a jumble of stone. The air is full of the noise of rushing water, heavy surf, and shouting voices. All but mine are issuing orders.

'Make sure your life jacket is on!' Only John is without one.

'Okay, when we get close enough to the beach, jump and swim for it.'

'Does everybody have shoes?' I pull mine from the mast where they've lived for four months. Shoes now feel so strange and confining. Over the open wound that still stands pink and oozing on Rick's ankle, he pulls a pair of socks. I tell him there are some high-top sneakers in the packing of the aft cabin.

He races below, rips the place apart, and comes up again. 'No good, I can't find them.' But Rick has a life jacket in his hand that he throws to John. 'Here, mate, put this on. What, do I have to always be your mum?'

John smiles at Rick as he slips on the jacket. For about three seconds, we are relieved by the unusual lighthearted ambience between the two foes. Then there is nothing left but to wait in our unspoken fear. John and Rick stand on the wing deck, hanging on to the rigging. Phil and I sit on the keel, grabbing the boat's backbone and centreboard slot, already braced for impact. I bite the side of my mouth with anticipation. I get up, climb down to the wing deck, stand for a moment, get back up on the keel again. We hang on as *Rose-Noëlle* rides the growing waves. They break against the weather hull to our back. She surges and we cling to her as if riding a giant bronco. She swerves, changing course, heading for a ridge of rocks that is sunk into the shoreline like a cleaver, cutting us off from the beach. We're not going to make it there.

But we might not even make it as far as the island ridge. Scattered boulders and reefs stretch a hundred yards to seaward of the shore. The ocean breaks over them. Waves pound through holes that it has punched into the land over millennia. Water floods back out, eddies, and seethes. Swirling currents grab *Rose-Noëlle*, yank her around, then twist her back again. 'We have to stay with the boat as long as we can,' John insists. There's no question now about going overboard. Alone in the water we will be pulverised to bits of scattered flesh. But if we stay aboard, the boat will certainly stop on the ledges. The sea, in a last brutal assault, will rip her apart and leave us clutching wreckage, facing her wrathful fists alone. Dead ahead now is a vast flattened boulder like a tipped table over which rollers wash.

'Brace yourself!' *Rose-Noëlle* quivers. A slow metallic moan emanates from within her body. It is the muted sound of the stub of her old mast that now hangs underwater as it meets, digs in, and plows the sea bed and begins to scrape along the rocks. A wave lifts us and the noise stops; then the wave drops us and the boat shakes as the stick screeches, twists, and folds. Twenty feet before we strike the table reef, we rise and fall again with a shudder as the metal mast rakes the rocks with a muffled unsteady noise of fingernails dragged along a blackboard. Ten feet, eight feet, five feet, another wave picks us up, pausing for a moment. I look down upon my mates, upon our ship, upon the rock upon which we will drop. I jam one hand in the hole in the keel. Rick and I reach toward each other, lock hands, and squeeze tight.

James Nalepka, Capsized, *1992*

SHEILA IN THE WIND

IN 1949, New Zealander Adrian Hayter, then a restless 35, resigned his Army commission in India. On August 12, 1950, in a 40-year-old 32ft gaff-rigged yawl named Sheila 11, *he slipped quietly away from Lymington on England's southern coast, towards Gibraltar, the Mediterranean and Red Sea, India, Ceylon, Malaya, Tasmania and New Zealand. Travelling from west to east, against adverse winds, under sail, the 'wrong' way. Beyond a year's sailing around the Solent, and brief childhood outings in dinghies, his blue-water yachting experience was nil.*

His extraordinary solo voyage was to take six years, and Sheila in the Wind, *the book that he published some years later, has become a classic of lone long-distance seafaring.*

After ten days storm-bound in Refuge Cove, on the south-eastern tip of Tasmania, with barely two weeks' supplies on board, he left on the 'last leg, the very, very last leg'. Twelve hundred miles away across the Tasman Sea lay his home town of Nelson.

Early on the morning of 23rd April I hauled in the two anchors and drifted out of Refuge Cove on puffs of wind; to leave such a place under sail seemed to be more in harmony with all I'd found there. The high granite ridge of the Promontory sheltered the water outside, until about 5 miles offshore a steady westerly picked me up and *Sheila*'s clean bow cleaved a way direct for home.

A week later sights confirmed that I had covered 420 miles, or a third of the distance to New Zealand. The winds had been cold and bitter, and leaking decks had soaked everything below once more; drifting acres of rain and flying spray kept me chilled to the bone, unprotected by the useless oilskins. I had re-sewn the seams, but the strong sail twine pulled out of the soft water-proofing material.

Then the wind turned east, dead ahead, against which *Sheila*'s Geraldton-cut mainsail was almost useless. This meant that I dropped below the distance-made, rations-allowed estimate, and so immediately adopted the emergency ration scale.

The adverse wind blew at half a gale for eleven days, and I arranged my three daily meals around the clock at eight hour intervals. Because of short rations every mile to the east was gold, so I sailed every hour of the day and night with only the barest snatches of sleep, and in the eleven days covered hundreds of miles to the north and south but only gained 80 to the east. It was a lot of work for so little, but as it turned out those few miles probably made all the difference between the success and failure of the whole voyage. Thus we may never know the value of the things we do, however small the gain or great the payment at the time.

The days were wild and wet, with low-flying cloud and curtains of rain; the nights were black as ink and bitterly cold, with what the Australians call a lazy wind. It's too lazy to go around you. Hunger was growing and greatly increased the effect of cold, when the mental reaction becomes worse than the physical. You feel despondent.

There seems to be a limit to what we are asked to bear, and perhaps when a thing becomes too much it simply topples over like a wave and levels off for a time. This seems to come about through some protective agency beyond our influence, but I'm not so sure of that. My diary enters this event:

'Turned on the radio just before 8.30 p.m. (7 a.m. GMT) for the first time to Radio N.Z. to get the Time Signal. And out of the radio came the clear notes of the bell bird – it brought back all my deep love of this country; I've said I'd never be able to live there and criticise it violently, but only because I love it so much. The bell bird brought back memories of earlier days. The purity of the sound seems to pervade all around it, including oneself, which is a very nice feeling. I'm going to make my home in New Zealand – it's the way I feel now anyway.' And for my own conversation I added, 'You smug ape, you'd make your home anywhere now.'

There used to be a lot of bell birds in a patch of bush just behind the house, and I knew they'd still be there. I knew also that the home and the fireside (to which my thoughts returned most vividly then) would be just the same. My father usually took a big rumpled chair on the far side, while my mother sat immediately in front near the table with a pile of socks and mending on it. And others of us had taken the other side opposite my father, to talk, read, or just stare into the fire. So many dreams had been born in that fire, perhaps after reading a stirring tale of the North-west Frontier, of sailing to far places and of storms at sea; and so many had come true.

The crowded mantelpiece too would be the same – my Gymnastics Cup, some cheap bronze medals we kids had won in various sports and borne home with such pride, all so unimportant, all so valued. And I felt sure a few opened letters would be pushed behind the clock – those were letters which anyone in the family could read. We had a 'thing' in our family about never reading anyone else's letters, and those left anywhere but behind the clock were as safe as in a vault.

Fair winds came with the bell bird's call and I gained another 200 miles to the east – and then came near-disaster.

The wind was mild in the morning, but during the afternoon a huge fan of cirrus ('mares' tails') and cirro-cumulus clouds spread outwards from the north, and a heavy swell came in from the same direction. The sun was cast in a livid, unhealthy haze. Around it ran a steel-blue halo, and when it set in the evening it looked like a ripe carbuncle. The weather steadily worsened during the night and all the next day, and the swell increased. These were all the text-book signs of a coming cyclone, and because the bearing of the wind did not change I knew that I was right in its path.

A cyclone is like a gigantic whirlpool of air with winds intensifying towards the centre, only in the 'eye' of the storm there is no wind but terrific seas, as great waves aroused by the winds on all sides converge to fling themselves madly against one another. It is mainly in this eye that the danger lies and it must be avoided at all costs.

The Pilot Book said of these storms:

'... and the high confused seas near the centre may cause considerable damage to large and well-found ships, while small vessels (for example, destroyers) have foundered.'

It didn't even mention *Sheila*! However because the path of these storms can be roughly assessed by the direction of the wind, it is possible to take action to avoid it if you have a fast enough ship; in a sailing ship the procedure is a little more complicated, and in my case meant scuttling away off course. I simply didn't have enough rations for such diversions, and anyway I knew that a cyclone in Latitude 40 was unlikely to carry the tremendous forces of those met in more tropical latitudes. So I decided to hold my course, having more confidence in *Sheila* to ride out a cyclone than in myself to live on nothing.

By dusk on the second day it was blowing gale force, and still increasing. *Sheila* lay hove-to under storm canvas, but at 9 that night I struggled to take it in before the still rising wind tore it to shreds or pulled out the stick. *Sheila* felt easier thereafter, steadied (without being over-burdened) by the tremendous wind in her rigging, and the only discomfort came with occasional breakers against which no small ship has protection.

Dawn came slowly through the dense rain, but at 10 a.m. the screaming wind stopped suddenly, the sky cleared overhead into bright sunshine, and we lay in the centre of the cyclone, enclosed by a huge beyond-horizon-wide circle of black clouds under which the storm still raged. There were only faint puffs of wind, but the seas were gigantic, rushing into each other, lifting into tall top-heavy triangles and flopping back to cause more trouble. I could do nothing to steady *Sheila* without wind, the un-rhythmic tossing and battering placing terrible strains upon her; during that day the eye of the storm slowly passed over us and the other rim approached.

We entered the other side just after dark that night, and flew east before the screaming rush under bare poles. It eased to gale force near midnight when I got on storm canvas, and replaced this just before dawn (when the wind eased further) by the closely reefed main and storm jib. I reckoned we covered 100 miles in the next fifteen hours, and at times when *Sheila* was lifted high on a crest and the full force of the wind hit her, she was flung far over on her side until half the sail was flat in the water. It was bad seamanship to sail so hard in such weather; the short rations impelled it, but it imposed the great strains and discomfort that bad seamanship always does. And so I had my cyclone.

The ration situation was poor, and just over halfway across the Tasman I had seven 12-oz. tins of meat and six 10-oz. tins of vegetables left. I'd been on the emergency scale for the last two weeks, one tin a day alternating between meat and vegetables to give variety. Only once did I succumb to the obvious common sense of mixing a tin of each together into a more pleasant stew, as a two-day ration. It is too difficult when hungry to face a lovely hot pot of such delicious stew, enough for the one good meal you need, and instead ladle out just one-sixth to draw it out into the full two-day ration it had to be. My meal times were 8 a.m., 4 p.m., and midnight, and there is a pitiful wail in my diary after the storm:

'Left the helm soon after dawn, and was so ravenous thought I'd have my breakfast then at 6 instead of waiting until 8. It was truly delicious, but mugger me, it's now 10 hours before I can have another.'

Followed a few days of winds from everywhere, all unpersistent and unreliable, in which I made what easting was possible, but in the fifth week out came a strong sou'-westerly. It had all the feeling of staying for several days, and with only 300 miles to go I determined to stay at the helm either until it blew out or until I reached New Zealand.

My object was to make a land-fall at Farewell Spit and get inside its protective arm, where in the comparatively sheltered waters of Tasman Bay my engine would take me the remaining 40 miles to Nelson if the wind dropped. Home – I just couldn't believe it; and yet to my surprise the idea of leaving that horrible life on salt water was tinged with sadness.

That wind held for three days. I know there was little time off for meals, such as they were; entries in the log are merely 'sailed till dawn,' and scrawled haphazard across the page whichever way the book had opened; and there is no mention of sleep, but I remember I did go below one night for three hours, numb with cold.

The night of 24th May was clear and moonlit. The main coast or even Aotearoa (the long white cloud) was not visible before dark, but by midnight I knew I must be close. At time a dimly visible shape appeared in the distant moonlight on the starboard bow; surely it couldn't be New Zealand, yet it could have been something. I wasn't sure.

The wind dropped two hours later, at 2 a.m., releasing me from the helm after an almost unbroken shift of three days and nights, so I went below to catch up on sleep before more wind recalled me.

A beautiful dawn came, the sea smooth, the sun warm, and the rugged bush-clad coast of New Zealand lay 20 miles to the south-east; the low-lying sand-hills of Farewell Spit lay about 40 miles dead ahead, but still under the horizon. There was one meagre meal left on board, six ounces of tinned peas, and as many cups of tea as I wanted without sugar or milk. So I sat on deck in the sun and dried out clothing, content with the world as it was because I couldn't do a thing to change it. The warmth and the stillness were heaven anyway.

There was enough petrol on board to carry *Sheila* as far as Farewell Spit in calm water, but what if the wind got up from ahead after 30 miles to leave me 10 miles short? It could then take another two days to get inside the Spit, and another two to Nelson. Hunger in itself is no great danger for a few days, just unpleasant, but the fatigue and weakness is dangerous. It only needs a slightly careless hand-hold or one without quite enough strength in it to let you fall overboard, to mention only one of the myriad forms weakness can take.

The alternative was to move in towards the coast and make Karamea, the nearest port and no further away than the Spit. It wasn't Nelson, but if the wind did go south after all, I could use it to make the Spit and still have my petrol intact; and if the wind came from ahead, with food in me I could take *Sheila* to Nelson later.

The wind came at noon, straight off the Spit, so I got on sail and headed for Karamea. I had no large-scale chart or Pilot Book of that coast (stupid economics), and only remembered that at school someone who came from Karamea had mentioned that ships called there for coal. If ships could enter so could *Sheila*. On arrival there that evening I discovered that over the years since I had left school the river had silted up the bar, and nothing could get in.

There was a big surge on the beach, too big to land in my pram, and although people were walking about within sight on shore I knew no one could get out to me. The bottom was good holding ground so I anchored for the night outside the breakers, had my last meal, and slept for 12 hours. The alternatives for the morrow were either to find a sheltered bay with a homestead or shell-fish or go another 80 miles down the coast to Westport, which had an established harbour.

Next morning, with my goal of years only a few hundred yards away – but with the breakers between, it might as well have been as many miles – I sailed south down the coast thinking of bacon and eggs. After about 15 miles I passed along spur running out into the sea and looking as if it might have a sheltered beach inside it, so I anchored just within the point with the idea of going ashore in the pram and collecting a sack of mussels. The beach was a mass of broken rocks on which the heavy surf broke angrily, and under the drizzle of cold rain it all looked very unfavourable, but suddenly I felt an over-powering urge to get ashore at any price.

My mind supported this idea as being the wisest course – Westport still lay a long way to the south, and the favourable wind might drop at any time to leave me in a worse situation than the first, out of petrol range of anywhere. But deep down was a small still voice, so far away I could pretend not to hear it but I couldn't still it.

'You're in a panic,' it said.

I laid out the second anchor, closed the hatches, and unlashed the dinghy. It was poised ready to go over the side but this voice, this feeling, made me pause; it was the same feeling of premonition that had stopped me plunging into the sunlit Mediterranean that morning when a shark followed astern without my knowing it then; it can also (I've found) mean I've forgotten something, like a door-key, and it always pays to pause.

'Of course,' I said to myself. 'The hanky.'

I pulled the pram back inboard, threw open the hatch, went below to the locker and took the child's hanky out from between the thickly-folded towel, still neatly pressed and dry. It made me smile to remember her serious gaze as she had stood before me.

'Do you promise?' And I had said, 'Yes, I promise,' and trusting me she had given her gift.

It was warmer in the cabin than in the rain outside, so I decided to have a final cup of tea before trying to get ashore, because it seemed highly probable that more than the rain was to wet me.

And while I drank that tea I took the opportunity to face that voice, because it still persisted. It said plainly that my chances of landing that light pram in that sea on those rocks, without damaging it or myself so much as to make return to *Sheila* impossible, were slight. And if the weather got worse *Sheila*'s anchors would not hold her.

'You're not going ashore for food,' the stillness said. 'You're in a panic and deserting your ship, and I'll ruddy well see you never forget it whatever stories you may hatch up, whatever fame the headlines give, whatever sympathy you receive.'

I had been on the lookout for some reaction to hunger and fatigue, and it is always near the end that distractions become strongest, but I had not expected them in this form.

So I finished my tea, put the hanky safely back in the folded towel, pulled the pram right inboard, up-turned it over the skylight and lashed it down, took in both anchors, and sailed for Westport.

It is not possible to state that the child's handkerchief and trust saved me perhaps from disaster, although certainly from a decision I would have regretted for the rest of my life; but it is equally impossible to deny it. Isn't this the child's fairy-tale, when a gesture of simple trust beyond any thought of reward turns the lowly beggar boy into a handsome prince; when a gentle kiss beyond desire awakens the sleeping princess and banishes the ugly witch under whose spell she lay; and the prince and princess live happily ever after? It's when we grow up and lay such stories aside that we lay aside their miracles too.

I arrived off Westport at three in the morning. Knowing the type of coast and that a river flowed through the harbour, I knew there'd be a bar across the entrance and that with the big swell it would be dangerous. The red and green entry lights were clearly visible, probably on the end of the breakwaters, but the red light seemed to be to starboard and the green light to port entering.

This is in accordance with the old system which changed soon after I had left England, and it seemed that Westport had not effected the change, which is opposite to the old – but I could not be sure. It's hard to explain the tricks that lights and angles can play at night, without a chart and not having seen the place in daylight – those lights could still be right, only appearing different owing to some angle in the breakwater I could not see; like the entrance lights into Bône which could have wreaked me.

It was worth having a closer look, so I eased *Sheila* in under sail; under sail because when the wind is steady and dangers lie close to leeward, sail is far safer than power and the ship handles better. Under power a drop of water or a bit of dirt in the carburettor jets – or some temperamental nonsense in the electrical system – can leave you bereft; under sail you can feel what a ship tells you, which is often what your eyes, ears, or even a chart cannot. The feel of *Sheila* to the waves, a feel words cannot explain, told me the situation was lethal; and being uncertain of the entrance lights I applied a golden rule – when in doubt get away the hell out of it, back to open water.

I headed out about a mile, hove-to, and stayed awake until dawn in case wind or current took me into danger. It was not wise to go further out to sea to sleep safely, in case a hard land-breeze came with the dawn and made it difficult to regain the port.

The drizzly dawn came slowly and I took *Sheila* close inshore to clarify the entrance. The river flowed strongly out of the harbour, its strength contained between two long breakwaters reaching out towards me, whereafter the outflowing water piled itself against the heavy incoming swell to form an area of high-reaching top-heavy breakers such as never happen in their normal state. So there again was my goal for the past six hard years and 18,000 miles, with such breakers in between that I would normally never have considered entering.

The longer I delayed the less likely would I be to make wise decisions, and the less strength with which to carry them out – *Sheila* needed my best as much as I needed hers. The weather might get better or it might get worse, when the bar would become unthinkable, and I had no food to stand off several days waiting for an improvement. The attempt had to be made and the sooner the better, but first I went below to make a last cup of tea, to consider all the factors that might arise and make the most careful plan for dealing with them.

The greatest danger of the breakers was not their size but their speed. Perhaps many have seen what happens to a light dinghy coming in to a beach on a surf – it is gripped by the forward edge of the wave and held in a speed which makes it uncontrollable, and the slightest deviation from off-straight forbids correction until the dinghy swings broad-side on to the wave, is toppled over and submerged. That was exactly the danger to *Sheila*, designed for a maximum 8 knots – those in-rolling seas were travelling at about 30 knots. And near the breakwaters, even if I could delay the broach-to, I would not be able to control direction, and to hit either of the breakwaters at 30 knots would be disastrous. And no swimmer could have lasted more than a few minutes in those seas and currents – I reckoned, in cool assessment, that I had a fifty-fifty chance of survival, and it was a bitter thought that in a few minutes it might all be over on the very threshold of my home.

I stripped off to shirt and shorts in case of a swim, because you never really know your chances and I'd certainly have no hope in the heavy clothes I was wearing. I then put two reefs in the mainsail, to give *Sheila* with that wind just enough power to drive her against the current with the minimum speed. The mizzen was furled in case a sudden gust swung her stern off course. I started and tested the engine, and let it run in neutral so it would give no extra speed and no spinning propeller would cause turbulence astern to upset a coming sea, but so it was ready for use once the shelter of the breakwaters had been reached. The wind was less there, and the two-reefed main would not have held *Sheila* against the out-going current; nor in that confined space would I be able to leave the helm to put on the extra sail needed.

It would have been normal seamanship to have trailed a heavy rope over the stern, so that its drag would lessen the chances of *Sheila* being carried forward with the speed of the waves; but the following seas might have swept it forward and around the propellor, to foul it and stall the engine when I did put it in gear. I had to be sure of that extra power when I lost the wind, or else be swept back into the breakers really out of control.

Then I again took the child's hanky from the locker, and buttoned it into the pocket of my shorts, so that whether I stepped ashore or my body was washed ashore trust itself would not be broken.

It was a very strange feeling deliberately and with calculation entering a situation which I hardly hoped to survive. For fleeting moments I knew it was to be death, but underlying, far down in my consciousness was a smooth, strong tide which I sensed was immune to all things, even death. And not to sense that tide was to panic, but that was mine to control and my only prayer was for the strength to do so.

All was ready. I lashed myself to the helm with a slip knot, closed all hatches firmly (with my warm clothes just inside in case I was to need them later), and turned *Sheila* towards the entrance and the breakers, placing her so that her bow pointed dead straight before the waves and into the dead centre of the entrance – and noted the compass course. Then I took her right to the very edge of the outermost breaker, keeping that compass course as accurately as possible; just before we got to the breakers her bow pointed 200 yards north of the northern breakwater.

Sheila answered as she always does under sail, turning as she lifted high on a big sea which broke with a roar only yards beyond, and I took her back into deep water to the distance of the original starting point.

Then I sailed south until the same compass bearing bore to a point ashore 200 yards south of the southern breakwater, plus a bit more. There was a drift up the coast which I had to allow for, because if I started from the wrong point and tried to correct on the way in, it would throw her off the dead straight before the seas at speed and she would become uncontrollable.

So in we went, and in seconds entered the breakers. *Sheila* lifted, surged forward quite happily, the broken crest climbed over the after-deck and spilled into the cockpit. She rode three waves beautifully until a monster bore down, so huge I felt there was no hope of survival, knowing that this one wave would decide the issue of the whole voyage. If I could maintain a dead straight course before it, it would carry us through the turmoil to the safety beyond, but if we wavered one iota, the very strength that could carry us through would annihilate us, either swinging us broadside on or into one of the breakwaters.

This was known as even then *Sheila*'s stern lifted, and I forgot the breakwaters, the entrance, all fear vanquished by inevitability as I pin-pointed my mind into the helm. With this I could no longer steer the course I myself wanted, but only maintain the course it would be disaster to evade.

Sheila became gripped in speed, her hull sucked down in the tide to decklevel; her bow wave was two solid masses of water, hurled aside so high I could see nothing beyond them, not even the light structures on the ends of the breakwaters. I could feel her balanced on the helm, which needed only a finger-tip to maintain with occasional gentle strength to correct tendencies about to develop; if these had developed, the strength of ten would not have saved her.

I was only half aware of the wonderful scene through which we roared – huge tangled masses of tortured water, glimpses of smooth-welling eddies, terrific noise, and through the soles of my bare feet I could feel *Sheila* vibrating in every plank. Never have I felt so at one with her, bringing that glorious surge of pure exhilaration and thrilling experience when you make powerful destructive forces not your enemy by mastery over them, but your own glory by attaining harmony with them.

Then the crumbling wave returned to its own, its destiny fulfilled, leaving *Sheila* in the centre of the channel between the breakwaters, balanced peacefully between the current from the land and the wind from the sea. I eased the gear into ahead, and as we moved sedately up the placid channel I pushed open the hatch and reached for my trousers.

'Thank God,' I breathed, 'I didn't try to land up the coast.'

Soon the channel widened and bifurcated, one branch leading up-stream to the wharves, and one to a sheltered lagoon in which small boats lay. I put the engine out of gear and took in sail, feeling every fold and reef point known so well, and going into gear entered the still harbour, which lay under the gentle, cool mist of a Sunday morning.

I again paused in the middle of the lagoon to look about and decide where the anchor or tie up alongside, and on the iron deck of an old dredge was a figure muffled against the morning cold. He waved me in, and as *Sheila* drifted alongside he took my ropes and made fast.

With his kindly welcome and congratulations came my own reaction, and I climbed up the iron side of the dredge, crossed a gang-plank on to New Zealand soil, as in a dream. My obligations to the Customs, Immigration, Port Health and others never entered my head.

My new friend, this stranger whom I somehow felt I'd known for years, took me to his nearby home. His family were out at early morning church, so he busied himself getting breakfast, pulling out dry clothes, stoking up the range for a hot bath, laying out a fresh towel and his shaving gear; and then he said,

'You'd better have a brandy,' and pouring out a medium tot he handed me the glass. I drank it slowly, and it made me feel more in a dream than I was already.

'I won't give you another,' he said. 'There's plenty there, but a cup of good hot tea will do you more good now.' And I think I was more grateful for the understanding of that denial than for anything else he gave me.

And soon I was on the phone to my people, to banish the fears they had borne unspoken for so long. And then the Port Authorities were on the phone to me.

The Customs were most kind, accepting my apologies for what was officially a grave transgression. The Port Health Officer collected me in his car, and on the way to his office a frantic desire for something swept over me – I'd had nothing with sugar in it for weeks.

'Stop at a sweet shop, please,' I said, 'even if I have to break it open.' But one was open and I rushed inside, only to return empty-handed.

'Don't you want it after all?' he asked.

'Yes,' I said, 'I'm longing for it but I've got no local cash.'

So this official went in and brought out two thick slabs of the most wonderful chocolate I've ever known. The brand was unimportant.

Others came. My old school in Nelson (I don't know how the news spread so fast) rang a local old boy, who came to offer anything he could and gave me a great deal of help. A fisherman, who looked as if he might be a bit of a wag normally, came and offered to look after *Sheila* if I intended going away for a brief visit home. It is asking too big a responsibility to leave *Sheila* in someone's direct charge, but he accepted it. (When I returned a week later to take *Sheila* on to Nelson, I found he and others had cleaned and dried her out, taken my salt-soaked blankets ashore, and his wife had washed and ironed my clothes. They cannot know what all that meant to me.)

I told my story to the local press. The editor took me back to lunch, and I found that his wife had rushed around the town to borrow a good steak, because she thought that would be best for me. And that paper wrote none of that exaggerated nonsense which to me is always a desecration. I know better than anyone else to whom the real credit for my safety lies, and to misplace that credit seems to include me in a claim I would not dare to make.

That evening my young brother and a friend arrived by car, having driven through from home; and the next evening the car drew up at the white gate of our garden. I tried to get out as if I'd only been for a drive into the village, and my parents came out with loads of Hayter reserve, their grins almost escaping their control and becoming tears, which didn't matter because we all knew they were there.

Then we went inside. The room was just the same, the fireside and the mantelpiece and the letters behind the clock; and I knew I'd never been away from the home they had kept so safe.

Adrian Hayter, Sheila in the Wind, *1959*

PART FOUR

Racing Ahead

THE EMERALD HIGHWAY

LEAH Newbold is one of the few New Zealand women to have sailed in the Whitbread Round-the-World yacht race, and the only one to have done it twice. Her 80,000 nautical miles also include two Fastnets, one Sydney-Hobart, one Newport-Bermuda, three trans-Atlantic crossings, and a host of shorter passages.

For the 1997/98 Whitbread race, at age thirty and now professional, she was watch captain aboard EF Education. *Sweden's 'Team EF' was the first to enter two boats, one with a male crew (the eventual overall winners), the other female. For the female boat, the race had its dramas, including losing their mast a thousand miles from Cape Horn and limping into Ushuaia, southern Argentina, where a new mast flown out from England was waiting.*

Earlier, on the first leg heading south, they were three days without water when their water-maker broke down. Then, in the icy southern ocean, near catastrophe when they almost lost their whole inventory of sails over the side . . .

The Cape Town stop-over was nothing short of hectic with a lot of work going on to prepare the boats for the first of the Southern Ocean legs. It was vital to give the boats a good 'going over'. The boats were pulled out of the water, hulls were checked for any damage, rudders dropped out and bearings checked, steering cables changed, winches pulled apart and cleaned, new running rigging installed and engines tuned. The masts were pulled out of the boats, and completely stripped to check all the fittings thoroughly.

I had a lot on, organising and co-ordinating the work programme with the shore-team, our crew and the *EF Language* crew. I was responsible for all the movements of the boat, lifting it, pulling the rig out and then getting on with my own work on the mast and some of the big jobs on the boat. The scheduling wasn't always very straight forward as we had to coordinate the timing around the two boats. We only had one cradle, therefore only one boat could be out of the water at one time. We had to pay extra money for the crane to do everything twice, so it was vital that we used the cranes efficiently. This proved to be a headache at times and we had to be very flexible to fit in with the guys' schedule. Fortunately Tim was pretty much in control of it all as he acted as the go-between for the two crews and he managed our time very well. Tim and his boys were responsible for any jobs on the boat that required repairing, like broken fittings or any structural damage, strengthening weak or fatigued areas, the installation of any new equipment and any building of new fittings. They were also responsible for the hull management and would decide when the boat needed new paint on the underside of the hull or any other major work done to it.

Tim, Freede and Magnus were kept extremely busy the entire time with the two boats and two rather demanding crews. They handled it all very well and were pretty good at accommodating all requests for both boats. Between them, they had an extensive knowledge of the workings of our boats and were helpful in any department if we ever needed their advice.

It was lucky that all the girls on our team were hard workers and they all knew what they had to do in their area before we were ready to go again.

Anna and Katie were always stuck in the sail loft working long hours shuffling the huge masses of kevlar around, repairing the damage inflicted on various sails and organising new ones making sure they were exactly right. We were fortunate to have a 'mobile' sail loft with our own sewing machines and sailmaking equipment which we set up in each port of call between our two shipping containers. It was a brilliant set up and saved a lot of headaches, which other campaigns experienced trying to find local sail lofts to work in. Again, it took careful management between the sailmaking teams from each boat to share the loft and the onshore sailmakers, Paul and Sam. I sometimes wonder how they managed with the metres and metres of sail cloth spread out on the floor with each person trying to find a space to do their work.

Keryn was my number one helper with any big projects on the boat or mast and she made my life easy due to her reliability and competence. Lisa worked mostly up to her neck in grease and diesel as she made sure the engines were in perfect working order. She had some excellent help from local engineers and managed to get the shaft on the generator fixed.

However, this took time and it wasn't fixed until only a few days before the re-start. She and I had a couple of late nights getting the damn thing back in order, but once it was done we were confident that we would have no more major problems with it.

I would liaise with Christine and keep her informed of how the work programme was going while she and Lynnath concentrated on weather routing and gathering important information for the next leg. We would only sail the boat two or three times before the re-start to check a few new sails and to make sure everything was up and running.

We had a crew meeting and discussed our performance on leg one and talked mainly of being disappointed in our result. We felt that we had made some expensive mistakes and we had to be more bold in making some radical decisions. We boiled this down to the fact that we had spent virtually our entire training period before the race sailing with the guys and perhaps this had prevented us from being brave and calling some of the shots ourselves. However, we were now on our own with no-one to help us in making those decisions, we had to be more confident in ourselves and go for it.

We were reasonably happy with our watch system, however we would have to make a few changes with the change in crew. Our watch system consisted of doing a six-hour watch during the day and four hours at night. It worked on a rotating basis. We split the crew for watches; there were two watch leaders, myself and Kiny, with one extra person each, then there were two groups of three, which left Christine and Lynnath to float – they didn't stand a watch as such. The grouping in leg one wasn't quite right, so we made a few changes.

The system worked with two groups of three spending half their watch with me and the other half of their watch with Kiny. It meant that we would have a change of watch every two or four hours and it also meant we only needed two people to cook – Bridget and Marleen. It sounds very complicated, but it worked well.

We would have two new crew join us in Cape Town with Rick and C.B. getting off. Rick was to jump on *EF Language* for the next leg to Fremantle. C.B. would re-join us in Fremantle to sail to Auckland with us. The two girls who replaced Rick and C.B. were Joan Touchette and Emma Westmacott.

We all knew Joan well as she had done some sailing with us previously, but she was not available for the entire Whitbread due to America's Cup committments. Joan is a big girl, as in tall and strong. She has massive drive and determination, is very straight forward and has a wicked temper.

But she fitted into our crew well and proved to be one of the hardest, most loyal workers on the team. She became a huge help to me onshore – I knew I could rely on Joan to complete her work perfectly with any task I asked her to complete on the boat. Onboard, her strength was a huge bonus and her helming skills in certain conditions were invaluable.

I didn't know Emma that well, but had heard great things about her sailing abilities and personality. She was taking time out of Tracy Edwards' Jules Verne project to come and do leg 2 with us. It didn't take long to work out just how good Emma was; I liked her attitude and her competitive nature. She was excellent on the helm and all-round brilliant on the boat. It was a shame she had to leave us in Fremantle, I would have been more than happy to have her on our crew for the entire race.

There was some disappointing news as we approached the second week in Cape Town and that was that *America's Challenge*, my good friend Ross Fields' boat, was to pull out of the race. They had run out of money due to some problems with the sponsor. This was extremely bad news for Whitbread, as the last thing they wanted was for someone to have to pull out of their race.

However, Ross was not prepared to carry on under-funded, as it wasn't worth it. I felt very sorry for him and his crew, particularly for the young guys on his boat who were doing their first Whitbread. I had vivid memories of my race almost being over at exactly the same stage last time round and I knew how devastated I would have been if that had happened.

It seemed bizarre that the guys who had helped us mostly in 1993/94, to make sure we didn't retire, were the ones that were going to have to retire themselves this time around.

Four of his guys were lucky enough to pick up positions on other boats. Some boats had sailed with eleven crew on the first leg and wanted to take twelve for the rest of the race.

Another surprise announcement just days before the re-start was that Chris Dickson, skipper of *Toshiba*, was resigning. They had not performed well on leg one and he resigned after he felt the pressure from *Toshiba's* crew that he was to blame for their poor result. A happy *Toshiba* crew announced that Paul Standbridge would take the role of skipper for the rest of the race.

It was definitely a stressful stopover for me, for everyone, and was made more so because it was shortened due to the leg down to Cape Town being so slow. With time to only have three days off, we weren't really rested enough for the next leg. However, we were looking forward to getting out there again and giving it heaps. The girls heading into the Southern Ocean for the first time were looking forward to the experience ahead. I was definitely looking forward to it, particularly because I felt so much more confident than last time and I knew we had a boat that would not let us down. It was up to us to sail it as hard as we possibly could.

We got over the start line in a good position again, spinnakers set to head down to the lay mark close to the beach, giving spectators a great view as we passed within swimming distance to the shore. There was a moderate breeze blowing and we all rounded the mark, hoisted our headsails and started to head southwest to get around the Cape of Good Hope. *Swedish Match* was the only boat to go out on a limb after the mark rounding and promptly headed offshore while the rest of the fleet made the fatal mistake of staying close to the shore. The breeze inshore virtually died out and we all sat becalmed as we tried to get around Sea Point and Clifton. It was incredibly frustrating, the entire fleet watched *Swedish Match* disappear on the horizon as we all jostled positions struggling to get our boats to move at all. *EF Language, Brunel Sunergy, Innovation*

Kvaerner and *Toshiba* were the first to get going again, followed by *Chessie Racing*, *Silk Cut*, ourselves and *Merit Cup*.

The first week was incredibly slow going, due to a high pressure system that was ridging over the fleet. The wind fluctuated, so we had an incredible number of sail changes as we went through the sail inventory at rapid pace. Apart from *Swedish Match* who were off in their own weather system and extending their lead way out in front of the pack, the rest of us stayed in visible range and we enjoyed some very close sailing next to the other boats. This was great for morale as we concentrated hard and every manoeuvre or sail change we made was performed perfectly so we wouldn't give any distance away to anyone.

We all continued to slowly head south; the weather gradually got colder, the breeze finally began to pick up and the fleet became more spread out.

At 48 degrees south, we passed Marion and Prince Edward Islands in daylight, both looking spectacular and inhospitable with their snow-capped mountains. It wouldn't be long before we would have the heater working overtime and we'd start dreaming of feather duvets and open fires!

Bridget had bought a good stock of gas this time so we could safely have one hot drink each watch, and toilet paper seemed to be in good supply too. We were looking forward to our first breakfast with hot porridge, which was a new addition to the menu for the cold leg.

Bridget had done a superb job with our food, she made sure that we were getting plenty of carbohydrates, fat and protein to account for the extreme physical conditions we were enduring. She had been advised to make sure we were eating up to 4,000 calories a day. Protein was hard to supply with freeze-dried products, but she gave us plenty of vegetables and occasionally we would have freeze-dried scrambled eggs for breakfast. As much as we moan about freeze-dried food, it is not that bad at all – it fills you up when you're hungry and provides adequate nutrients and vitamins. To boost our energy intakes, we also had nutrition bars and replacement drinks that were excellent for providing a useful snack.

We were well into the second week before we started doing some fast downwind sailing. With the six hourly schedule coming in giving each yacht's position, we could see that a few of the boats in the front of the fleet were picking up the pace as they had obviously hooked into a frontal system. It is amazing how boats only twenty miles ahead of you can suddenly get into a weather system which helps them to take off. Before you know it, they are doing three or four knots faster than you are as they extend their lead and you try to work out from the weather maps what they're in and why it missed you.

However, before our first day of hard downwind running we were still in good company. *Silk Cut* and *Chessie Racing* had been in our sights all day and *Merit Cup* were very close behind us, but we couldn't see them. As the night drew in and we lost sight of the others we enjoyed 24 hours of fast, furious sailing with a fractional spinnaker up. It was great Southern Ocean conditions, big waves, lots of wind, grey overcast sky and grey sea.

The wind instruments were reading 30-36 knots of windspeed, but it felt like more. The air and wind feels so much heavier than what it says down in the Southern Ocean, it is very dense air – almost eerie. Driving the boat down the big waves was super fun, we'd often get completely soaked as the bow of the boat dug itself into a wave. Water rolled along the deck and into the cockpit where we would be up to our knees in water; often we found ourselves clasping onto solid objects so that we wouldn't be washed to the back of the boat. On the wheel, I'd grab it tight and brace myself for the onslaught of the powerful rush from the massive volume of water. Wearing safety harnesses was imperative, with the boat screaming along so viciously and such an amount of water coming over the decks, moving around was dangerous. Downstairs, moving around was no easier; it feels like you are on some mad ride at a fun fair and every care must be taken not to be thrown off balance as you load on the layers of gear before going outside.

Sitting in the Nav. Station is like sitting in a flight simulator; the noise from the water rushing by the hull and the churn of the winches above your head is a constant reminder of the forces from the conditions outside. We were getting great speeds and I broke my record from the previous leg as we went down a great wave and topped 30.2 knots. It felt fantastic and seemingly easy as the boat surfed along with the wave; everything became unloaded and it felt as though we were flying. We were certainly on the edge though, and after a couple of wild broaches and breaking a bit of gear, we needed to reef the main. We didn't want to risk a violent crash that would end up costing too much time. We were in seventh position, which we were pretty happy about, and we didn't want to lose any miles.

We were expecting this weather to last at least a week and were getting psyched for the hard week ahead when the breeze suddenly died down again.

It was quite bizarre, and most unlike Southern Ocean conditions. As the breeze died down to around sixteen knots and the sky cleared, the wind went ahead and we found ourselves putting reaching sails up. We knew *Merit Cup* was still close and someone finally spotted them on the horizon behind us.

We kept a close eye on them and used the radar to monitor if they were making any gains on us. After an hour or so, it was clear that they weren't making any impact on us and we noticed them suddenly pulling their sails down. This was a little odd but we found out later that they had massive weed around their keel and one of their guys had to jump over the side, into the freezing four-degree water, to clear it off. They then hoisted their spinnaker and sailed on a lower course than us and that was the last we saw of them for the rest of the leg.

As we headed into the furious fifty latitudes, the breeze freed up and we were happy to raise the masthead spinnaker again. The most windspeed we would see was 26 knots, somewhat disappointing, but the waves were still big and we continued to sail at good speeds. The weather seemed somewhat mild and it wasn't even that cold. The wet was the hardest thing to overcome, it didn't matter that we had the best wet-weather gear available, it was impossible to keep the continuous flow of salt water out.

Our heater had broken down after only two days of use, so now there was no way of drying any of our gear. It was awful getting out of our bunks and putting on wet socks and wet outer layers. Mind you, as soon as you stepped outside it would take only seconds before you were soaked from head to foot anyway.

Before I went up on deck I would always go and visit Lynnath or Christine in the Nav. Station to get an update and to learn whether any new pieces of information had come in while I was asleep. I would get a run down on what the weather was expected to do during my watch so that I could be prepared for sail changes or a course change. Sometimes there would be some bright news from a message received from another boat or someone on shore. This was always a welcome relief to lighten up the isolation we felt in the deep dark south! When I got up on deck I would sit next to Kiny for five or ten minutes discussing the conditions and what it had been like for her watch. She would describe how the boat was feeling and the characteristics of the wind from the previous few hours. Anna came on watch with me and she would discuss the sail trim with Katie. We would all talk about the options of what sail might be used next, if the wind changed. When I was happy with the set up, Kiny and Katie disappeared downstairs and left us to it.

We were pleased to see that we were keeping up the same speeds as most of the fleet. This was a little surprising as we thought that the heavy downwind sailing might prove to be a weakness for us. However, in time we learnt that we were able to sail just as quick as the guys in any downwind situation. It was only when we would end up sailing certain reaching angles that we were severely disadvantaged.

Silk Cut was going faster than everyone else though and she set a new monohull world record for a 24 hour run during this period. She covered 449.8 miles, which broke the record of 425 nautical miles that *Intrum Justicia* set in the 1993/94 Whitbread.

The call for a gybe from the navigator in heavy downwind sailing is the one call the crew hates to hear. It can be quite hairy in big seas in Whitbread 60s and in most cases it is better to play it safe, which involves dropping the spinnaker, gybing the boat and then re-hoisting the spinnaker. In essence, you lose very little time, rather than risking doing it with the spinnaker up, crashing and wasting more time than you need to. We had previously done some good, safe gybes and we were ready to go ahead and do another one when Lynnath asked us to gybe so we could start heading north towards Fremantle.

We had the masthead spinnaker up and it was blowing between 20 and 25 knots which is generally a pretty safe windspeed to keep the spinnaker up through the gybe. Everyone was awake, with nine of us on deck getting ready to gybe. We made a crucial mistake which was one that we would never make again. With all the headsails stacked on the weather rail, rather than putting them downstairs for the gybe, we put them on the leeward rail and tied them down. We didn't think they would be any problem there.

Christine called for the gybe when she was comfortable on a wave. As the main was grinded into the middle and the runners were pulled tight, the spinnaker collapsed and when it filled again with a big puff of wind, Christine lost control of the boat and we were thrown into a violent broach. There was nothing she could do as she wrestled with the wheel to try to correct the boat. With all the sails on the leeward rail, this was disastrous because they all ended up in the water when the boat was on its side during the broach. With the weight of the waterlogged sails we couldn't right the boat and by now the spinnaker was flapping madly out of control too. Helplessly, we watched the sails on the leeward side disappear under the water, ripping the stanchions out of the deck; we saw the lifelines go limp as the side of the boat was swallowed under a large volume of water. Fortunately the sails were tied on very well, so even though it seemed that they had all been wiped completely off the boat, the ties holding them on had simply stretched to their limits and the sails were, remarkably, still attached to the boat but hanging dangerously over the side.

It didn't take long for the rest of the crew to scramble up on deck, pulling on their jackets and harnesses as they came out of the companionway. The first thing we needed to do was to get the spinnaker down and onboard before it destroyed itself. Once that was back on board, the boat righted itself, but the waterlogged sails, weighing well over a ton, were still hanging over the side. We had to work quickly because, if the ties gave up, we would lose our whole headsail inventory to the depths of the ocean. We put halyards on whatever sailbag holders we could, but we couldn't move the whole lot without getting some rope around the entire stack. We needed someone to get into the water to get the rope around.

There wasn't a lot of time to debate who was going over and I volunteered quickly. I had my survival suit on, which is like a dry-suit and completely watertight, a life jacket and a tether, and braced I myself as I leapt over into the freezing waters. I gasped as the icy water hit my face – the only part of me that was exposed. I had to quickly forget the icy shock and turn my attention to the huge pile of sails lurking above me.

The girls handed me a rope and, as the boat rolled on a wave, I shot under the pile of sails to pass the rope around them. It was quite scary to say the least, diving under the sails and the side of the boat as they rolled on the waves, but I realised that there was no time to be scared, I had to just get on with it. I knew there were eleven willing on-lookers above me and that I could easily get out from under the pile in an instant. It took a couple of attempts before I could thread the rope between them and the side of the boat and back up to the eager hands waiting above me. Once I got a second rope around and my mission was complete, two of the girls leant over and pulled me out of the water – over the pile of sails as if I was weightless – and they threw me into the safety of the cockpit. Within minutes they were able to attach a couple of halyards to the ropes and on a big roll of the boat the sails were heaved back on board. A huge cheer and a massive sigh of relief went around the boat as we all looked at each other and realised how lucky we were to not lose a single sail into the blue depths.

I went downstairs and got out of my survival suit. I was happy to see that it worked and I was completely dry underneath. However, I was beginning to get very cold and I spent a few minutes getting myself warm as everyone started to get the boat up and running again. The boat was a mess, every bit of rope available had been pulled out and used in the rescue mission, downstairs looked like a bomb had gone off with gear, and the spinnaker we had pulled down, scattered everywhere.

I went back up on deck as soon as possible to help get the main back up and another (smaller!) spinnaker up to get us going again. Once we had picked ourselves up, shaken ourselves off and were on our way again, we could see that we had sustained no major damage, except the stanchions which had been wrenched out of their bases making the lifelines ineffective on the starboard side. However, we rigged up some jury lifelines and continued to be astounded at how lucky we were in getting out of the situation without any real wounds. We also realised how stupid we had been in not putting the sails downstairs and not going the safe route. We lost over two hours during the incident and were bitterly disappointed in our performance. We were to later learn in Fremantle that we weren't the only ones to have such an experience, and everyone had learnt similar bitter lessons.

Our luck had taken us a little further than emerging lightly from a disaster – we were fortunate to not lose any miles to our nearest competitors who were *Merit Cup* only 30 odd miles ahead of us and *Brunel Sunergy* who were behind. However, we had been heading for a 24-hour run of over 400 miles and our little 'incident' prevented us from achieving this. It was a long day for everyone, Anna and I had the worst of it because it was the end of our watch when we gybed and by the time we were up and running again and we had cleaned up downstairs, we were due to go on our six-hour daytime watch. We threw back a couple of black coffees and did our watch; we'd been working for fourteen and a half hours before we were able to get into our bunks for a coma sleep.

The following morning, after another good 24-hour run, Anna and I were on watch again. We had the spinnaker up and Anna was steering when she screeched, 'Oh my God, look ahead!' The sight before us was incredible. There was a pod of 30 or more pilot whales stretched out across the sea in front of us, leaping out of the water, coming straight for the boat.

'Which way shall I go?' Anna yelled.

'I dunno, just hold on!' I said to her, watching the whales in fascination. Fortunately, as we met, the whales parted around the boat and they disappeared behind us in an instant. It was one of the most incredible things I've ever seen at sea; they must have been travelling at twenty knots themselves.

After a couple of days of heading northeast and getting into the mid 40 degree latitudes, the weather started to warm up and we started counting down the miles to Fremantle. We were looking forward to the sky clearing, as we hadn't seen stars or the sun for quite a few days now, and the grey of the sky and sea was becoming rather tedious. There were only 80 or so miles separating *Merit Cup*, *Brunel Sunergy*, and us. *Merit Cup* was definitely within striking distance and *Brunel Sunergy* was snapping at our heels, so we had to keep concentrating and pushing hard. We had a nervous period where the wind dropped off and we had a headsail up for a few hours but fortunately this didn't last long and we soon had the spinnaker up again enjoying some nice down-wind sailing.

We had one great eight-hour run averaging 16.7 knots and the most pleasing thing was that we were going faster than both *Merit Cup* and *Brunel Sunergy* keeping us in the running with them.

While we still had four days to go, *Swedish Match* was the first boat across the line in Fremantle. Their initial break from the fleet right at the start paid off hugely over the entire leg of the race, an amazing achievement.

Our last 800 miles into Fremantle were frustratingly slow, which was affecting us three at the back of the fleet. After the fast, action packed days we'd experienced getting us this far, the ten knots of boatspeed we were achieving now seemed so boring and slow especially when the rest of the fleet had started to finish. *Innovation Kvaerner* added another second to their first leg result, *Toshiba* with their new skipper was third, *Silk Cut* was fourth with *EF Language* having a tough Southern Ocean leg, coming in fifth. *Chessie Racing* finished sixth.

We definitely needed our sense of humour to get us through the last couple of days into Fremantle as the wind seemed to play havoc with our sanity while we struggled to maintain a ten knot average towards the finish line. Fortunately *Merit Cup* and *Brunel Sunergy* were still out there with us and experiencing the same frustrations – it was painfully slow. We were all dying to get back to civilisation once again, but we still had to finish in front of *Brunel Sunergy* which seemed to be getting some wind from behind and was gaining on us as we closed on the finish. *Merit Cup* kept their lead and finished seven hours ahead of us and we crossed the line at 0645 reasonably pleased with our performance. *Brunel Sunergy* came in only an hour behind us as they made a last minute charge and closed the gap considerably in the last 50 miles of the leg.

There was little time to enjoy any festivities when we arrived, and once we had been to the press conference, I took the boat around to the Fremantle Sailing Club with some crew and a few stragglers on board the boat. Along with the help from our shore-team, we stripped the boat completely before we were able to go to our apartments, shower and enjoy a cooked breakfast at the yacht club. At 1530 that same day, I pulled the mast out of the boat with Dave White and a couple of other crew. We were determined to get into the work programme straight away so that we could afford to have some time off during this stopover. Most of the fleet was already out of the water sitting in their cradles with their masts out and people were already working hard. This was a strong reminder of how different the race was compared to that four years ago. In the 1993/94 race, boats and masts were only pulled out three or four times in the entire race. This time we could already see that it was going to happen in almost every stop-over.

It was not worth taking any risks and everyone was doing complete overhauls and thorough inspections of their boats. A lot of boats had sustained a fair amount of damage during leg two, so everyone had another tight schedule ahead of them.

Leah Newbold, The Emerald Highway, *1999*

BIG RED – THE ROUND THE WORLD YACHT RACE ON BOARD STEINLAGER 2

THE 1989–90 *Whitbread Round the World yacht race was to be the one in which Sir Peter Blake finally triumphed for New Zealand, after two previous attempts in* Ceramco NZ *and* Lion New Zealand. *It was the contest that pitted two great Kiwi ketches and two race-hardened Kiwi skippers against the best maxis the world could throw at them.*

New Zealanders still remember the finish at Auckland in January 1990, at the end of the leg from Fremantle. Incredibly, by North Cape, during 3000-odd miles of hard sailing, a match race had developed between Blake in Steinlager 2 (Big Red) *and his former watch captain Grant Dalton in the white-hulled* Fisher & Paykel *(eventually to finish the whole race a magnificent second.) South of Kawau Island, with the two vessels flying their spinnakers and mizzen staysails, virtually neck and neck, a vicious little southerly squall hit, deciding the contest in Blake's favour. Glen Sowry and Mike Quilter recall the start from Fremantle and the Kiwi yachts burning off the opposition as they hammered homewards across the Tasman Sea and around North Cape . . .*

On the eve of the race start from Fremantle we had our usual pre-race briefing amongst the crew. Peter did not have to tell us the importance of the forthcoming leg to Auckland. If there was one leg of the race that we wanted to win, this was the one. No Kiwi yacht had ever been first into Auckland before and we were all fired up to make sure *Big Red* led the fleet into the Waitemata Harbour and across the finish line. However, we had no illusions as we knew that Dalts and his crew on *F&P* would be very hungry for a win, especially after the disappointment of the second leg.

Mike showed us, on the charts, the course and the likely route we would take along the way. He had been regularly to the Perth weather office and had the latest predictions, which were explained at length so that everyone on board knew exactly what to expect. Some of the other boats perhaps did not understand the importance of a solid game plan. It was equally important that the navigator be flexible, as the strategy needs constant updating throughout the leg as new weather information is received.

The morning of the start produced the first rainfall we had seen since we had arrived in Fremantle. The good news was that this was accompanied by a fresh westerly air flow in place of the usual southwesterly sea breeze which the locals refer to as the 'Fremantle Doctor'. This meant that instead of a beat into the wind leaving Freo, we would be on a very fast reach with the wind from abeam.

Milling around before the start, prior to hoisting our sails, we could not help but smile at Pierre Fehlmann, standing at the helm of *Merit* dressed in his bright yellow wet-weather gear as the rain pelted down, nonchalantly puffing away on a huge cigar, oblivious to his surroundings. To make the most of the start for the spectators, the local Whitbread officials sent us first to a turning mark off beautiful Cottesloe Beach, followed by an eight-mile beat out around Rottnest Island, before reaching southwards.

Fehlmann, obviously benefiting from his cigar, got the best of the start to lead *Big Red* around the first mark, with *Fishpie (F&P)* snapping hard on our heels. On the beat out across Gage Roads to Rottnest, Brad called into play some of the 'Kiwi Magic' he learnt racing in these waters on *KZ-7*, to see us picking some good shifts to be right on *Merit*'s tail for the turn south, with *F&P* and *Rothmans* 300 metres astern.

The wind increased to 35 knots, which, combined with the big seaway running, gave us an abrupt reminder that we were back into it again. *Merit* was proving to be difficult to overhaul in these conditions and we remained abeam of the Swiss boys until dusk, when they speared off to leeward of us into the darkness. Throughout the night we monitored *F&P* and *Rothmans* astern of us on the radar. *F&P* was easy to keep track of as she remained exactly 200 metres astern, which had us looking over our shoulders the whole time to see her navigation lights, looking like a pair of red and green eyes following us. During the night Peter and Mike had a few anxious moments as we negotiated Cape Naturalist and its associated reefs. In total darkness and the breaking seas glowing white, it was very hard to see exactly where we were, so the radar and Satnav were glowing red hot from constant use.

Dawn on day two revealed *Merit* in front and to leeward, while *F&P* was still behind us. The wind strength was right up and, if anything, the seas had built even more, which was making for some extremely fast sailing. Undoubtedly reaching in these conditions is the wettest point of sail. A feature of Farr's Whitbread designs is the flared bow, which prevents the boat from nose-diving excessively. Another result of the flared bow is that the bow wave is tossed up and away from the hull, which means that large volumes of water can be blown across the flush deck, resulting in crew members who closely resemble drowned rats. To come on deck without full wet-weather gear, as Mike did on occasions for a quick smoke, is about as sensible as walking through a car wash in a business suit.

The bumpy conditions made for a distinctly subdued atmosphere on board as we all slowly developed our sea-legs once more. Therefore, there was not quite the same enthusiasm at meal-times. Because of the amount of water coming across the deck, it was necessary to keep all of the hatches shut, with the result that the interior of the boat became very stuffy. BC, who never failed to produce a meal whatever the circumstances, was finding the conditions particularly unpleasant. As he stood in the heaving galley stirring the stew, he had his head down the sink throwing up at the same time. There was much conjecture, judging by the appearance of the stew, as to whether he made it to the sink!

Throughout the morning we were to play a game of cat-and-mouse with *F&P*, as she would attack and we defended. The roles were reversed on a couple of occasions as we exchanged the lead. *F&P* first broke through on a spectacular surf no more than 50 metres to windward of us. In the pale light we could see Keith Chapman helming *Fishpie* as he finally hooked onto the right wave. The sight of a maxi with five sails set surfing down the face of the grey seas at over 20 knots with water being thrown everywhere was unforgettable.

Shoebie was on the helm of *Big Red* and did not enjoy being passed by the enemy on the white boat. With both the standby and regular watches on deck we counter-attacked, searching for every wave that would gain us back precious metres. Again and again we scorched down the seas with the spray flying everywhere, almost reducing visibility to nil as we surfed up to within a couple of metres before being forced to bear away to leeward of *F&P*. We were trimming all five sails constantly as we tried relentlessly to break through. We eventually found the elusive wave and in a blast of spray we gave the white boat her own medicine back as we blasted over the top of her and into the lead. *Merit* and *Rothmans* were unable to hold the duelling Kiwis and by the end of the day they had both disappeared over the horizon behind us. It was becoming apparent that we had one hell of a fight on our hands for the 3400-mile 'sprint' home.

Christmas Day arrived and was something of a non-event on board *Big Red*. We thought of our families back home sitting down and tucking into the roast turkey and leg of ham. In a continuation of our weight-saving policy we had no fresh food 'treats' or champagne on board, as most of the other boats had, to celebrate the day. We even went to the extremes that no Christmas presents were allowed on board as they were too heavy, so we had opened all of our presents in Fremantle before starting the leg. We were highly amused later to see video footage off some of the other boats who had celebrated Christmas with all the trimmings. Our Christmas dinner was the usual freeze-dried gastronomic delight; on this occasion it was curry and rice with a dessert of hot custard and sponge cake.

The conditions were still bumpy and we were making very good progress across the Great Australian Bight when the highlight of Christmas Day occurred. *Fourtuna*, which was obviously enjoying the strong winds, had sailed over the horizon from behind with a spinnaker set, and was a mile off our leeward beam when she wiped out in spectacular fashion. She got knocked down so far that it was a case of 'now you see me, now you don't.'

We were beginning to wonder if the wind was ever going to ease away when after five days we were still experiencing a very fast, albeit wet, ride. Mike was forever being asked when the wind was going to moderate as weather maps with conflicting scenarios were fed out of the weather fax. On the fifth night we just about smashed into *F&P*'s stern, as our paths converged once more. Ross was on the helm as we scorched down a large wave with the deck enveloped in spray, giving us very little visibility, when *F&P*'s illuminated transom suddenly appeared no more than a few metres in front of our bow. As we sliced across her transom with our hearts in our mouths, we decided that it was an awfully big ocean and it was not entirely necessary to be right on top of *F&P* the whole time, so we separated by a couple of miles.

It was something of a relief when the wind did finally moderate on day six, as we were all beginning to resemble gorillas with our arms stretched longer from the incessant strain of steering the boat when it was fully powered up. On numerous occasions, we had needed a 'shot-gun' helmsman to stand by the leeward wheel ready to help pull on the wheel if the helmsman could not manage on his own.

During the extended period of strong winds, Alain Gabbay's *Charles Jourdan* had blasted into the lead. Her moment of glory was short-lived as both *F&P* and *Big Red* overhauled her in the light winds that followed as we approached Tasmania. *F&P*'s navigator Murray Ross had called a few good shots and the white boat led us around Tasmania and into the Tasman Bay by seven miles. With *F&P* just on the horizon in front of us, Brad decided it was time to 'point the bone' at her. Whenever Brad did this it was usually the kiss of death to the recipient of his curse. This occasion was to be no different.

Rothmans was still a threat to us, 25 miles astern, while *Merit*, with a damaged steering system, was a comfortable 85 miles behind. Our confidence was soon eroded as we were becalmed off the ironically named Storm Bay on the east coast of Tasmania. *Merit* picked up 60 miles on us as we sat in sight of *F&P*, going nowhere and rapidly losing our sense of humour. The breeze began to filter in again from astern as squalls developed behind us. Our biggest concern now was to make sure that *Fishpie* did not wriggle away from us during the night.

New Year's Eve arrived and was celebrated with the same lack of enthusiasm as Christmas Day. It did not seem natural to be sitting becalmed with no wind, worrying about where the opposition was, when all of our friends were partying hard ashore. Trae decided that if he could not have a drink, then he would at least pretend he was having a high old time. At the midnight change of watch he stumbled out through the main hatch, tripped over winches and sheets, and slurring his words, stated that 'thish ish the best New Year'sh Eve I've had in-hic-agesh.'

The first sched of the new year was listened to with more than the usual interest. Whenever we had a slow 12-hour run in light winds, the next sched would be listened to with a degree of apprehension. Did the other boats have similar conditions or had they 'jagged one' and got away from us? To our relief we had, in fact, gone extremely well overnight to pull 14 miles out of the white boat and move into a seven-mile lead. With 800 miles to Cape Reinga and a large high-pressure system giving light winds to the whole Tasman Sea, we were going to be in for a tense time until the finish.

Our match-race with *F&P* continued the whole way to Cape Reinga in very light conditions. It was a constant see-sawing effect as first she would carry the breeze up to us and then we would wriggle away again. We were forced to show *F&P* our winning technique in light winds as we attempted to hold her at bay. Instead of trying to carry a spinnaker downwind in light airs, we had discovered while training in Auckland before the race that we were much faster sailing downwind with a light genoa set, keeping the apparent wind forward on the boat. This was a technique that Peter and Mike had learned on the trimaran and had won us the leg into Fremantle.

One hundred miles out from Cape Reinga we had *F&P* tucked away three miles astern as we monitored her constantly on the radar. There was a startled yell from Marko as he saw a blip racing across the screen. We could not figure out what it was until we looked up and saw a RNZAF Orion flying over the top of us. At least it wasn't *F&P* switching into hyper-drive. Our biggest concern was now *Rothmans*, which was right in on the Northland coast and in a position to sail around us if the wind swung in direction. That was all we needed – a wild card as well as *F&P* to worry about.

Approaching Cape Reinga early in the morning of day 13 there was great excitement on board. We had our first glimpse of Godzone since we had flown to England six months earlier. Apparently the boys on *F&P* were just as fired up about coming home as they caught up to within 200 metres of us before we caught a wind shift and stretched back out to a three-mile lead. As we rounded Cape Reinga we got a taste of what was to come. Local fishermen were out in force and the cape itself looked like a grandstand with hundreds of people watching the epic match-race between their two Kiwi boats. 'Huey' had smiled on us and the wind had remained constant to put *Rothmans* ten miles astern. They now had their own private battle with a much-improved *Merit*.

Sailing across the top of New Zealand to North Cape the watch system was cancelled. Auckland was only 200 miles away and it was going to take a lot of work on our part to make sure we were first home. There would be plenty of time for sleeping after we had won this leg. Once around North Cape we had the wind behind us for the sprint down the Northland coast. As night closed in, our eyes were constantly on *F&P*; the last thing we could afford to do was let her separate from us. Approaching Cape Brett, the wind began to freshen just as *F&P* did a Houdini disappearing routine by turning off the navigation lights. A sharp call over the VHF radio telling them their lights were off had the desired effect and we spotted her again, although she had gybed away from us towards the shore while we couldn't see her.

Throughout the night we defended our lead jealously as, gybe after gybe, we covered their every move. By dawn the adrenalin level was reaching maximum amongst the crew as we sailed past Whangarei Heads and an early morning reception committee. At this time Blakey took the helm, where he was to stay until the finish with Brad calling the tactics, while the trimmers concentrated on extracting every ounce of speed out of *Big Red*.

We held *F&P* one mile astern as we blasted past Flat Rock off Kawau Island. The number of boats out to meet us was incredible and spurred us on as *F&P* carried a freshening breeze down to close the gap. The atmosphere on board was totally electric as we willed the finish line closer. The sky over Auckland was starting to look ominous, so Mike went down to the nav station to listen to the radio for any updated weather reports. At that moment a listener had called Newstalk 1ZB from Titirangi, saying a southerly front had just passed through. That was all it took for Blakey to order a small genoa to be made ready and for everyone to be ready to drop the spinnaker at a moment's notice.

Peter's twenty years of ocean-racing experience paid huge dividends in one dramatic minute as he screamed '*Get rid of it!*' the instant we saw the wind change on the water a mile in front of us. We worked like men possessed to drop the spinnaker and mizzen staysail before the squall hit. Dalts and his boys, trying desperately to catch us, were not as prepared and were caught with their spinnaker still up and were soon in big trouble. It was impossible not to detect a strong note of satisfaction in Blakey's voice as he said 'Got the bastards.'

With the initial fury of the squall past and our one-mile lead over *F&P* restored, we were able to enjoy the sail from Whangaparaoa along the East Coast Bays to the finish. The rookies on board who hadn't sailed a Whitbread before could not believe the spectacle that was unfolding in front of us as boats of every shape and size came out to welcome us home. Even those of us who had experienced an Auckland Whitbread finish, could not believe the incredible enthusiasm of the thousands of Kiwis who had braved the shocking weather to watch *Big Red* make history.

It was fortunate that it was raining as we sailed up the harbour as it helped to disguise the damp eyes amongst the crew. The emotions we experienced crossing the finish line off Orakei Wharf were impossible to describe. Turning the corner into the arrival berth at Princes Wharf was overwhelming and we were stunned by the reception that these people were giving us. Amidst the cheers and clapping of the crowd was a fantastic big red boat with 15 very proud Kiwis lining her deck. We were home!

Glen Sowry and Mike Quilter, Big Red – the Round the World race on board Steinlager 2, *1990*

ENDEAVOUR – WINNING THE WHITBREAD

AUCKLANDER Grant Dalton had built up a reputation as a fearsome and fearless crew of Whitbread maxi yachts – on the Dutch yacht Flyer *and as watch captain on Sir Peter Blake's* Lion New Zealand *– before he got to mount his own challenge to win ocean racing's ultimate trophy. On board* Fisher & Paykel, *he pushed Blake on* Steinlager 2 *every inch of the way in the 1989–90 race.*

For the 1993–94 race Dalton was back with another white-hulled ketch, the 29.50m Bruce Farr-designed New Zealand Endeavour, *carrying his country's high hopes of notching up another Kiwi win. He led the fleet in to Punta del Este from Southampton by a winning margin of more than eight hours. Ahead lay the notorious second leg to Fremantle on the western Australian seaboard, 7558 nautical miles through the icebergs and wild unforgiving storms of the southern ocean.*

Dalton went on to win the overall event, and to beat Steinlager's *fastest elapsed time by more than eight days, but in the southern ocean his campaign very nearly came to a crashing and inglorious end. The first two days out of Punta del Este, the crew apprehensively settled in their watches and routines in mostly light airs . . .*

On day three we were soon shaken out of our trance when a dramatic increase in both wind strength and sea size, and an equally dramatic decrease in temperature, heralded our arrival into the Southern Ocean.

The next day a sequence of events occurred that prompted us to call this Spike's Big Day. As the dull dawn light began to break up the dark sky, an increase in wind strength necessitated a spinnaker peel. Spike, as the on-watch bowman, climbed out to the end of the spinnaker pole to clip the tack of the new sail onto the pole. While he was hanging onto the outboard end of the pole some six metres above the roaring bow wave, the topping lift supporting the outboard end of the pole was inadvertently released. The first that Spike knew of the problem was when he found himself suddenly plunged into seven-degree water. Still clipped onto the end of the pole, he was being dragged at speeds in excess of seventeen knots. With the spinnaker pole pinned against the sidestays, and Spike spending more time below the water than above it, there was frantic activity around the mast as crewmen struggled to bounce the topping lift up and pull him clear of the frigid water. After what seemed like an eternity, the spinnaker pole and the bedraggled bowman were eventually hoisted clear of the water. If ever we needed any reminding that prudence and care were needed in this part of the world, it was reinforced by this incident.

To cap off Spike's day, he was called upon to retrieve the spinnaker, which was jammed at the top of the rig in 40 knots of wind. After his experience earlier in the morning, it was amazing that we managed to get him off the deck at all, but Spike is one of that rare breed – a bowman – who thrives 30 metres up a violently moving mast.

No sooner had Spike returned to the deck, having successfully retrieved the jammed spinnaker, than he took the helm. Within a matter of minutes, he launched the boat down an enormous wave, recording a new speed record of 28.4 knots.

As the fleet headed on the great circle course towards Fremantle, the temperature continued to drop at an inversely proportional rate to the increasing latitude and the days became longer, until we had no more than six hours of darkness. The sun, however, was mostly absent, but on one of the rare occasions it made a guest appearance, Hermie donned sunglasses at four thirty in the morning while trimming the spinnaker. Some of us were not convinced that he was not just trying to look cool.

A pitch-black night can turn a relatively easy daytime deck job into a major mission. In order to preserve the helmsman's all-important vision, torches are kept to a minimum, so tasks tend to take a lot longer to perform and there is an increased margin for error. Shortly after midnight on our fourth night at sea, one such mishap occurred when Dalts' watch gybed the boat in 25 knots of wind. With Shoebie's standby watch up on deck to help out, everything was set for the manoeuvre. As Dalts called 'Gybing' and began to turn the boat through its arc onto the new starboard gybe, things began to go wrong in the back of the boat.

Unfortunately, the mizzen sheet had overridden when it was loaded onto the self-tailer, the device on top of the winch that enables the sheet to pull itself in as the winch turns. Such an override is one of the yachtsman's biggest enemies, as it winds the heavily laden sheet into an impossible tangle. Calls of 'Ease the sheet!' from Dalts, as the mizzen filled with wind on the new gybe and began to screw the boat into a broach, were returned with an anxious response of 'I can't!' from Shoebie, who was frantically trying to untangle the override. Dalts' plaintive yells to sort out the mess were drowned out by the noise of the angrily thrashing sail cloth.

BC, who had been on deck for the manoeuvre, thought that perhaps Dalts had just discovered that he still had the rental car keys in his pocket and had decided to return to Punta to give them back. Trae, an aspiring musician, decided to write a song about the broach. Sung to the tune of Englebert Humperdinck's 'Please Release Me', it went something like this:

> *Please release me, let me go,*
> *For I am trying to steer one five ooooohhhh.*
> *We gybed and the mizzen wasn't let go.*
> *Please release me, come on, boys, let me go.*
> *With the helm hard down, Daltsy's arms started to grow.*
> *He screamed for f . . . 's sake give me some floooooohhhh.*
> *All I wanted was to gybe and go.*
> *So please release me, come on, boys, it's time to go.*

The afternoon after our impromptu turn back towards Punta, the wind freshened and changed direction, giving us an extended period of 'blast' reaching. This term comes from the fact that reaching across the wind under jib top is both very fast and extremely wet. In these conditions we took on the appearance of drowned rats, as the boat surged down moving walls of the Southern Ocean at speeds well in excess of twenty knots. For the helmsman, it was a case of lining the boat up on the wave then dipping his head to avoid the spray lashing his face.

Hands became blocks of ice by the end of a four-hour watch on deck at high latitudes. Many of the younger guys had bought flash dry-suit diving gloves in England before the race. The 'vets' had told them these were not necessary, but we had obviously forgotten how cold it got down south. After one particularly cold watch, Foxy arranged to borrow Trae's bright-orange 'wonder gloves' for the agreed fee of providing him with all the alcohol he could drink in one night once we had arrived in Fremantle. It is amazing what you will do to stay warm.

If standing a four-hour watch on deck in these conditions was akin to living on a half-tide rock in a storm, life down below decks was not a whole lot better. A combination of the ever-present condensation dripping off the deck head and the large volumes of water that pour down the hatch when a sail was being lowered down below resulted in the interior being perpetually soaked. On one occasion, Hermie drove the boat under spinnaker down one particularly steep wave and straight into the back of the next. The cockpit was filled to the brim with freezing water, a good percentage of which went down into the interior of the boat through the partially open hatch. He had obviously decided he was a U-boat commander but had forgotten to shut the hatches before diving.

At 50 degrees south, after three days of blast reaching, we enjoyed a welcome reprieve in the form of some clear skies and lighter winds. Mike was a little concerned that we would be caught out by a ridge of high pressure and hung out to dry, as we were one of the northerly boats in the fleet. Memories of *Fisher & Paykel* scorching away to a big lead over *Steinlager 2* were hard for Mike to forget, and he was studying the weatherfax maps with increasing anxiety. As luck would have it, the ridge and its associated light winds trapped the boats further to the south. When things were going well for us, with our lead increasing at each six-hourly sched, Mike was the most popular guy on the boat. It is all very well to be sailing the boat hard and fast up on deck and driving it to its full potential, but if the navigator makes an error of judgement in his analysis of the water, all the toil can be for nothing if the opposition is in better wind.

Despite the clearer skies and lighter breezes, the temperature still remained extremely cold. As dusk fell on our ninth day at sea, the temperature snapped to below freezing and the whole boat was soon covered in a coating of ice from the masthead to the deck. Even our masthead wand, which measures wind speed and direction, froze up and had to be retrieved and thawed out over the galley primus. In these conditions, moving around the boat became dangerous, with our thick rubber boots slipping and sliding all over the slick and lurching deck.

By now we were well and truly into iceberg territory, and a member of the standby watch was constantly sitting in the nav station keeping an eye on the radar for any bergs that may be in our path but invisible in the darkness. The big ones are relatively easy to pick up as ghostly green blips, but the smaller chunks of ice that have been broken off the main iceberg are a constant worry. These are known as growlers and can be as small as a car or as big as a house.

While they are potentially dangerous, icebergs are one of the features that make the Southern Ocean a wonderfully spectacular place. The sight of huge seas crashing against the vertical cliff faces of these bergs, enormous albatrosses with three-metre wing spans skimming the wave tops behind the boat, and the half-terrifying, half-exhilarating sailing makes this part of the globe irresistible.

New Zealand Endeavour proved to be considerably faster in the heavy running and reaching conditions that are so prevalent in the Southern Ocean than her predecessors, *Fisher & Paykel* and *Steinlager 2*. This was largely due to her being some seven tons lighter than the older boats, so we were able to fly full-size spinnakers and big mizzen gennakers in 35 knots of wind. The fact that we could carry all of this sail further up the wind range meant that we had to do so if we wanted to stay in front of our maxi opposition and to foot it with the flying Whitbread 60s. It was tempting to say, 'Let's back off for a while and lay it safe,' but whenever we succumbed, we found we'd lost time when the next position sched came around. Of course, we weren't alone in this compulsion to drive the boat to the edge. When the fleet arrived in Fremantle at the completion of this leg, there was no shortage of horror stories of knee-knocking rides and gear broken in high-speed wipe-outs.

After days of living on board a boat in such exhausting conditions, you start to look for anything to take your mind off the sailing. On *Endeavour* this often involved accusations of that most heinous of crimes – chocolate and biscuit theft. It had become apparent that someone was going into the food locker and taking a few biscuits out of the packet on the sly. After some detective work, it was deduced that the culprit was a member of Dalts' watch, and eventually Trev was caught red-handed. It seemed suspicious, though, that Shoebie's watch, who were without doubt the leading perpetrators in food crimes, had been doing all of the investigations.

Their credibility was soon blown away when they tried to corrupt Lowlife with contraband smuggled on board by Trae. One day when we were approaching Prince Edward Island at the midway stage of the leg, Lowlife discovered the 'Foodtown' watch eating peanut slabs and looking like cats slurping cream. Offered the remaining slab, Lowlife – quite out of character – refused it and proceeded to make public the dastardly deed. For the rest of the leg there were accusations and counter-accusations of skulduggery while 'Peanut and the Chocolate Slabs', as Shoebie's watch were referred to in the logbook, defended themselves.

The Whitbread race committee had installed Prince Edward Island as a course mark in an attempt to prevent the fleet from getting too far south. This was not a particularly successful move, because before and after rounding the island the fleet ventured as far south as it has ever gone on this leg in search of stronger winds.

As we reached into the bleak island in low overcast and 30-knot northerly winds, BC observed that Prince Edward must have been very unpopular at the time with the Queen to have such a desolate place named after him. Rounding the mark, we pulled on the canvas and ran south again. With a lead of about 65 miles over *Intrum Justitia* and 118 over *Merit Cup*, we were eager to keep the boat at full pace to preserve our hard-earned advantage. At the halfway stage of the leg, we were very happy to have built such a solid margin particularly over the Whitbread 60s, who had been relishing the heavy conditions.

Foxy's watch, with Dalts and his team on standby, enjoyed a roller-coaster ride for the next four hours with an average speed for one hour of over nineteen knots before things began to get a little hairy. A sudden squall had the boat sitting on a solid 27 knots before Foxy yelled in a less-than-controlled voice, 'Get the mizzen gennaker down – now!' Throughout that night we scorched through the darkness and by the time dawn came, everyone's nerves were stretched taut.

Shortly after dawn, a wind shift of 40 degrees made for some very tricky sailing, as the boat ran across the large seaway at an awkward angle, with each wave picking up the stern and screwing us around each time. After a brief respite, the wind increased in strength and it was decided to peel to the full-size heavy-air spinnaker to avoid blowing out the 1 1/2-ounce sail we were flying. Burt was hoisted up to the halyard-exit sheave to 'lock' off the halyard in order to take the weight off it and avoid chafe and possible breakages. No sooner had he reached the top of the rig when a wave slammed the boat from the leeward quarter, throwing it into a violent broach. The danger in this case is that as soon as the boat rounds up towards the wind by more than a few degrees, the massive mizzen gennaker and mizzen load up the stern, dramatically accelerating the broach.

As soon as the boat began rounding up, all Foxy could do was try to slow down the broach as the power generated by the mizzen rig spun the boat into the oncoming waves, leaving it lying on its side with the sails violently thrashing. While all this drama was happening, Burt hung on grimly at the top of the main mast, which was swinging through an arc of 10 metres.

Dalts began to lower the mizzen gennaker halyard to depower the boat and enable it to regain its footing. While the standby watch attempted to pull the massive sail on board, a wave snatched the foot and swept the sail over the stern. It became a giant sea anchor, pulling at the top of the mizzen rig and placing the mast under enormous strain. Too much strain: with a sickening graunch and metallic bang, the mast snapped clean off at the third spreaders.

As the gennaker was hauled on board, the scene on deck was as if a bomb had just gone off. Dalts stood at the base of the mizzen looking plaintively up at the broken top of the rig crashing against the remaining section and could only mutter, 'Oh no! Not the mast . . . not the mast.' Once Burt was lowered safely back down, there came the nauseating realisation that we were in very deep trouble, with 3,500 miles still to sail to Fremantle in a severely depowered boat.

A shocked crew began the depressing job of cleaning up the carnage. The first priority was to get the expensive lump of scrap metal down from the top of the stump of the mizzen. This was a very tricky operation, handled by Burt in his usual professional manner. With the broken section of mast crashing around his ears as the boat pitched and rolled in the large seaway, he spent two hours aloft with a hacksaw cutting away the thick rod stays. When the mangled rig was secured on deck, a storm spinnaker was set on the main mast and we resumed our course towards Fremantle, at a very reduced pace. The remainder of the day was spent cutting down some of the mizzen sail inventory to get what we could out of 'Stumpy', as the shortened mast became nicknamed.

From the time of the broach, no one had a moment's rest for the next 24 hours as we were immersed in the task of trying to get the mizzen working again after a fashion. It was probably the best cure for the depression we were all feeling, and kept us from dwelling on the question, 'Have we just lost the whole race because of this one broach?'

Dalts and Lowlife began to calculate how much time we were likely to lose before arriving in Fremantle, and whether it would be an insurmountable deficit for the rest of the race. BC, as always, did a great job keeping everyone positive about our prospects. His log entry about summed things up: 'Ah, what a f . . . g day, first the All Blacks lose to the Poms, then our little world caved in temporarily for this leg. Who knows, there are still plenty of days left, so keep your chins up, blokes, we can still beat the bastards yet . . . fantastic efforts all around so far.'

Trae and Moose worked like men possessed as they cut down and resewed a wide selection of sails to squeeze an extra fraction of a knot out of our wounded boat.

It soon became apparent through the scheds that we were rapidly losing our handsome lead on the fleet. We became resigned to losing time, the only question being, 'How much?'

With less than two legs of the race complete, three of the four maxi ketches in the race had broken or severely damaged their mizzen masts, and we began wondering when *Merit Cup* would join the list of casualties. Fortunately for Fehlman and his Swiss crew, they were to never join the less-than-illustrious club.

Unbelievably, three days after the broach we still led *Merit Cup* and were a good distance ahead of *La Poste*, although losing ground to both. Daniel Mallé faxed condolences, saying he did not want to beat us in this fashion. Daniel need not have worried – we had no intention of lying down and playing dead just yet.

The demolition derby continued when the youngsters on *Dolphin and Youth* were faced with a broken rudder, not a comforting prospect in the middle of the Southern Ocean. Fortunately for Matt Humphries and his multi-national crew, they were able to stop at the French meteorological base on the Kerguelen Island to build an emergency rudder to get them to Fremantle. But the woes of *Endeavour* and *Dolphin* were to prove to be little league compared with the drama that was about to unfold in the depths of a severe Southern Ocean storm in less than 24 hours time.

On a typically drab day, with constant rain and winds of 30 to 40 knots, we were blasting through the murk towards Australia when the familiar 'beep, beep, beep' of the Satcom C announced some electronic mail had just been received. Mike felt a sudden chill as he read the message from Ian Bailey Willmot, the Whitbread race director back in England, announcing that one of the Whitbread 60s, the Italian yacht *Brooksfield*, had activated its emergency EPIRB device. An EPIRB is only ever used in dire emergency, and transmits the distressed vessel's position and identification code by satellite to search and rescue authorities around the world.

Within minutes we received a similar message from Canberra asking *Endeavour* – the duty yacht for the day – to try to contact *Brooksfield* to ascertain if she was, in fact, in distress. Mike immediately attempted to call *Brooksfield* on the SSB radio but heard only an ominous silence. Hurried fax messages were sent off to the Whitbread office and search and rescue in Canberra informing them of the situation. An immediate response asked *New Zealand Endeavour* to co-ordinate a search within the fleet.

With the nearest land 2,000 miles away, we were out of aircraft range and there was no shipping in the area, so it was up to one of the Whitbread yachts to attempt to locate *Brooksfield*. Dalts was woken from his off-watch sleep to work with Mike communicating with the other yachts in the fleet. The two nearest *Brooksfield*'s last EPIRB position were *La Poste* and *Winston*. Both Daniel Mallé and Brad Butterworth agreed without hesitation to stop racing and head back into huge seas and winds that were gusting to 50 knots.

As we ploughed on through the storm-force conditions, we were all lost in private thoughts contemplating what had happened to *Brooksfield*. We hoped like hell they were all right and that it had been a false alarm, but in the conditions we were experiencing it was easy to believe that something had gone very seriously wrong and that the Italians were doomed. The prospect of them being forced to abandon the boat for life rafts or trying to hold onto an upturned hull did not bear thinking about. While *Winston* and *La Poste* turned back to look for a needle in a haystack, the leading yachts, including *Endeavour*, were faced with massive breaking seas, screaming winds and driving sleet. But as we went into 'survival mode' for the night, *Brooksfield*'s plight was always in the back of our minds.

Shortly after midnight, with the storm at its peak, Shoebie was trying to keep the boat upright as she careered down foaming seas. On one such rapid transit down a moving mountain of water, a wave broke into the deck and washed Brad back into the windward steering wheel. The impact smashed the carbon-fibre wheel, leaving Shoebie lying on his back on the cockpit floor with the remains of the wheel still in his hands. In the darkness it took a moment for the others on watch to realise what had happened before Shoebie yelled, 'Someone grab the wheel!' There was a frantic unclipping of harnesses as the crew tried to reach the wheel down to leeward. Remarkably, the boat resisted the temptation to broach and stayed on track for the ten seconds it was driverless. To cap the night off, we tore the mainsail, cracked a winch pedestal and broke a stanchion. Shoebie's finale was a spectacular flight in his sleeping bag as the boat heeled steeply, ejecting him from his bunk. Luckily his trajectory was not interrupted by any of the beams or posts that littered the boat's interior.

After this drama, the dawn produced a steadily moderating breeze, which gave us the opportunity to repair the night's damage. Although the wind was dissipating, an enormous seaway continued to throw *Endeavour* around as if we were in a giant washing machine. Within a couple of hours, however, the good news came that *La Poste* had found *Brooksfield* and everyone was safe and well. It transpired that they had broken their rudder shaft, which in turn had started to smash a hole in the bottom of the boat. The Italians had managed to stem the flow of water by jamming a bucket wrapped in a bunk squab in the hole before the interior was completely flooded. All of their electronics had been swamped, so they had been unable to communicate their plight.

While *La Poste* escorted *Brooksfield* under emergency steering towards Fremantle, we continued racing towards the finish, losing big mileage in the lighter conditions near the West Australian coast. We were amazed to be able to hold off *Merit Cup* until we were less than 400 miles from the finish. Pierre Fehlmann must have been incredibly frustrated to have been unable to put some big time on us in our under-horsepowered state. Our saving grace was the predominantly fresh reaching conditions that had prevailed from the time we broke the mast until the last few days, when the wind lightened. With sufficient breeze, we had not been too badly underpowered, despite the drastically reduced sail area on the mizzen. We were, however, losing consistently on the leading Whitbread 60s, notably *Intrum Justitia*, which had given the fleet a lesson in Southern Ocean power sailing.

After 26 days of living in wet and smelly wet-weather gear in a closed-up boat, it was a relief to encounter some warmth in the last couple of days of the marathon from Puna del Este. Spike commented in the log that it was 'nice to see BC and Lowlife on deck, it must be getting bloody smelly down there', to which BC replied, 'This boat smells like a dog kennel.' The wet socks that had been worn for ten days and were now lying festering in the bilge made for an aroma that can only be experienced on board a Whitbread boat at the end of a long leg.

Having held *Merit Cup* off for twelve days since the mizzen had broken, we had to remind ourselves as she overtook us that we were very lucky to have lost as little time as we did. At the time of the dismasting, we had thought it likely that we could lose up to 24 hours on *Merit Cup* and the leading Whitbread 60s. To finish as close as we did was more than we could have hoped for. Our last day at sea was spent running up the coast in light to moderate tail winds, exactly the conditions we were most vulnerable in. As we approached Rottnest Island at dusk, we caught a glimpse of the Spanish Whitbread 60

Galicia Pescanova on the horizon ahead of us. Lawrie Smith and his pan-European team had sailed a strong race to win the leg overall from Chris Dickson's *Tokio*. The press dubbed *Intrum Justitia* the 'Silver Bullet', as they had set a new 24-hour record for the monohull of 425 miles. Even so, we had managed to keep the deficit down to 8 hours, 18 minutes behind *Intrum Justitia*, and 1 hour, 46 minutes adrift of *Merit Cup*.

As a crippled New Zealand *Endeavour* approached the finish line in Fremantle in the balmy late evening, there was a collective sigh of relief amongst the guys. The second leg through the Southern Ocean is hard enough without the added drama of breaking the mast. Not only were we still in good shape for an overall victory, we had stuck together as a team. Spike hit the nail on the head when he commented soon after stepping onto dry land, 'There's nothing like a good battle to really pull a team together.'

Grant Dalton and **Glen Sowry**, Endeavour – Winning the Whitbread, *1994*

COURSE TO VICTORY

RUSSELL *Coutts, C.B.E., a Bachelor of Engineering who learned to sail as a child in a P class revelling in the variable conditions of the Paremata Harbour north of Wellington, was at the helm of* Black Magic *when New Zealand lined up for the America's Cup races off San Diego on May 6, 1995. As reputably the world's number one match racing skipper, world youth champion in 1981, Olympic gold winner in 1984, helmsman (with the German team) of the 1993 Admiral's Cup, Coutts really had only the Everest of yacht match racing left to achieve.*

Led by Whitbread veteran Peter Blake, with Coutts as skipper and a hand-picked and race-hardened crew, the Black Magic *team blazed their way through the preliminary Louis Vuitton Cup, brushing aside all-comers, including the highly-favoured Italians, Australians, French and Japanese: 37 victories and only one loss.*

Then it came down to New Zealand's old foes, Dennis Connor and Paul Cayard, in a borrowed boat. Stars and Stripes *had won Connor the challenger's berth, but it was the supposedly faster* Young America *that was his last and clearly desperate card to play against the storming Kiwis.*

You might think that after four months of racing, a boatload of very experienced sailors who have raced all round the world would be pretty used to making our way out to the race course once again. But I recall that on May 6, 1995, the morning of the first race of America's Cup XXIX, there was an electric excitement flowing through Team New Zealand.

As I arrived at the compound that morning, I noticed stacks of faxes, letters and telegrams, all wishing us good luck. The phone never stopped ringing. Crowds of spectators, many wearing the trademark red socks, gathered outside our docks and yelled encouragement. We knew that as many as a dozen planeloads of Kiwis had arrived in the past few days.

No, this wasn't your typical race day. This was why we were here. This was what we had planned for, worked for, waited for, for more than two years . . .

this is what all of New Zealand had waited for since that day in 1984 when a small group got together and asked each other if there was any possibility our little nation could put together an America's Cup team.

On the tow out, we passed shore fronts lined with cheering people. All around us were boats headed for the race course. Overhead a plane flew by us streaming a banner behind reading: 'Take it home, *Black Magic, NZL-32*.' Boats loaded with New Zealand flags raced by us. Others had large cardboard cutouts of the kiwi pasted to their hulls. Everywhere we looked, we saw thousands of people waiting to witness this first race, waiting to see who had got it right.

Aside from excitement, we felt well prepared. We thought we had the boat at its fastest and, despite our 37–1 record compared with our opponent's 20–17 score, we were not overconfident. There were still enough memories of what happened in Fremantle against Dennis, when New Zealand had a similar record, to keep us in check.

When we got to the race course, the scene was unbelievable. Boats everywhere, horns blasting greetings and support, news and television helicopters circling above, press boats filled with photographers and cameramen circling us on the water.

Simon and I have long had a saying between us, whether we're in a great race or at an unusual social event or at a Rolling Stones concert: 'Where would you rather be right now?' When the answer comes back, 'Nowhere,' there's a good chance you are in the right place at the right time.

Looking around at the scene, checking out the wind, at that point registering about 15–17 knots, I said to the guys, 'Look at this scene, where would you rather be right now?' The question didn't need to be answered. There was no doubt in my mind that this is exactly where everyone wanted to be, exactly where I wanted to be.

My only concern was that the boat was pounding in pretty steep waves. The possibility of gear failure was high. We had a brand new heavy-air mainsail on board; when the breeze began blowing 17 knots, we changed to it. Having the sail on board was another indication of how prepared we were. This sail was designed to handle winds above 25 knots and although the boats certainly shouldn't be racing in that type of wind, we didn't know what we could expect from this race committee. We were no longer dealing with the challenger officials. The people running the America's Cup races were officials of the San Diego Yacht Club and their representative was our opponent.

The wind gusted to about 19 knots a few times well before the start of the race, but then dropped to below 15 and we changed back to our original main. I steered for the growing spectator fleet to sense some of the atmosphere and to get used to our surroundings. We were cheered everywhere we went, by the Kiwi faithfuls and Americans as well.

It was something of an odd sensation to find support from the Americans. I think some of it was a reaction to the controversy the Cup had brought to town coupled with the skulduggery of the defender series. The three boats in the two-boat finals had caused a great deal of consternation to the sport's observers and many American publications editorialised that such shenanigans were ruining the event.

We had drawn the port end of the line to enter the starting box, and, in this type of stiff breeze, I began thinking, 'This isn't perfect.' In a chop like the one we found ourselves in, our boat did not manoeuvre well and I thought we had to avoid downspeed tacking if we could. I was wondering if Cayard would try to dial us up at the start and try to push us into a downspeed situation.

I went through the pre-start for perhaps the twentieth time in my mind. Bob Rice and his team had told us that shortly after the start we should be prepared for the wind to move right. At this point, we never even thought about getting a second opinion. Bob and the gang had been spot on in almost every race we'd had, particularly over the past two months. There was just no question; if he said move right my only response was: 'How far?'

So we wanted to come off the start line to the right of the Americans and then go right when the breeze dictated. Being on port was okay, as long as we could get to the right without their using their starboard advantage to block us.

As we entered the starting area, we sailed past them and I noticed Paul behind the wheel staring at us as if he were in a trance. It was an unusual moment, one I can neither describe nor explain. I'm not sure if he was trying to psych us out or if he was psyched out by us. Rick Dodson was also surprised by the unusual behaviour and gave him something of a stare back.

I gave a slight wave as if to say, 'Isn't this great? The first race of the America's Cup . . . ' but there was no reaction. He just kept staring. But there was no time to give the snapshot much thought.

We circled a little bit, but avoided any tight manoeuvring. Dennis and his team had never raced this boat and they were playing it somewhat conservatively. When the gun went off, we had managed to get to the right of them and to windward, but we were closer to them than we wanted to be. We were a little further behind the line than them but, all in all, happy with the start. Starting so close to them in a windward position, we were expecting to be forced to tack off to the right. But the wind had already gone right a little and we decided to wait for a short time.

In less than a minute, the breeze started clocking further right, just as we'd been told. We went with it as did *Young America*. The two boats were sailing at about the same speed, but it was already evident we were sailing higher. Schnack looked under the boom and said, 'Boy, this is going to be a quick America's Cup.'

The wind shifted between 15 and 20 degrees in our favour and we began to stretch out a lead. But then the breeze settled down, so did the Americans, and they were going along just fine. Schnack took another range reading and said, 'Well, maybe not as quick as I thought.'

We got to the first mark in the lead by 31 seconds. As expected, our upwind speed had served us well once again. But we suspected we were racing a boat that had been set up for downwind speed. We were now about to see how successful she was.

We noticed immediately that there was a huge difference in the type and shape of spinnakers flying on the two boats. As we sailed down the first run, *Young America* came at us like a freight train. She kept coming and coming, closer and closer. I began thinking this could be a real concern. If they could keep close to us on the upwind legs, they would definitely threaten us downwind, and the final leg on the course was downwind.

As we approached the mark, we had trouble with the spinnaker pole during a couple of gybes. That may have left an opening for *Young America*. I started thinking, 'This is not the time to be having spinnaker problems as we try to protect an inside overlap, coming into the bottom mark.'

But a little luck came our way and we opened up just a little breathing space to get around the mark a couple of boat lengths in the lead. Our 31-second lead had been reduced to 12 seconds. We'd have to put together a good weather leg to stretch out enough so the next run wouldn't damage us too badly.

And then it all came together. All the work, all the testing, all the guessing, all our confidence in the boat. The breeze died a bit to come into the range in which *Black Magic* performed best, and we simply sailed away with the leg and the race. At the second windward mark we were 42 seconds ahead and then we gained on each following leg to win by 2:45. It was a tremendous performance.

Not too much was said on board as we crossed the line. There were some 'Well dones' and we shook hands, but we knew we needed four more wins to take possession of 'the Auld Mug'. But if we weren't saying much, after what had just happened, I doubt there was anyone on board *Black Magic* who didn't know in his heart of hearts that we were going to win this regatta. It was simple and it had just been proven: we had the faster boat.

Following the race the opposing camp made a few statements to the effect that they were hoping for lighter breezes and smoother seas. But when they made the switch from *Stars & Stripes* to *Young America*, they had said they had done so specifically because the Pact 95 boat was a stronger performer in the type of conditions we encountered in the first race.

The results of the race had to be extremely discouraging to the Americans. They obviously believed *Young America* was a better boat than the one which had got them to the dance, but once inside the party they had discovered not much more than the make-up was different on their new date. But with only six days to get to know her, we wondered how they could expect much more.

The press had reported that the Americans were having some trouble getting used to the new boat. It wasn't set up the same as *Stars & Stripes*; the boat was narrower, the boom was lower and the winches were in different places were only a few of the differences.

'It was a tough day when you really needed to know your boat,' Paul Cayard was quoted as saying. 'It was like two races in one. The first two legs it was really close and I thought, "Terrific, it's going to be a great series." Then the rest was a blowout. I saw some reasons why they got ahead, but I also saw some Kiwi speed. Maybe they were nervous in the beginning and then finally got it rolling.'

Well, maybe. But maybe we just had a boat that sailed even faster once the conditions changed in the latter half of that race.

The following day was a scheduled lay day during which both teams were back on the ocean, testing. Race two was on a Monday, and the Americans left their dock on their new and different boat, with new and different uniforms to new and different send-off music. Dennis was big on thematic music. He loved the theme from the movie *Top Gun*, and in the days of the semi-finals and finals of the Citizen Cup, when he was clawing away to stay in the game, the send-off music was the Bee Gees' 'Staying Alive'.

This morning the tune wafting across San Diego Harbour was 'I Still Believe'. Apparently the new uniforms, white in colour instead of their traditional navy blue, were the result of a last-minute order that was filled incorrectly.

Neither the boat nor the uniforms nor the music made much difference. Nor did Dennis Connor taking over the wheel about two-thirds through the race. *Black Magic* was simply devastating. Perhaps our boat took exception to the Americans saying they were waiting for better conditions to do well, apparently the hopes of our opponent didn't sit well in either case. We were behind at the start, but Bob Rice and his team had once more given us the right weather information and, after catching the first shift to the right, we took the lead, added to it, and put together an incredible 4:14 thrashing of the boat that was claimed to do better in lighter and smoother conditions – just what was on the course today. We crossed the finish line some 42 lengths in front of the Americans. It was the worst defeat of a defender since 1871, when Britain's *Livonia* beat the US yacht *Columbia* by 15:10.

I don't suppose there was anyone who had observed the first two races of the 1995 America's Cup match who held out much hope for the defenders – there didn't even seem to be much hope among the defending team itself. Following the race, their navigator, Jim Brady, said at the press conference, 'We thought we sailed the boat pretty close to its potential today.'

Bill Trenkle, Dennis Conner's long-time operations manager, was quoted in a local paper as saying: 'That was hard for our guys. We're not used to that kind of a stomping.'

Paul Cayard was already thinking about the next America's Cup and looking towards the South Pacific. In an interview with Angus Phillips of the *Washington Post*, the American helmsman said: 'Change is always good. The Kiwis have been at the top of the sport for ten years. They've won the Admiral's Cup and they've been at the top of this event. So it was long overdue for them to get into the Cup match. They'd be great hosts, very enthusiastic. The venue probably will be more exciting, with more variable weather conditions.'

Inside our compound we were happy to read comments like these, but no one had handed us the trophy yet. If we were to prove Paul correct and be great hosts four and five years down the track, we had to win three more races.

It was apparent at the start of race three that the two teams had different views of where the better wind and wind shifts would be. We took the right side, they took the left and we crossed the line on split tacks. Almost immediately upon crossing, the wind came our way and so did *Young America*, quickly realising their mistake. At the first cross we tacked with our stern just clearing their bow, prompting them to raise a penalty flag claiming we had tacked too close. The on-the-water umpires didn't agree, signalling with a green flag that no rule had been infringed.

A short tacking duel followed until we decided to go for straight-line speed. I asked, 'Which way do you want to break out of this guys?'

'Protect the right,' was the call from Murray. I turned the wheel, pulled out of the duel, and drove straight up the course. We thought *Young America* might have been a little quicker in manoeuvring and we didn't want to be caught in a downspeed situation. The first two races had proven our boatspeed superior, so why play their game?

We turned the first mark ahead by 20 seconds and headed for the left side of the course. Cayard then rounded and ran to the right side. If we were racing by the book, we would have gybed over and covered them but in light, shifting winds, that strategy can be more risky than not covering at all. Murray and Rick were discussing the situation, watching the Americans, talking to me, looking back at our opponent, talking to each other. At this stage in the regatta, I had total confidence in the afterguard. I concentrated on steering the boat fast and following their advice on when to turn and where to take the boat.

'I like our chances on the left better,' I heard one of them say.

'Me, too. If we gybe back at them now we will be out of phase. It's safe to keep on this course.'

Some may have considered our tactics something of a gamble, but the decision paid off. We added a full minute to our lead and they never got closer. Race three to the Kiwis by 1:51. Two to go.

After the first two races, the papers were filled with speculation about whether Dennis made the right decision in changing boats. That story was getting old, but Tom Whidden threw some humour into the discussion after being asked at the press conference what they could do to stop us. With a straight face, the American tactician, one of the best in the world, answered: 'I think the two big improvements made in the rules this time are that there are nine races instead of seven, which should work to our advantage. And the second rule is the one which says the defenders and challengers swap boats after every third race.'

For a moment the room went silent while the press wondered how they could have missed this new dictum. Then the joke was realised and the room burst into laughter. Tom, still with a straight face, asked: 'Oh, did I get that wrong?'

As the laughter died, I couldn't resist. I leaned into the microphone and asked a question of my own: 'Don't you think you guys have swapped boats enough?'

That brought forth another round of laughter. Unique within the world of sports, press conferences at the America's Cup and on the match-racing circuit always have representatives of all teams on a single dais at the same time. In other sports, it's rare that two tennis players are in front of the same camera at the same time or two rugby coaches face each other in the press room. Our interviews almost always generate a provocative comment or some revelation or good humour, even in the face of defeat. Tom's wit was appreciated.

Race four may have exemplified the skills of Team New Zealand better than any of the previous 41 races we had entered during 1995. The routine of checking every piece of equipment before we left the dock had kept us relatively free of gear breakage. Our pre-race strategy meetings helped all of us understand what we would try to do out on the race course. The weather team, at this point, was close to being deified in all our eyes and we unquestionably followed their every word of advice.

So, in those respects, race four was not unlike all those that had come before. But it was a particular incident that illustrated to me why our afterguard was the best in the business and I attribute a large portion of our victory to them. *Young America* could have and probably should have led the race at the first mark.

We came off the starting line and went left. Our weather intelligence had predicted a shift to the left and we wanted to be in position to take advantage of it. It did indeed occur, but five minutes after it was predicted to do so. As we sailed further and further out towards the layline, the breeze was clocking more and more to the right, giving *Young America* the advantage. For the first time in our series, the Americans crossed ahead of us. This is just what Paul Cayard had been waiting for. Earlier, he had told the press that if he could just get ahead of us on the first leg, he stood a good chance of holding us off for the rest of the race.

While looking at *Young America*'s stern for the first time was new, the attitude remained calm aboard *Black Magic*. We'd followed other boats before and got past. All those experiences did was bring out more confidence in our team and in our boat.

We'd been told the wind would come left, and it did. We were getting closer and closer to the layline and the wind continued to move left but not enough for us to pass *Young America*. We wanted to avoid the situation where we'd get to the layline and they would tack to cover us and build on their lead. So we tacked towards them and the wind lifted us, which was not what we needed. That meant that when they tacked, they'd be in phase with the wind and they would force us out of phase.

That's just what happened. They tacked on top of us, forcing us to tack, and they put some more distance between the two boats. As soon as we got back to speed, we tacked again to take up position on their hip as they were on the favoured course and we didn't want to spend much time on the opposite tack. We needed to keep the race as close as we could. No gambles today.

A minute or so later, they tacked towards us and, just as the two yachts were about the meet, our guys in the cockpit picked up a big breeze on the left-hand side. This was the wind our weather team had predicted.

I turned to the afterguard of Jones, Dodson, Schnackenberg and Butterworth and said, 'Now we're really in the cart. They're going to cross us, keep going to the breeze, tack, and they're gonna be gone. What do we do?'

I started thinking maybe we should tack underneath them, which would have kept us close to them but probably behind at the first mark.

'Keep going,' I was told. The tactical minds of our strategists agreed with each other and I wasn't about to do anything but follow their advice.

What must have happened was that our guys saw the breeze just as we were approaching *Young America* and they figured the Americans may not have picked it up.

A lot is going on in the cockpit as two boats approach each other. Match racing has often been called a chess game on water in which you have to think several moves ahead. Their conversation on board at the time must have been focused on the impending cross and retaining the starboard tack advantage for the rest of the leg. Had they seen the new wind, the decision would have been easy – keep going.

But that's not what they did. They tacked on us, away from the new pressure, allowing us to immediately tack away towards where we saw the wind. As soon as we tacked, I looked at the afterguard, smiled, and said, 'We're ahead now.' We weren't at that moment but we soon would be. They had made a brilliant call. They had stayed on station looking for breeze. They had not been distracted by what was happening at that very moment in the race. And, they had total trust in the weather team so they knew where to look. We caught the breeze, it lifted us towards the mark, and within minutes we had surged into a four or five boatlength lead. When we got to the mark, we turned with the biggest lead we'd had against *Young America* at that point, 1:09. Race over.

At the press conference the men representing the defenders looked and sounded beaten. Short of some massive catastrophe in which we lost both our boats, no one was believing the Americans could win five races before we won one more. Paul Cayard spoke for the team and probably best expressed their feeling of futility when he said: 'I'm not to the point of crying, but I've never been in a race where I felt I had so little control over the outcome. I don't even feel like I'm in a sailboat race.'

We knew from similar comments the defenders were reeling. Tom Whidden, who's been with Dennis for more than 20 years and has been calling tactics in America's Cup races longer than anyone, told a reporter: 'This race was won five or six months ago. The Kiwis were focussed when they arrived here last November and they've stayed at it. We never guessed the entire defence effort was so far off the pace. We can't even engage these guys in a race.'

Before the start of the fifth race we had a slight scare when our starboard primary winch decided to go on strike and the Cunningham track pulled off the mast. Shore boss Tim Gurr, alias 'the Rat' – who had not been out on the water in his whole time in San Diego – rushed out from the compound to personally make the repairs. As he worked furiously to fix the breakages, Joe Allen and Simon Daubney proceeded to give him a bit of stick. 'Ratty, in case you didn't know, that boat over there is the American boat we are racing.'

'Shut up you guys.'

'And that point over there is Point Lorna, and that's Mexico down there ...'

'Shut up you guys.'

'And this here is our America's Cup boat.'

'SHUT THE — UP!'

'Ratty, I was sailing off this coast in *Pendragon*, when you guys were boys, too young to be yachtsmen.' *Pendragon* was a famous Laurie Davidson boat that won both the Three-quarter Ton Cup and the One Ton Cup. Joe and Daubs' behaviour did show that the attitude on board wasn't that tense on the final day of the America's Cup. The truth is, the Rat and the rest of the shore team had built a fantastic pair of boats and had detailed them perfectly. Joe, Simon and anyone else chipping in, enjoying giving the Rat some lip, were really saying, 'Thank you'; proof that Kiwi teams are 'culturally different.'

This concluding race was not unlike our first encounter. In about 10 knots of wind and sloppy seas, *Young America* stayed close to us on the first upwind leg and we didn't add much on the first run. But then some bad luck for the Americans sent us on our way to the collect the Cup. *Young America*'s jib halyard broke and the headsail crashed to the deck. By the time they got back to full speed, we were 59 seconds ahead and impossible to catch. We won the race by 1:50, completing a clean sweep.

This was also the race that Meaty was caught waving at the television monitor positioned just in front of the huge grinder. Daubs was asking the big man to grind coming into the last mark and when nothing happened he looked over and noticed Meat directing a thumbs-up at the camera. 'What the hell are you doing Meaty?' We later discovered that the faithful grinder from all our America's Cup efforts, had devised a hand signal to advise his wife that his lunch had been prepared just how he had wanted it on that last day!

I've said throughout that statistics don't tell the full story, but perhaps these will give a more definitive picture of just how dominant *Black Magic* was:

Our 5–0 score was the greatest margin of victory in the 144-year history of the America's Cup. The rules were different in 1987 when Dennis Conner won 4–0 as a challenger against Australia, but his average margin of victory per race was 1:39 and he never won a race by more than two minutes. Our average victory in the Cup match was 2:52, with three of the races won by more than two minutes.

Against *Young America*, *Black Magic* led at all 30 marks, gaining time on 25 of the 30 legs. In more than 13 hours of sailing, the black boat followed the Mermaid for less than half an hour. There were only two occasions in the entire series that *Young America* crossed in front of us.

Our 42–1 overall record was the best ever posted by any America's Cup team. Our average margin of victory in all our races was 3:06.

We gained time over the opposition in 77 percent of the 260 legs we raced. We were in the lead on 93 percent of those 260 legs.

We spent approximately $US15 million on our two-boat programme. The three United States syndicates spent some $US55 million.

The population of San Diego county is twice the total population of New Zealand.

Not one member of Team New Zealand left the programme.

And so the fourth time was a charm. Team New Zealand built on what Michael Fay and Chris Dickson and Roy Dickson and Laurent Esquier and Rod Davis and Bruce Farr and David Barnes and a thousand others on board and ashore had done over the past 11 or so years and we accomplished the goal every Kiwi challenge had had since 1984. We did it because of what came before us, because of what collectively we'd learned on the oceans and in the design rooms and tank testing facilities and sail lofts of the world. We did it because we put the team first and we learned to trust each other totally. We did it because we all had a say in what we thought would make the boat go fast. We did it because we'd been to Admiral's Cups and One Ton Cups and dinghy world championships and the Olympics and the match-racing circuit and the Whitbread Round-the-World races and races on Auckland's Waitemata Harbour. We did it because we had an entire nation behind us. And most of all, we did it because two black boats were faster than anything any other nation could come up with.

Pure magic? No. Team magic? Probably. A magic time? Most definitely.

Russell Coutts in Paul Larsen, Russell Coutts: Course to Victory, *1996*